AF576512

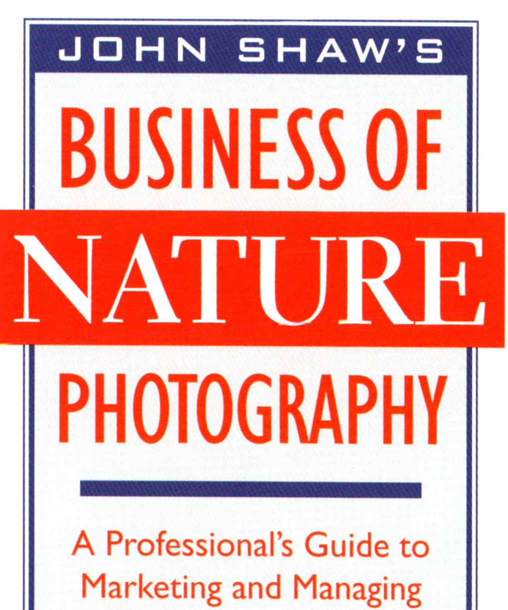
JOHN SHAW'S
BUSINESS OF
NATURE
PHOTOGRAPHY
A Professional's Guide to
Marketing and Managing
a Successful Nature
Photography Business

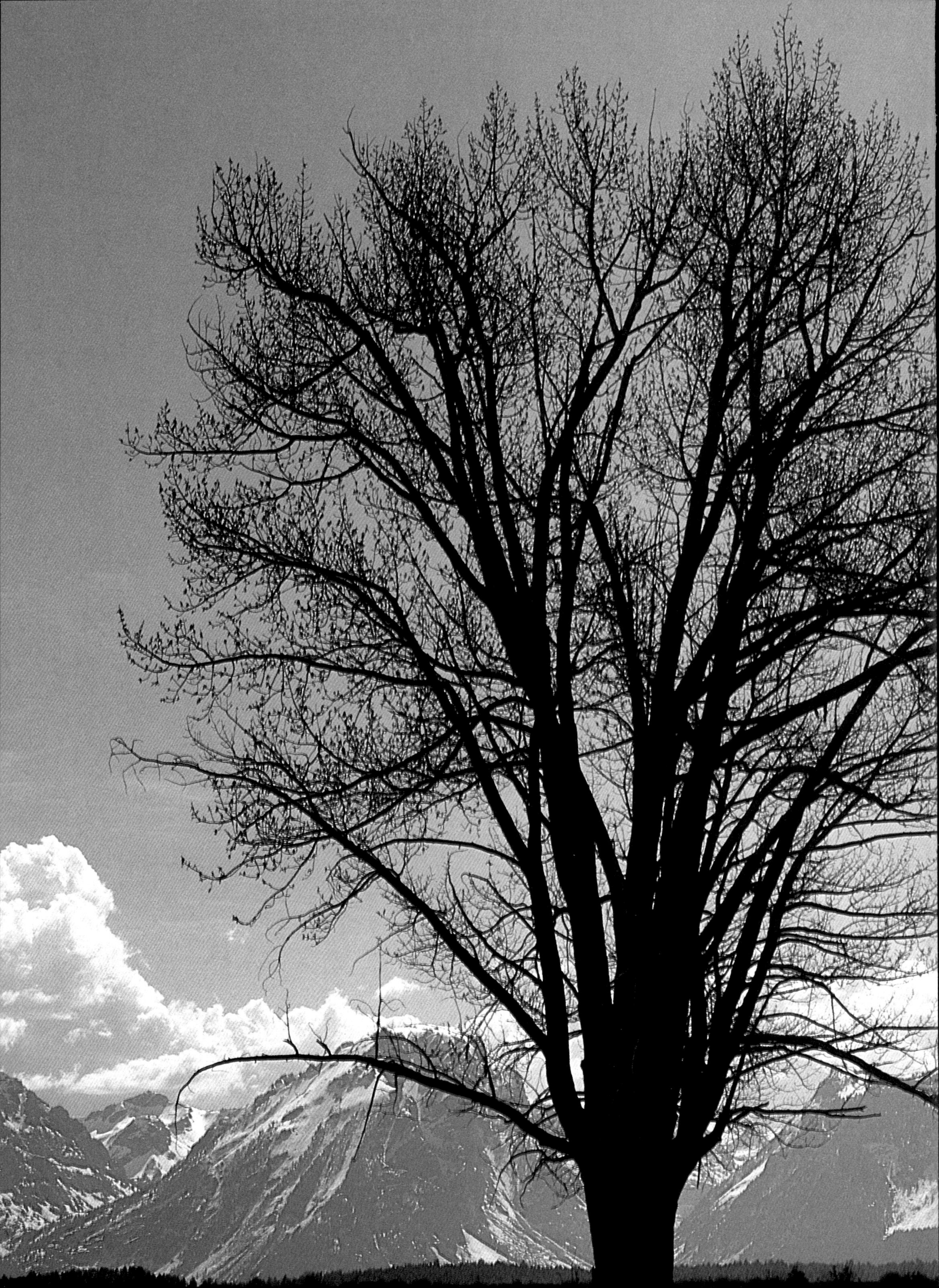

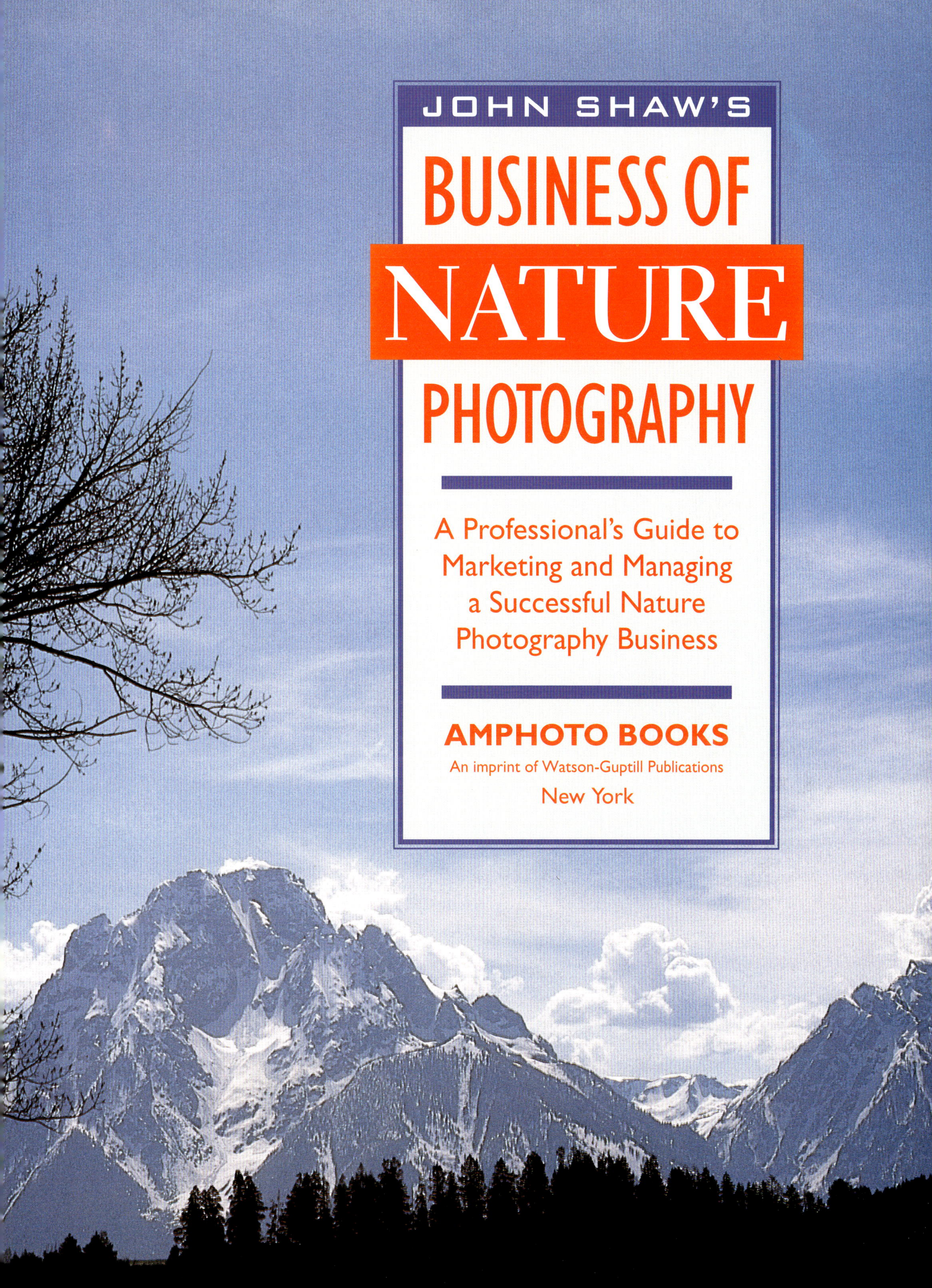
JOHN SHAW'S
BUSINESS OF
NATURE
PHOTOGRAPHY
A Professional's Guide to Marketing and Managing a Successful Nature Photography Business
AMPHOTO BOOKS
An imprint of Watson-Guptill Publications
New York

John Shaw, an internationally acclaimed nature photographer, is the author of four best-selling Amphoto books: *The Nature Photographer's Complete Guide to Professional Field Techniques* (1984), *John Shaw's Closeups in Nature* (1987), *John Shaw's Focus on Nature* (1991), and *John Shaw's Landscape Photography* (1994). He lives in Colorado Springs, Colorado.

Title page:
Cottonwood tree silhouetted against the Teton Range, seen from near Oxbow Bend.

Opposite page:
Alpine sunflower growing between tundra rocks, Mt. Evans, Colorado.

Contents page:
Clouds over mountain ridge at sunset, Olympic National Park, Washington.

First published 1996 in New York by Amphoto Books
an imprint of Watson-Guptill Publications
a division of VNU Business Media, Inc.
770 Broadway, New York, NY 10003
www.watsonguptill.com

Library of Congress Cataloging in Publication Data

Shaw, John, 1944–
[Business of nature photography]
John Shaw's business of nature photography : A professional's guide to marketing and managing a successful nature photography business.
p. cm.
Includes bibliographical references and index.
ISBN 0-8174-4050-X
1. Photography—Business methods. 2. Nature photography.
I. Title.
TR581.S53 1996 96-31125
778.9'3'068—dc20 CIP

Manufactured in Italy

First printing, 1996

5 6 7 8 9/04 03 02

Senior Editor: Robin Simmen
Editor: Liz Harvey
Designer: Jay Anning
Production Manager: Ellen Greene

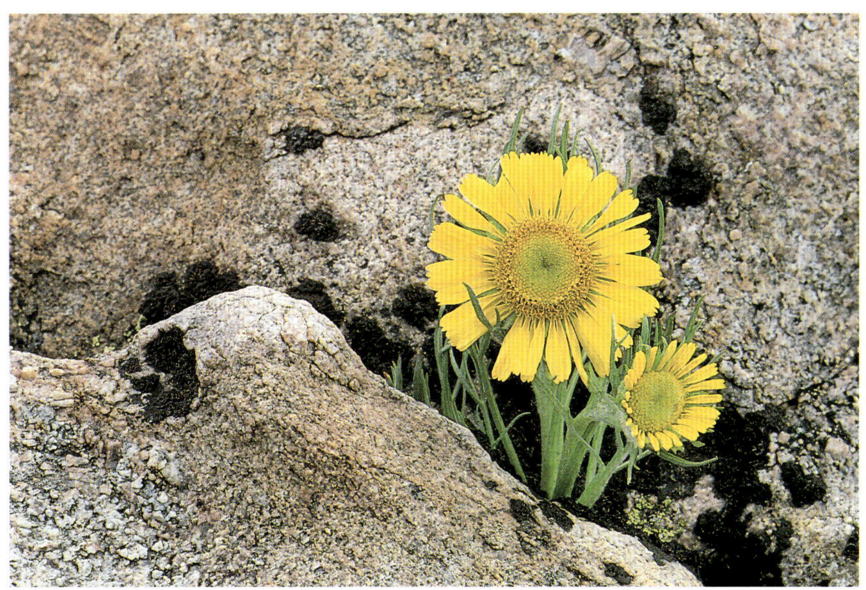

Acknowledgments

My sincere thanks to the many people who in their capacity as editors helped me develop in my career. I'm pleased to count them as friends as well as business associates.

Karen Altpeter, freelance editor

Bob Dunne, *Ranger Rick*

Nick van Frankenhuyzen, Michigan Natural Resources

Ann Guilfoyle, AG Editions

Martha Hill, *Audubon*

Larry Mishkar, NorthWord Press

John Nuhn and Steven Freligh, *National Wildlife*

Judith Parsons, *Ontario Naturalist*

Robin Simmen, Amphoto Books

Tom Stack, Tom Stack and Associates

Barry Tannenbaum, Nikon

Norman Tomalin and Linda Waldman, Bruce Coleman, Inc.

Gordon VanWoerkom, *Birders' World*

Steve Werner, *Outdoor Photographer*

CONTENTS

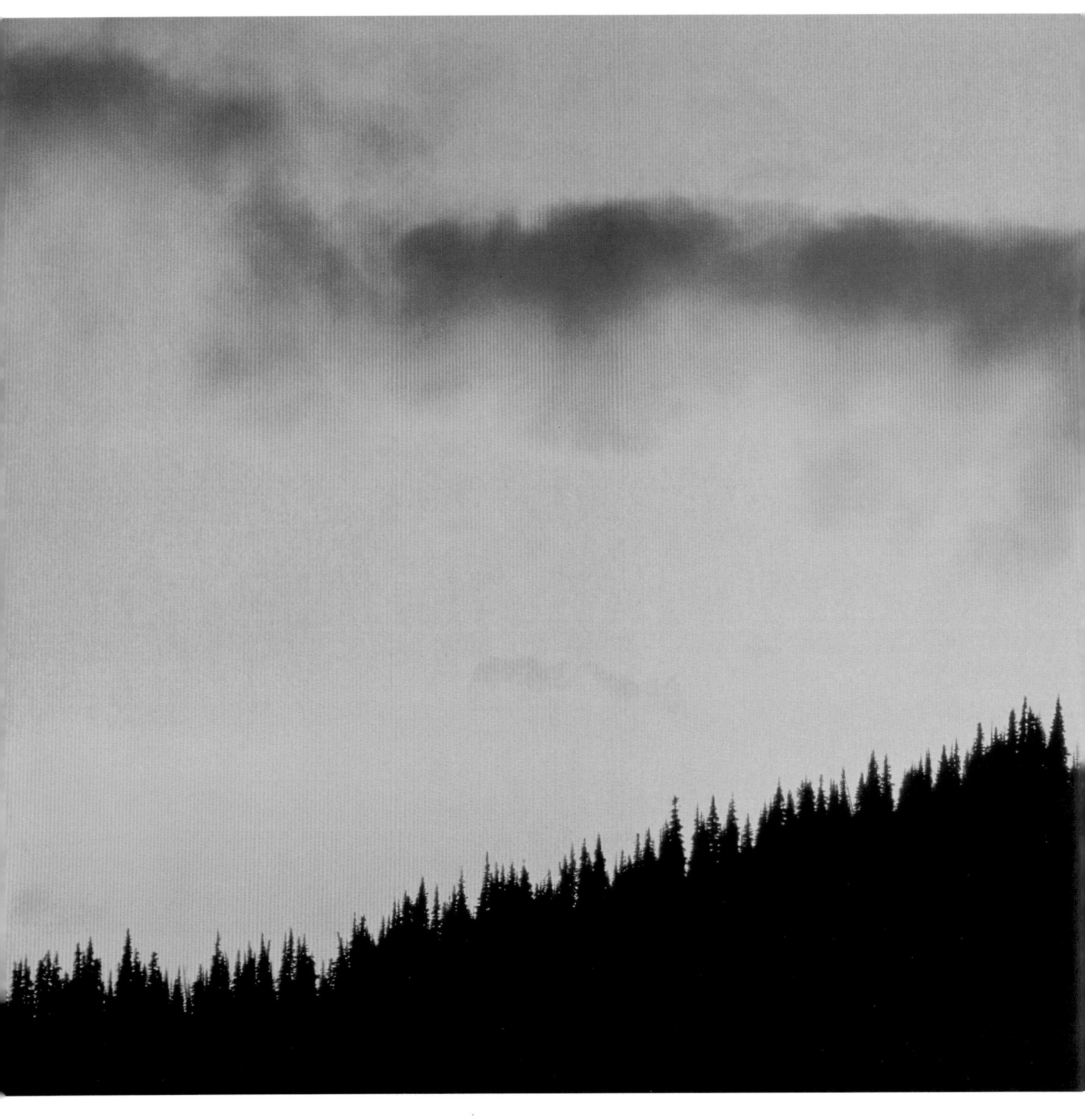

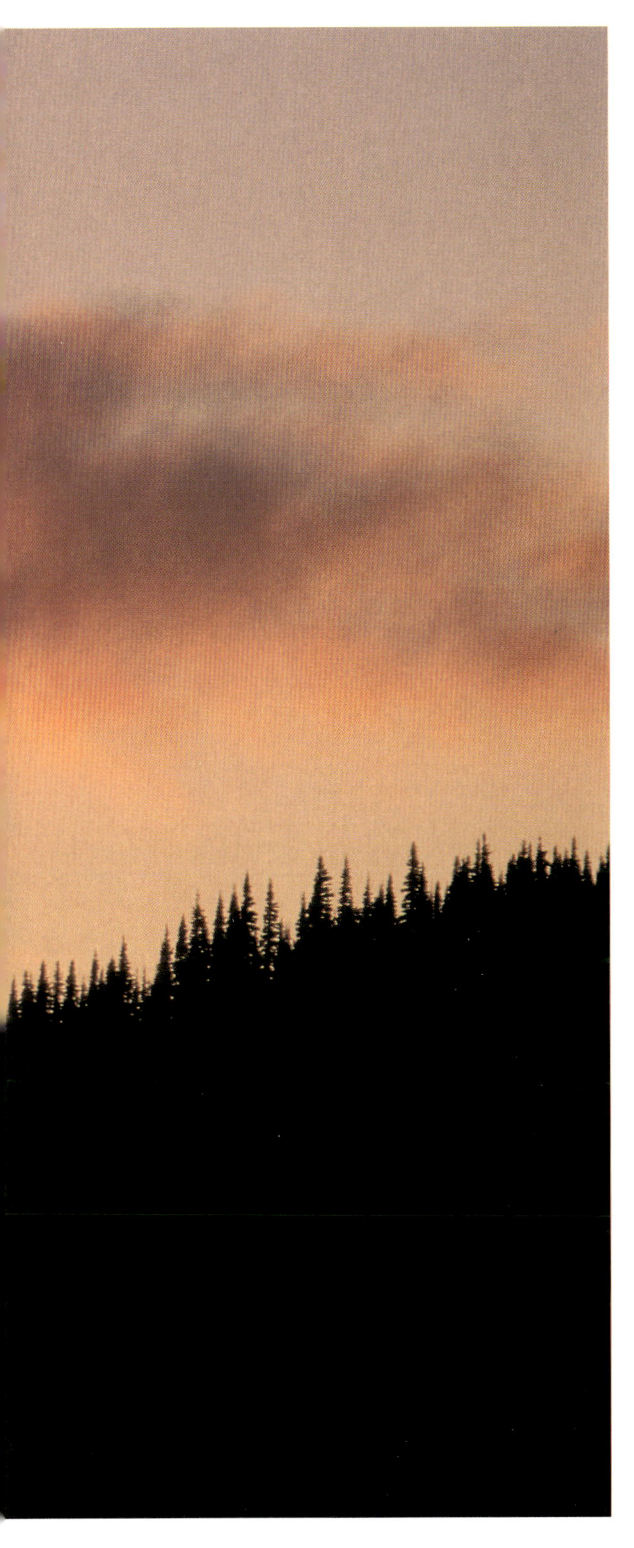

INTRODUCTION 8

CHAPTER ONE
GETTING STARTED 10

CHAPTER TWO
OFFICE WORK 32

CHAPTER THREE
FINDING CLIENTS 52

CHAPTER FOUR
SENDING OUT SUBMISSIONS 78

CHAPTER FIVE
WRITING AND PUBLISHING 94

CHAPTER SIX
MONEY MATTERS 112

APPENDIX
An Overview of Digital Imaging 133
Software Options 136
Handling Rejection 137
Suppliers 138
Miscellaneous Resources 139

Glossary 140
Bibliography 141
Index 143

INTRODUCTION

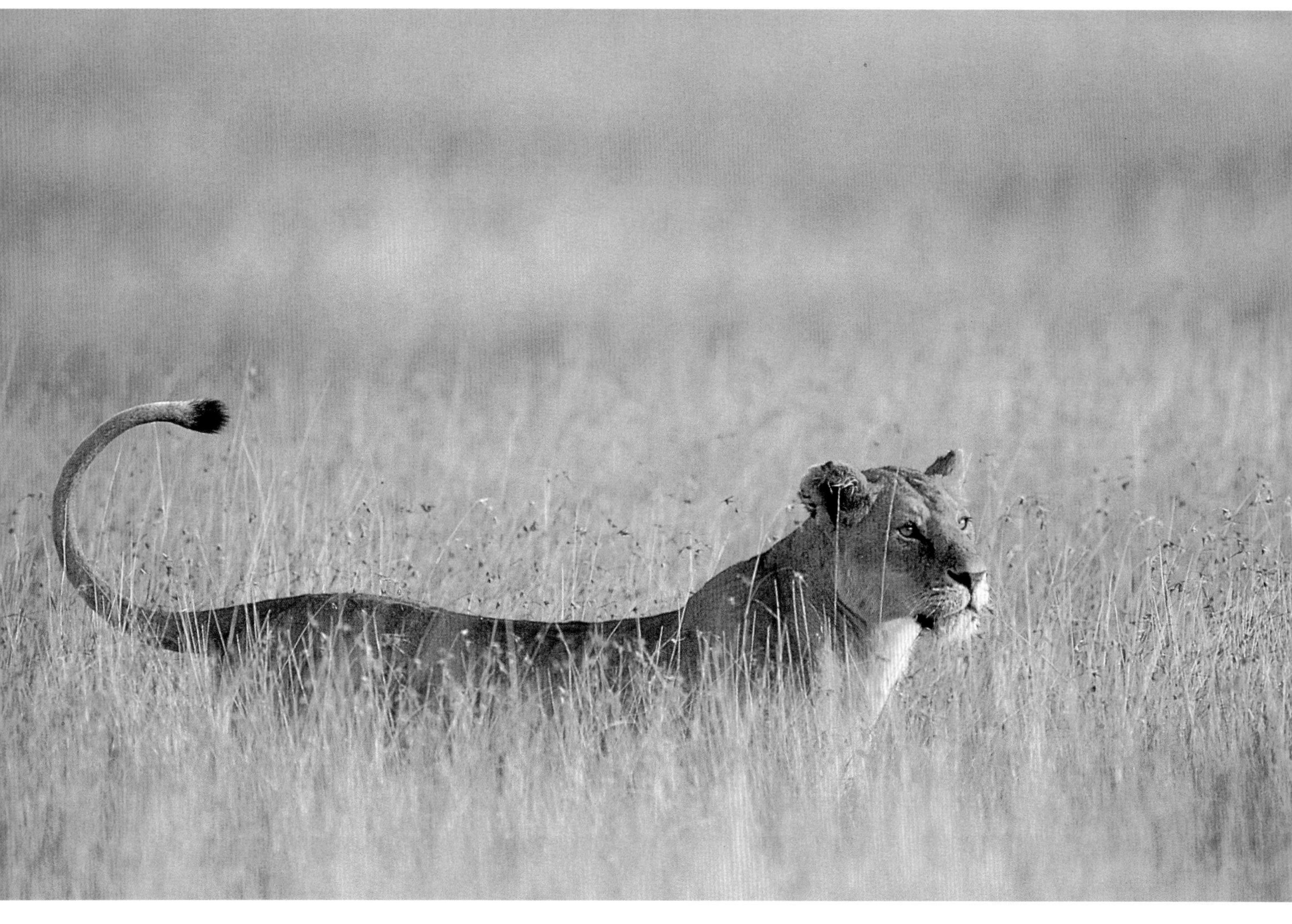

Lioness hunting in tall grass, Masai Mara National Park, Kenya. Nikon F4, Nikon 500mm lens, Fujichrome 100.

You've won several awards at camera-club competitions with your bird photographs. An entertaining slide show you presented for a business group was well received, and several people actually purchased prints of pictures they saw in the show. You're starting to think that perhaps now it is time to take the plunge and become a professional nature photographer. Indeed, you already feel the excitement, knowing that *National Geographic* will call, telling you it has heard about your photography. Consequently the magazine wants to send you to Kenya for six months of shooting with all expenses paid—in addition to a base salary of $5,000 per month. Well, dream on. That isn't how the business of nature photography operates.

Nature photography as a business is demanding and competitive. Being able to take a few good pictures isn't enough; you have to be able to produce many quality images week after week, month after month, year after year. You must stay technologically current, both in your photographic endeavors and in your office procedures. And above all, you must be able to professionally market your images. The world's greatest pictures won't be published if they languish in your files at home. Getting pictures into print is a business and, if you want to publish more than just a rare photograph now and then, you must approach it as such.

So the very first question I'll ask is, "What do you want to accomplish?" Do you want to see just a shot or two printed in a national magazine? Perhaps having a picture in one of the prestigious calendars is more what you had in mind. Possibly a career change is part of your plans. I strongly urge you to sit down and define on paper as specifically as possible exactly what it is you want to do. When you write this out, be as honest with yourself as you can be.

I've been in business full-time as a nature photographer for about 25 years. Indeed, photography (and photography-related activities, such as writing this book) is my one-and-only source of income. Markets for my work include magazines, books, calendars, posters, cards, advertisements—the whole range of printed materials for which natural-history photographs are used. I don't concentrate, and I've never concentrated, on selling photographs as prints that people would hang on a wall. I shoot primarily for reproduction on the printed page, not for the prints made in a darkroom.

I'm telling you this in order to define what this book is and isn't about. This book won't help you at all in selling photographic prints at the local art fair; I don't do that, and I know nothing about doing so. What I cover, as thoroughly as I can, are all the steps in getting natural-history photographs published in the print media, such as magazines, calendars, and books. These steps include setting up an office, organizing and filing your photographs, finding suitable markets, submitting pictures to editors, and getting paid for the use of your photographs.

I discuss all of these topics from one perspective: how I run my own office. I don't presume at all that my way is the only way; indeed, I know many successful nature photographers who have very different business practices than I do. But I do tell you what has worked for me over the time that I've been in business and what procedures I've developed. Take these practices as starting suggestions only, and then tailor them to your precise needs and requirements.

Let me remind you that this book is about professional *nature* photography and only that; it isn't about commercial studio photography or fashion work or mainstream advertising photography. Marketing nature photography is a specialized niche business that I think is distinct from all other areas of professional photography.

I don't delve deeply into the mechanics of taking pictures in this book. If you seriously want to market your nature photographs, you need to have the highest technical standards; good photographic technique is imperative if you must produce more than that one lucky shot. I see this book as a companion piece, an extension if you will, of my previous books. If you want more technical information on the how-to of photography, please read those works carefully. I suggest that in particular you go through my last book, *John Shaw's Landscape Photography*, because the technical and aesthetic discussions in that book apply to all of nature photography.

And finally, I would like to make one suggestion. I think that the photographers who have a deep and abiding affection for their subject matter produce the best nature photographs. Being completely market-driven in your photography—in other words, being concerned only with whether or not a picture is salable—leads to a coldness of attitude that I for one don't want to possess. Adhering to the highest ethical behavior in terms of how you treat your subject matter, how you actually take your photographs, and how you deal with editors and clients will let you state honestly and unequivocally, "I love my job."

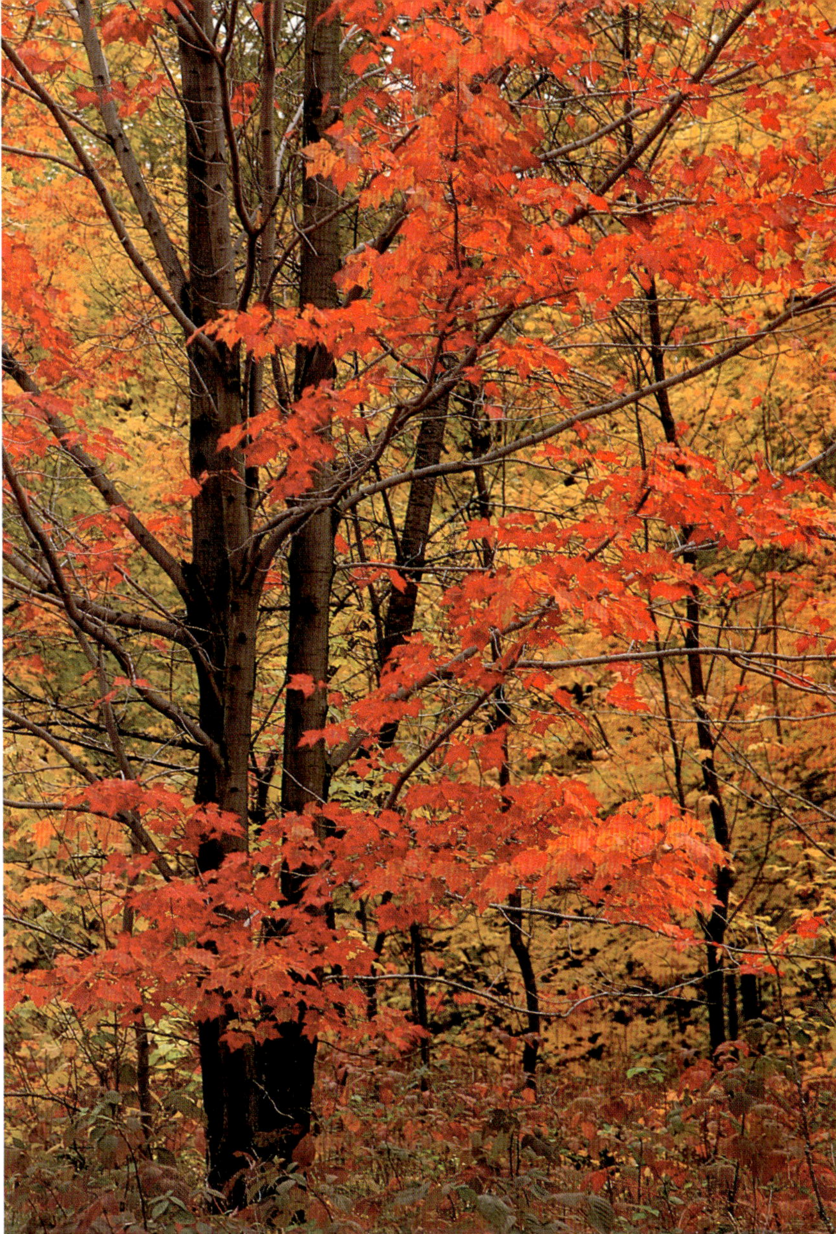

Red maple tree in autumn, Michigan. Nikon F4, Nikon 50-135mm zoom lens, Fuji Velvia.

If you want to sell photographs, they must be aesthetically pleasing and technically perfect. For this shot of an autumn red maple, I composed carefully while shooting with quality film, good optics, and a heavy, solid tripod.

CHAPTER ONE

GETTING STARTED

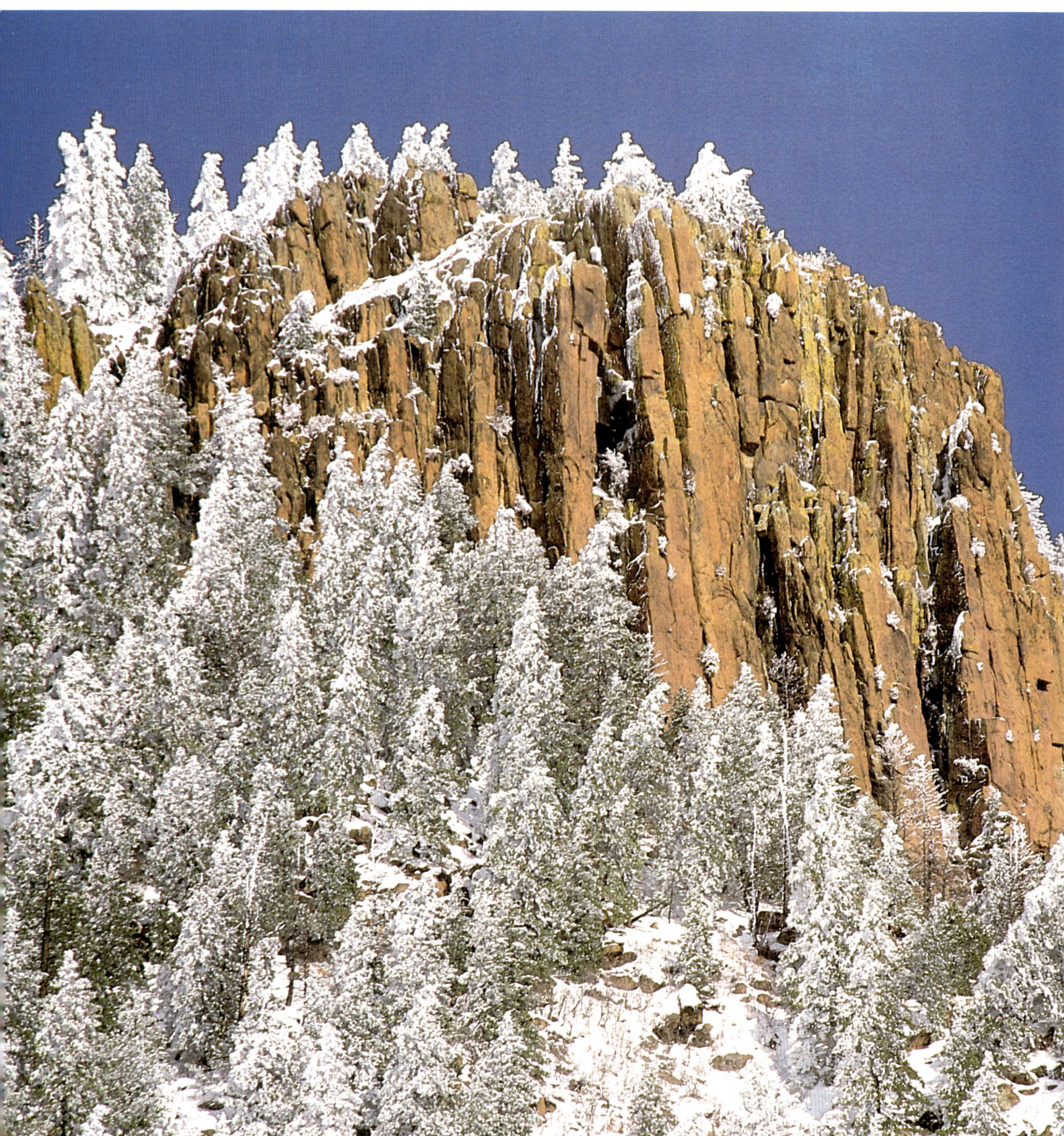

Snow on pines and rock face, Colorado.

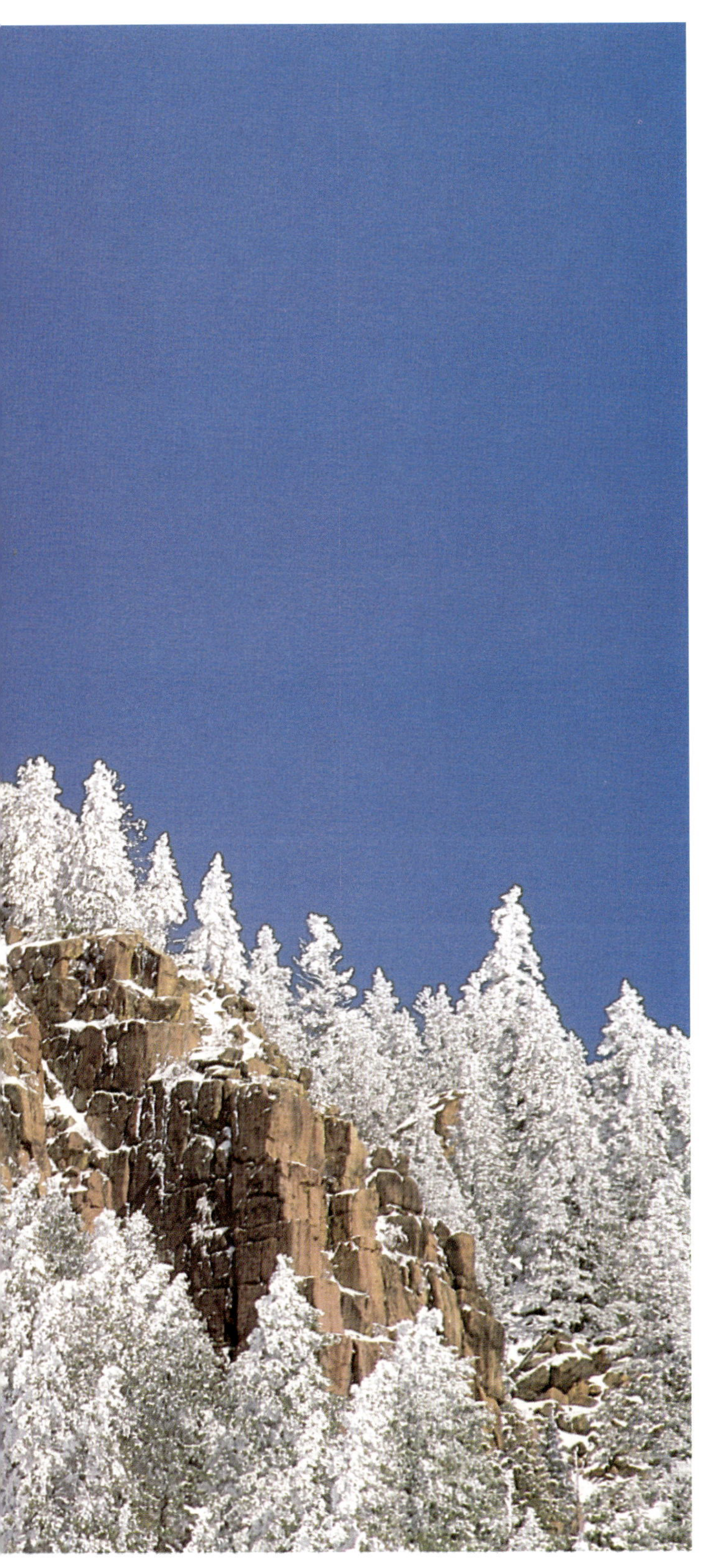

BEGINNINGS

Before you can sell images, you need to have some images to sell. Although this sounds all too obvious, I've run into quite a number of people who have asked about becoming professional nature photographers. When I've inquired, in turn, as to how many pictures they have in their files and of what subjects, their response has been, "Oh, I don't have many good pictures yet. I'll take a lot of them when I contact magazine and book publishers, and they send me to scenic locations."

That isn't the way the natural-history photographic market works. Almost all of the nature pictures you see published today are pulled from photographers' stock files, not shot on assignment. For practical purposes—and especially for photographers starting out—nature-photography assignments are nonexistent. Magazine and book publishers have neither the time nor the money to support photographers in the field while they shoot a natural-history event. True, there are some assignments, and book publishers pay out some advance money, but you shouldn't count on these dollars. The way to get started in the business of nature photography, and the way to stay in business, is to take a lot of pictures and then to market them aggressively yourself.

Basically, a *stock photograph* is one that was taken at an earlier time and is available for use by a client (but generally not as an outright sale). So how many stock photographs do you need in order to break into print? Exactly one. But that photograph has to be precisely what some editor requires at a certain moment in time. Furthermore, not only does the editor need to know about your picture, it must also be readily available at the exact moment it is needed.

Realistically, the number of photographs you must have in your file in order to start marketing depends upon your ambitions. If you want to see only one photograph published somewhere, sometime, then you certainly need far fewer photographs than the person whose dream it is to become a professional nature photographer. Remember that professional photographers may have to support a spouse and/or children, pay a house mortgage and other bills, and still cover the overhead of running a photography business. Needs vary greatly, which is why I urge you to precisely define your goals.

If your desire is simply to see your work in print, to have one or two photographs published, then I think you must have at the very minimum a few hundred top-notch, first-class, knock-your-socks-off photographs. Making your living through your photography is another story, and it calls for you to answer many preliminary questions. First of all, you must put a dollar value on "making a living." How much money do you need? Will your photography be your only source of income? Are you married or single? Do you have children to provide for? What lifestyle do you want to be able to support?

Suppose that you would like to make a net income (after expenses) of $50,000. What are some of your expenses as a professional photographer? Start off with the obvious: equipment, film, and processing. Do you currently own all the camera equipment you need? Buy that autofocus 600mm *f*4 lens you've been thinking about, and you'll have to gross an additional $10,000 just in order to pay for it. Equipment has to justify itself; the lens starts making money only after its initial cost is absorbed.

Shoot the lens enough to make it pay for itself, and another Catch-22 factor comes into play: time. You'll have to spend quite a number of hours using that lens in the field to take the images you need to sell in order to pay for the lens. But this is time you now no longer have available to make a profit with the other equipment you already own and have finished paying for.

Shoot 1,000 rolls of film a year (which isn't much for a professional photographer), and you'll need to gross another $12,000 or so to cover the film and processing costs. Travel to Alaska to shoot all that film through that new lens, and now you have airfares, car rentals, lodging, meals, and incidental expenses. I still haven't mentioned insurance (both for yourself and for your equipment), the cost of an office (computers, printers, file cabinets, etc.), telephone bills, courier accounts for sending photographs to clients, reference books to identify what it is you've photographed, and so on and so on. You can see that professional photography, like most businesses, is one in which overhead can be enormous. While it isn't hard to gross $50,000 a year in this business, it is even easier to spend $51,000 a year doing so.

Back to my question as to how many photographs you need in your file to be a professional photographer. The answer is it takes thousands of photographs to make thousands of dollars. A very rough equation that stock agencies often use (see page 72) is that you're doing well if you average $1 per year per transparency. That is, if you want to gross $50,000 per year through an agency, then you need roughly 50,000 photographs on file to do so. Since agencies ordinarily assess 50 percent of monies received to handle photographs, cutting out the agency would reduce the number of pictures required in half. In this situation, you would need about 25,000 pictures to gross the same $50,000. Remember two essential points here: first, this is just a very rough estimate to give you some idea of numbers; and second, I'm talking about *gross* income, not *net*.

I've always said that you can obtain marketable photographs two ways. One is to take pictures of subjects no one else has photographed. For example, the first person who gets scientifically verifiable pictures of Bigfoot or of the Loch Ness monster will have no trouble marketing the shots. It

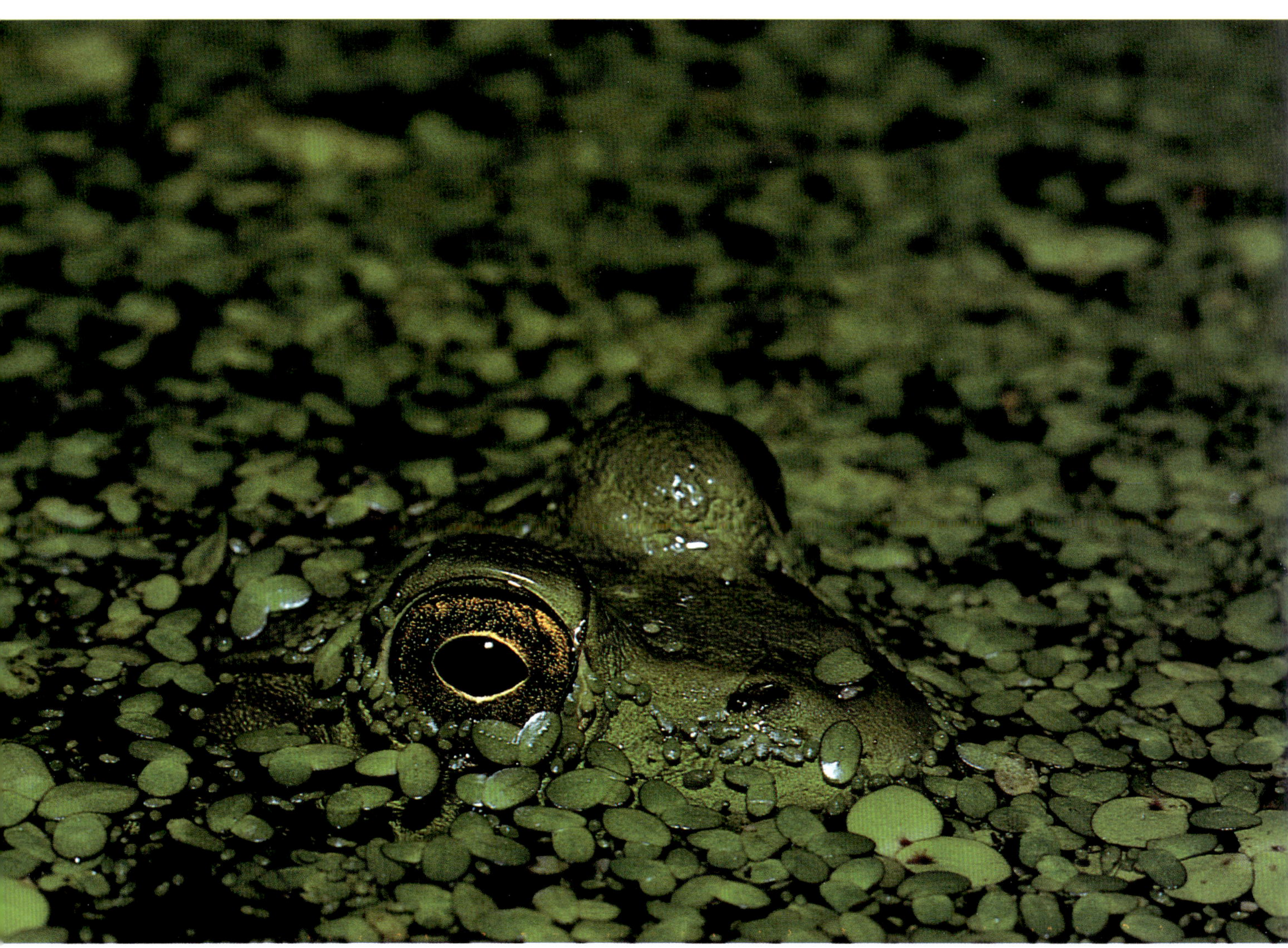

Green frog in duckweed, Michigan. Nikon F2, Nikon 105mm macro lens, Kodachrome 25.

A vernal pond about a mile from where I lived in Michigan was the setting for this shot of a frog.

wouldn't matter if you took the pictures with out-of-date ISO 400 color print film that had been sitting in the sun for a year or two, using a cheap, no-name 400mm lens handheld, and then made duplicate slides for distribution. Because no one else on the planet has similar photographs, you would be paid a great deal of money for them. But what do you do during all the years while you're waiting around for Bigfoot to appear? And what do you do once those pictures have been used?

The other way to get published is to take pictures of subjects many people have photographed, but to do so with the highest technical and aesthetic excellence, then to show editors specifically how to use the resulting photographs. For example, everyone photographs sunsets, colorful autumn leaves, and evocative landscapes. Your shots must be technically superb since your competition's images will undoubtedly be. If you're going to compete with other photographers, you have to be at least as good as they are. This is especially true if you want to publish in the major national magazine, calendar, and book markets.

Of course, you can always get pictures into print if you aim at the lowest markets. Your local community newsletter will welcome any picture it can get—and it most assuredly doesn't pay for these images. *Your Magazine*, circulation 20, will publish anything but *National Wildlife* magazine, circulation about 1,000,000, is another story. Indeed, the undertaking of getting published in just such markets as *National Wildlife* is the subject of this book.

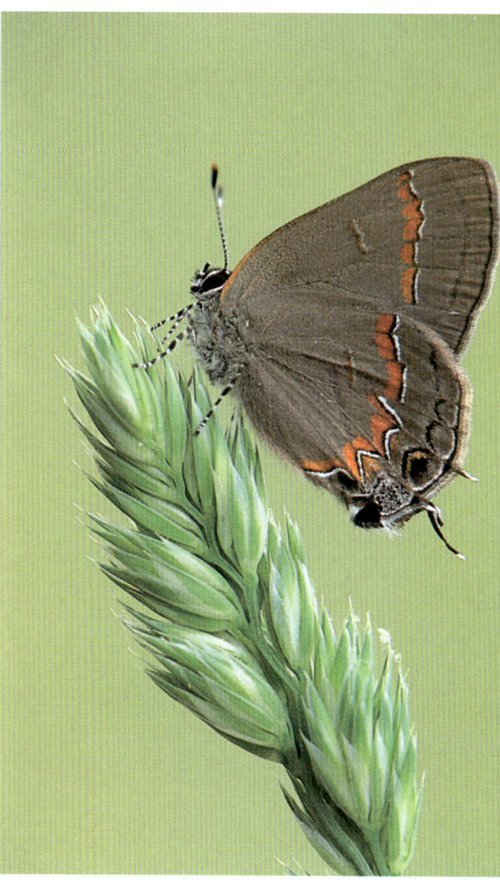

Red-banded hairstreak butterfly, North Carolina. Nikon F4, Nikon 105mm macro lens, Fuji Velvia.

You really don't have to travel to the ends of the earth to take salable nature pictures. The butterfly was photographed close to home; I actually found it sitting on my garage door one day. I flushed it into an adjoining field before photographing it with a handheld flash rig.

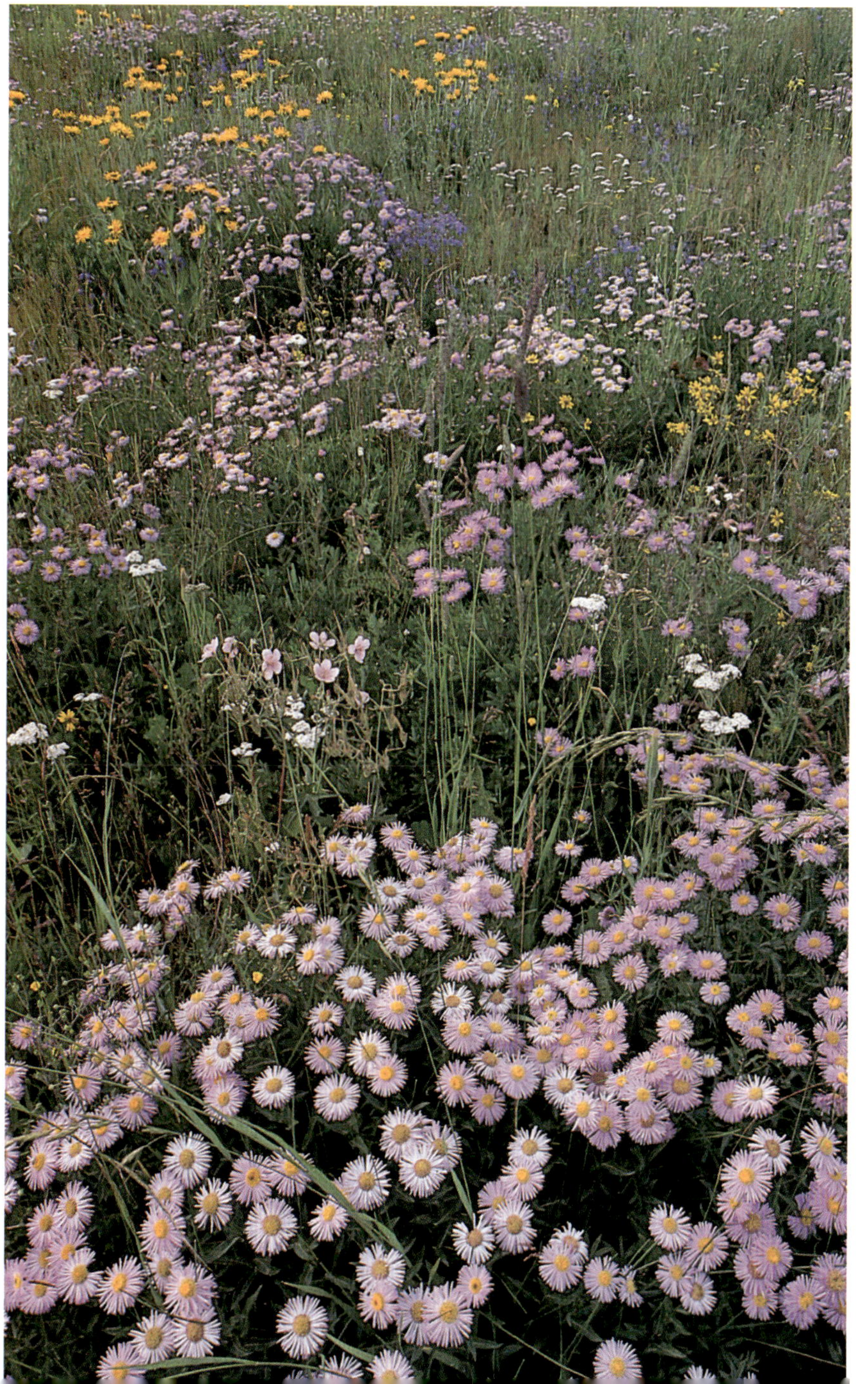

Summer meadow of fleabane, asters, and sunflowers, Colorado. Canon EOS-1, Canon 45mm TS-E lens, Fuji Velvia.

The summer meadow, a magical location in late July, is only a short drive from where I live.

PHOTOGRAPHIC EQUIPMENT

Your first order of business is to go out and take some pictures. To do this you obviously need some camera equipment, but what? A lot depends on the subjects you want to photograph: the grand landscape, birds and mammals, intimate nature details, wildflower portraits, etc. If you're reading this book, I can assume you're already photographing, so for a start just use whatever equipment you already have. If you're contemplating seriously marketing your work, I can easily be much more specific: start out with 35mm SLR equipment.

The Advantages of 35mm

Why not shoot larger-format cameras—for example, 2¼-inch square, 6 x 7cm, or 4 x 5 inch—rather than 35mm cameras in order to obtain more sharpness and detail in your pictures? Well, there are some pluses and minuses with larger-format cameras when compared to 35mm. It is true that the larger the film format, the more detail can be rendered at any enlargement size. But, and the following are major "buts," 35mm cameras are easier to operate in the field, have viewfinders that show the image right side up and unreversed, have extensive lens options, are readily obtainable, aren't grossly expensive, have many film choices easily available, are relatively inexpensive to shoot per frame, and can be used to photograph subjects ranging from extreme closeups to the broadest scenic.

Larger-format cameras have some of these attributes, but not all. Consider, for example, a typical 4 x 5 field camera. The groundglass shows a relatively dim view of an upside-down, backwards image, which takes some getting used to. While this type of camera is great for slow, studied landscape photography, it has some limitations due to lens choices. An 80-200mm zoom lens on a 35mm camera gives much longer equivalent focal lengths than those of the lenses most view camera photographers own.

You can't photograph wildlife with a view camera unless you're taking a landscape shot that includes animals—and then the animals better be completely still. Tight closeups aren't very practical in the field either. Consider that a full-frame shot of a dandelion made with a 4 x 5 camera is actually about a 4X magnification photograph, while with a 35mm camera you're shooting at roughly life-size.

Why not a medium-format outfit then? Well, if you want to photograph wildlife at all, the few lenses available won't be adequate. The longest lens offered for a Hasselblad is a 500mm *f*8, which is roughly the equivalent of a 300mm lens on a 35mm camera. The problem with an *f*8 lens should be obvious: it doesn't allow a lot of light for you to focus with or to shoot by. To achieve the effect of a longer lens with a Hasselblad, you must add a 2X teleconverter; this yields a 1000mm *f*16 lens. Birds and mammals aren't the most active in high-noon light. In addition, the weight, size, and bulk of most medium-format systems work against them for field use.

Begin with a 35mm system and, if you want, add another format in the future. I know of few working nature photographers who started out with larger-format cameras and who now work only with them. Almost everyone uses 35mm to some degree. After all, how many pictures can you produce with your camera? The business of nature photography is a volume business, as you'll see. Under the best of conditions, how many 4 x 5 images can a photographer shoot during the course of a month? Far fewer than the possible number of 35mm frames.

Let me break this down further, to cost per frame. As of this writing, an individual frame of 35mm color slide film costs approximately 30 cents for the film and processing, while each sheet of 4 x 5 film costs about $3. Shoot 4 x 5 film, and your overhead for film and processing is instantly 10 times higher than that of 35mm film. This means that either you have to find markets that pay 10 times better rates or you have to make 10 times the number of picture sales.

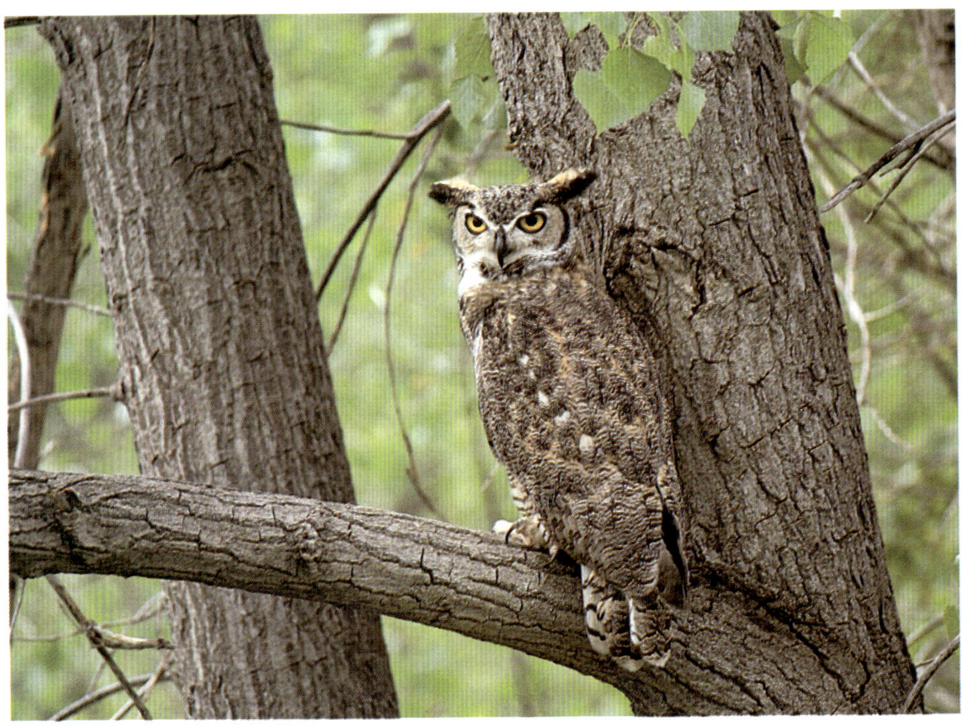

Great horned owl in cottonwood tree, Colorado. Nikon F4, Nikon 500mm lens, Fujichrome 100.

Wildlife photography is far easier with 35mm equipment than any other format as lenses are both varied and readily available. I made this shot with a 500mm lens, although a 400mm or a 600mm would have yielded similar results.

Actually the cost per salable frame of 4 x 5 film is even a little higher: 35mm film comes back from the lab already mounted, while 4 x 5 film doesn't. You must purchase stock frames, then take the time to mount each and every sheet of film before you can send it to a client. And, as in all businesses, time is money.

I'm not suggesting that you shouldn't consider shooting with larger-format cameras. Far from it. But I've heard beginners comment that you must shoot large format in order to sell landscape photographs. This simply isn't true. My career has been built around 35mm; in fact, well over 95 percent of my income is from sales of 35mm photographs. I've shot other formats—6 x 7cm, 4 x 5 inch, 6 x 17cm panoramic—and will continue to do so, but 35mm is what makes my house payments.

Selecting a 35mm System

Notice that I said to start with a 35mm *system*. If you're going to be serious about nature photography, you want your camera equipment to be able to grow as your interests grow. You can produce salable images and make your living with any 35mm camera currently on the market. The actual brand of camera is immaterial. However, I urge you to purchase the very best lenses you can afford. A camera body is basically just a light-proof box that houses the film. A built-in exposure meter or flash or motordrive are just accessories that manufacturers add to their cameras. The technical quality of your pictures, though, can only be as good as the quality of your lenses.

If you are on a limited budget and are faced with the choice of an expensive camera body and cheap, off-brand lenses or of a non-top-of-the-line camera body with better lenses, definitely opt for the latter. Given a choice, I would stick to the major-brand camera manufacturers' lenses, as these tend to be optically superb and mechanically reliable. This last point is critical if you're planning on earning a living with your cameras.

I would be far more concerned with the reliability and ruggedness of a camera than with its brand name. There seems to be a photographic natural law that camera malfunctions are directly proportional to the difficulty faced in getting repairs made. To check on reliability, you can contact local camera-repair shops and ask how often its staff works on specific camera models.

You can also ask professional nature photographers why they own certain pieces of equipment. Locating these photographers is actually easy, although getting to these places might be difficult. Check out Alaska's Denali National Park in late August, Florida's Ding Darling National Wildlife Refuge in February, or Colorado's San Juan Mountains in late September. By the way, one of the best justifications I know for purchasing high-quality camera gear is that once you own the best, you have no one but yourself to credit or blame when your pictures turn out well or fail.

But don't let not owning certain equipment at this time limit your photography.

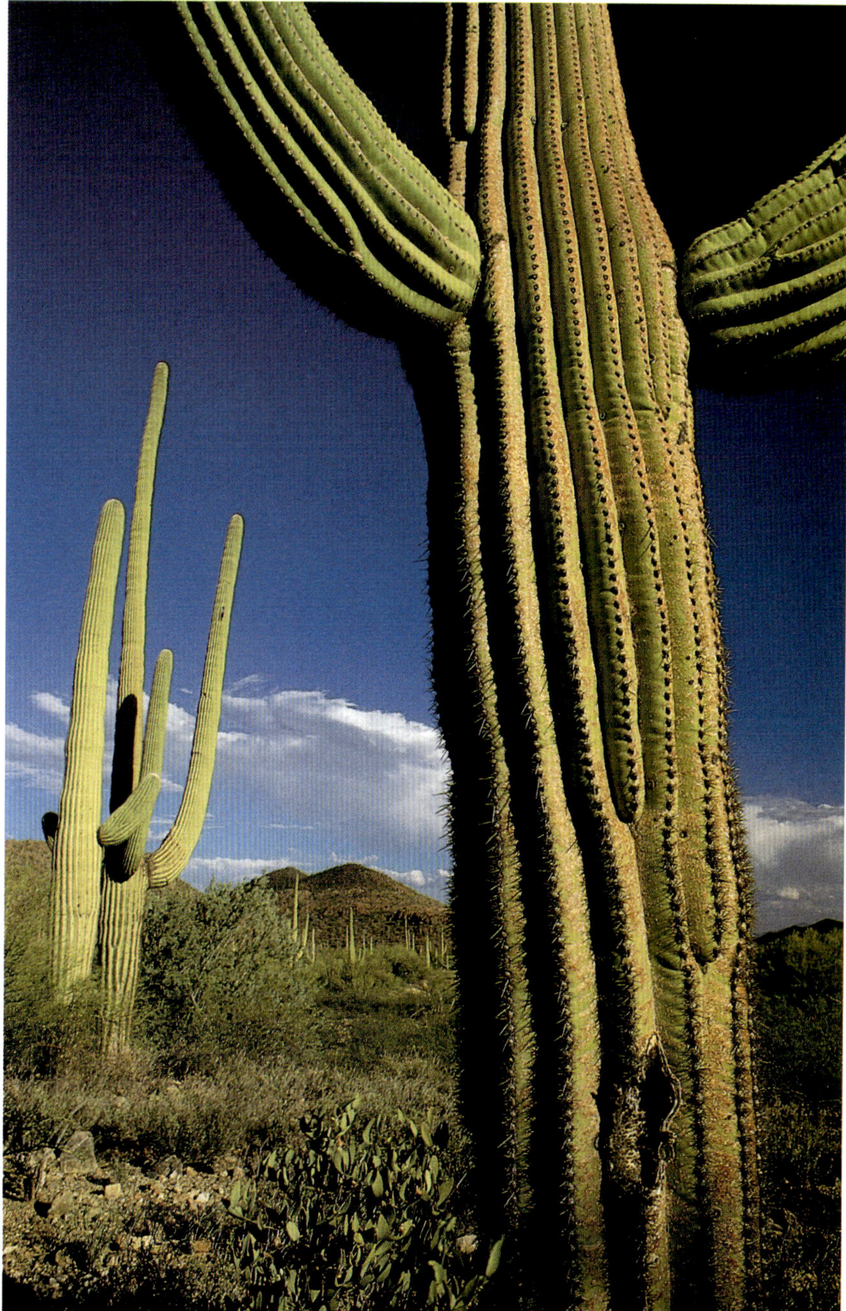

Saguaro cactus, Saguaro National Monument, Arizona. Nikon F4, Nikon 24mm lens, Fujichrome 50.

One of the joys of 35mm photography is that lenses are available in many focal lengths. You can photograph everything from wildlife to wide-angle scenics using the same camera system.

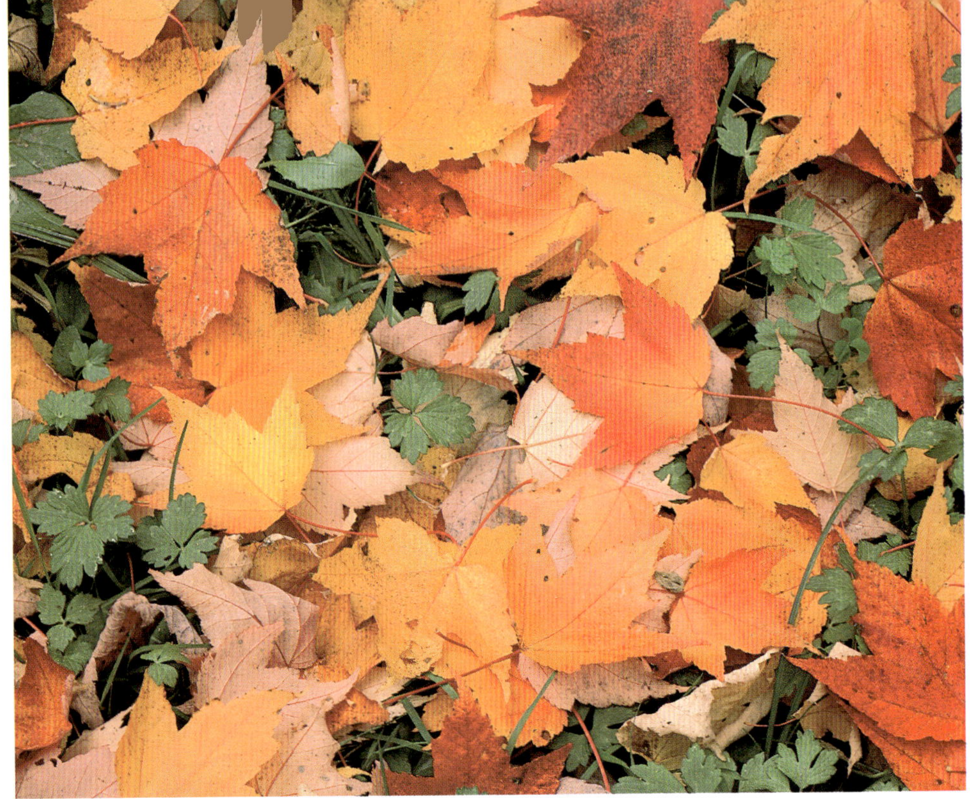

Autumn red maple leaves, Monongahela National Forest, West Virginia. Pentax 6 x 7, Pentax 135mm lens, Fujichrome 50.

I made this shot in the 6 x 7cm format. I must admit that having a transparency you can view without using a loupe is appealing.

Many photographers—and I count myself in this group—fall into the trap of believing that if they only had another lens or a different camera body, their pictures would show a vast improvement. Most of the photographers I know tend to be equipment junkies, always wanting another lens or two. The sad truth is that more equipment generally means exactly that and nothing more; you just have more equipment. Learning to use the equipment you already own to its fullest potential is what really makes a difference.

The Essentials

All camera equipment is *not* created equal. This is especially true in the world of 35mm cameras since so many different models with various features are on the market. Each of the major camera manufacturers offers at least three or four distinctly unique camera bodies, along with all sorts of accessories. What to do? Well, I think that certain pieces of equipment and some specific camera features are necessary to have if you intend to photograph as a profession (see the chart on page 19).

Total Exposure Control

I can't imagine attempting serious work without being able to control exposure precisely as I want. I like using a camera that allows completely manual control of exposure settings along with autoexposure modes. If you do want to use a fully autoexposure camera, make sure it has a total autoexposure compensation system. At a minimum it should provide two full stops of compensation on either side of the metered value, in half-stop increments (third-stops would be even better). Full-stop autoexposure settings don't permit the fine-tuned exposure control required for shooting color slide films.

Total exposure control also means a having a full range of shutter speeds available. The top-end speeds of 1/2000 sec., 1/4000 sec., 1/8000 sec., and even faster are meaningless. I don't think I've ever used a speed faster than 1/1000 sec., and it is hard to remember the last time I even used that shutter speed. If you're photographing birds and mammals in the field and you're using a film such as Fuji Provia or Kodak Lumière, the correct exposure in blazing, full sunlight for a frontlit subject is 1/1000 sec. at *f*/5.6. I would much rather use this shutter speed and have some depth of field to make sure my subject is all in focus, than crank the shutter up and shoot at 1/4000 sec. at *f*/2.8. In truth, I do most of my bird and mammal photography at speeds far closer to 1/250 sec.

When you shoot landscapes and close-ups, you commonly work stopped down to around *f*/16 or *f*/22 for extensive depth of field. An ISO 50 film, even in full sunlight, is properly exposed at 1/60 sec. at *f*/16, but rarely would you ever shoot a scenic in such light. Most of the time you'll be working at very slow speeds because some of the most beautiful illumination occurs early and late in the day.

In fact, the shutter speeds I want most on a camera aren't the fast speeds but the slow ones. Many current camera bodies offer timed shutter speeds as long as 30 seconds, although sometimes these speeds are available in only selected exposure modes. You can certainly use a camera that has no marked speeds slower than 1 sec. by doing the old "one-thousand-and-one, one-thousand-and-two" routine with the shutter-speed selector set on "Bulb." The 2 sec. speed will probably be your most variable; after that you can always use a watch for timing. However, newer cameras with built-in slow shutter speeds are far more convenient, especially when you're working in the field in bad weather. It is easy to lose track of what you're doing photographically when your teeth are chattering.

Depth-of-Field Preview

I wouldn't recommend any camera for serious nature photography that didn't have some provision for depth-of-field preview. This feature enables you to stop your lens down to your shooting aperture, thereby permitting you to preview the depth of field that will appear in the final photograph. Ordinarily when you look through a lens you're viewing with it wide open at its maximum aperture; you're seeing the depth of field of that *f*-stop, not the *f*-stop you've selected to use for your exposure. I want to see exactly what my pictures will look like on film, and not just guess about the results. Aside from fast-action subjects, I use the depth-of-field preview before almost every photograph I take.

A Complete System of Lenses

At the very minimum if you're going to photograph a full range of natural-history subjects, you need lenses covering the range from 24mm to 300mm. Whether or not you own them, having both wider and longer focal lengths available for your camera brand, say from 20mm to 600mm, would be ideal.

You don't need to buy every prime focal length in this range. In fact, I would urge you to consider zoom lenses if you're just starting to purchase equipment. Fifteen years ago the quality of zoom lenses was so-so at best, but this isn't true any longer. Today's zoom lenses are superb, especially in the middle-focal-length range. For professional work I would certainly avoid too extreme a zoom range, such as 28-200mm, because it is impossible to make one lens do everything well. Besides, carrying only one zoom lens to cover a number of focal lengths is an invitation to disaster in the field. What if the lens breaks?

On page 19 you'll find my recommendations for a basic starter 35mm outfit, with two possible lens combinations. The first requires more pieces to cover the complete range of focal lengths, but I would prefer the first outfit since if the long lens malfunctioned, I would still have focal lengths extending to 200mm. With the second outfit, I would be restricted to a maximum focal length of 70mm if the longest lens quit.

Of course, these are absolute minimal lens choices. If you're interested in shooting many closeups, add a 105mm, or better yet, a 200mm macro lens. As soon as possible, you should also get a longer telephoto lens, either a 400mm or 500mm.

So far I haven't mentioned lens speed, which is the maximum aperture of a lens. I see no reason to own really fast lenses—those around *f*1.4—for nature photography because you'll almost always be shooting stopped down. My fastest lens is a 35mm *f*2, but the lenses I carry and use the most often are *f*3.5 and *f*4. However, for longer focal lengths, 300mm and up, buy a relatively fast lens, no slower than *f*4. Remember, the speed of a lens is relative to its focal length. So *f*4 is fast for a 500mm, fairly normal for a 200mm, and abysmally slow for a 50mm. Don't purchase any lens slower than *f*4 if you can avoid doing so.

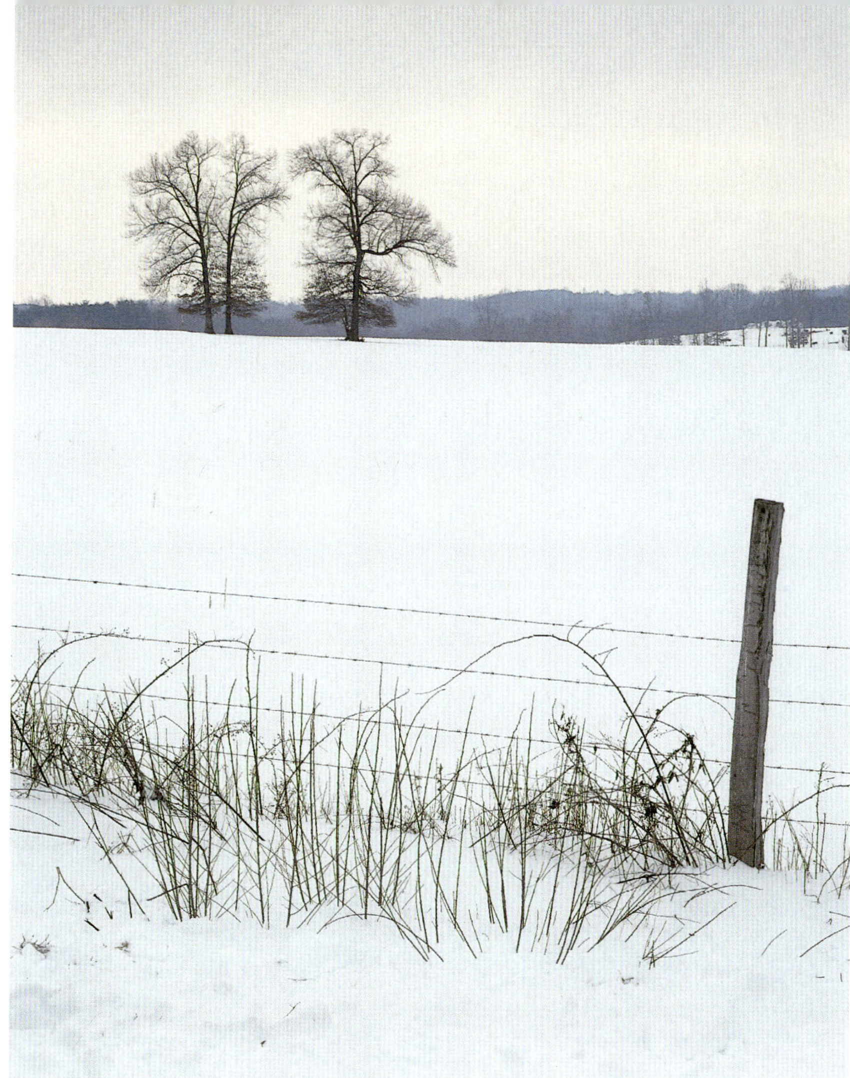

Winter field, North Carolina. Pentax 6 x 7, Pentax 55mm lens, Fujichrome 50.

Photographers often use formats larger than 35mm for landscapes and landscape details, such as this cold midwinter scene. But these cameras really aren't suited for extremely tight closeups or for photographs requiring very long lenses.

Tripods and Heads

Without a doubt, the best photographic accessory you can buy is a good-quality, sturdy tripod. If you want to exponentially improve the technical merit of your photographs, use a tripod. I don't know of any working professional nature photographer who doesn't shoot every picture possible with the camera firmly mounted on a tripod.

Be aware, though, that not all tripods are created equal. In fact, I find that most tripods on the market today aren't suitable for nature photography in the field; they are too short, too flimsy, too awkward to use, and too apt to pinch your fingers. Unfortunately most photographers seem to go through the same succession of tripods. First they buy a cheap $39.99 tripod, then a month after than they buy a $59.99 special, then a year—and much frustration—later, they finally buy a quality tripod. Do yourself a favor, and skip right to a good one. The following suggestions are in my order of preference.

The Gitzo 340, 320, and 410 models are relatively heavy tripods. More professional nature photographers probably use Gitzo tripods than any other brand. The reason: they work.

The Bogen 3021 and 3221 are twins, the chrome and black-anodized, versions respectively, of the same tripod. Lighter and much less expensive than Gitzos, Bogens are probably the second most used tripod by pros. If you are more than 6 feet tall or if you often use lenses with focal lengths of 400mm and up, you should buy a Gitzo tripod. The two Bogens are neither tall nor sturdy enough for really long lenses.

Regardless of the tripod, you'll have to add a head, either a three-way pan/tilt head that offers independent movement in each axis, or a ball-socket head that provides free movement in all directions when the ball is loosened. I would strongly urge you to add

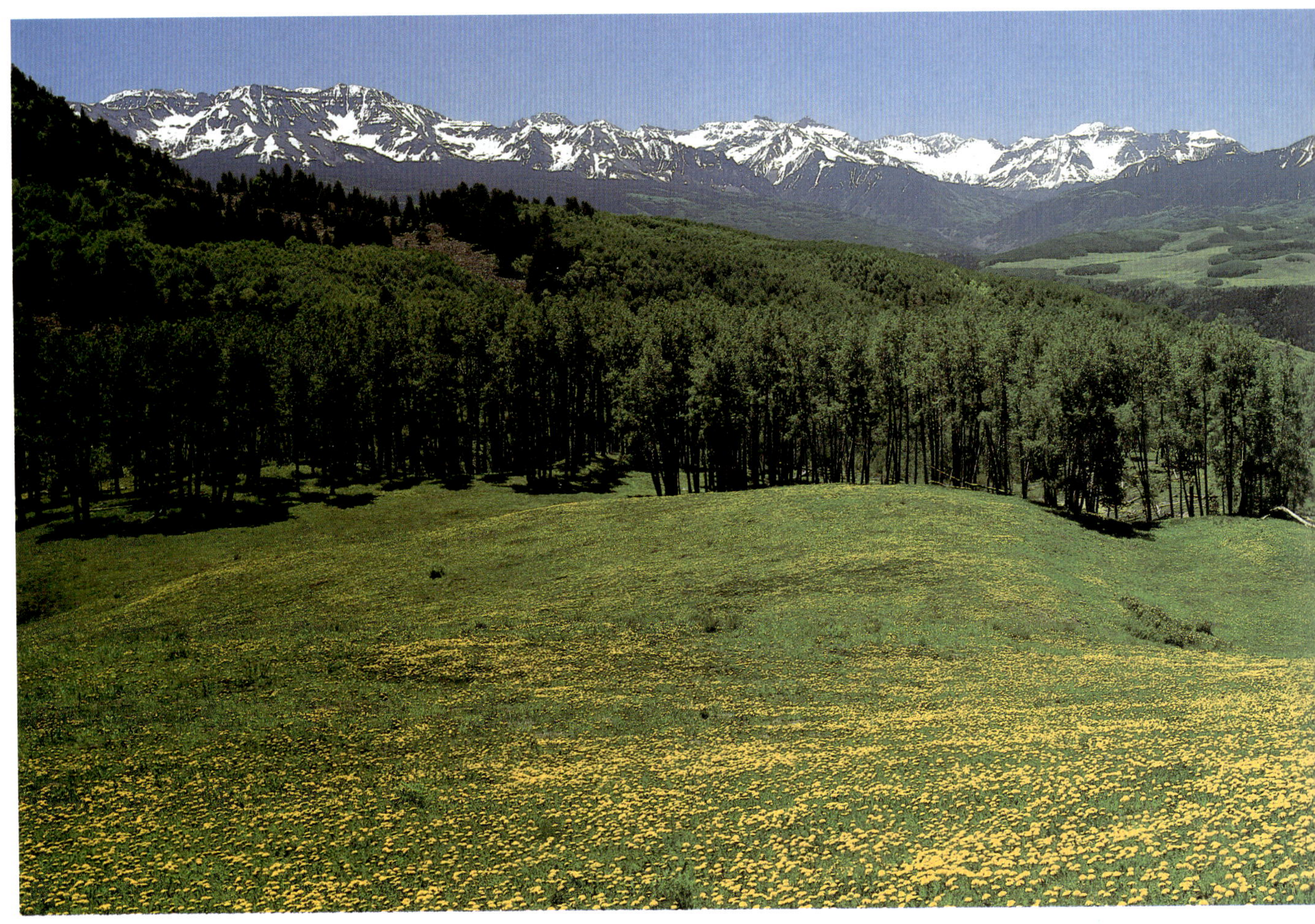

Mt. Wilson and the San Miguel Mountains, Colorado. Fuji G617, fixed Fuji 105mm lens, Fuji Velvia.

Here is a good application of a special format, in this case the 6 x 17cm panoramic. As much as I like working with this camera, it wouldn't be my first choice in equipment if I wanted to sell photographs. It doesn't offer TTL viewing or metering; you get only four shots per roll of 120 film; depth of field is limited with a 105mm lens; and f/22 is the sharpest point on the lens.

a quick-release system to any head you use. The de facto professional standard has become the Arca-Swiss dovetail system, which is used by a number of manufacturers besides Arca.

Mount quick-release plates on all of your camera bodies and lenses, and leave them on. I'm amazed that some photographers buy one plate and try to move it from lens to lens. This isn't a "quick-release" system; it is a "slow-release but quick-frustration" system.

There are several decent three-way heads on the market, including the Bogen 3047 and some of the larger Gitzo heads. Actually I am far more partial to quality ball heads, especially for any bird and mammal photography.

Two distributors offer Arca-style quick-release plates and adapters that are custom-made to fit specific lenses and cameras. I highly recommend using custom plates rather than the generic, one-size-fits-all plates supplied for the ball heads listed. (For more specific information about these accessories, contact Kirk Enterprises and Really Right Stuff—see the listing on page 139).

Additional Accessories

While two camera bodies, a selection of lenses, and a sturdy tripod are the core of your equipment, you'll probably want to add other accessories to your starter set. These include flash units, filters, remote releases, teleconverters, and other lens modifications.

Be careful, though, not to get overloaded with equipment. Owning more equipment definitely won't make you a better photographer. I can't stress this point too emphatically. Equipment by itself doesn't take pictures; the very best optics on the market can't produce pictures without being used correctly. It is much better to have less equipment and to use it well, than to have tons of equipment and to use it badly.

The secret of taking salable photographs isn't what equipment you own, but how you use it. Technique—how you use your equipment in the field—is the deciding factor. The best cameras and lenses used haphazardly will produce sloppy photographs, while mediocre equipment that is wielded with strict attention to technique can produce exquisite images. Nothing, however, is a substitute for photographic vision.

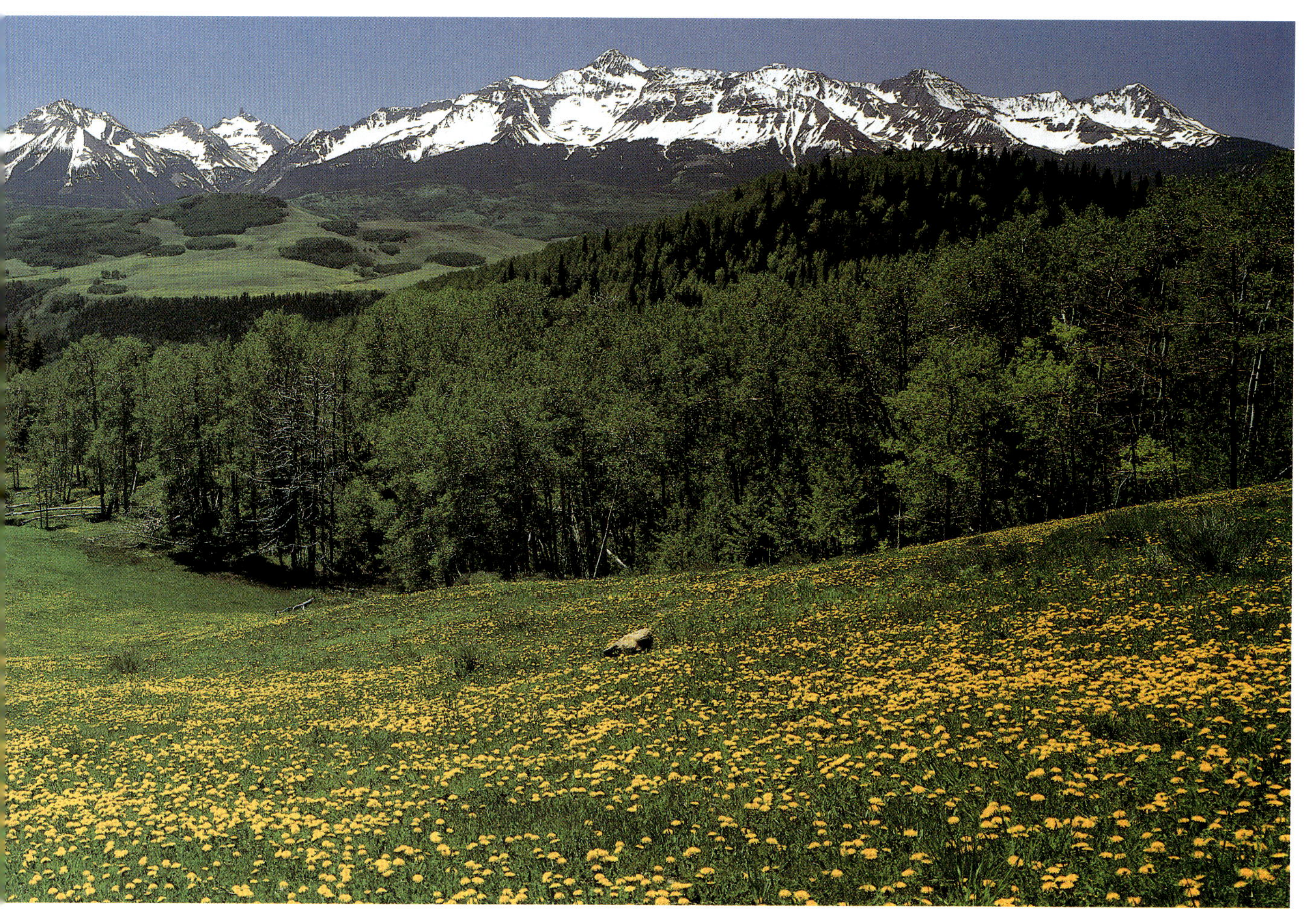

A BASIC 35MM STARTER SET

Even for a basic starter 35mm outfit two camera bodies are an absolute necessity for professional photography. Here are my recommendations to round out a basic outfit:

Basic lens set
24mm
35–70mm
70–210mm zoom or 80-200mm zoom
300mm

Optional lens set
24mm
28–70mm zoom
75–300mm zoom or
100–300mm zoom

Tripods
Consider one of these models:
Gitzo 340, 320, and 410R
Bogen 3021 and 3221

Tripod heads
Here are three models I recommend:
Arca-Swiss B1
Studioball QR
Foba Ballo QR

Additional accessories
Here are some other accessories that I think you'll want to add to your basic outfit as soon as possible:

1.4X teleconverter for your longest lens

Powerful TTL flash unit with its off-camera cord

Quality glass polarizing filter and an 81A filter, in sizes to fit all your lenses

2-stop graduated neutral-density filter

Remote release

Extension tube(s)

Two-element closeup lens (one of the Nikon T-series of closeup diopters) for your long zoom

FILMS

No one film is perfectly suited for all subjects, in all lighting conditions. In addition, all photographers have their own preferences when it comes to color rendition, grain, and sharpness of individual films. But if you want to market your photography to books, magazines, calendars, and, someday, advertisements, I can easily generalize about the films you should use.

First of all shoot transparency, or slide, film exclusively. Many newspapers today use color print film, but almost all the nature-photography markets demand color slide films for reproduction. Forget about black-and-white film—except for your own enjoyment. After all, how many black-and-white nature pictures do you see published in a year's time? If editors really need a black-and-white shot, a print can be made from a color slide, but a color slide can't be made from a black-and-white negative. For the record, it has been well over 10 years since I've even had an editor ask about converting a transparency to black and white. So shoot color slide film.

Film Speed

Next, favor film with the slowest speed—the one with the lowest ISO number—that you can use in any given situation depending on the light and the subject. If you can shoot an ISO 50 film, don't use an ISO 200. But if you need ISO 200 speed film, don't use ISO 400 film. This is generally true with some provisions. Kodachrome 25 is certainly one of the sharpest, least grainy films on the market, but professional nature photographers rarely use it any more.

As of this writing E6 process films in the ISO 50-100 range dominate the market. These films include Fuji Velvia and Provia, and the Kodak Ektachrome films. The reasons: they rival Kodachrome 25 in terms of both sharpness and grain but at one or two stops faster speeds, and they have pumped-up color saturation. Like all E6 films, they can be developed at hundreds of local processors. However, you need to be selective in your choice of labs. Why spend lots of dollars on the best equipment only to skimp by using a discount processor?

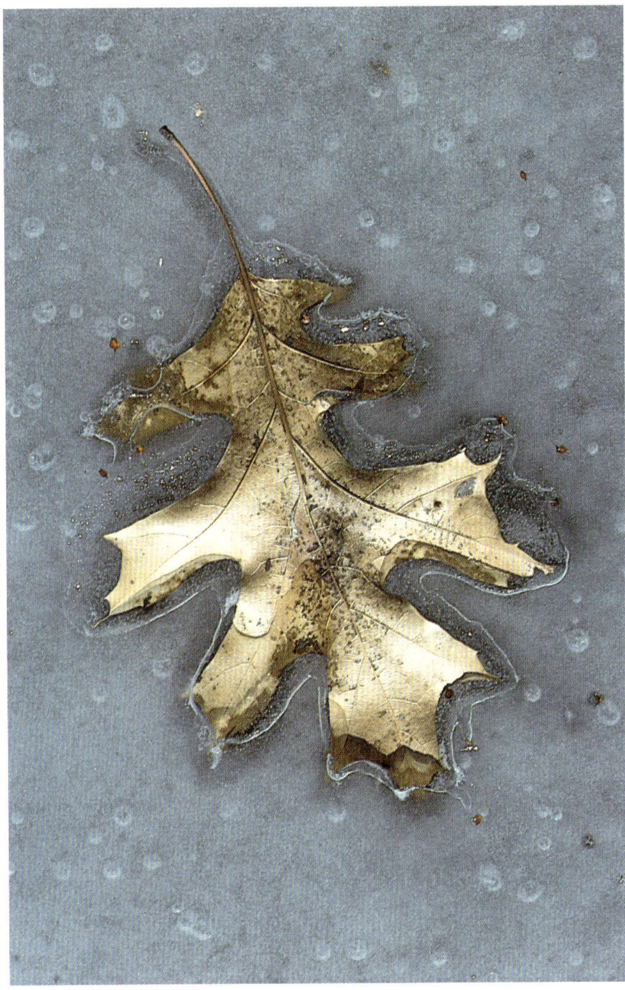

Oak leaf in ice, Michigan. Nikon F3, Nikon 105mm lens, Kodachrome 25.

Here is a perfect subject for a slow film, such as Kodachrome 25. The leaf isn't going anywhere, the light is even, and the colors are muted.

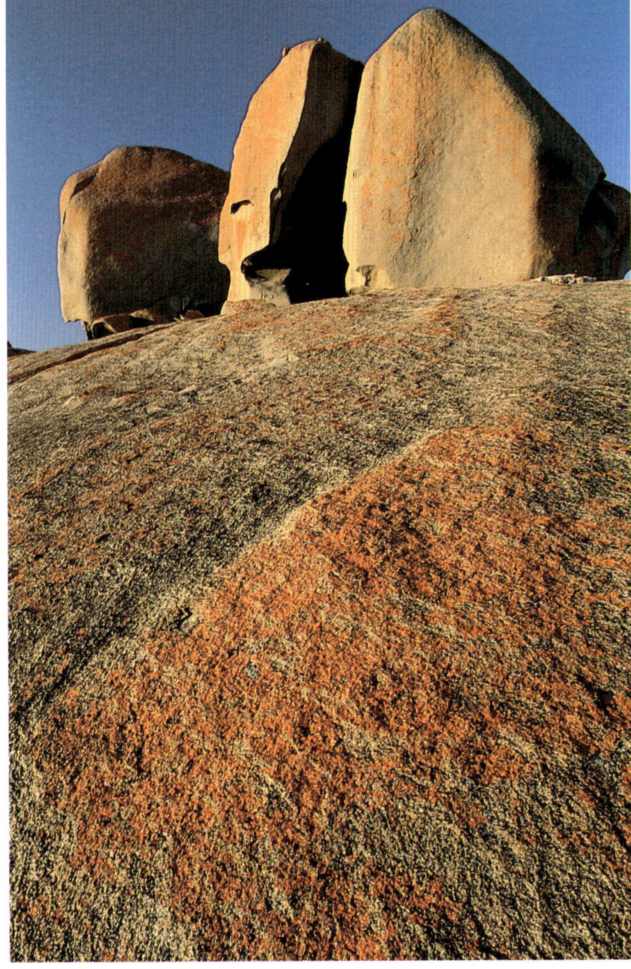

The Remarkable Rocks, Flinders Chase National Park, Australia. Nikon F4, Nikon 20-35mm zoom lens, Fuji Velvia.

Velvia has become my standard landscape film, as it has for many other nature photographers. I like its color palette.

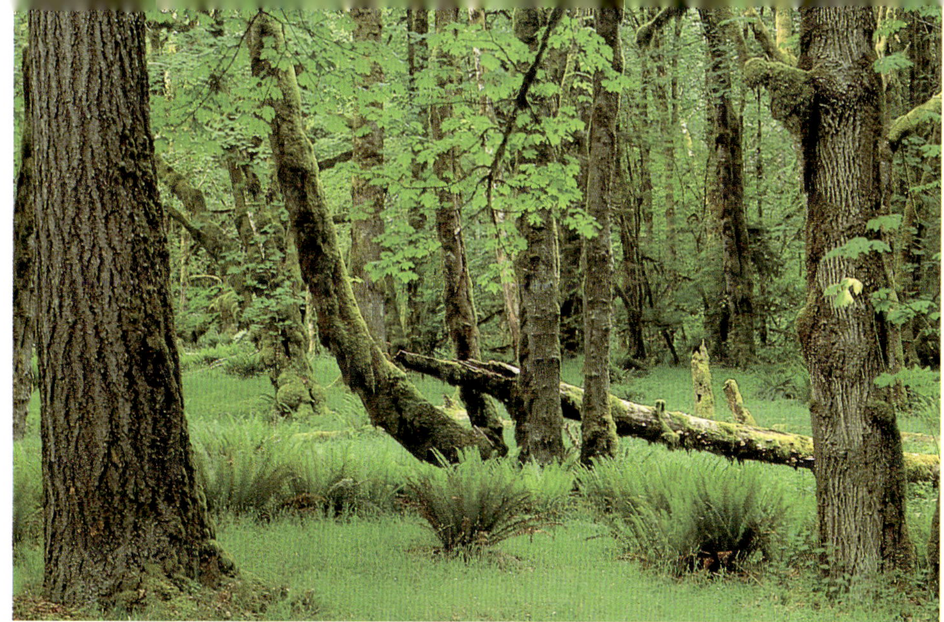

Bigleaf maples and sword ferns, Elwah Valley, Olympic National Park, Washington. Nikon F4, Nikon 80-200mm zoom lens, Fuji Velvia.

Here is another photograph done on Velvia film. I chose this particular film to record the lush delicacy of the greens.

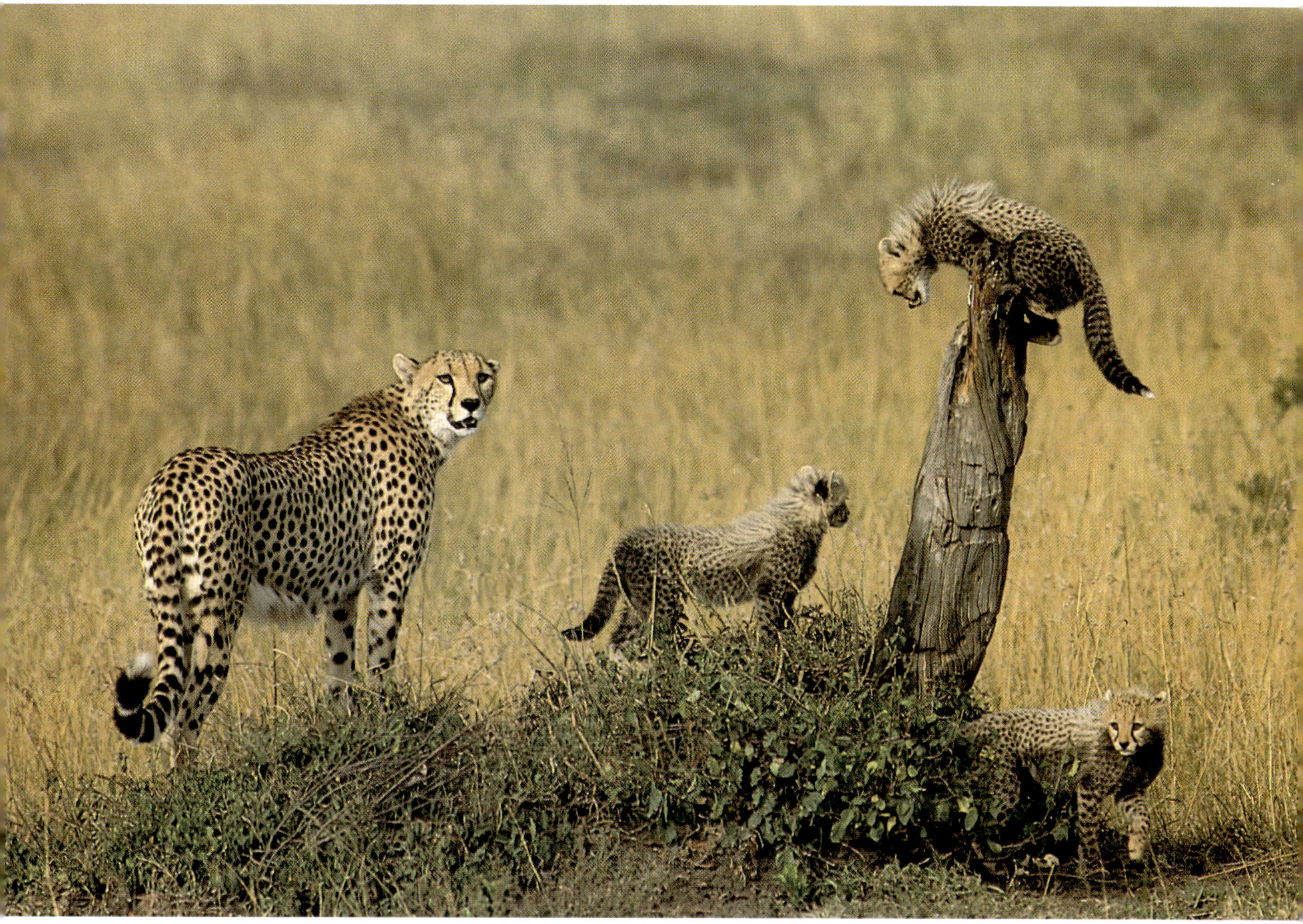

Female cheetah with 6-week-old cubs, Masai Mara National Park, Kenya. Nikon F4, Nikon 500mm lens, Fujichrome 100.

For most bird and mammal photography, you'll want to use a slightly faster film than Kodachrome or Velvia. By shooting this image on ISO 100 film, I was able to gain one full shutter speed over Velvia, which helped stop the motion of the cheetahs.

Editors are going to look at your film, not your equipment. Find a good lab.

Many amateur photographers have asked me which films provide the most realistic color rendition, as if "realism" is a criterion for choosing a film. It isn't. Like lenses, all films exhibit a color bias one way or another. Film doesn't see the world the same way the human eye does; for one thing all films can record only an extremely compressed contrast range when compared to human vision.

Amateur Versus Professional Films

What about professional films as compared to amateur films? Forget about these names as both versions are certainly salable, although some emulsions, such as Velvia, are available only under the professional label. All films change color balance as they age. Amateur film is marketed with the assumption that it won't be exposed and processed promptly after it is purchased. More likely a single roll will contain pictures from Easter, the Fourth of July, and Labor Day. Consequently amateur, or consumer, film is released onto the market quite early in its color life.

Professional films are meant to be exposed and processed quickly. This is why they're marketed at their optimum color balance. These films can cost considerably more than their amateur counterparts, by as much as $2 to $3 per roll.

But you do get something for your money. In the Kodak line, professional films are manufactured to a tighter tolerance, 1/6 stop rather than 1/3 stop in ISO speed. Fuji's professional films are actually on a different base with a slight fog in it that, according to the company, helps maintain detail in the highlight areas when the images are printed by photo-mechanical reproduction.

Both Kodak and Fuji professional films are usually kept under refrigeration (to slow the color shifts that all films go through before processing) until they're sold. They should then be processed fairly soon after exposure. But don't be paranoid about the necessity of continuing to keep the films refrigerated. I've carried professional films on trips during which they haven't been refrigerated for a month or two, and I've never noticed any deterioration. But I certainly wouldn't recommend leaving any film, professional or amateur, locked in your car's trunk while you're shooting in Arizona's Saguaro National Monument in July. Take the usual film precautions, and you'll have no problems with the professional films.

If I specialized in advertising photography, I would be much more careful as to how I handle my professional films. I would probably refrigerate the film until a day or so before shooting it, and process it as quickly as I possibly could after exposure. After all, I would want to maintain precise color balance.

Consider the following example. You're shooting for a major client whose product has a certain identifiable color, such as the yellow of Kodak's film boxes. You would want to make sure that the film you used would be consistent in color rendition from roll to roll, and that today's photography and tomorrow's photography match. That is what the client is paying you to do. That Kodak yellow box had better be Kodak yellow in the final picture. But suppose you're shooting a nature photograph. What exactly is the correct color of an autumn maple tree or of a sunset?

Actually I can think of two good reasons to use professional films, aside from the fact that some emulsions are only available under the professional label. The first is consistency from roll to roll. It doesn't really matter if the film's color balance or designated speed rating is slightly off so long as it is consistent. You can correct for color balance if necessary, and set your meter's ISO at whatever number you think yields correct exposure. I find that professional films are generally consistent once you get past the first six months or so after they're first introduced into the market. Like almost all products today, it takes a while for all the quirks to be worked out.

The second compelling reason to use professional film is a little more directly business oriented: your competition will be using these films. I firmly believe that in business you have to be at least as good as your competition. And in the photography business, you must be at least equal to other photographers in technique, aesthetics, and marketing. Any edge I can get over other professional photographers in any of these areas means I can sell pictures and stay in business. Consequently I'll do anything,

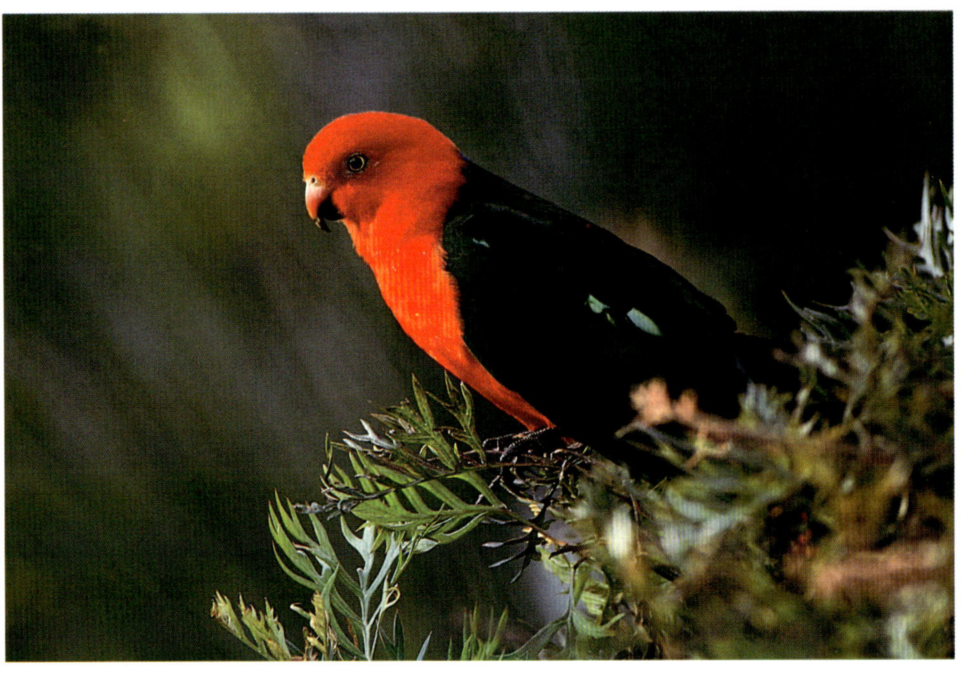

Male Australian king parrot, Lamington National Park, Australia. Nikon F4, Nikon 400mm lens, Kodak Lumière 100 pushed one stop.

At times you simply need fast film in order to use a shutter speed high enough to freeze your subject's motion. Even though I was using my 400mm lens wide open at f/13.5 to photograph this king parrot in dim light, I still needed to push-process my Lumière film one stop, to an effective ISO 200 speed.

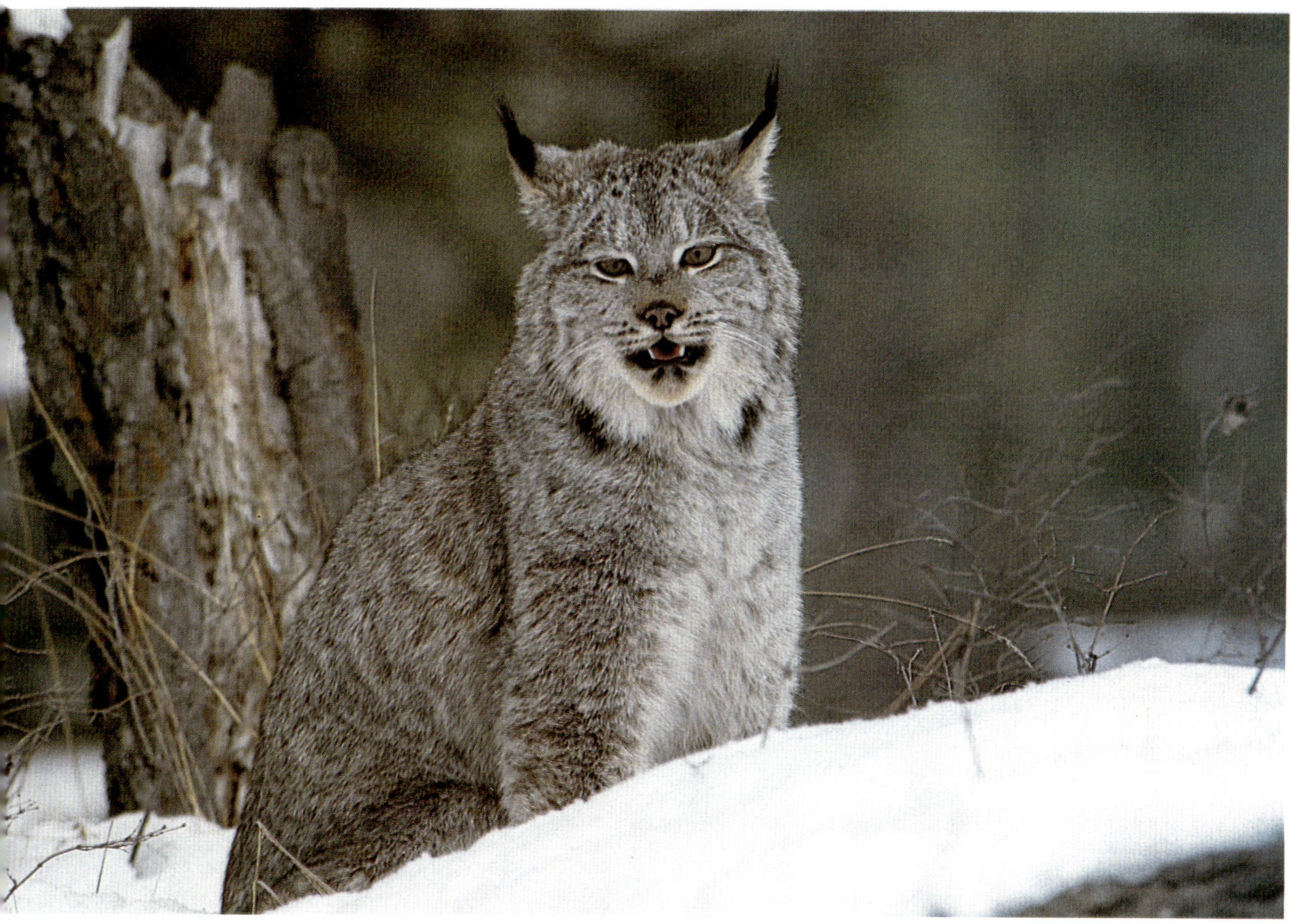

Lynx in winter, Montana. Nikon F4, Nikon 500mm lens, Kodachrome 200.

Ordinarily, I would push ISO 100 film one stop to get an effective 200 speed film if I were photographing animals and needed the extra speed. However, I much prefer using Kodachrome 200 in dull, flat, midwinter light. The film is very sharp although rather grainy. I think it records the whites of snow quite well while retaining some warmth in the browns and gray of animals.

ncluding spending a few dollars more for professional films, to maintain my position.

As I've said many times, my dream is that all other professional nature photographers handhold their cameras, use ISO 1000 film pushed a couple of stops, and then make duplicate transparencies to send to editors. If you were to combine this with business letters written in pencil on paper ripped from a spiral-bound notebook, my submissions would look much better than those of the competition.

One final film note concerning a non-standard film. Eastman 5247 is a movie film that several labs heavily promote as a universal film, offering slides, prints, and negatives all from the same stock. Is it marketable in the nature field? Yes, but only if you want to publish in the smallest, lowest-paying, bottom-of-the-barrel markets that probably don't even pay for photo usage. If you want to see your work printed anywhere else or if you're considering seriously trying to market your work, don't use this film. Shoot Kodak and Fuji transparency films in the ISO 50-100 range exclusively.

Slide Mounts

Given any choice of mounts whatsoever, you should ask for cardboard slide mounts rather than plastic mounts when your film is processed. As digital scanning for color separation becomes more commonplace, the type of mount will have little difference. Currently, however, the creation of standard four-color separations requires film to be removed from the slide mount and placed on a scanner drum that rotates at a very high revolutions-per-minute (RPM) rate. Your film is easily removed from a cardboard mount with no harm to the film itself. The cardboard is slit, the mount peeled apart, and the film taken out to be scanned. Afterward the film is replaced in the opened mount and returned to you, whereupon you have the job of remounting the transparency. (For a source of card board self-sealing mounts, contact The Stock Solution—see page 138.)

It isn't quite such a neat job with plastic mounts. Too often the plastic is snapped open, leaving sharp, jagged edges to scratch the film as it is removed and reinserted. Film endures enough wear and tear in the process of being handled by yourself, editors, and separators without adding potential problems.

WHAT EDITORS WANT

As I've already said, most published nature photographs are pulled from photographers' stock files, and the rules for successful stock photography are simple: quality, quantity, variety . . . and more of these three. Stick to the highest technical standards, shoot a lot of film, and take variations of each composition if possible, including both vertical and horizontal framing. Picture editors look first for proper exposure and for razor sharpness. These are the two most important technical aspects of successful photography.

Accurate Exposure

Proper exposure means knowing that color slide films can record a tonal range of about five stops from textureless white to detailless black, then using this knowledge when exposing your film. Proper exposure also means recording subject tonalities as you want them to be recorded: medium-toned subjects are rendered as medium-toned, light-toned subjects as light-toned, and dark-toned subjects as dark-toned. Proper exposure also means holding detail in your subject's highlights, but at the same time whites should indeed be white while blacks should be black.

You may have heard the old adage about underexposing a little to saturate the colors. This is no longer valid, particularly with the current group of E6 films. Underexposed pictures simply are muddy, dark photographs with limited detail. Learn how to achieve correct exposure. (For an explanation of correct exposure and how to achieve it, study the "Exposure" section in one of my earlier books, *John Shaw's Landscape Photography*: Amphoto, 1994).

Sharp Focus

Critical focus is essential, too. Don't evaluate your slides by projecting them. After all, you're just evaluating how good your projection system is and, quite frankly, few projection lenses have camera-quality optics. Besides, the intense light and heat from a projector can cause fading of a slide's colors, especially if it is projected for any length of time. Slides can also be scratched by a projector's changing mechanism. Critical focus of an image is almost impossible to assess, even though the image is enlarged when projected. Instead use a quality loupe and a light table to check sharpness (see page 36).

Many amateur photographers believe that the printing process improves photographs. This just isn't true. In fact, it does just the opposite, as do all processes that yield a second-generation product. It is true that with the latest digital software, pictures can be manipulated, but few nature-photography markets have either the time or the money to do major digital retouching. If your pictures aren't sharp to begin with, they won't make it past a photo editor's initial cut.

When a vertical-composition 35mm transparency is printed at full-page size, it must be enlarged roughly 800 percent, while a double-page spread needs about 1,700 percent enlargement. At these magnifications, the lack of sharpness in images becomes readily apparent. Unsharp photographs, if used at all, can only be printed small.

You can obtain sharpness by always shooting with your camera mounted on a sturdy tripod at a shutter speed/aperture combination suitable to your subject. Make sure that you can actually see a sharp image through your camera. You may want to change the focusing screen in your camera (an architectural grid screen helps in keeping horizons square with the world) and to adjust the eyepiece diopter-correction now common on most viewfinders. By the way, using an autofocus camera and lenses doesn't guarantee sharp images. Fuzzy pictures of common subjects just won't get published, but you'll quickly become known as a poor photographer.

It took me a long time to realize that to picture editors, a photograph really means a physical space on a page that must be filled

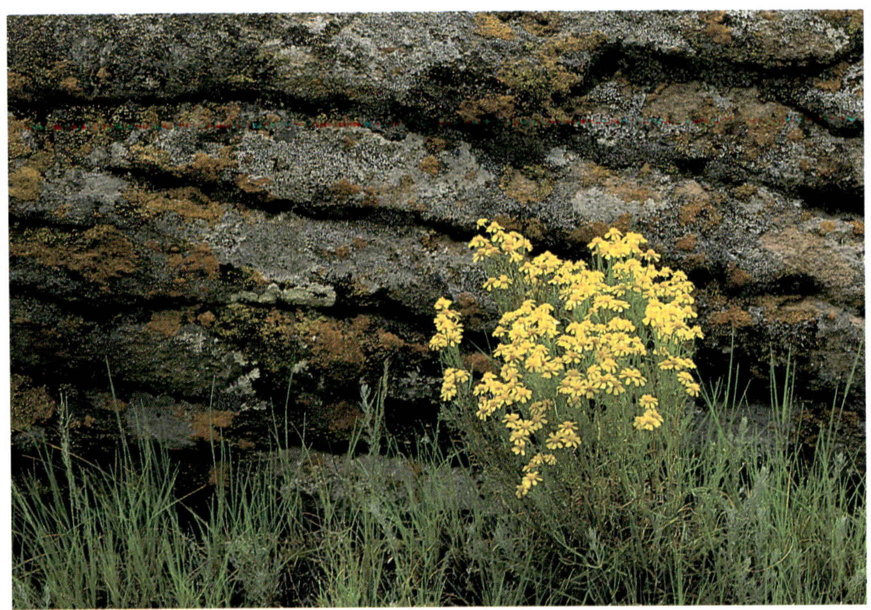

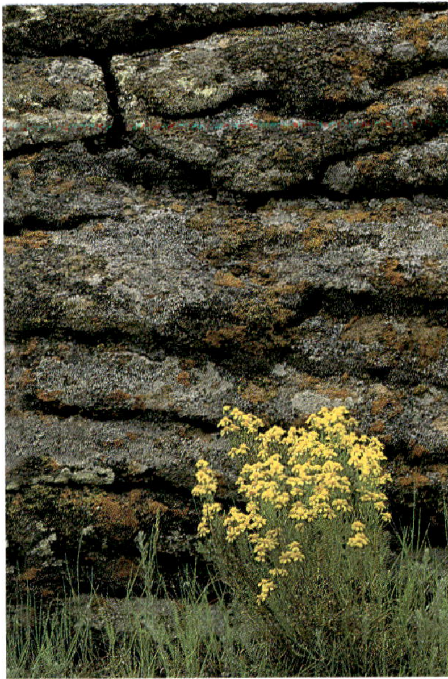

Butterweed and lichen-covered rocks, Colorado. Nikon F4, Nikon 200mm macro lens, Fuji Velvia.

It is helpful for picture editors to have both vertical and horizontal versions of the same subject, even of something as simple as this butterweed and rocks.

with an image. This means that the editors need both horizontal and vertical image choices. They might also have to crop into your composition and will do so without your consent. Picture editors carry none of the emotional baggage concerning the images that we photographers do. The editors don't care that this frame is one of your favorite shots, they don't care that it was taken with the latest equipment, and they don't care that your mother likes the shot. Photo editors must have a quality image, and they must have it before their deadline.

Furthermore, photographic quality doesn't equate in any way whatsoever to the time and effort you've expended in taking the picture. Perhaps it took you three hours to get close enough to those ducks to photograph them; meanwhile you had to crawl through muddy ditches filled with stagnant water dragging 50 pounds of equipment. So what? Does that make an out-of-focus, underexposed photograph any better? No.

Photo editors do need your good photographs since almost all published work today is from freelance photographers. (Name a national publication other than *National Geographic* that uses natural-history photographs and that has staff photographers. Can't think of any? Neither can I.) These editors want and need quality pictures and will use them if they are right for the current needs of the publication. But keep in mind that photo editors at major magazines see about 100,000 images in a year's time. Too many of those pictures will be just plain bad or at best mediocre.

Let me define mediocre. These are ordinary pictures of ordinary subjects presented in an ordinary manner. In other words, mediocre pictures are similar in both content and quality to hundreds of other photographs that the picture editor has already seen. If you shoot images that are artfully composed, beautifully lit, and informative, editors will remember your work. Make your photographs evocative and exciting, and you'll be published.

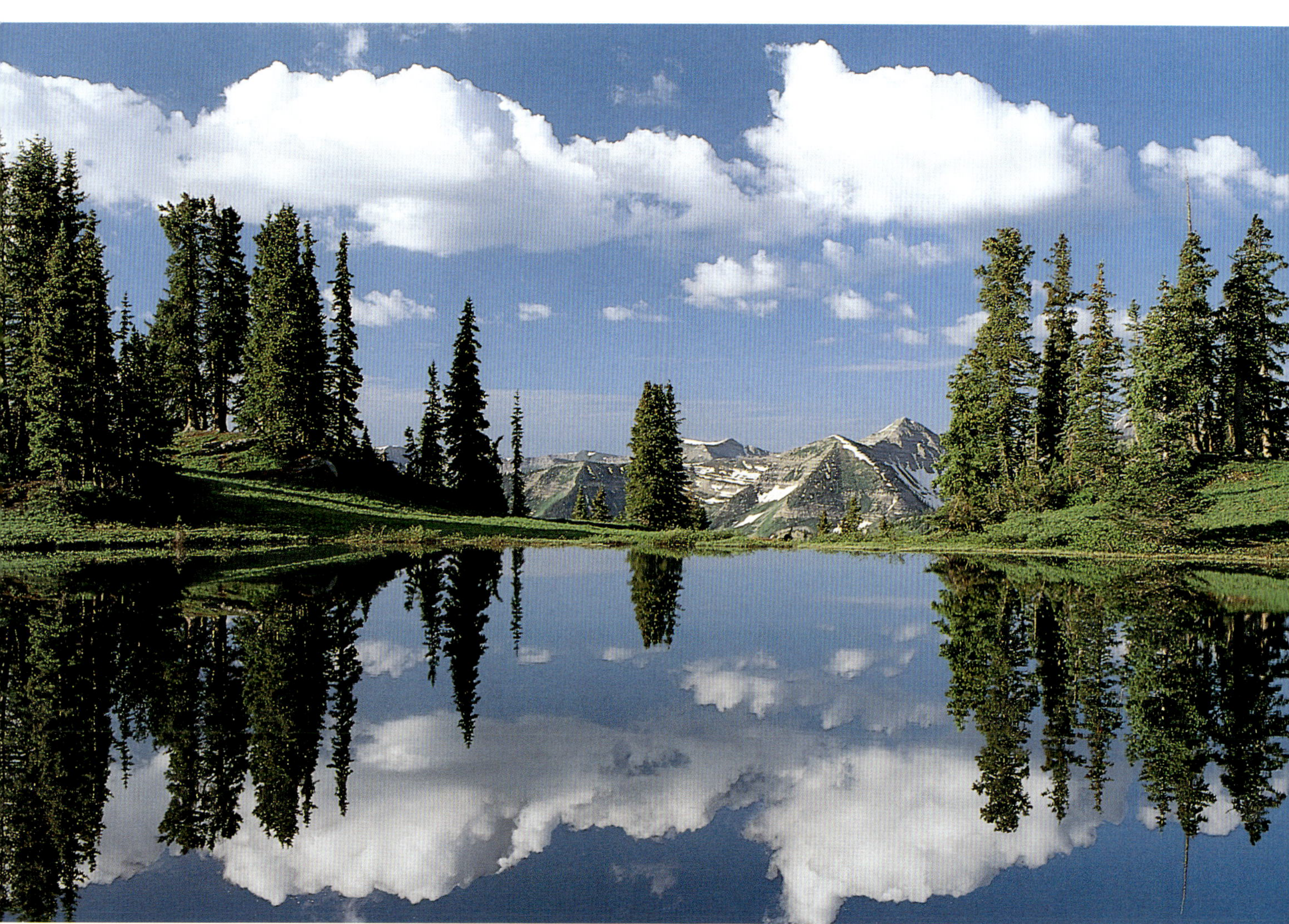

Alpine tarn and reflections, Gunnison National Forest, Colorado.
Nikon F4, Nikon 35mm lens, Fuji Velvia.

Technically this photograph is just what a photo editor wants: correct exposure—the white clouds are indeed white and the deepest shadows, black—and razor-sharp focus.

Big Cypress National Preserve, Florida. Nikon F4, Nikon 50-135mm zoom lens, Fuji Velvia.

Big Cypress National Preserve adjoins Everglades National Park; this shot shows the cypress with new spring leaves and bromeliads, along with willows and cattails. Notice the even light of an overcast day. The same composition shot on a bright, sunny day wouldn't be salable due to the extreme contrast range.

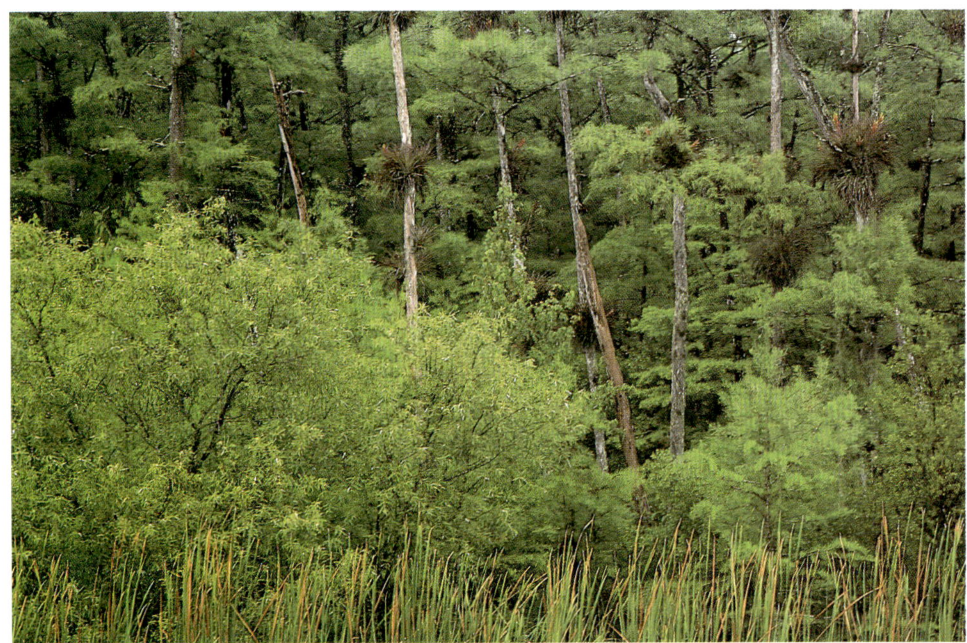

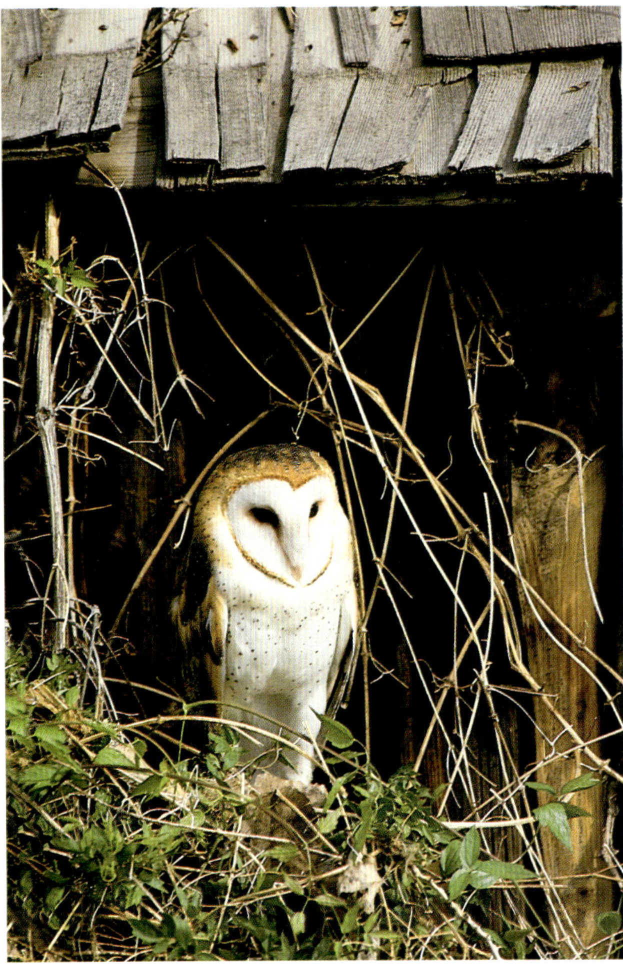

Barn owl, Colorado. Nikon F4, Nikon 500mm lens, Fujichrome 100.

This barn owl could be used as a stand-alone subject, yet there is room for a photo editor to crop the image if needed.

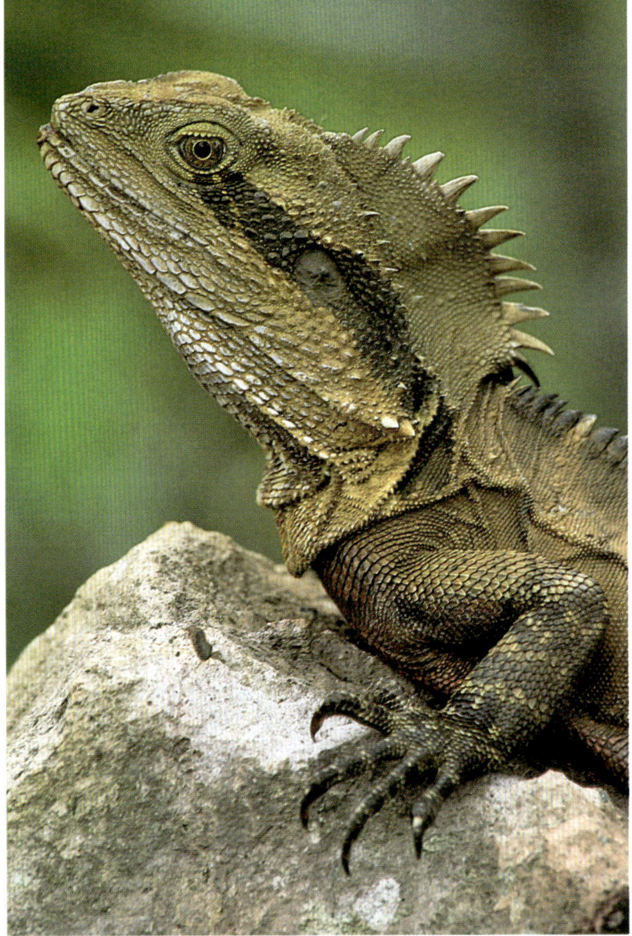

Eastern water-dragon lizard, Australia. Nikon F4, Nikon 300mm lens, Fuji Velvia.

I zeroed in on this water-dragon lizard's most prominent detail, its striking head crest, in order to create an image that a publication might be interested in.

WHAT SUBJECTS TO SHOOT AND HOW TO SHOOT THEM

It is very easy for me to tell you what to photograph. Just shoot whatever subjects you enjoy photographing. However, it isn't as easy for me to tell you what subjects are salable.

The Specialist Approach

Most photographers making significant sales from their nature work fall into one of two categories. There is the specialist who photographs only a limited range of subjects but has thorough coverage of these subjects. These photographers make few sales, but when their specialty is needed they have all the shots. For example, imagine someone who photographs only the life history of several bat species. How many bat photographs are published each month? Not many, but when a photo researcher wants a bat picture, that photographer's name is sure to come up and the photographer will make good sales.

You can apply this specialized approach to living creatures, locations, inanimate objects, or whatever aspect of natural history most intrigues you. Photograph just one location, such as the Konza prairie in Kansas or Arches National Park in Utah, in great depth, and you'll soon be know as a source for those pictures. But the danger here is that if you specialize too much, editors will have a hard time thinking of you when they need shots of other subjects.

I know this from firsthand experience. Early in my career I got pigeonholed as a closeup photographer because of a portfolio of my closeups in a widely published book. Indeed, I did take a lot of closeups, but I also shot a broad range of other subjects. I had to go to great lengths explaining to editors that I also had files on grizzly bears, African birds and mammals, New Zealand rain forests, and many other topics. The irony is that at the time, I'd had more bird photographs published as covers than any other subject in my file.

If you limit yourself to certain common subjects, you'll have difficulty selling pictures due to the number of people photographing these exact same subjects. Five such topics come quickly to mind: wildflowers; sunsets over the ocean; elk in Yellowstone; national-park scenics taken from marked overlooks (the road sign says "Photo opportunity ahead!"); and large Florida wading birds, such as herons and egrets, photographed in the Everglades or at

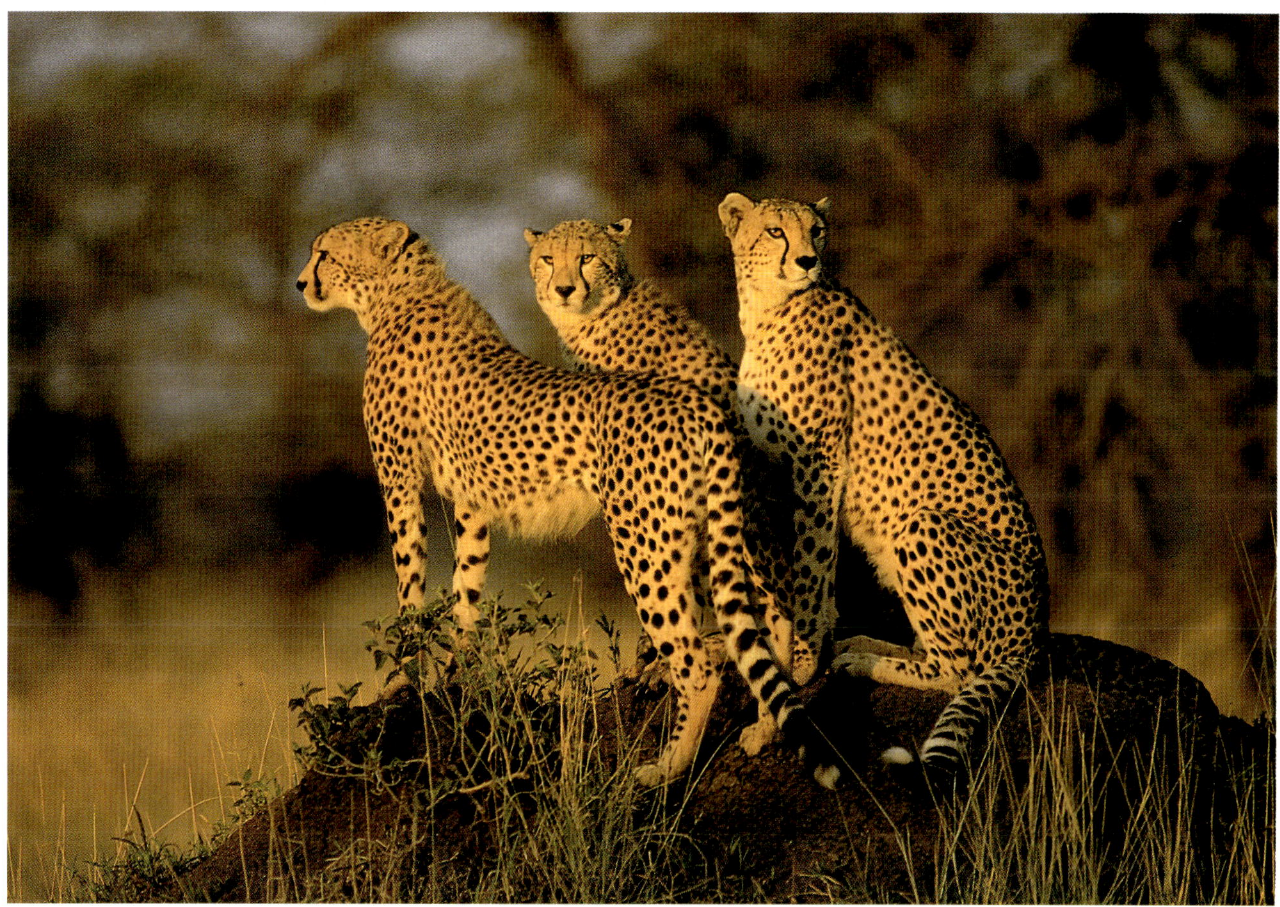

Cheetah family group on top of termite mound, Masai Mara National Park, Kenya. Nikon F4, Nikon 500mm lens, Fujichrome 100.

It is certainly exciting to be able to photograph cheetahs in Kenya. However, actually making a living selling pictures would be difficult if cheetahs were the only subject you photographed.

These diverse subjects range from the straightforward to the poetic, to the abstract. Having such variety in your file opens up the possibility of selling pictures to multiple markets.

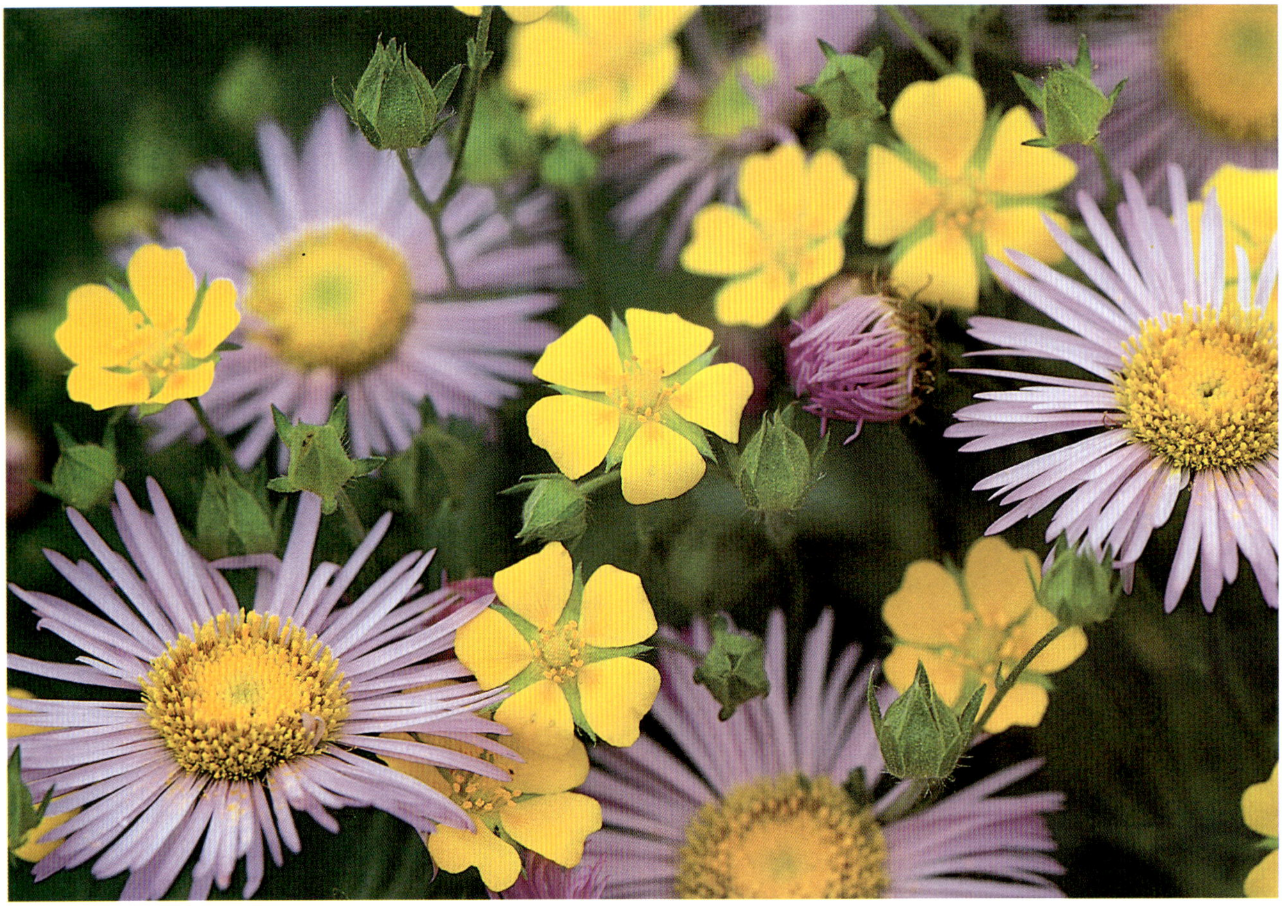

Summer flowers, fleabane, and buttercups, Colorado. Nikon F4, Nikon 200mm macro lens, Fuji Velvia.

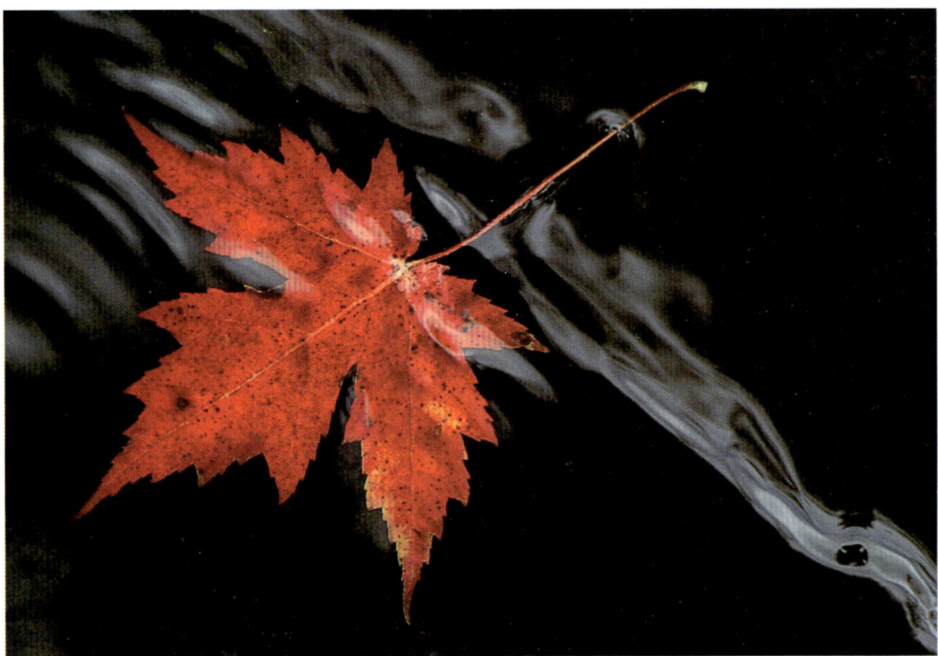

Autumn silver maple leaf at edge of stream, Vermont. Nikon F4, Nikon 200mm macro lens, Fuji Velvia.

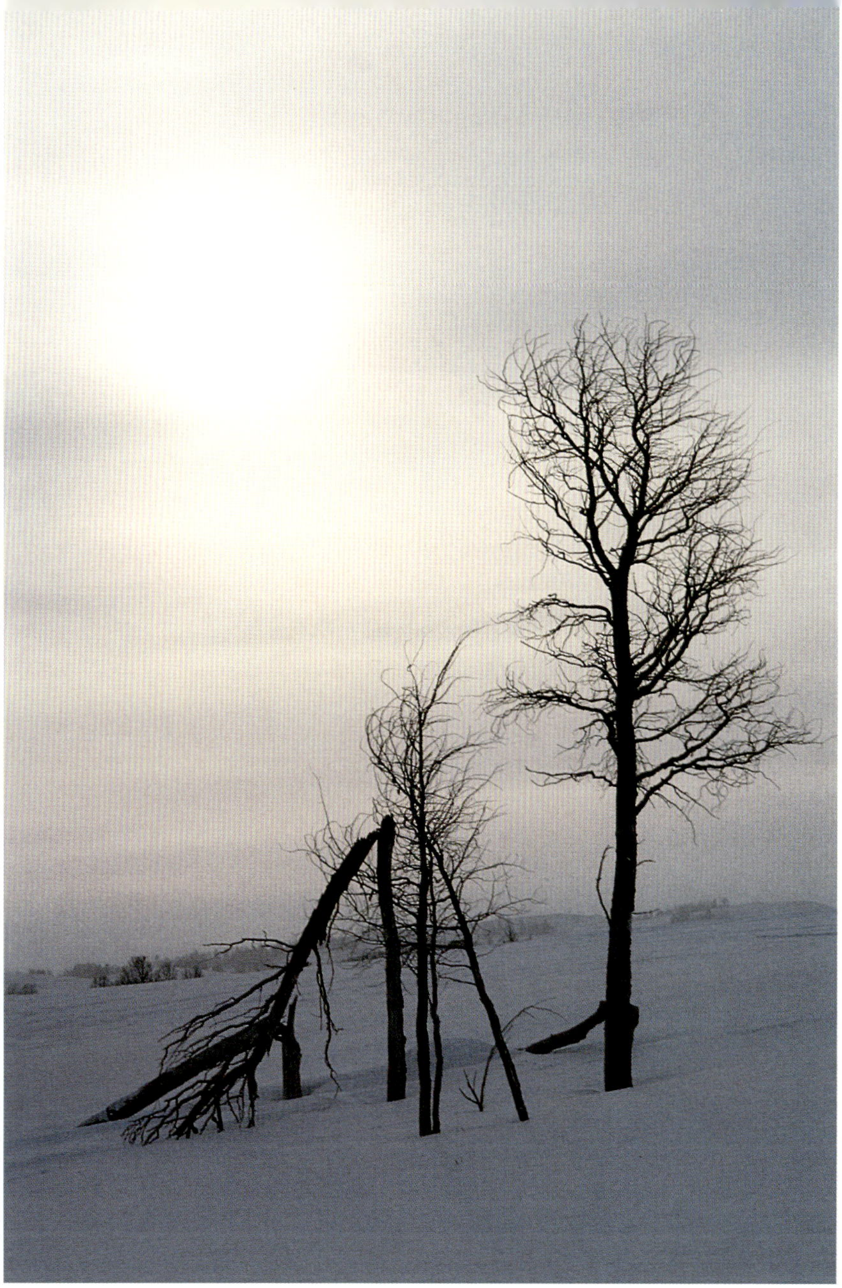

Winter sky with dead aspen trees, Yellowstone National Park, Wyoming. Nikon F4, Nikon 80-200mm zoom lens, Fuji Velvia.

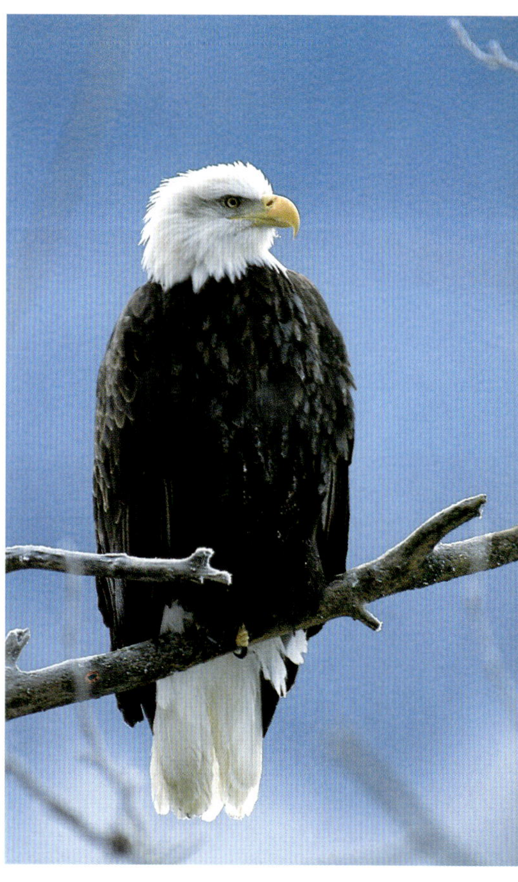

Bald eagle and frost, Chilkat River Valley, Alaska. Nikon F4, Nikon 500mm lens with 1.4X teleconverter, Fujichrome 100.

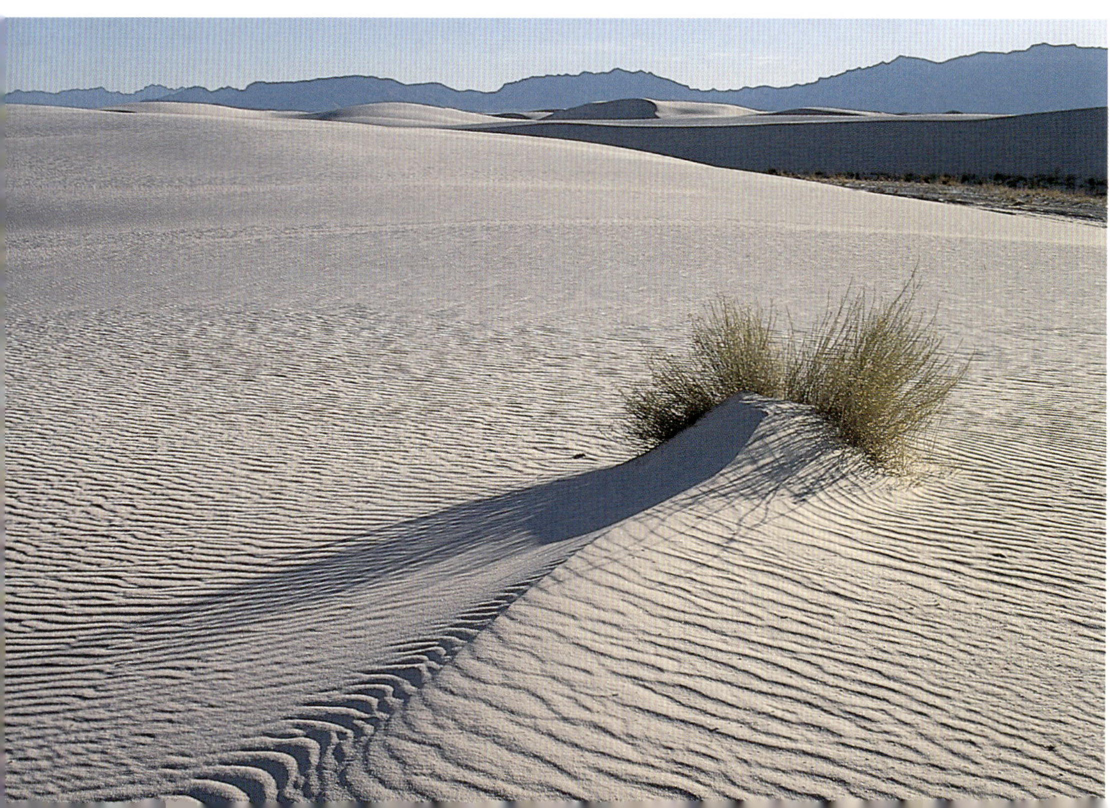

White gypsum sand dunes, White Sands National Monument, New Mexico. Nikon F4, Nikon 24mm lens, Fuji Velvia.

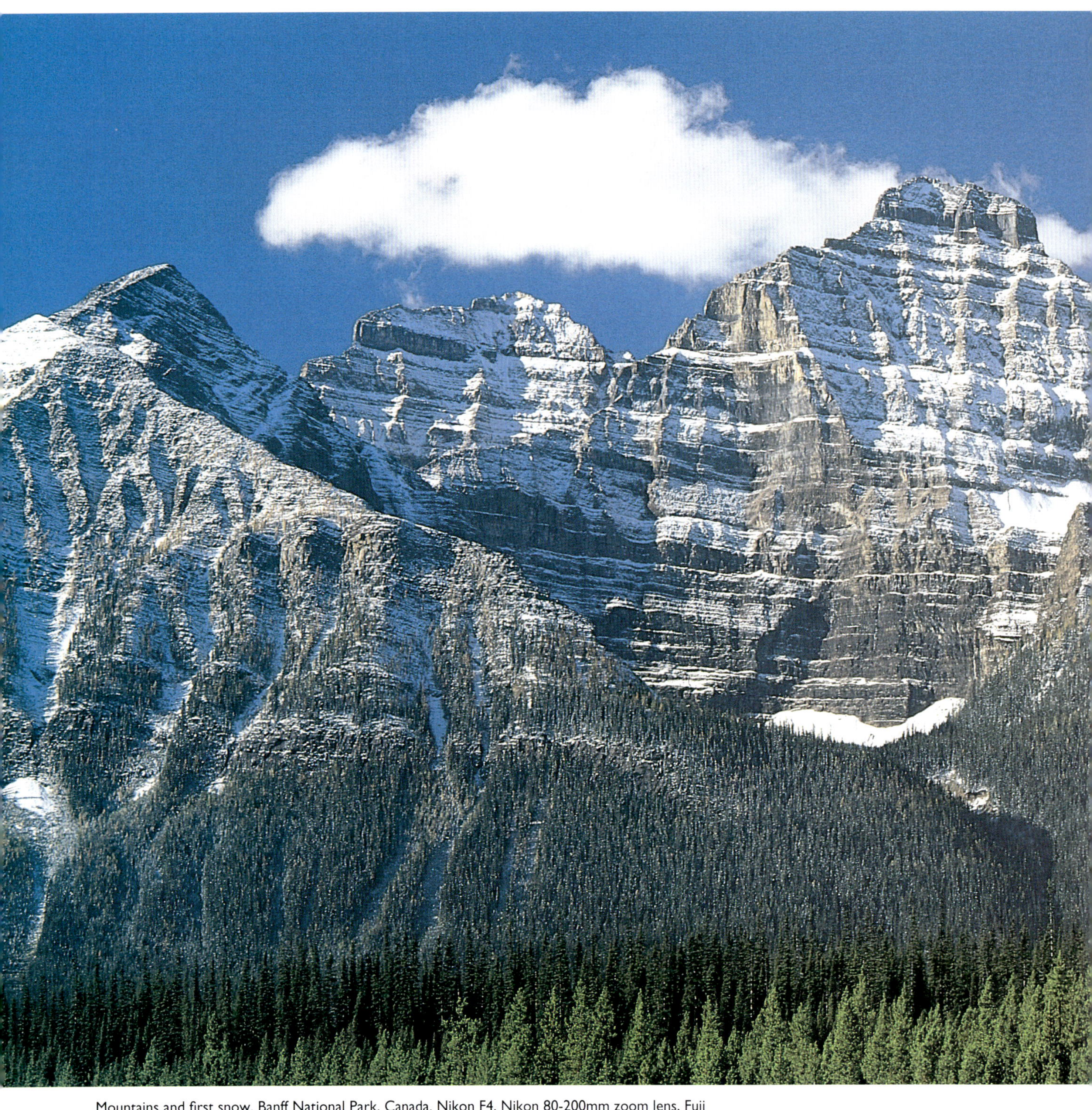

Mountains and first snow, Banff National Park, Canada. Nikon F4, Nikon 80-200mm zoom lens, Fuji Velvia.

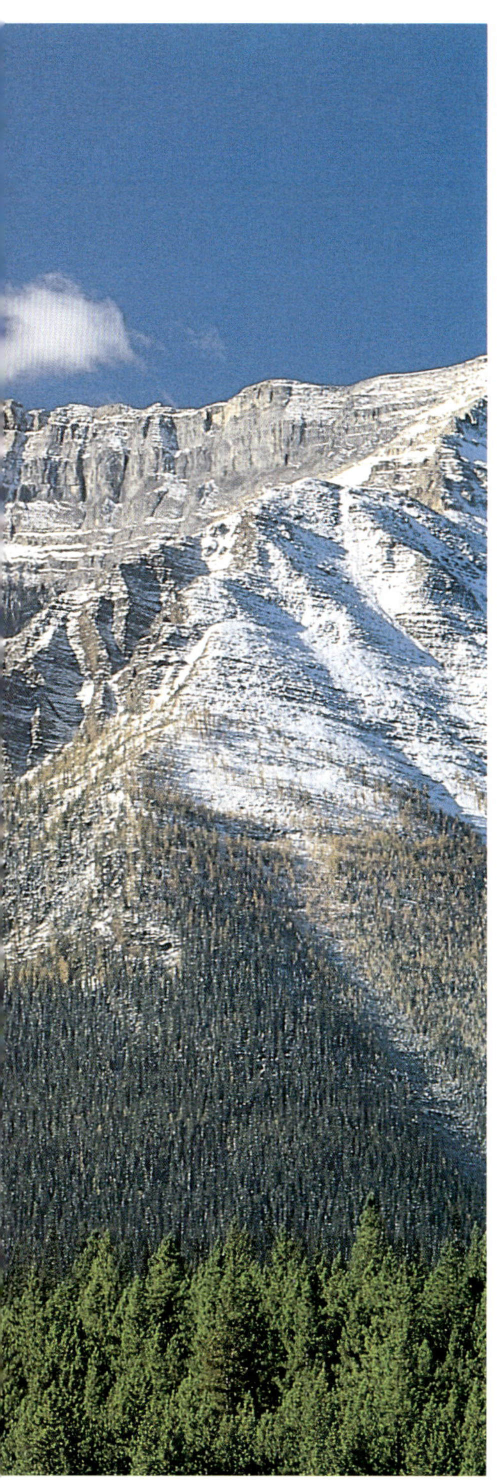

Ding Darling National Wildlife Refuge in Florida. Thousands of photographers have photographed all of these subjects over and over and over, and consequently the pictures are hard to market as stand-alone shots. You certainly should have these subjects in your file, but your file shouldn't contain only these subjects.

The Generalist Approach

Unlike specialists, generalists photograph the broadest range of nature topics, from mountains to mosquitoes and everything in between. This is what I do, and what I would recommend you do, too, if you want to publish widely. You might not be able to fulfill every picture request, but broad coverage means you'll have something to sell to many different markets. I think that the more you diversify in your photography, the more chances you have to market your photographs. And the more you diversify in your markets, the more chance you have of financial success.

One good method of deciding what to shoot is to do some market research. Go down to your local bookstore, and look through as many current books and magazines as you can to find which use the type of photographs that you take. What subjects are being published? Do you have similar coverage? Do you have in-depth coverage? Are your photographs distinguishable from the pictures in the books and magazines, or are yours just more of the same?

And the next time you visit a national park, check out the postcard and book racks in the visitor center. Jot down all the distinct features of that location, then photograph all of them at different times of day in different light with different lenses. Ten good shots from Arches National Park doesn't mean that you have an Arches National Park file; 300 or 400 frames means that you are on your way.

Another method is to pick up a college biology textbook and study the pictures used in it. How can you illustrate biological principles better than the pictures published in the text? You need more than one photograph for each concept. So, do you have variations on a theme? If not, make a list of what you need to shoot in the future.

The following example explains what I mean by thorough coverage. Every biology, botany, and ecology book published (and almost every magazine that deals with biological stories) requires illustrations of ecosystems or biomes. Some broad names of distinct biomes include:

- Tundra
- Northern conifer forest (taiga)
- Temperate deciduous forest
- Temperate rain forest
- Temperate grasslands
- Chaparral
- Desert
- Tropical rainforest
- Tropical scrub forest
- Tropical grasslands and savanna
- Mountains

Do you know what typifies all of these biomes? If you want to submit pictures to the biology book market, you must know. Consider deserts. In North America there are four different desert communities: the Great Basin desert, the Mojave desert, the Sonoran desert, and the Chihuahuan desert. What are the distinguishing features of each? What plants and animals do you find there? Where are archetypal locations?

Suppose that you're photographing the eastern deciduous forest in autumn. This is another way of saying "New England fall color." But there is more to photograph than just hillsides of pretty colored leaves. How about individual trees, or tight sections of leaves just starting to turn color, or the period of leaf-fall when half the trees are bare, or ferns and other plants in the autumn?

And what about the eastern deciduous forest community in other seasons? You'll need to shoot wildflowers in the spring; leaf buds opening on the trees; the forest canopy in the summer; streams lined with mossy rocks; birds and mammals, and life histories if you can; butterflies and other insects; nonflowering plants; dewy spider webs in late summer; leaf veining patterns—the list goes on and on.

Mammals can be salable subjects, but photographers concentrate on the same few species: elk, deer, and bison. Small mammals are particularly overlooked. Strictly in terms of sales, you would do far better to photograph shrews, star-nosed moles, deer mice, kangaroo rats, and red squirrels than working most big-game mammals. Ten good frames of each would sell over and over again.

CHAPTER TWO

Office Work

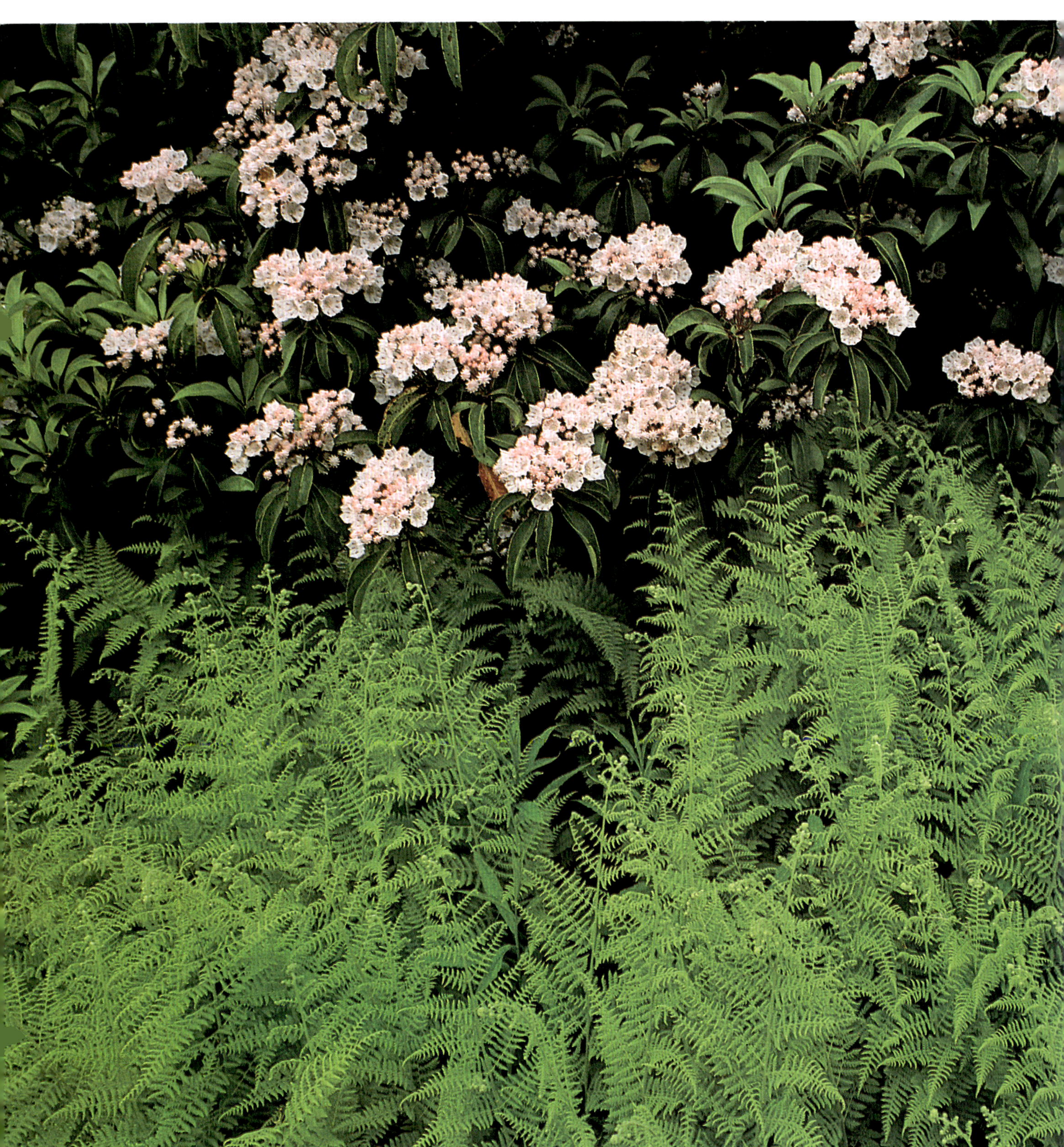

Hay-scented fern and mountain laurel, North Carolina.

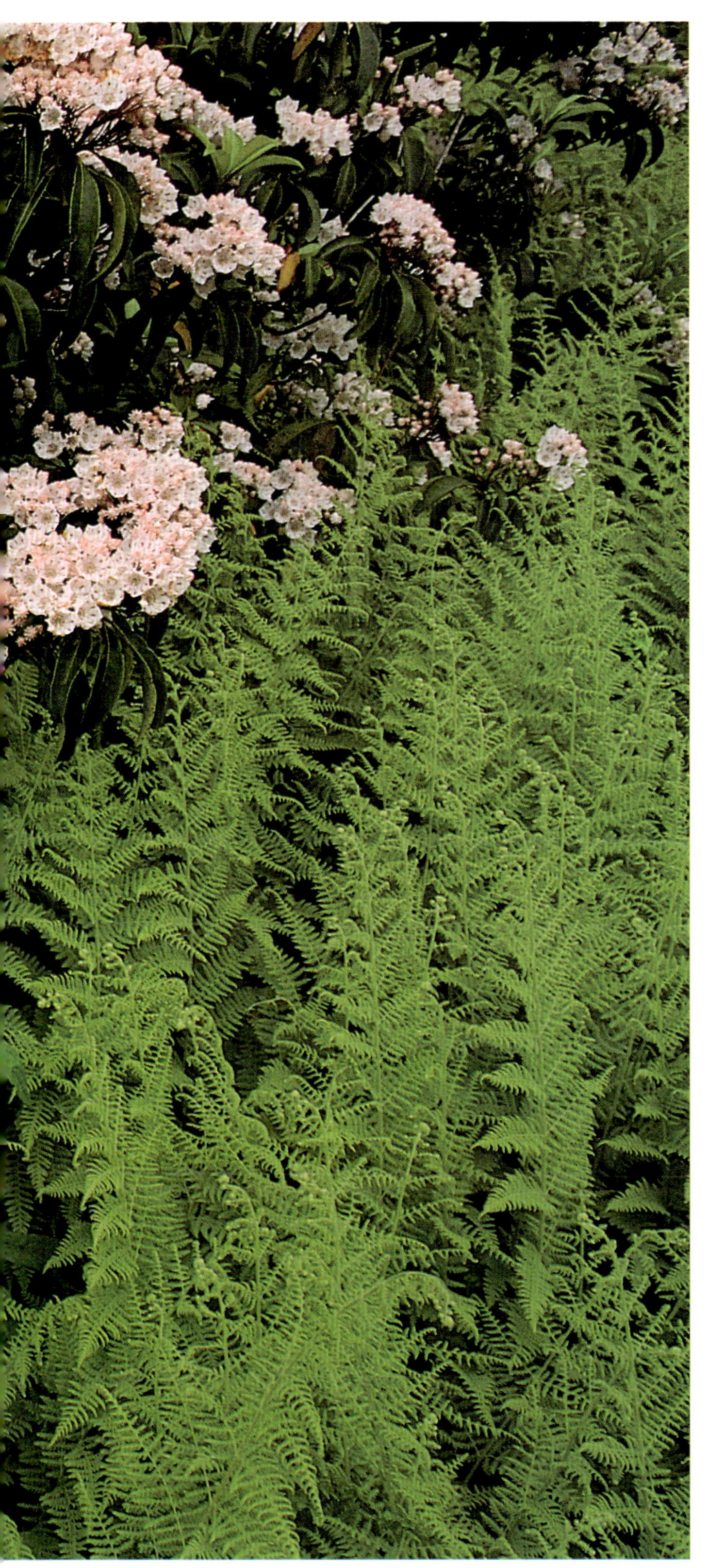

THE PHYSICAL SPACE

When I started freelancing full-time in 1970, my "office" was a huge, old, manual typewriter sitting on a desk from a thrift store, along with an address book listing editors and publishers. I can remember thinking how efficient and technologically current I was when I purchased an answering machine.

Well, times have changed for all of us. While you certainly don't need a suite of rooms at the finest office address in town, you do need a physical office space in order to run a business. This can be as basic as the spare bedroom in your house or as fancy as room in an office building. Just remember that office overhead, including the cost of commuting to the site, comes out of your profits.

Most professional nature photographers I know actually run their businesses out of their homes. This is less expensive than having a separate office, and the nature-photography business is unique in that you almost never have a client in your office. Business is conducted long distance: you ship photographs to buyers. Actually having someone visit my office, other than family and friends, is so rare that I can count a year's worth of business visitors on one hand. My Federal Express route driver has been in my office more than all my clients put together.

For years I put up with an office in the spare bedroom or in the den. Then I built a house and, as part of the plan, designed one entire floor to be given over to my business. A large, open space serves as a main office, complete with desks, light tables, slide files, and computers. Small rooms are devoted to office-supply storage, photo-equipment storage, and a workspace for shipping and packaging that doubles as a location for the copy machine. I must admit that having a physical area set up as a pleasant and effective business space has actually helped my state of mind when I'm forced to be indoors. Still, I would rather be outside taking pictures.

Office Supplies

You don't have to build a formal office to get started. All you need are some basic supplies. Start with stationery and forms. Even if your office is only a cleared space on the kitchen table, you need to present yourself to your customers as a real business. All your correspondence should be typed on a letterhead, not handwritten. I've received handwritten letters on notebook paper from people wanting to be hired as assistants; needless to say, I immediately toss these letters into the wastebasket.

You'll also need some business cards. Since your contact with clients will take place mostly through the mail, a small supply should last a while. Any print shop can provide you with these. Eventually you'll want an invoice form, also run on your letterhead. At first, simply use the standard preprinted invoices available at any office-supply store. You'll want a self-adhesive mailing label with your name and address printed on it, too.

Don't go overboard when you get these supplies. I've seen expensive stationery from beginning photographers who have never sold a shot. I've also seen many more do-it-yourself-on-the-computer letterheads from working pros.

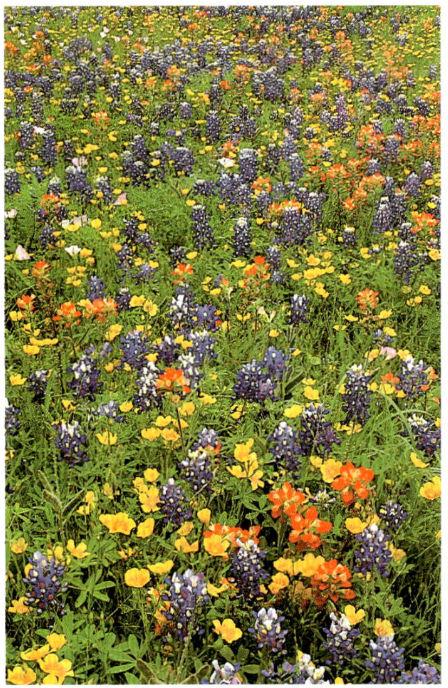

Bluebonnets, yellow flax, and paintbrush on spring prairie, Texas. Canon EOS-1, Canon 45mm TS-E lens, Fuji Velvia.

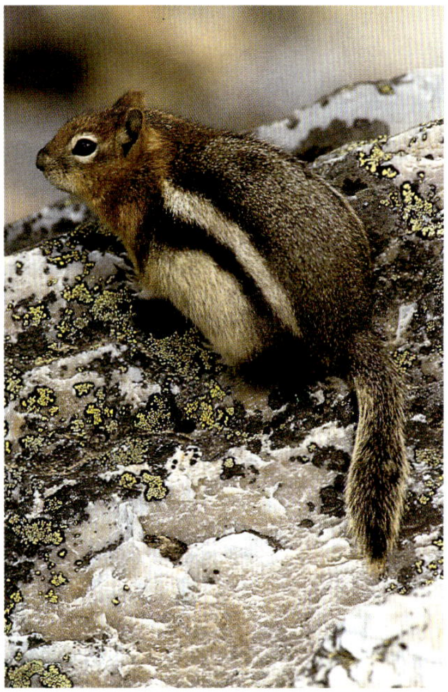

Golden-mantled ground squirrel, Banff National Park, Canada. Nikon F4, Nikon 500mm lens, Fujichrome 100.

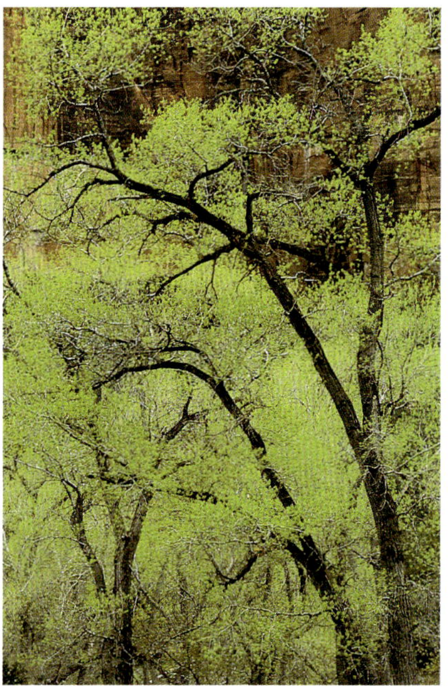

Fremont cottonwood trees in spring, Zion Canyon, Zion National Park, Utah. Nikon F4, Nikon 50-135mm zoom lens, Fuji Velvia.

You'll need a separate workspace to caption and label slides, to store your photographic files, and to put submissions together. If an editor called requesting these pictures, could you put together a submission and present it in a professional manner?

You should also buy a stash of standard office supplies: letterhead and envelopes, good bond paper for manuscripts, cardboard mailing flats (see the Calumet Carton Company listing on page 138), corrugated cardboard stiffeners for mailing slides, and miscellaneous items like rubber bands and sealing tape. Keep a supply of tear-resistant envelopes on hand, as well as shipping forms from Federal Express or Airborne Express (or whichever shipper you want to use). If you set up an account with the carrier, you can have your name and address information printed on these forms, which are free. You'll also need material from the Postal Service, including certified- or registered-mail forms, return receipts, and customs forms if you plan to send packages overseas.

Office Equipment

In addition to typical office supplies, you have to get some standard office equipment. You might already own some or have access to some for use. Some needs are obvious.

Buying the Basics

You'll want a desk and chair (or at least a clear workspace when you're starting out), a light table, and file cabinets to hold both your paperwork—you're running a business, so you always have paperwork to file—and your slide collection.

If you are truly serious about marketing your work, you should plan for future growth and for more business when you purchase any electronic office machines. The right office equipment can save time and money if used properly.

At the very minimum, you'll want a typewriter, for filling out multi-part forms if for nothing else. Learn to type, as business runs on typed correspondence (well, computer-keyboard-inputted correspondence anyway). Get rid of your old manual typewriter no matter what your financial circumstances; even the cheapest electric model from the local discount store will output better-looking type. No business today has a manual typewriter.

Two more office items are so fundamental that I almost forgot to mention them: a telephone answering machine and a standard Rolodex. The business of nature photography runs via the mail and the telephone, so make sure your clients can reach you at all times. Because the telephone is often your first contact with a new client, you should answer it in a business-like and professional manner. Don't let your children answer your business phone. After all, would you think of purchasing top-quality materials from a company whose telephone is answered by a 6-year-old?

Be sure to speak with your local telephone-company representative about all the services the company offers. When you pay just a few dollars a month, you might be able to get such options as voice mail (an answering machine even when your line is busy) or distinctive ringing (two numbers on the same line so you can separate business and personal calls). As your business grows, you'll probably have a separate business line, a dedicated fax line (see page 35), and more. Just remember, you must be able to justify all of these expenses.

Having a simple Rolodex next to your telephone is a necessity. Besides the usual names, addresses, and telephone numbers you might want to add the clients' 800 numbers, Federal Express account numbers, secretaries' names, fax numbers, and for foreign listings the time-zone difference. I also keep cards on many other photographers. If I can't supply a photograph when a picture editor calls, I try to be as helpful as I can in responding to the request. I think that is simply good business practice.

Investing in a Computer

Next, buy a computer and some software. If you want to do more than just sell an individual picture now and then, buy a computer. If you want to be in the business of nature photography, buy a computer. For almost all of your office requirements, you won't need the latest models with the biggest hard drives and the most memory. But in any business, a computer is no longer a luxury. Don't even think about doing anything with digital imaging at this stage; I'm assuming you want to take pictures, not spend hours on end sitting before the computer.

Computer prices keep plummeting, while features expand. The two computers in my office are 486 model PC machines with 210-megabyte hard drives. Although they are several years old now, they are just fine for day-to-day office work. Most of the software programs I own are written for DOS, but as I get into Microsoft Windows more I'll upgrade the hard drives.

Why do I have two computers? For several reasons. First of all Andrea, my wife, is my business partner, and she works full-time in this office. She needs a computer, and I need a computer. Second, we swap computer files continually, essentially backing up one hard drive onto the other so that if anything happens we won't lose data. Both computers have a complete record of our business files. For that matter we run backups onto disc of important files, such as our database, tax records, and submissions, and store these separately. Third, I can't conceive of running a business without a computer, so I have an extra one, just as I have an extra camera body.

The other hardware you'll need is a printer. I suggest buying a laser printer. The output of laser printers looks great while their prices keep dropping. As of this writing, a good-quality, low-end laser printer retails for less than $500 from my local discount office-supply house. Laser printers enable you to run graphics, scale type fonts larger or smaller, and with the right software do desktop publishing and page layout.

Of course, you'll need software programs to run on your computer. Minimally, you need a database program and a full-featured word-processing program; however, I would buy an accounting program, and perhaps a tax program, as soon as possible. Additional programs for every application you can think of are available; just contact any software outlet or pick up one of the zillions of computer magazines on the market.

USING SOFTWARE PROGRAMS

Three basic types of office software—database, word processing, and accounting—can make running the business side of your work a lot easier. Here are some of the applications for each type of software:

Database
Photo-filing information
Submission records
Copyright sales records
Invoicing
Mailing lists
Client lists

Word processing
All business correspondence
Stock lists
Magazine and book manuscripts
Mail-merge features for mass mailings
Slide labels
Mailing labels
Letterheads
Business cards
All office forms
Model and property releases

Accounting
Bookkeeping
Profit and loss statements
Expenses by client
Financial record keeping
Monthly/yearly budget plans
Cash flow
Business reports for credit institutions

Purchasing an accounting program has been one of the best investments I've made in both return for the dollar and time saved. As the owner of a small business, you don't need a top-end program. In fact, in my two-person office, Andrea and I use the personal version of Quicken (a $40 program!) to run our entire business accounting. We combine this with the yearly federal TurboTax program because the income and expense categories transfer directly into the tax program. Computers are wonderful tools for these applications.

If you've purchased a new computer recently, the odds are that it came with a fax/modem and a fax program bundled in. You can receive any sort of fax so long as your computer is turned on and the program is running. You can view faxes on your monitor screen or print them out, depending on the capabilities of your printer. But you can't send out anything via fax that wasn't first generated through your computer. For example, you can't fax your signature at the close of a letter with a fax/modem.

Eventually you'll want to purchase a separate fax machine. This isn't necessary when you're starting out selling nature photographs, but once you have one you quickly get hooked on its usefulness. Basically, a fax machine lets you have 24-hour-a-day instant mail service. You can send and receive stock lists and photo requests, as well as business correspondence.

EDITING SLIDES

When processed film arrives at your office, the first stage of business is to edit it. Here is all the equipment you need: a transparency viewer, which is usually called a lightbox or light table; a camera-quality loupe, which is a magnifier; and a wastebasket.

Using a Projector

To edit your images, you might want to run through your film quickly with a projector and a stack loader, just to get an overview of the images. Very honestly, I never do this as I would have to set up the screen, dig out the stack loader, and clear off a place to set the projector down. Besides, as I've noted earlier, when projecting images you always run the risk of scratching the film or fading the colors.

My main objection to editing by projection is that you really can't determine much about slides when you project them. Deciding whether or not an image is absolutely sharp is hard because it involves the screen surface you're projecting onto. Is the film properly exposed? Projected slides will appear overexposed, underexposed, or properly exposed depending on your projection setup and how dark the viewing room is. If the projector is too close to the screen, everything will appear overexposed; if it is too far away, all of the images will look underexposed.

And if you project slides in a totally darkened room, even severely underexposed film will look fine after a few minutes. The irises in your eyes will open up, just like a camera lens, to compensate for the lack of light. Consequently the projected image will seem to be properly exposed.

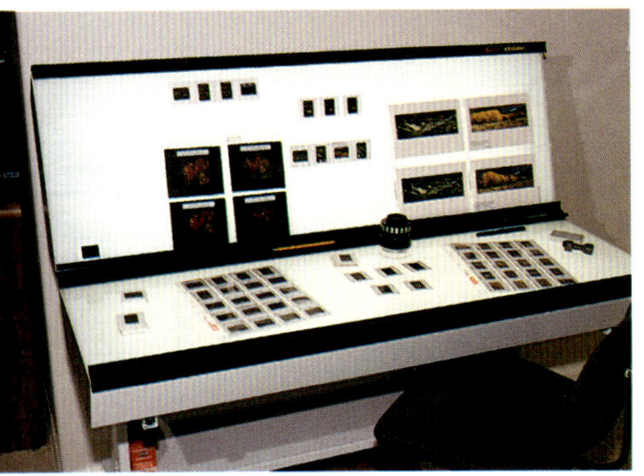

These transparencies of different sizes are on my lightbox. I attached plastic strips on the rear of the box to hold the film on the angled surface.

It is also difficult to compare two or more slides when you're projecting a single image at a time. If you've taken several frames of each composition and shot several compositions with only slight variations, which frame is the best? How can you remember what one picture looked like when you saw it 10 slides ago? Trends in your photography will also go unnoticed. By this I mean shooting mainly horizontals, tilting all horizons in the same direction, or always dividing the frame in half compositionally. These tendencies are far easier to discover when you look at many slides side by side all at once than when you project them one at a time.

I want to edit and to evaluate my slides in the exact manner in which photo editors will look at them. If all editors projected slides, I would project slides, too. But I've never known any photo editor to rely on projected images. Use your projector to give a slide show to your friends; edit your slides with a light table and a loupe.

Using a Lightbox

A lightbox, or a light table, is simply a backlighted surface on which you place your transparencies for viewing. You can easily construct one. Build a wooden box, and mount fluorescent fixtures under 3/16-inch-thick, white Plexiglas, so that the tubes are spaced about 12 inches apart and 4 inches below the surface of the Plexiglas. Make sure to get photographic 5000K daylight color-corrected light tubes; these are available through any electrical-supply house. Paint the inside of the box matte white.

A better option is to buy a lightbox specifically made for photographic purposes. Judging correct light intensity is quite difficult with a homemade light table. If you are serious about publishing your nature images, you should purchase a quality light table, which will come with the correct bulbs installed and be built to produce the industry-standard intensity. By the way, don't waste your money on the little slide sorters sold in many discount houses. Because a single incandescent bulb illuminates the sorters, they are off-color; hot-spot badly, which means that they are much brighter in the center than at the edges; and give off slide-damaging amounts of heat.

Lightboxes and light tables come in all shapes and sizes, from small to large, and in various configurations for flat, angled, or upright viewing. I strongly suggest purchasing one of the larger-sized light tables since it will have the surface area you need to spread out several rolls of film all at once. Suppose you come back from a major shoot and have a lot of film to edit; in this situation you want to be able to compare as many shots as possible at one time.

The light table I use is 4 feet long and 16 inches wide, the largest Acculight Viewer/Editor commonly sold. (I actually own two of these.) The Acculight light table is probably as much an industry standard as any other light table available and, as light tables go, is relatively inexpensive. Acculight makes a stand that holds two lightboxes together: one is flat, and one is angled in the back. The flat surface is easy to work on—pens, loupes, and transparencies don't slide off the surface—while the angled box gives me a location for selected images.

I did, however, have to modify the angled lightbox a bit. (Acculight sells a spillproof overlay to hold 72 slides on the angled box, but I didn't like it.) I purchased some 1/4-inch-square Plexiglas rods from a local plastics supply house and attached them to the angled light surface with a strong glue, spacing them 1¾ inches apart. I can now set 24 slides on each row. This is a great organizational help when I'm pulling a submission or putting together a slide show.

The Process

Start editing your film by spreading out an entire roll of processed slides on your light table. Cull any slides with obvious technical mistakes. Then use a camera-quality loupe to evaluate each image. I'm always amazed that photographers will spend thousands of dollars on cameras and lenses,

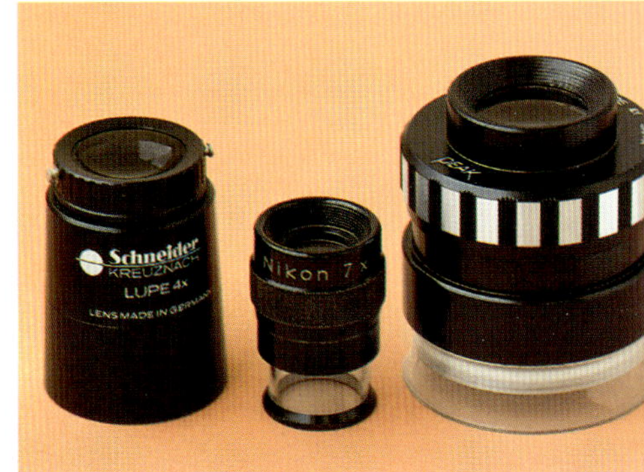

A selection of quality loupes, all of which can be focused.

spend thousands more on travel to exotic locations, and then evaluate the resulting photographs with a $10 loupe with one plastic element. The loupe that lives in more editorial offices than any other is the Schneider 4x. I much prefer the Peak 4x (model 1990), but I keep a Schneider in my office. Every editor I've ever watched evaluate film has used a 4x loupe, so if that is how picture editors are going to look at my work, then that is how I want to also. I've heard a number of photographers advocate using more powerful loupes, 8x or 10x, for normal use.

Pick up a good loupe in this magnification range so that you can check your slides for perfect sharpness and exact focus, but definitely get a 4x. The best loupes offer a means of focusing the optics for your eyesight, which both the Schneider and the Peak do. You want this feature on any loupe you use since you'll be spending hours staring at slides through it. Camera-quality loupes are somewhat expensive, costing somewhere between $100 and $200. But because they don't have any moving parts to wear out, your loupe should last the rest of your photographic life.

To examine your images, place the loupe directly on each slide lying on the lightbox. Carefully evaluate each and every slide for sharpness, correct exposure, and good composition. Some of your shots will jump out at you right away as good graphics, but others will be disappointing. Throw away any shot not up to the best technical and aesthetic standards. Edit ruthlessly.

I know from experience the temptation to keep "almost" shots, ones that are just slightly out of focus or not quite as strongly composed as the best images. Photographers fleetingly believe that time will fix the problems, that if they just wait another week to review the film, the image will have come into focus and rearranged itself into a stronger composition. Of course, this just doesn't happen, no matter how much they wish it would. Don't keep bad photographs. As you work, keep in mind the old joke that the difference between a professional and an amateur photographer is the size of the wastebasket next to the light table.

Actually you can keep missed shots if you want to. Simply file them in a folder labeled "Photographs to which I'm emotionally attached but which I'll never send to an editor." Your reputation as a photographer is built on the images an editor sees. Send out mediocre images, and you label yourself as not knowing the difference between good pictures and bad. Send out only the best photographs, and your reputation is made. You want editors, when they see your submission still in its envelope, to eagerly anticipate seeing more of your wondrous images. You certainly don't want them to sigh heavily as they toss the unopened package into the "rejects" pile.

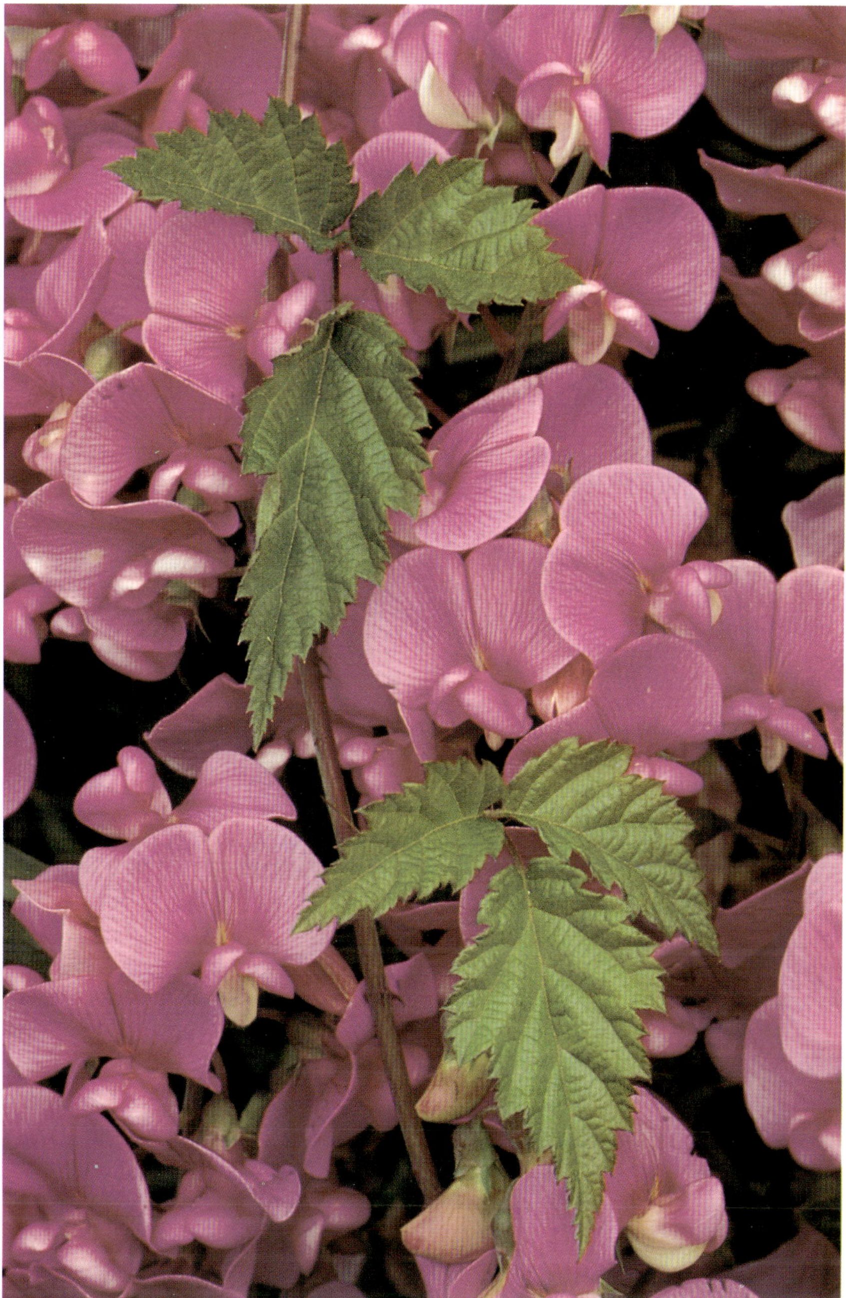

Blackberry leaves and everlasting pea, Washington. Nikon F4, Nikon 200mm macro lens, Kodak Lumière 100X.

When this transparency is viewed through a quality loupe, its sharpness is obvious.

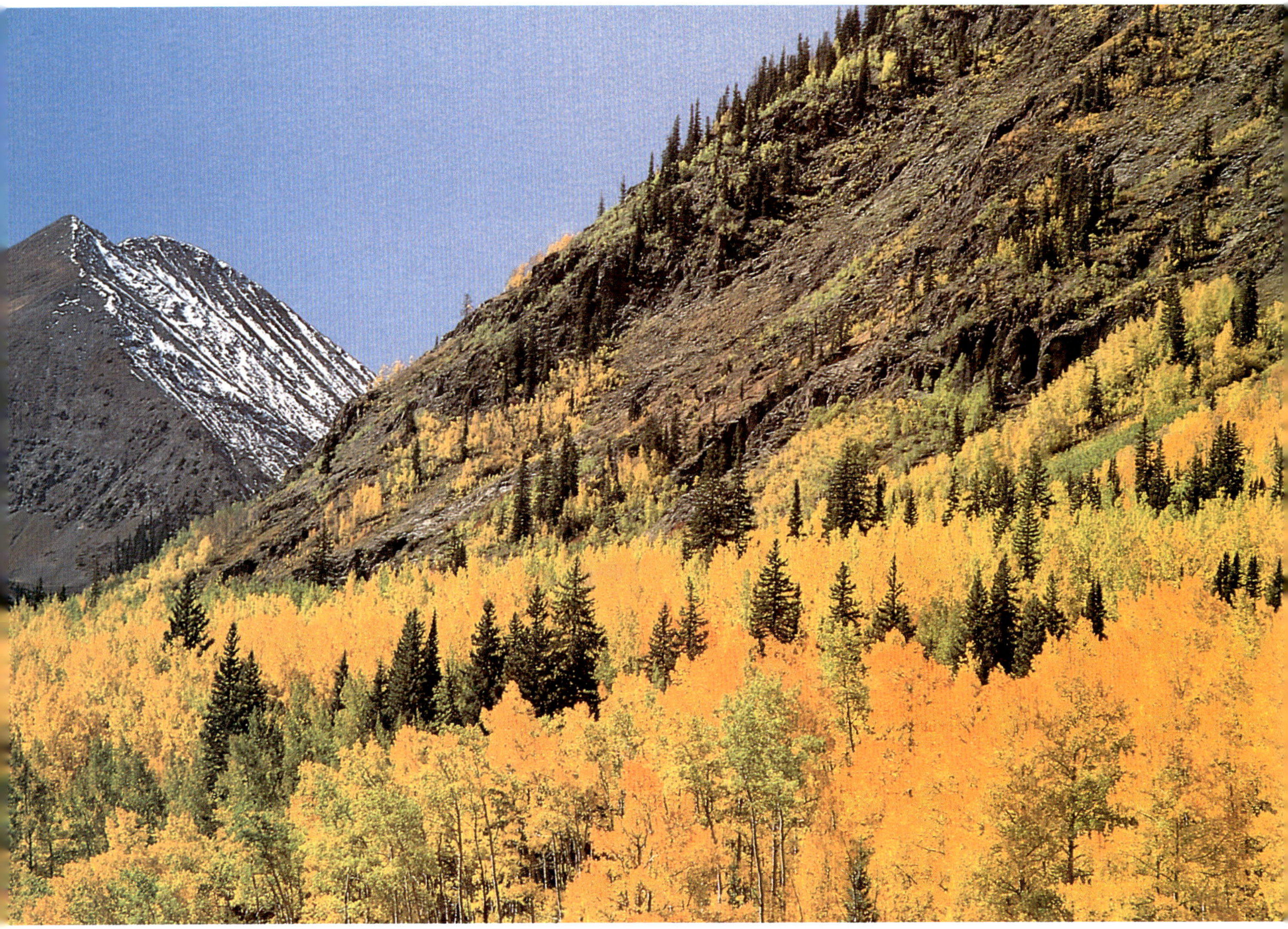

Autumn aspen trees, Colorado. Nikon F4, Nikon 50-135mm zoom lens, Fuji Velvia.

Picture editors always look for razor-sharp focus when they evaluate photographs. This is especially important with 35mm film if the image is enlarged for use as a full-page illustration or a double-page spread.

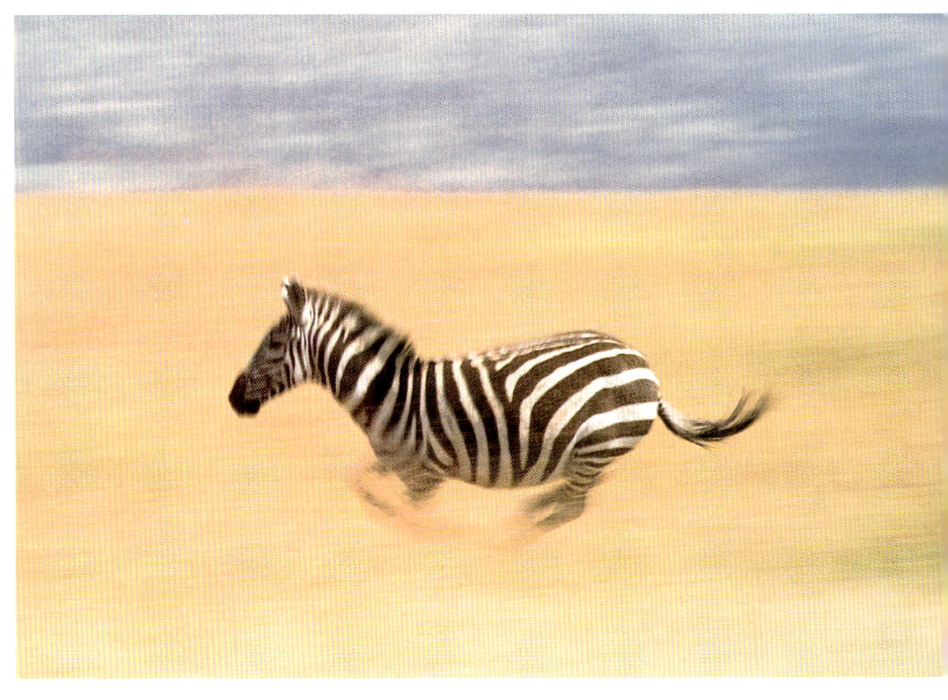

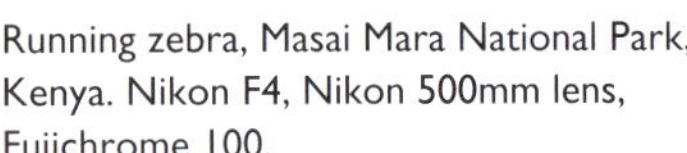

Running zebra, Masai Mara National Park, Kenya. Nikon F4, Nikon 500mm lens, Fujichrome 100.

The difference between deliberately blurred photographs and those that are unintentionally out of focus should be apparent. Here the blur is a means of representing movement in a still photograph.

CAPTIONING SLIDES

After you edit your slides, the next step is to label them with your name and to caption them. Right now I'm assuming for convenience that all the slides you're keeping will be filed in your own office. Perhaps someday you'll be placing film with a stock agency. Almost all agencies have a distinct manner in which they want film labeled; a staff member will tell you how to present your film, and you'll need to follow these instructions. (However, signing on with a stock agency comes much later in your business career. For more information see page 72).

The Copyright

Do the easy part of identifying your slides first. After the edit, put your name and ©, the copyright symbol, on the mount of every slide you keep. This copyright sign warns any potential users that they may not reproduce the image without first getting permission from you, the copyright holder. The simplest way to do this is to get a rubber stamp made: © JOHN SHAW. Use a typeface small enough so that it fits along the narrow side of a slide mount without intruding into the wide portions of the mount. You might need both wide sides for caption information.

Putting your name on the mount in this manner certainly is easier when you have a short name like mine. I urge you to use your own name here, and not a business name such as "Prairie Earth Studio" or "North Woods Photography." This little name stamp acts as advertising for you, reminding picture editors exactly who to contact for more great images. Make sure your name pops easily into their minds.

Don't place your address or telephone number on the mount unless you intend never to relocate again. I've moved several times since I started my business, and even after notifying clients of a new address with multiple fliers and cards, I still have film returned to previous addresses. And don't use a line on the mount that reads something like "Photography by John Shaw." After all, can't an editor tell that this is a photograph? Why take up space with the obvious?

I don't include the year in my copyright notice. Technically you own the copyright to a work at the moment of creation, when you press the shutter. The copyright law protects photographs even if there is no © notice on them, but I would strongly urge you to use the copyright symbol. So why don't I add the date on my slide mounts? Because it makes the slides seem old. I'm still actively marketing photographs I took early in my professional career, 25 years ago. This will sound strange, but a photo editor once commented about a picture marked with the year it was shot, "I don't want an old shot of autumn leaves. I want a new shot." Now, autumn leaves are autumn leaves, and I don't think they change styles ("Red's out this year, dear."). The photograph the editor was referring to was 4 years old. While I don't cover up the date my processing lab places on the mount, I do nothing to draw additional attention to when I took the photograph.

Writing Captions

After stamping your name on the mount, you need to caption the slide. A caption is as much information as you deem necessary to help someone understand the photograph. Don't make assumptions, such as "everybody can recognize a white-tailed deer," because everybody can't. Be as specific as possible; the more information you give about your photograph, the more possible uses for the shot.

Les Line, the former editor of *Audubon* magazine, once acted as photo editor for a book on wildflowers across America. He later commented that one of the most difficult aspects of the project was getting accurate picture descriptions. He received photographs with vague captions, such as "pretty red flower." If at all possible, caption each slide of a biological subject with both its common and Latin names; for landscapes, include the names of any prominent geographical features.

Be wary of using only common names for plants since these vary from place to place. Consider the shrubby trees of the genus *Amelanchier*; the trees are also locally known as serviceberry, juneberry, shadbush, shadblow, and sarvis. Which one is correct? Similarly, the pink lady's slipper orchid is also called stemless lady's slipper orchid or moccasin flower depending on locality, but there is no doubt about the identity of *Cypripedium acaule*.

Learning how to identify subjects is critical. You'll become a better nature photographer if you become a better naturalist. Picture editors shouldn't have to wonder about the subject of a photograph. Is that a picture of a female mallard, a mottled

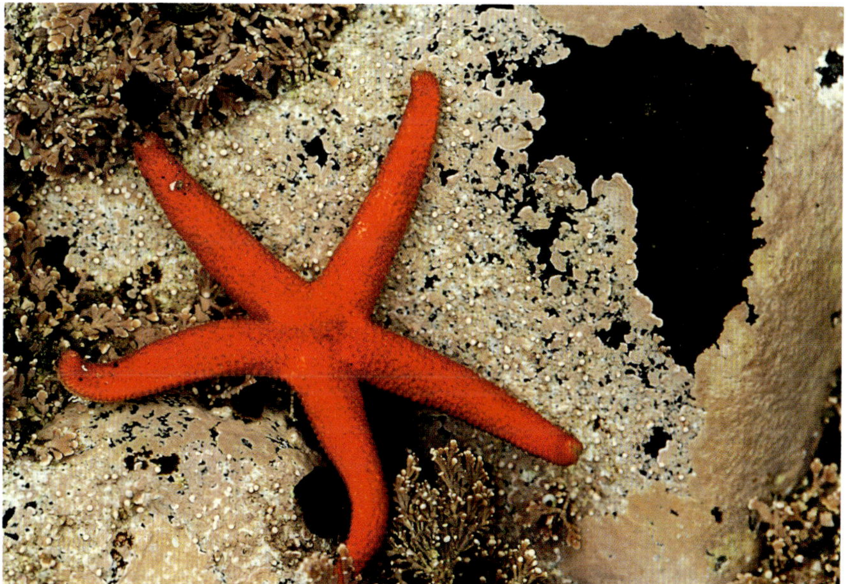

Red starfish in tidal pool, Olympic National Park, Washington. Nikon F4, Nikon 200mm macro lens, Kodak Lumière 100X.

A little research enabled me to identify this starfish down to its species name, Henricia levluscula. *The park naturalist at the Olympic National Park Visitor Center steered me to a tidal-pool guide book sold there. For just a few dollars, I can now easily key out many of the other creatures I photographed along the ocean's edge.*

duck, or a female black duck—and what is it doing? A working assumption for you when captioning is that editors know nothing about nature and have never traveled anywhere. Now tell them what they're seeing in your photograph.

You'll need a reference library of sorts. Basic field guides, such as the Peterson series, the Golden Guides, or the National Geographic bird guide, are the place to start. Your local nature center probably has some specialized books that will help you identify esoteric creatures. Every national park and national monument has a bookstore in its visitor center filled with local information, plus maps of the park marked with the names of prominent features. Whenever I travel I try to purchase any local field guides or checklists that I come across. Thus, my little library includes such titles as *Wildlife of the Falkland Islands*, *The Lizard-Watching Guide*, and *The Butterflies of Trinidad*. The more information you have available when you write a caption, the more potential uses for your photograph.

Suppose you did label a shot "pretty red flowers." Who would buy this photograph? Someone looking for "pretty flowers" or for "red," but that is about it. If you caption it "Paintbrush on Texas spring prairie; the Hill Country near Austin; *Castilleja indivisa*; April," you can still sell it as "pretty flower" or "red." But look at all the other possibilities that have arisen: you could sell it for "prairie," "Texas," "springtime," "midwest," "wildflower," "Austin," "seasonal," or "April," among others.

Work up your captions as soon as you get your film back if possible. First of all, you'll remember what the picture is of. Three years from now you might not—I should say probably won't—remember which mountain you photographed or if a particular African antelope is a bushbuck or a waterbuck. Second, if you suddenly need to submit the image quickly, your work will have been done. And third, someday assistants might be pulling slides from your file for submission. Will they know what this subject is? Don't get behind with captioning because it is very hard to catch up.

Where you physically write the caption information is up to you. Some photographers favor a separate caption sheet with all the information tied to numbers on the slide mounts. I don't do this unless I have a request for very specific photographs and am asked to do so. I put as much information as possible right on the slide mount itself. After all, a separate sheet of paper with caption information can be easily lost, but, I hope, my slides won't be. Editors also won't have to go back and forth between slides and caption sheets.

If you do caption the mounts, you can use standard abbreviations, such as "AK" for "Alaska" or "NP" for National Park. But spell out any words that might be questioned. Don't use slang, and don't be cute in any captions.

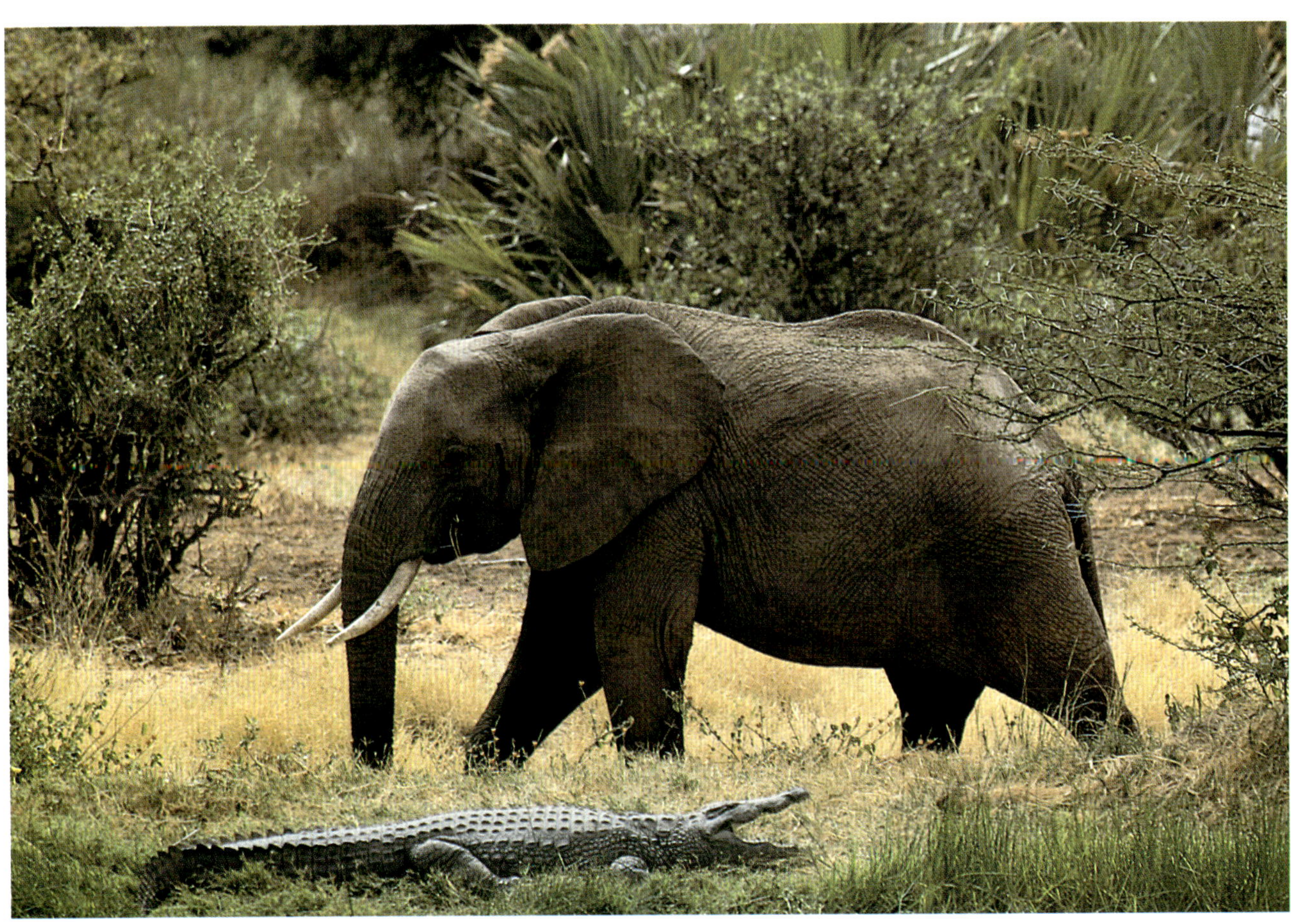

African elephant and crocodile at waterhole, Samburu National Reserve, Kenya. Nikon F4, Nikon 500mm lens, Fujichrome 100.

The caption information for this photograph includes where it was taken in case a photo buyer is specifically looking for "Kenya" or "Samburu National Reserve" shots.

I know that it is difficult to write captions directly on the slide mounts themselves. If you do caption by hand, print with an India ink draftsman's pen rather than with a ballpoint pen, pencil, or felt-tip marker. You want letters that don't smear or rub off, and ink that doesn't run on the cardboard mounts.

Far better than handlettering a caption directly onto the mount itself is printing on a stick-on label that you then affix to the mount. My favorite labels, which I get from SlideScribe (see page 138), are the perfect size for the wide portion of standard 35mm slide mounts. Although these labels are available in different colors, I wouldn't suggest using anything but plain white.

Even better than writing by hand on labels is using a typewriter or computer to print directly onto them. This creates a much cleaner, neater, and more professional-looking label, thereby adding to the business-like image of your submission. By using a small typeface, you can fit a lot more information on one label than handlettering permits. If you use a typewriter, the smallest typeface usually available is 15 pitch, or 15 characters per inch. Allowing a little room at either end, you'll have about 25 or 26 characters per line. If your typewriter supports eight vertical lines per inch, you'll be all set because a standard SlideScribe label holds three lines at this spacing. With three lines of 25 characters each, you'll have 75 character spaces to write a caption. Not bad.

But by far the best way to label slides is to use a computer and printer. The many slide-labeling programs on the market today range from very plain and simple to fancy and complex. Some are included with photo database programs, and others are available as stand-alone labeling programs (see the list on page 136). If money is no object, you can even buy a computer/printer combination that will actually print directly onto your slide mounts. This is the TRAC Slidetyper system, and available models print between two and five lines of 22 characters via an inkjet printer. However, the price for this convenience is out of reach for most nature photographers: Slidetypers start at about $850 and run up to around $4,500.

Do I use such equipment or special slide-labeling programs? No. I do caption my slides using my computer to print stick-on labels, but my "label program" is the exact same one I'm using at this very moment, my word-processing program. This happens to be WordPerfect. I use this by choice over any other slide-labeling program for several reasons. First of all, I already own it and know how to use it. Second, it offers many standard word-processing features that most slide-labeling programs don't, such as word-wrapping text around the end of a line or moving text flush right if desired. With the correct printer I can also get all sorts of special characters, such as ♂ and ♀. Third, given the right printer I can get far more information onto my slide label than any other manner permits.

I've run my caption labels two different ways, switching methods as I upgraded my printer. Using roll labels on a tractor-fed printer is easy. I formatted each individual label as one very small page only three lines long (set your top margin to "0," and printing starts immediately on the top line). For convenient access I saved the page form as a macro. The smallest type my dot-matrix printer supported was 20 cpi, so when I called up the format I had a page with three lines of 45 character spaces each. To make a label I typed in whatever information I wanted, positioning the text wherever I wanted on the "page."

To print just one label, I keyed in "print page" one time. For many identical labels, I keyed in "print page" as many times as necessary. After each label the printer rolled the next one into place. Then I peeled off the label and stuck it on the slide mount.

Since I started computer labeling, I've upgraded to a laser printer (which I must admit I like much more than my old dot-matrix printer!). The same slide labels are available from SlideScribe in sheets for laser printers rather than rolls. Refer to your software's instruction book as to how to format for sheets of mailing labels, and you'll be all set. Every full-featured word-processing software program supports labels; just follow the instructions. I'm running four lines on each label, using a proportional font at 6 pitch. It is quite legible, neat, and professional-looking.

The only trick to remember with WordPerfect and most other word-processing software programs concerns the number of labels you want to print and where they're physically located on the sheet of labels. Enter "print page" and only the first label in the upper left corner is printed as the sheet goes through your laser printer. Most word-processing programs treat labels as a series of pages in a document rather than as individual items. If you use "print document" instead of "print page," you'll have all the labels for which you've typed captions.

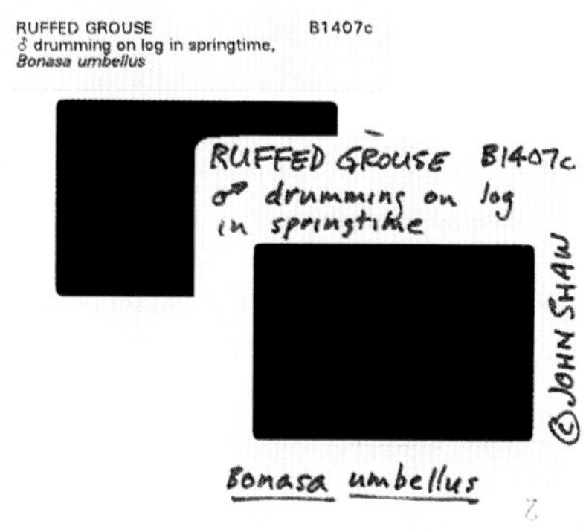

Here are two identically captioned slides. On one slide mount the information is handlettered, while the other has a computer-generated and printed label. Notice a difference?

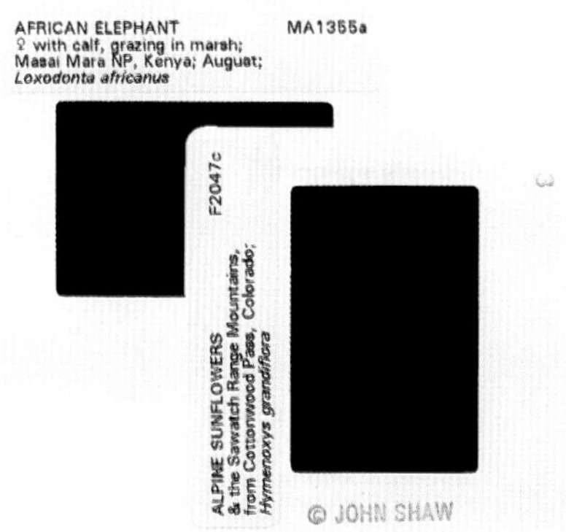

To caption both vertical- and horizontal-format slides, I run SlideScribe labels through my laser printer, which I've set for four lines of text. This produces a very legible label.

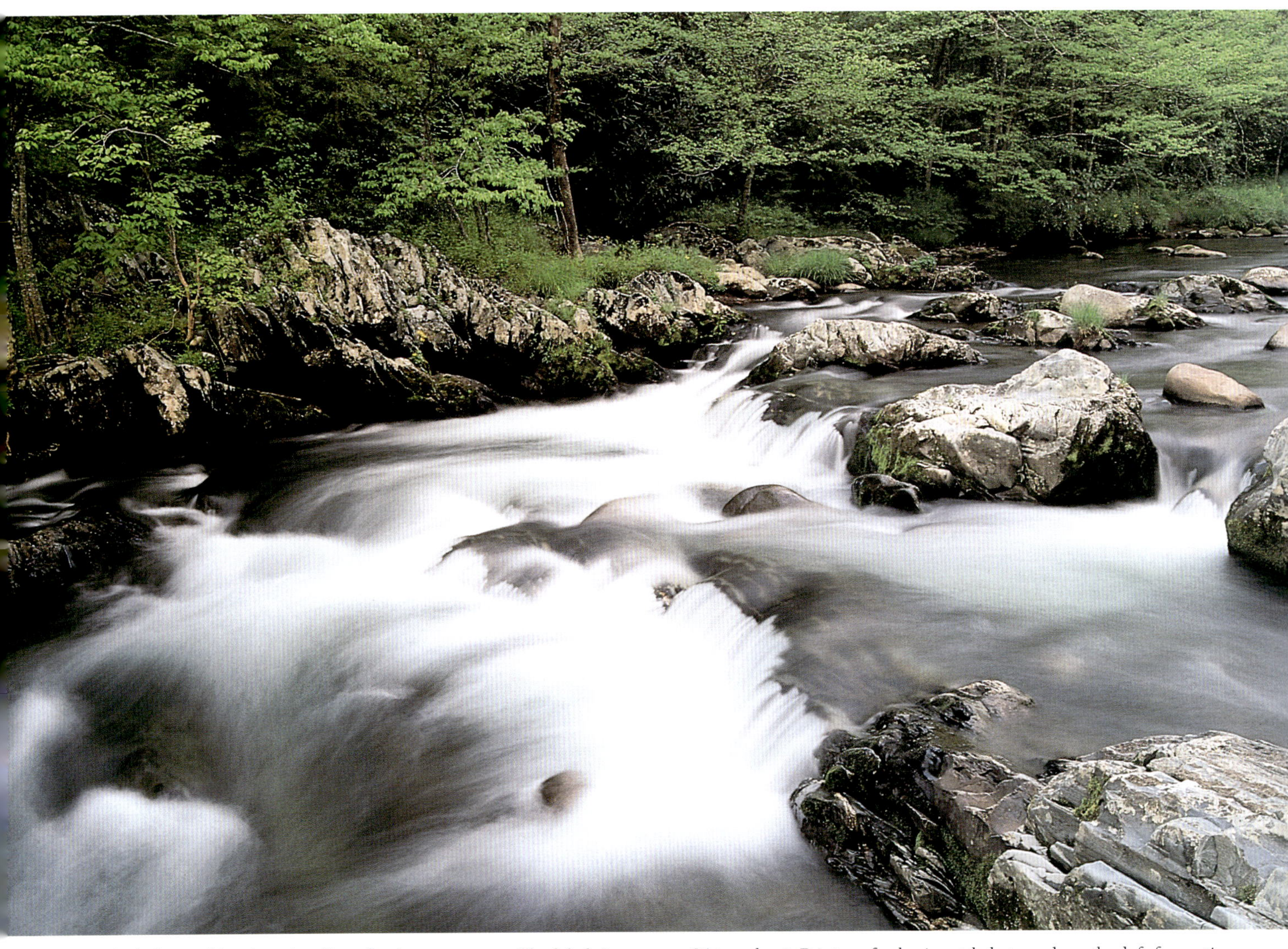

Little Pigeon River in spring, Great Smoky Mountains National Park, Tennessee. Nikon F4, Nikon 35-70mm zoom lens, Fuji Velvia.

Without specific caption information, this photograph could be of almost any stream in the eastern United States. But identifying the location makes it far more salable.

The labels I use come 84 to a sheet. Print just a few labels, and you'll end up with a partial sheet. No problem. Simply put in some blank "pages" to get down to the location you want, and then type away. That isn't hard at all. Suppose I have a partial sheet of labels. I just count how many have been used (and since they are on the page in rows of four this is pretty simple) and start captioning with the next number. If 16 have already been used, I need to start typing when the computer screen tells me that I am on "page" number 17. This isn't a big deal.

Position the labels on your slide mounts so that they can be easily read when the slides are on a light table. Spread out your film on your light table so that the images are correctly oriented: the blank side of the slide mount should face you. My label always goes in the same position, on the top of the slide for horizontal shots and on the left for verticals. For that matter, my name stamp is always on the right margin for horizontals, the bottom of vertical photographs. This is habit, nothing more. Place your captions and copyright notice anywhere you want so long as they are easy for an editor to read. No information should be on the reverse side of the mount unless absolutely necessary as undoubtedly it will be overlooked.

By the way, have you noticed that I haven't mentioned adding photographic information to the caption? Believe me, most photo editors don't care that a picture was taken with a 300mm lens at 1/500 sec. at *f*/5.6. They're concerned with the image itself and not how you shot it. You might like to keep track of this information, but don't waste your time including it on the slide mount.

ORGANIZING SLIDES

As part of organizing your slide file, I strongly urge you to add a unique file number to each individual photograph. This is a lot of extra work, and I know many successful professional photographers who don't number their slides. But an inventory numbering system enables you to follow each and every image as it passes through clients' hands and, with some sort of data-retrieval system, to quickly find any individual shot. And thanks to the numbering system I use, my office grosses roughly an additional $8,000-$10,000 per year simply because Andrea and I can track slides instantly both in-house and out-of-house. (I explain this in more detail later when I discuss dealing with clients—see page 53).

Filing Slides

If your total "good photo" file comprises only 1,000 slides, it will be pretty easy for you to find any one frame just by looking through all of your pictures. This won't take long at all. But suppose you have 10,000 slides of all sorts of subjects: birds, animals, landscapes, travel destinations, wildflowers, and so on. You want to make a submission to a magazine, and you know that somewhere you have a great vertical shot from Rocky Mountain National Park with an elk standing in the midst of autumn aspens. Can you find it easily? Or let me jump way ahead to the day when you have many submissions out with publishers. You sent out a submission of 247 photographs, but when it is returned there are only 246 slides accounted for in the package. What shot is missing?

Numbering systems can be as basic or as complex as you want to make them. Almost all photographers I know who number their slides tie their numbering system in with their storage system. After all, what is the use of an inventory number on a slide if you can't find the slide in the first place?

Most photographers group and store images by subject, such as "Birds," "Bears," and "Butterflies." I urge you to take the extra time needed to carefully consider the ramifications of any classification plan before you jump into using it. It doesn't matter at all how you file your slides or how you number them, so long as you find your system easy to use. But you should plan for the future when your slide collection is 10 times bigger than it is now.

A simple system involves numbering the slides according to the slots on the slide page in which they're filed, and then to store the pages by separate category. For example, suppose "B" stands for the "**B**irds" category. The first shot in your bird file, then, is **B-1-1**; that is, **B**irds, **1**st page, **1**st slot. The next frame is B-1-2, followed by B-1-3, B-1-4, B-1-5, etc. The last frame on the first slide page is B-1-20, so the next picture is B-2-1 (Birds, 2nd page, 1st slot).

Many photographers carry this even further, breaking "Birds" down taxonomically or by groups, such as "Seabirds," "Owls," "Hummingbirds," and "Raptors." The problem I see here is that I would have to have lists posted everywhere in the office to keep track of all the subcategory codes. Does B-W stand for "Birds-Waterfowl," "Birds-Wrens," "Birds-Waxwings," or "Birds-Warblers"? If you keep breaking down categories, soon half your slide labels will be taken up with numbers, such as B-WPK-SS-RN-3-18 (the 18th slide on the 3rd page of Red-naped Sapsuckers in your Woodpecker division of Birds). Have too many categories, and you'll have a zillion subdivisions, with only a few slides in each. After all, how many P-T-N-QWT (Plants, Terrestrial, Nonflowering, Quillwort) photographs will you ever have?

Another numbering system breaks down subjects first by location, and then by type of subject. For example, you could assign each continent a number, then each country on that continent a sub-number, and then each major city a sub-sub-number. This could be followed by a subject code for what's going on in that city, in that country, on that continent. For example, 3-11-12-5-37/5-3 could stand for Africa, Kenya, Narok, Maasai, child/5th page, 3rd slot. Whew! It would take me far too long to figure out exactly which numbers stood for exactly which topics. And I just hope that a country never changes its name. After all, where is the USSR? And EG and WG are now just G since the Berlin Wall came down.

Long ago I decided I wanted a simple, mindless system that took minimal brainpower on my part to use. I've stuck with the same basic system since I started numbering slides, and so far, so good. Bear with me here, as some of my procedures will become clearer after you read the next section on databases.

I file all my slides by category, and in each category, by sequential number. My categories are quite broad, and I lump many subjects together. I use a letter-number-letter code (uppercase letter, number, lowercase letter). The first letter (or letters) denotes the general category. This is followed by the number of a slide filed sequentially within that category, which in turn might be followed by another letter denoting multiples of the same exact shot. Here are some of the roughly 30 categories I have:

M	Mammals
B	Birds
F	Flowering plants
N	Nonflowering plants
NP	National Parks (North America)
FC	Fall Color
PA	Patterns
MA	Mammals, Africa
SK	Skies and sky phenomena
R	Reptiles and herptiles

Not too complex, right? I can look at a photograph and without much thought at all say, "Yes, this is a picture of a mammal" or "No, that's a bird in this picture." The one- or two-letter category code is then followed by a sequential number. The first shot in my "Fall Color" file is FC1, followed by FC2, FC3, etc. FC175 is the 175th distinct image in this file. Suppose I took quite a few frames of this composition—I shot multiple, in-camera, duplicate originals, that is—and I want to keep four of these identical images in my file. I add a lowercase "a," "b," "c," and "d," etc., after FC175; thus, I have FC175a, FC175b, FC175c, and FC175d. The reason I do this is straightforward. If I'm looking for a certain photograph and it's being used somewhere, I want to know if I have an identical frame of it.

The page-slot numbering system does have a drawback. How do you know if FC-17-12 is the same as or is different from FC-17-11 or FC-17-13? If there is no lowercase letter, I know that the picture is a one-of-a-kind shot, or at least I've put only one version into my file.

If I were starting over, I wouldn't use lowercase letters. Even with a laser printer, a lowercase "b" looks too much like a "6." Instead I would probably use a decimal or dash version for identical frames, something along the lines of FC175.2 or FC175-2.

Out of habit I number all my slides in the upper right corner of the label, flush with the

These three photographs represent various categories in my filing system: "Winter Scenics," "National Parks," and "Mammals."

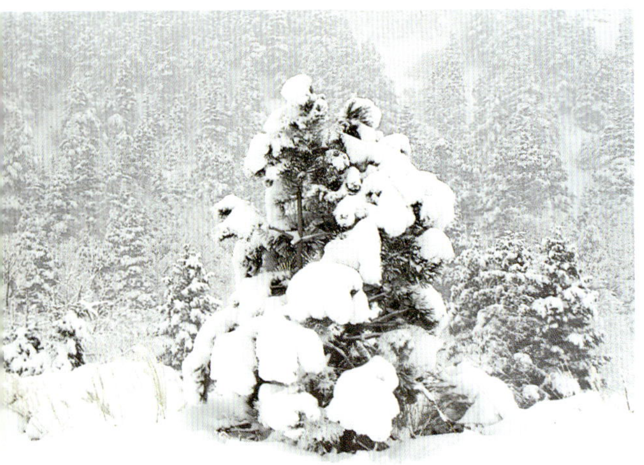

Ponderosa pine in snowstorm, Colorado. Nikon F4, Nikon 55mm lens, Fuji Velvia.

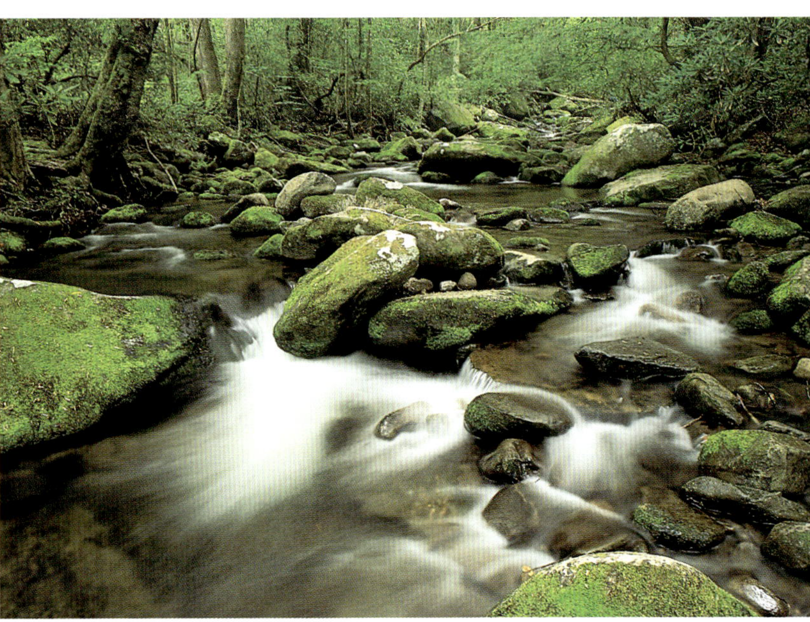

Roaring Fork in spring, Great Smoky Mountains National Park, Tennessee. Nikon F4, Nikon 20-35mm zoom lens, Fuji Velvia.

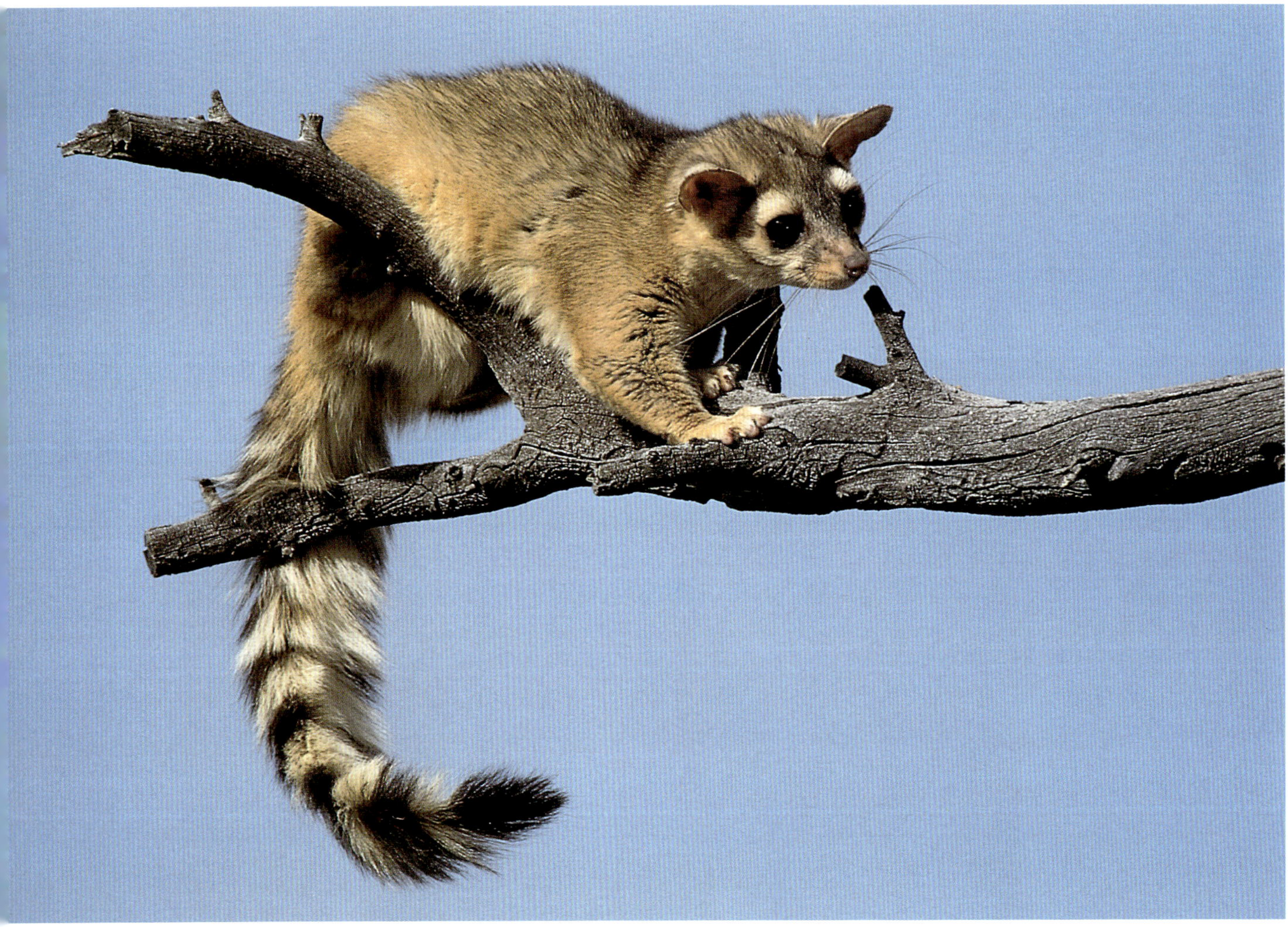

Ringtail (or Miner's Cat), Utah. Nikon F4, Nikon 400mm lens, Fuji Provia.

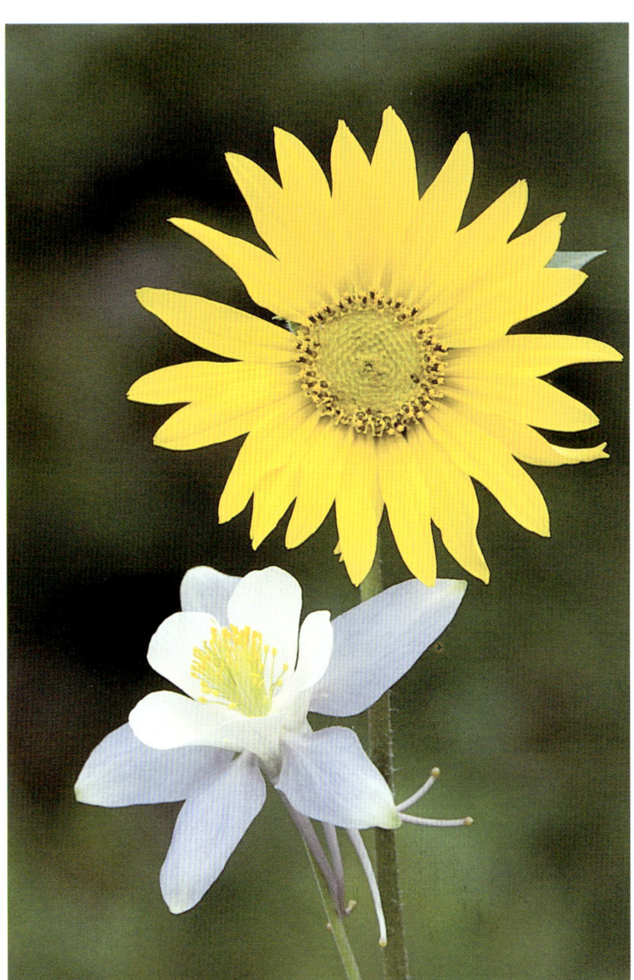

Here are examples of photographs filed in my "Flowering Plants" and "Insects" categories.

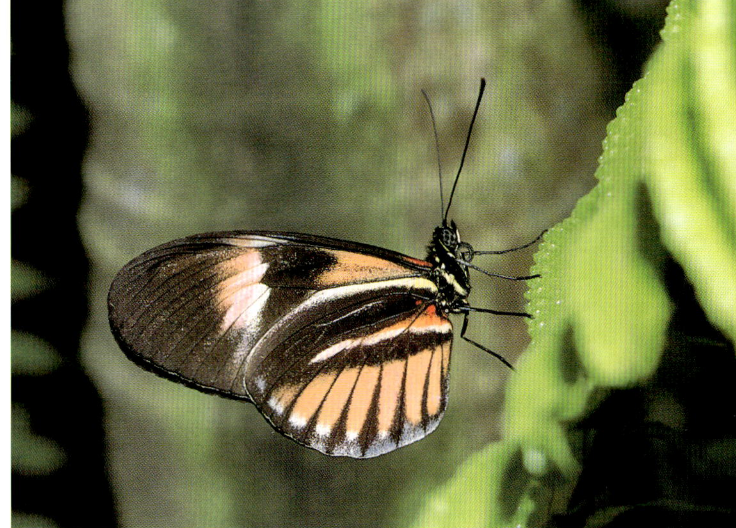

Heliconius butterfly on fern frond, Florida. Nikon F4, Nikon 105mm macro lens, Fuji Velvia.

Summer flowers: columbine and mule's ear sunflower, Colorado. Nikon F4, Nikon 200mm macro lens, Kodak Lumière 100.

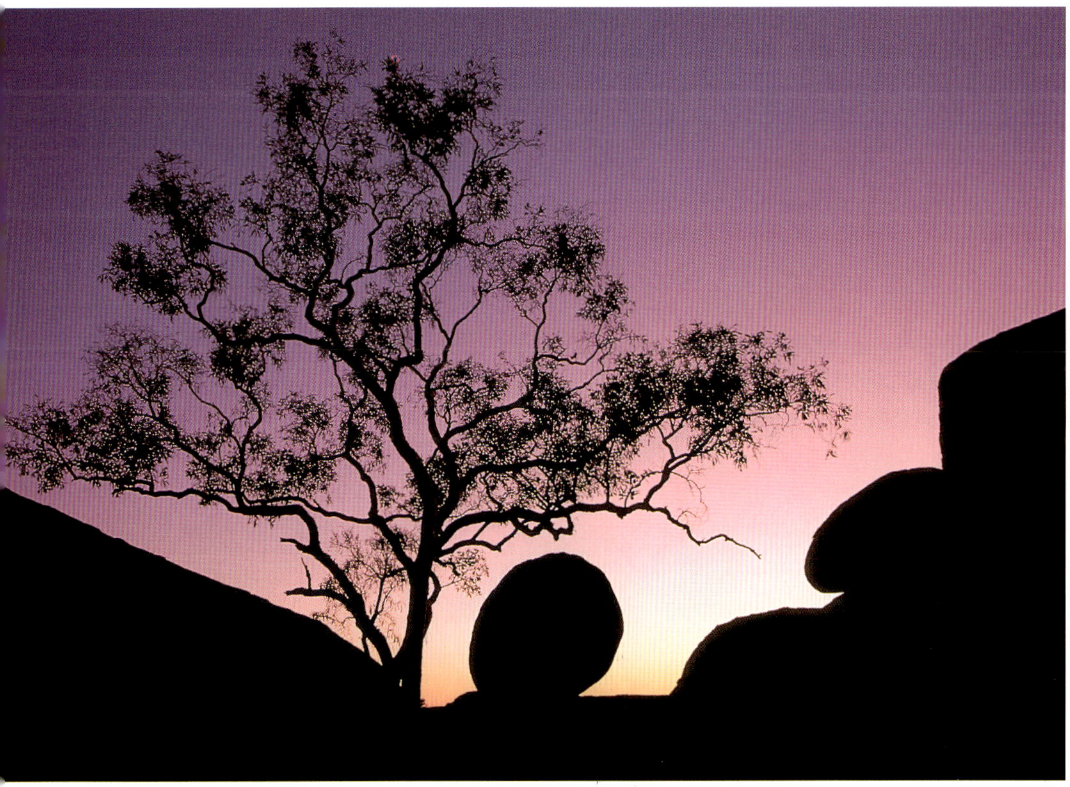

Eucalyptus tree silhouetted at twilight, at The Devils Marbles, Northern Territory, Australia. Nikon F4, Nikon 20-35mm zoom lens, Fuji Velvia.

Since I don't have many pictures of certain areas and probably never will have, I lump together all my general landscape, flowering-plant, and detail shots. This grouping includes pictures that I've shot in such far-off places as Australia. I do, however, have separate files for "Mammals, Australia" (MAus) and "Birds, Australia" (BAus).

right margin. This is meaningless, but that is the way I've always done numbers. Pick a method you like, and stick with it.

Once I've numbered my film, I file the slides by sequential number in those archival slide pages. Then I drop 10 filled slide pages, with a total of 200 slides, into a regular-letter-sized, office, hanging-file folder in my four-drawer file cabinet and label the file folder's standard plastic tab as to what is in it. Quite a few photographers hang each and every slide page separately using hanger bars that run through the slide pages. I've always thought that slide pages alone are too slippery—or at least I keep dropping them—whereas file folders are easy to hold. Each file folder holds 200 slides, and each drawer conveniently holds about 5,000 slides, for a total of roughly 20,000 slides per file cabinet. On the outside of each drawer is a card with information as to what is in the drawer.

Suppose I want to find slide number M3784b. First, I look in the "Mammals" file cabinet, in the drawer that happens to be labeled Mammals M2740a-4522c." Inside I find the file folder with the tab number M3755-3891a, and then find the page with slide M3784b in it, right after M3784a. Easy.

Storing Slides

I've seen slides stored in all sorts of ways, from slide boxes stacked in suitcases, to Kodak projection trays, to expensive cabinets with vertical racks of slides. I'll dismiss the suitcase idea out of hand. Forget the slide-tray method. It is impractical and inefficient. After all, a collection of 10,000 slides would require going through 125 standard Kodak trays. And as for fancy cabinets, remember that expenses quickly eat up any profits—and showing a profit is why you are in business.

When I first started photographing, I kept my slides in metal slide-file boxes that held about 300 slides per box in individual slots. Once I'd accumulated 20 boxes, I saw my folly and graduated to a steel-drawer system from an audio-visual supply company. Each drawer had a plastic egg-crate type insert that held slides in groups of 50. Unfortunately this meant that I was always handling a pile of 50 separate slides. About the umpteenth time I sprayed them all over the floor, I realized that I'd made another mistake.

I now store all my slides in archival slide pages that hold 20 slides per page. Today almost all slide pages are archival. But make sure that you avoid any you come across made from PVC plastic. These slide sheets are instantly recognizable: they are stiff, thick plastic pages with that "new-car" smell. Using slide pages means that each slide, which is encased in its own little pocket, is protected from fingerprints, scratches, and dust. Instead of handling each and every individual slide, you can work with 20 at a time without touching the film. I much prefer top-loading slide pages for their ease of getting slides in and out of the pockets.

I store all my slide pages in standard, metal, four-drawer, office file cabinets. They are relatively inexpensive and readily available, and, made of metal, are bugproof and have no glue fumes to react with the film. By the way, expensive fireproof cabinets for slide storage generally aren't worth the expense. They'll keep papers from burning, but transparency film will still bake or even melt. (If you have an extra frame or two of your best shots, you might want to store them in a safety-deposit box at your bank. This is an easy and inexpensive means of fire protection. Rent a large box, and fill it with slides. You'll then have a second picture file to fall back on if the worst happens.)

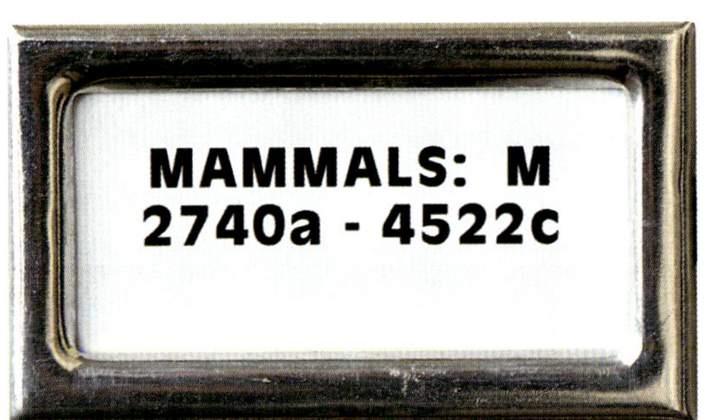

A card on each of my file cabinets indicates exactly which slides are filed sequentially in the drawer.

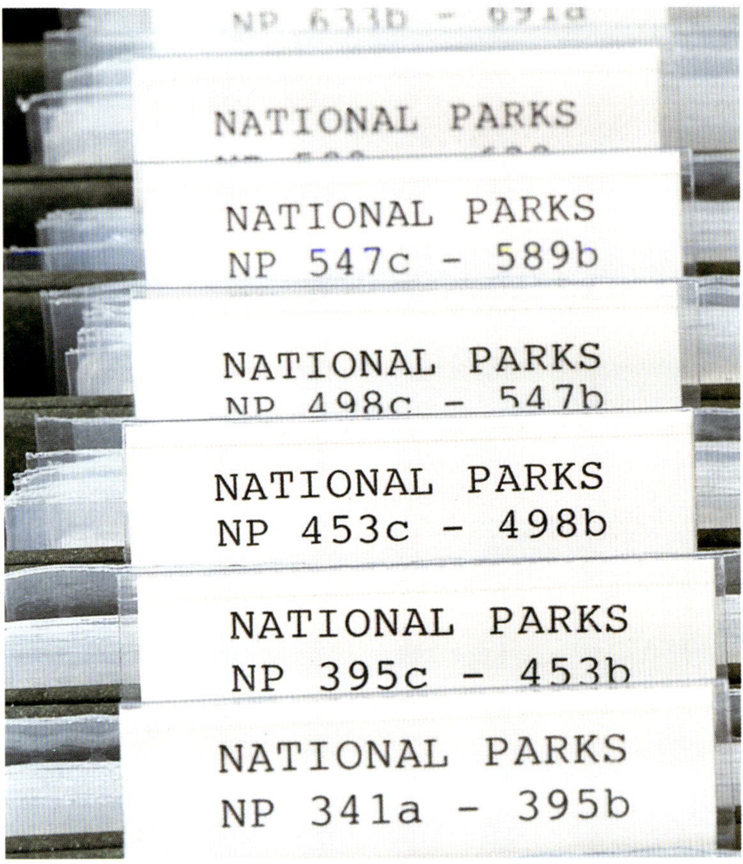

When you open the first file drawer in my "National Parks" file, you see these file-folder tabs, which indicate the slides in each folder. However you actually store your slides, whether in a file cabinet or slide trays or in special AV boxes, you must make sure that the actual piece of film rests in a vertical position. This way, the larvae of a group of minute beetles, the Dermestidae, will fall off the slides rather than eat the emulsion off the film.

COMPUTERS AND DATABASES

At this point, you've captioned and numbered your slides and safely filed them away. The obvious problem now is how to find any one specific photograph. You can, of course, scan through all your slide pages until you come across the shot you want. A visual search works just fine, especially if you have a small number of slides in your collection, or if you are in and out of your files so often that you've memorized almost all the images. But what happens when another person has to find a specific photograph? What is the point of numbering slides unless you use the numbers?

When I started out in business, I needed a means of finding photographs, so I developed a basic database just one step up from visually looking through all my slides. I created a card file, similar to the card-file indexes you'll find at the local library. I took standard index cards, captioned them as to specific subjects, and then wrote slide numbers on the cards.

For example, I had a card labeled "Robins" and on it were the numbers of all my robin photographs. Since I didn't file all my robin shots together, these numbers weren't sequential. My "Robins" cards looked something like this:

ROBINS
B13, B91abc, B241, B242,
B243ab, B330abcd

But suppose I had a photograph, slide number B477, of a robin's nest with the eggs showing. I also had a "Nests" card and a "Bird's Eggs" card, so B477 was listed on both of these cards, as well as the "Robins" card. Of course, the "Nests" card listed slides of other birds species besides robins, so to find one shot I sorted through pictures of grouse, sandpipers, flycatchers, and turkeys. My slide filing system got out of hand even more as I continued to shoot. Eventually I had more cards than photographs, so most of the time I ended up looking through all of my slides to find a particular shot. I began to wonder why I bothered with a card file at all. Then I bought my first computer, and life became much easier.

For several reasons I strongly—let me repeat, **STRONGLY**—urge you to buy a computer if you don't have one. You'll need at least an electric typewriter for general office correspondence, and writing with a word-processing program on a computer is

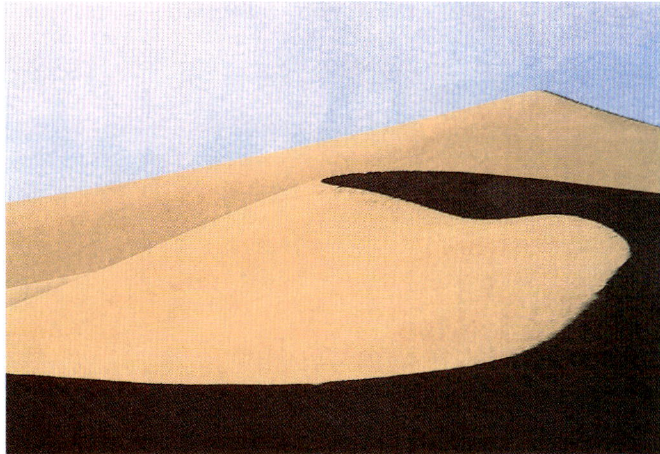

Sand-dune pattern of sun and shadow, Great Sand Dunes National Monument, Colorado. Nikon F4, Nikon 300mm lens, Fuji Velvia.

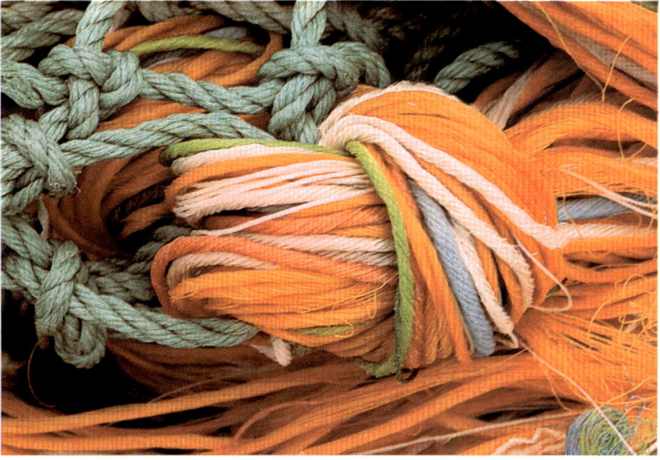

Nylon fishing-net pattern, Oregon coast. Nikon F4, Nikon 105mm macro lens, Fuji Velvia.

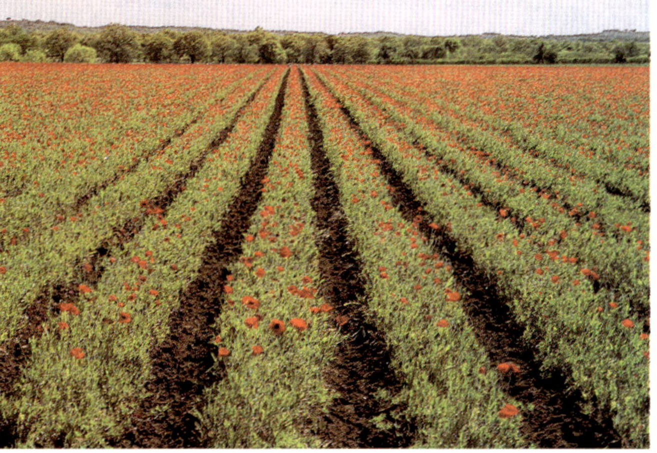

Commercial poppy farm, Texas. Canon EOS-1, Canon 90mm TS-E lens, Fuji Velvia.

These three photographs are all indexed and physically stored in the same category in my filing system even though they are of radically different subjects. The file category is "Patterns." To find one specific shot, I let my computer do the work of sorting out the pictures, utilizing the descriptive information I enter in my database.

exponentially easier than using a typewriter. In my office the typewriter is used only for filling out multiple-part FedEx forms.

With a word-processing program you can easily write business letters and magazine articles, mail form letters to clients, label slides, and so on. (Later on you'll see that you can use the computer to track your submissions, keep your accounting books, and do your taxes—see page 128). Quite honestly, I can't conceive of running a photography business or any small business without at least one computer.

You don't need the latest, fastest, largest computer system although you might be tempted to buy one because prices keep coming down while available features keep increasing. As mentioned earlier, I'm writing this book on a 486 computer with a 210-megabyte hard drive. At this point my computer, which is a couple of years old, is almost outdated technology, but it works perfectly for all my office needs. Some day in the future I'll undoubtedly upgrade my equipment, especially as digital manipulation of images starts to affect my business. I see no reason to do so just yet.

The computer simplified tasks for me in terms of finding slides because I also bought a database program. The many database programs available today range from the extremely basic ones, which are little more than list organizers, to complex databases, which can link multiple kinds of information. Program prices also reflect this diversity, starting at $20 or $30 and going up to thousands of dollars.

Currently all sorts of databases are designed strictly for photography businesses, from keeping track of studio expenses to organizing picture collections. Many of the latter also generate slide labels, although often you must use their label-information format or purchase a specific brand and size of labels. Many of these programs are complex and require quite some time to set up, and even more time to learn to operate.

I wanted a program that was easy to learn and simple to use. I'm not a computer whiz. I didn't want to spend hours on end learning how to operate a program when I could be out photographing, and I didn't want to spend a fortune for software. At the same time, if I was going to set up a database, I didn't want to be limited in how I searched the data since I didn't—indeed couldn't—know what I needed to find until I was asked a question. How could I know what a picture editor was going to want until the request came in?

The database software I bought wasn't designed for a photographic slide file, but it has worked perfectly over the years. In fact, I used the exact same basic program for 10 years before updating it, and then I just went to the next version of the same program. My original software program was called *Nutshell*, the upgraded version is *Nutshell Plus II*, and an upgraded upgrade called *UltraPlus* is available. Nutshell is a flat file manager, while the two "Plus" programs have

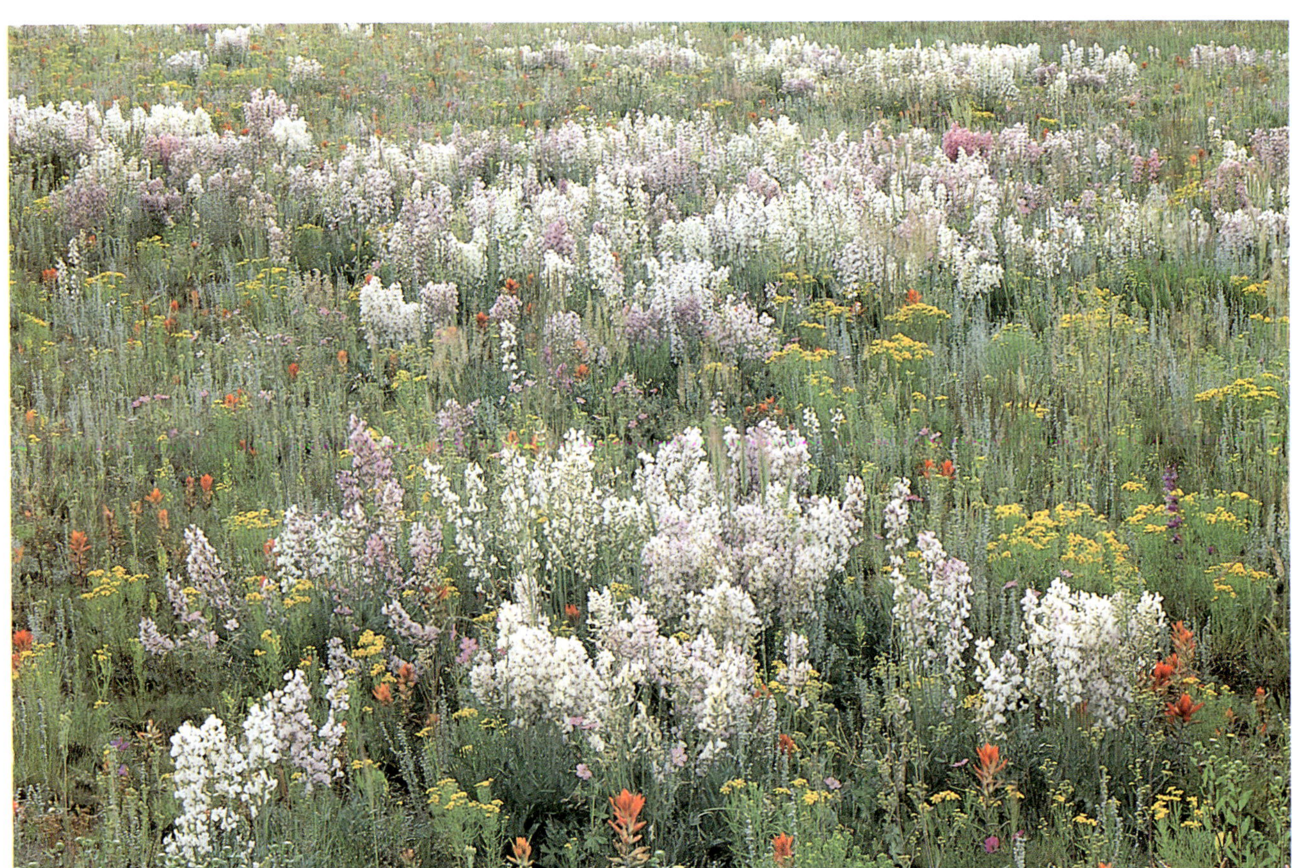

Locoweed prairie, Colorado. Nikon F4, Nikon 105mm lens, Fuji Velvia.

I can find this photograph and similar ones by running a computer search through my database for different criteria. Searching for the word "Prairie" in the subject field would yield this shot's record along with those of hundreds of other pictures of prairies. By specifying some additional search parameters, such as "Locoweed," "Colorado," and "Horizontal," I can narrow down the choices.

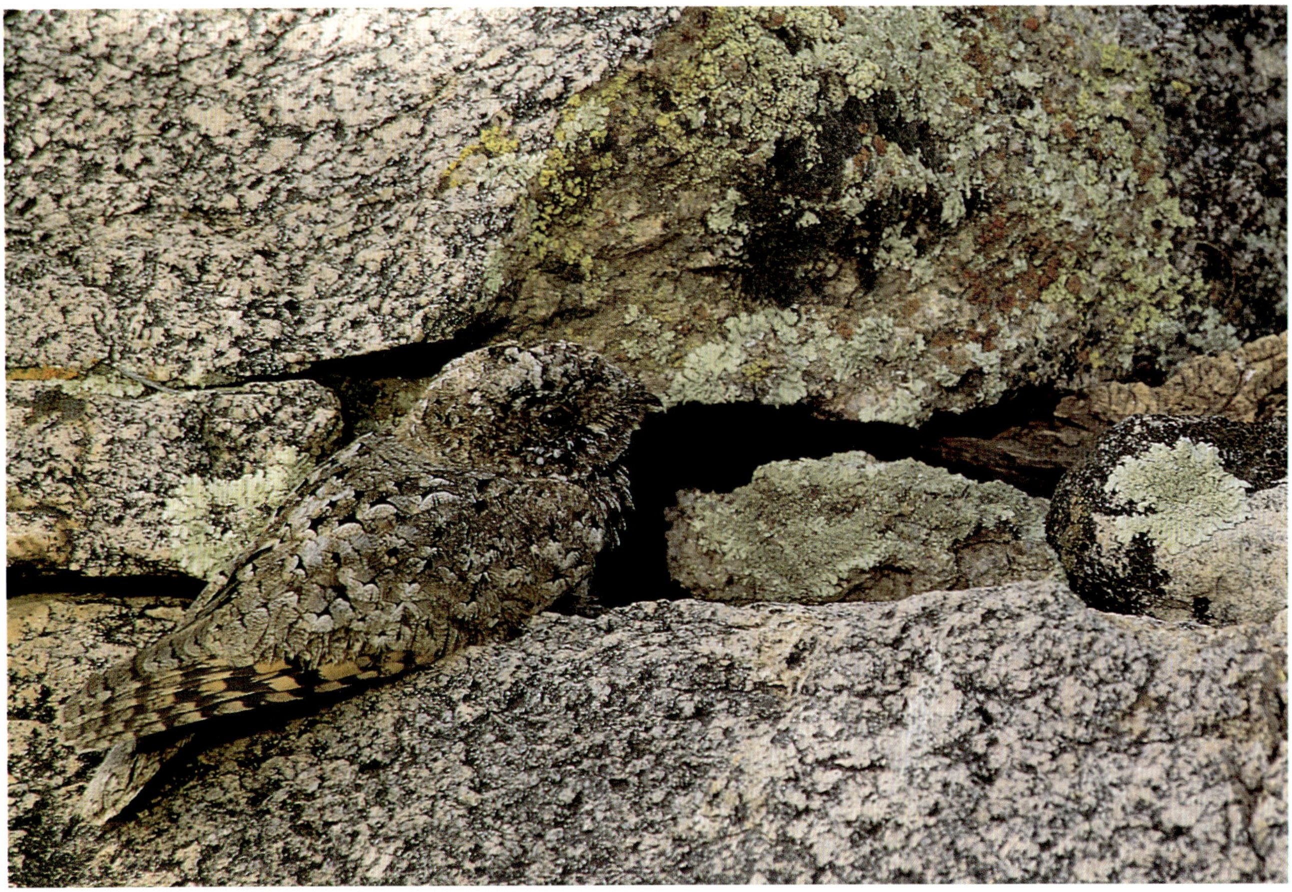

Common poorwill roosting camouflaged on lichened rock, Arizona. Nikon F4, Nikon 300mm lens, Fuji Velvia.

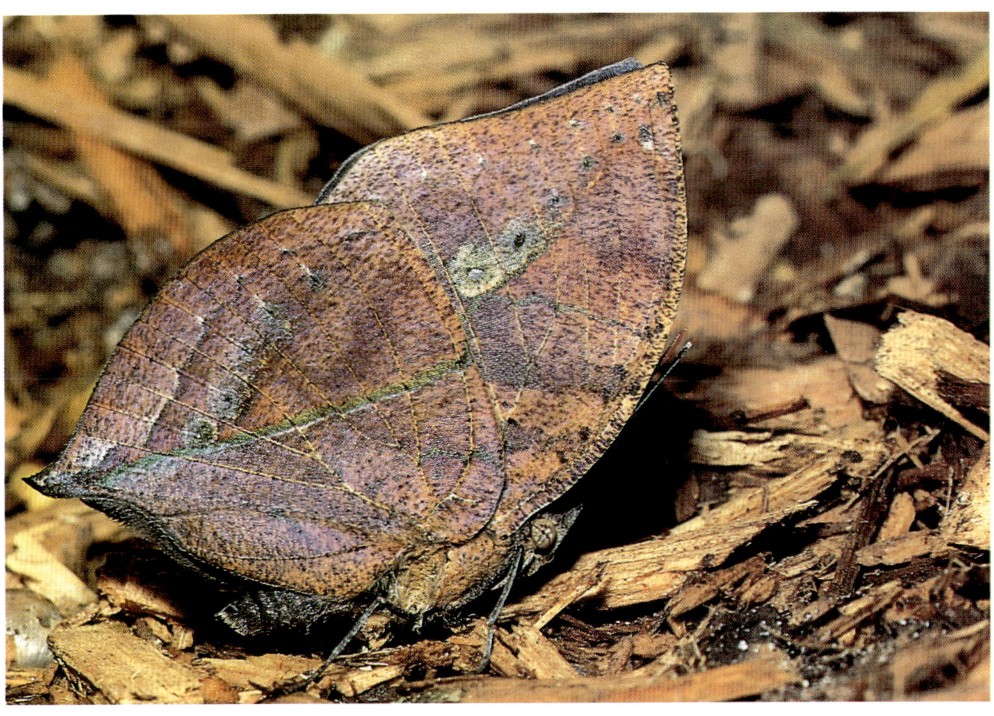

Indian leaf butterfly showing "mudding" behavior, Florida. Nikon F4, Nikon 105mm macro lens, Fuji Velvia.

Here are two seemingly unrelated photographs of a bird and a butterfly. However, a good database description of the subject and an easy-to-use slide-filing system enable me to quickly find these two shots. All I need to do is search for "Camouflage."

relational capabilities (see the listing on page 136).

All three programs are designed for use with DOS machines only (sorry Mac users) and, in fact, have minimal equipment requirements. I highly recommend the Nutshell database. In truth, after years of using Nutshell I can't think of any features that seem to be missing. If I had to purchase database software for my office today, I would buy the exact same program once again. If you're considering purchasing software or if you're setting up a database using software you already own, keep in mind the following features of Nutshell and Nutshell Plus II, which have been a big help to me (I haven't tried Ultra-Plus).

Ease of Use

Nutshell is quite easy to learn and use. I was up and running in about an hour the first time I used the program, and I was a real computer novice then. You simply pick what you want to do from menus; you don't need to learn any complex computer commands.

Flexibility

Nutshell enables you to add, delete, or change information at any time, quickly and easily. You can alter the size of your data fields and create as many fields and records as you have disk space for. If at some later date you need to change the contents of the database or the screen layouts (how the data appears on screen), you'll find that it isn't a big deal. All your information will reappear in the new format.

Unlimited Display Capability

You can arrange your information in the format that you want. And you can create and store as many formats, as many screen layouts, as you like and switch back and forth among them. Each layout can utilize any or all of your data fields, which you can in turn arrange on screen in any way.

Indexing Capability

This is the major reason I like the Nutshell programs. Every word and every number in your database are automatically indexed. This means that at any time you can find, sort, view, or copy information in any field in any record. I can search for any information at any time, not just for a limited number of key words or key fields.

To open a new file, you simply type a new filename at the first screen and define the fields for that new file. You create fields by typing a name and then choosing one of six possible data types: text, number, date, calculation, summary, or time. Once you've completed this step, you simply arrange the data fields on your computer screen the way you want them to appear. In addition, you can make data fields fit certain validation parameters, such as "unique" or "must enter."

So far this has been a rather wordy overview, and I know at this point you're asking, "Okay, Okay. So how do you actually use this program?" Each of my categories (Birds, Mammals, Patterns, etc.) is a separate data file, but all records in all files have the same informational fields and appear the same way on screen. I record the following important information about every image:

- The slide file number
- The number of duplicate frames, if any (remember, in my system these are actually multiple original frames)
- A description of the photograph
- The season you took the picture, if it is relevant
- The location where you shot the image: sometimes this is specific—for example, the name of a national forest—and sometimes just a state abbreviation
- The year you made the photograph (this is only a memory aid for me as it triggers recollections about other subjects I might have shot on the same trip)
- Whether the photograph is a horizontal or vertical

Although this is how I happened to arrange the fields, you can set up your records and your display screen any way you wish.

Adding a slide to the file is just a matter of filling in the blanks. I know what slide number to type by adding "1" to the "# of records" in the upper right. I have the "Slide number" field set up as a "must enter, unique" field, so that I don't accidentally type duplicate numbers. The rest of the fields are self-explanatory, except that "Subject" actually has room for several lines of text. The more I can describe the slide in detail, the better.

Right now I can hear some of you noting that I have to type some information twice: once on the slide label, which I do in WordPerfect, and once here in my database as the "Subject" field. Yes, that is correct, but there is a reason I do it this way. In the database I add a lot of information to "Subject" that is absolutely unnecessary on the slide mount. For example, a slide label might read "Canada geese," while the database reads "3 Canada geese in flight against blue sky, full frame." After all, just by looking at the slide a picture editor would know that there are three geese in the picture, that they are flying, that the sky behind them is blue, and that they fill the frame.

I add information to the datebase because I've actually had requests for shots of birds against a blue sky, and even for certain numbers of animals in the frame. In fact, once I was asked to illustrate the numbers for an elementary children's book, showing countable subjects that children would recognize, such as one rabbit, two ducks, and three pretty flowers. Finding these photographs was easy, thanks to the information I'd typed into my database.

To find a particular photograph, I simply open the file and hit "find" at the bottom of the screen. The same screen layout that I created shows up; I then enter any or all of the criteria I want to find. Suppose a photo editor calls with a request for a vertical shot of a cottontail rabbit in a cornfield. I open "Mammals," enter "cot rab corn" (I could spell out all the words but why bother when Nutshell can find any character string?) on the "Subject" line, and "V" on the "V/H" line. Nutshell pulls up all records that match these parameters, and I look in my file cabinets for the slides in their sequentially numbered locations. Simple.

Suppose that the editor had asked instead for either cottontail rabbits in a cornfield or deer in a flowery meadow. Rather than running two separate searches, Nutshell offers an "also find" command, which enables me to pull up all the records at once.

Another advantage is the program's speed. I had a telephone request yesterday for shots of tiger beetles standing isolated on sandy backgrounds. I opened my "Insects" file to search through roughly 4,000 entries. It took longer for me to enter the search criteria than it took the computer to run the program. I had my list of slides in about three seconds. To be honest, I actually did the search while chatting with the editor on the telephone, and then told her exactly what species I had and in what poses. I made the sale.

The speed of a data search is helped by how I number my film and enter the information. Remember that if I have five identical shots, they all receive the same file number followed by different extensions, which are lowercase letters. All five frames are just one record in Nutshell; each record is of a unique image, not necessarily a unique slide. All of my file categories have far more actual slides than indicated by the numbers on the slide mounts. For example, my "Buildings" category goes up to slide number Bu897; I have 897 distinct images of old barns, schoolhouses, and rural churches. But the category has about 2,500 actual slides.

Here is another question you're probably asking yourself: Where do I file a picture of an elk, standing among golden quaking aspens, taken in September in Rocky Mountain National Park, with autumn asters prominent in the foreground? Do I file that shot under "Mammals," "Fall Color," "National Parks," or "Flowering Plants"? The answer is that it doesn't matter at all. When I label and number a slide, I make an arbitrary decision about the photograph by asking myself what is most prominent in the picture. If I glanced at the image, would I say that it was an elk shot or a fall-color shot or what? I number the slide and file it in some category, and then let the computer sort it out. I don't worry about storing all my elk shots together in one category or all my cardinals in another. I let the computer do this for me.

Yes, this is a lot of work, although in actuality it isn't as time-consuming as it sounds. I see no reason to bother with numbering slides unless you go ahead and set up some sort of database to make use of the numbers. If I didn't use a database but filed my slides into multiple categories and folders, I would spend quite a lot of time sorting and arranging slides. I would then take more time looking through all those slide sheets to find specific shots. Instead, I spend time entering information into the computer. I think both methods take about the same amount of time. With two people working, one person describing the photograph and the other keying information into the database, they can easily enter 250 to 300 slides per hour into the database.

CHAPTER THREE

Finding Clients

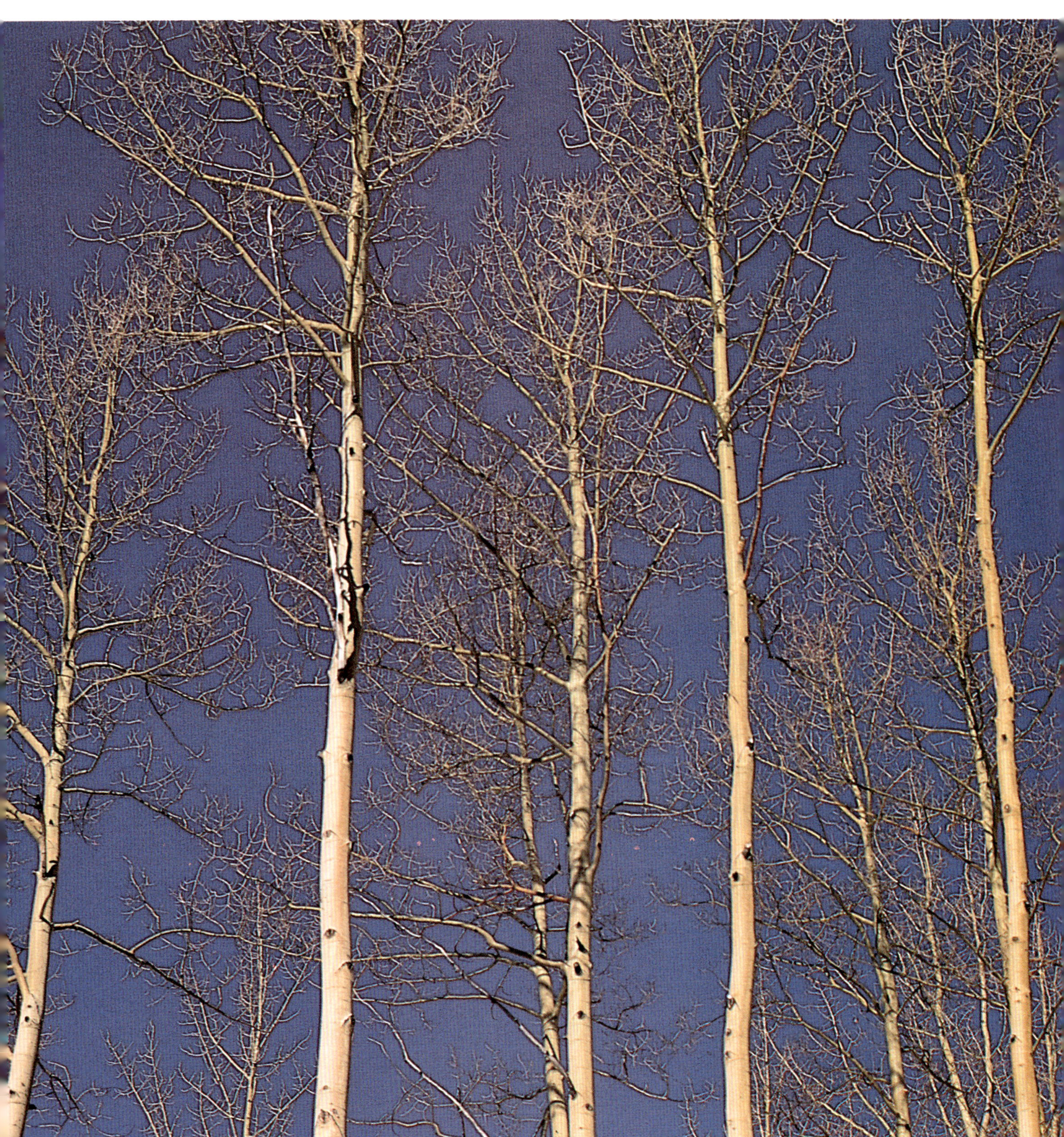

Quaking aspen trees against winter sky, Colorado.

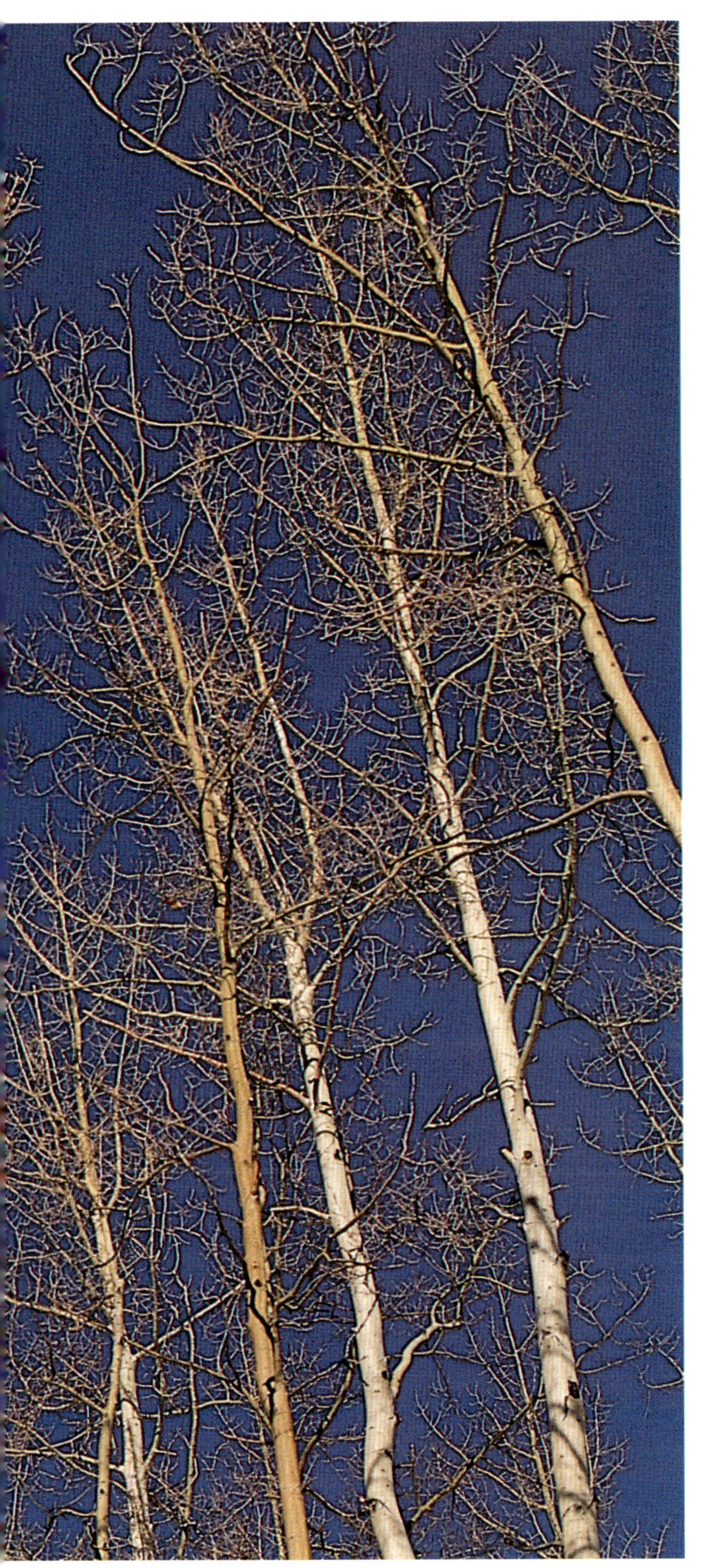

CONTACTING CLIENTS

In order to sell natural-history photographs to publishers, you have to find some clients. This is rather obvious, so the first questions to seek answers to are: (1) Who actually uses nature photography? and (2) In what manner are the photographs used? There is an easy way to conduct this research. Just look around you. Every magazine, calendar, book, and product that uses nature photographs had to first obtain those pictures from a source. That source might as well be you.

Keep a small notebook with you at all times, and jot down any and all information about who actually published the product. Sometimes this information is easy to find. For example, magazines have a masthead page that lists the editorial offices and personnel. At other times you'll have to do a little sleuthing to uncover the information. Most calendars have a company name and address, and perhaps a telephone number, prominently displayed. All books list the publisher; if the address isn't given, your local friendly bookstore can easily pull it from *Books in Print*.

You can glean a lot more information from reference sources. The most popular listing of photography markets for beginners—and probably the most easily obtained sourcebook—is *The Photographer's Market*, an annual publication that is available through any bookstore. Next, you should work through *Literary Market Place*, an extensive listing of book publishers. In the reference department of a major library you can find a number of other specialized books that are useful in locating names and addresses, although a small library might have access to these through Interlibrary Loan Service.

Once you have a name-and-address list, you need to go back to your computer to develop a generic form letter. Almost every business that purchases photography from an outside source has some sort of printed guidelines covering its photo-submission/photo-purchase procedure. Write a "Dear Photo Buyer" letter to every potential market on your list, asking it to send you its submission guidelines both for photographers and for writers. Include a self-addressed, stamped envelope (SASE) for its convenience.

Why ask for both sets of guidelines? The best way I know of breaking into the business of selling photographs—let me repeat: **the best way I know of breaking into the business of selling photographs**—is to write articles to go along with your photographs (see Chapter 5 on page 94). You might as well gather as much information as possible.

You'll receive back one or two pages outlining if the company accepts unsolicited photograph submissions (it might work exclusively with stock agencies rather than with individual photographers), what subjects are needed, how material should be presented, any recurring deadline dates, to whom the material should be submitted, and most important the rates it pays. Read this specification sheet carefully.

Does the client accept 35mm transparencies? Almost all markets do, but why tie up someone's time in returning your work if the company wants only large-format images? Will it accept work from anyone or must you be a previously published photographer? What sort of caption information does the client want? Does it accept any

Of the submission guidelines for three magazines shown here and on the following pages, note that two discuss only picture submissions; you should ask to receive writer's guidelines also.

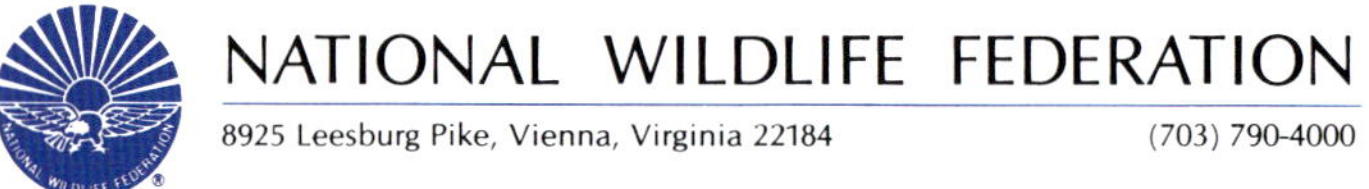

RANGER RICK MAGAZINE

PHOTO GUIDELINES

* **Does Ranger Rick accept color slides?**

  Almost 100% of photos used are original transparencies.

* **What color format does Panger Rick use?**

  Any size transparency.

* **What about color prints?**

  No. Printing quality using transparencies is sharper, cleaner and more brilliant.

* **Does Ranger Rick use any black and white?**

  Only on rare occasions when color is not avaiable.

* **Photo payment information**:

  Front cover....$1,000
  Back cover..... $550
  Full page........$500
  Two-page spread..&750
  Half page.........$350
  3/4 page..........$425
  1/4 page or less..$300

* **What rights does Ranger Rick purchase?**

  One-time reproduction rights for our North American editions. Payment is made three months prior to publication and the photos are returned as soon as the printer's work is complete.

* **What does the Photo Director look for in a transparency?**

  Must be extremely sharp with acceptable depth of field. Subject of image must be clearly defined using proper lighting and exposure (no dark or washed out images.) Strong color and overall visual impact are important.

* **What subjects is Ranger Rick looking for?**

  a) Wild animals, from mammals and birds to insects and microscopic life. Prefer photos shot in the wild to zoo shots. Subjects in captivity should look as natural as possible.

(continued on back)

Picture-submission guidelines for *Ranger Rick* magazine.

b) Pets children would keep. Gerbils, dogs, etc. - but no wild creatures turned into house pets.

c) Humorous nature subjects.

d) Weather, geology and other natural history aspects. No scenics, flowers or mushrooms.

e) Children (ages 6 to 14) interacting with wildlife or pets, involved in ecology or environmental problems, having a fun time in outdoor recreation. Always interested in cultural diversity among children.

f) Adults doing exciting things related to wildlife ecology, science, environmental problem solving.

* **What about captions?**

  In most cases, all we need is subject identification. Include scientific names if appropriate.

* **What about story ideas that are supported by photos?**

  We are always interested in complete packages - ones where a collection of images follow a specific theme.

* **How do I submit my photographs?**

  Please be sure to protect your material with cardboard and other protective packaging before mailing. Include a self-addressed, stamped envelope of proper size so that we can return the images to you as quickly as possible after my review. Send the package to my attention at the address shown on our letterhead.

* **What happens if Ranger Rick loses my photographs?**

  We cannot assume responsibility for unsolicited material.

  However, we do accept responsibility for requested material while it is in our hands. If by any chance transparencies are lost or damaged by us we will negotiate the real and fair market worth. We do not accept delivery forms with binding prices and conditions.

* **Does Ranger Rick pay holding fees?**

  We never have, as we try to return unsuitable material as soon as possible, usually within two weeks of its arrival.

Thank you for your interest in Ranger Rick magazine. I look forward to reviewing your submission soon.

Stephen B. Freligh
Photography Director

Picture-submission guidelines for *Nature Photographer* magazine.

NATURE PHOTOGRAPHER

"The Magazine for People Who Love to Photograph Our Natural World"
P.O. Box 2037
West Palm Beach, FL 33402
(407) 586-3491 · FAX (407) 586-9521

Advertising Sales in the East
3M Pattis
122 East 42nd St. Ste. 2707
New York, NY 10168
(212) 953-2121 FAX (212) 953-2128

Advertising Sales in the South, Midwest, West, & Canada
Nature Photographer Publishing Co., Inc
P.O. Box 2037
West Palm Beach, FL 33402
(407) 586-7332 FAX (407) 586-9521

NATURE PHOTOGRAPHER Submission Guidelines

NATURE PHOTOGRAPHER is an international photography magazine published six (6) times a year. The focus of *NATURE PHOTOGRAPHER* is photographing in the wilderness throughout the world. We are looking for two to five articles per issue that discuss how to improve technique (e.g., submit thorough, well-planned "how-to" articles) for all aspects of nature photography in the wild, including macro subjects,wild flowers, wildlife, landscapes, underwater, and nature abstracts. Looking for travel destination articles and unique photo location pieces which include how-to information. Please, no pets, images of wild animals that have been obtained by feeding the animals (birds at backyard feeders are acceptable for publication), wildlife "setup" shots, zoo shots, or shots of animals confined in any way (this includes insects, reptiles, and amphibians). No game farm "rent-an-animal" images accepted. *NATURE PHOTOGRAPHER*'s regular departments are staff-written and include interviews, field notes, wildlife images, wild lore, conservation articles, and equipment reviews. The one exception to regular departments beings staff written is Photo Techniques and Gear which is written by various experts in the field of photographic techniques and those who are well familiar with photoraphic gear. We welcome queries for this department.

QUERY BY LETTER FIRST! Please, no phone queries. *NATURE PHOTOGRAPHER* maintains high editorial standards. Upon our acceptance of a queried idea, the manuscript will range from 750 words to 2,000 words. Please submit all articles double-spaced and printed on a letter-quality printer. No draft-quality dot matrix!

We review 35mm, 2-1/4 x 2-1/4, 6x7, and 4x5 transparencies. (NO GLASS MOUNTS ACCEPTED.) We only review or accept color prints for publication which were taken by by young people between the ages of 5 yrs. and 18 yrs. All submissions made by adults must be on slides/transparency film. All submissions must include the photographer's name, address, and subject identification on the slide mount or on the back of the black and white print. Transparencies should be presented in clear slide saver sheets. We do not review slides packed in their yellow Kodak boxes or wrapped in tissue. Please limit your submissions to 40 or less. Quality is better than quantity. IMAGES FOR COVER CONSIDERATION MUST BE VERTICAL, SHOT IN THE WILD, AND DRAMATIC. Black backgrounds or excessively dark backgrounds DO NOT WORK for our covers.

Our review schedule for slides is as follows):

Review for Mar./Apr., May/June and July/Aug issues (Spring & Summer images) - 11/1
Review for Sept./Oct., Nov./Dec., and Jan/Feb. issues (Fall and Winter images, including tropical scenes and wading birds photographed in southern destinations during winter) - 5/1

NOTE: PLEASE HOLD ARTICLE SUBMISSIONS FOR TWELVE MONTHS. WE HAVE SOME ARTICLES ALREADY SCHEDULED THROUGH 1996 and INTO 1997.
PLEASE HOLD SLIDE SUBMISSIONS UNTIL 4/15/95. WE WILL BE REVIEWING FALL & WINTER IMAGES AT THAT TIME.

-2-

A self-addressed stamped envelope (SASE) must accompany all submissions. If you do not include an SASE with your submission, we will not return the work. We only hold work submitted without a self-addressed stamped envelope for 6 mos. After 6 mos work submitted without a self-addressed stamped envelope is destroyed.

We do not pay holding fees. We cannot return shipping memos and postcards included with submissions.

You need to pack your submissions properly to protect your work during shipping, both to *NATURE PHOTOGRAPHER* and back to you. We recommend that you use a cardboard mailer larger than your prints so that they arrive undamaged. Please do not tape to the point that it is almost impossible to get into your package. It is fine to secure your package with tape, but remember that you also want us to be able to access the contents of your package. Your return mailer must also be large enough to hold the transparencies and/or black and white prints submitted. We suggest that you ship your work by certified mail or registered mail, and you need to include all paperwork for your return package.

If we accept your idea, we will either have color separations made from the slides selected for publication or convert the slides to black and white prints if the article or a portion of it is to be printed in black and white. Slides must be publication-quality duplicate 70MM transparencies or original 35MM, 2-1/4 X 2-1/4, 4X5, or 6x7 transparencies. *NATURE PHOTOGRAPHER* reserves the right to reject prints or slides of unacceptable quality.

NATURE PHOTOGRAPHER will take first rights on all materials accepted for publication. However, we do review previously published material, as long as six months have elapsed since its initial publication.

Although *NATURE PHOTOGRAPHER* will do its best to insure the safe handling of all submitted materials, *NATURE PHOTOGRAPHER* and Nature Photographer Publishing Co., Inc. do not assume liability for materials that may be damaged while in transit or in our possession. Again, we strongly recommend that you submit publication-quality duplicate slides or black and white prints.

NATURE PHOTOGRAPHER and Nature Photographer Publishing Co., Inc. does not accept the premise that any transparencies, prints, or negatives are worth a minimum of $1,500. *NATURE PHOTOGRAPHER* is not responsible for submissions in transit. Furthermore, *NATURE PHOTOGRAPHER* is not responsible for submissions in our possession beyond their material cost (material cost limited to $5.00 for each transparency, $3.00 for 5x7 prints, and $6.00 for 8x10 prints). *NATURE PHOTOGRAPHER* does not pay holding fees or research fees. Unless approved in writing before the arrival of the photographs, *NATURE PHOTOGRAPHER* and Nature Photographer Publishing Co., Inc. cannot, and *NATURE PHOTOGRAPHER* does not acknowledge the terms and stipulations on delivery memos and other paperwork accompanying the submission of photographs. Packages of slides submitted with conflicting delivery memos are returned unexamined. If any slide or slides receive damage during color separation, the color separator's liability is limited to $250 per slide.

Payment rates: $75 - $150 for package, text and photographs. Single photo rate $15 to $30. Front cover $100. Magazine printed in 4-color and B&W. You can expect to receive your payment after publication during the first month of issue date in which your work is published. Payment for reprints is 75% of article rate.

Please address all article queries to Evamarie Mathaey, Publisher/ Editor, and photo submissions (slides and/ or B&W prints) to Helen Longest-Slaughter, Photo Editor, NATURE PHOTOGRAPHER, P.O. Box 2037, West Palm Beach, FL 33402-2037 -- Telephone - (407) 586-3491 FAX - (407)586-9521. Office hours are Eastern Standard Time 8:00 am to 4:00 pm Mon through Fri. Call only if absolutely necessary, please.

Picture-submission guidelines for *National/International Wildlife* magazine.

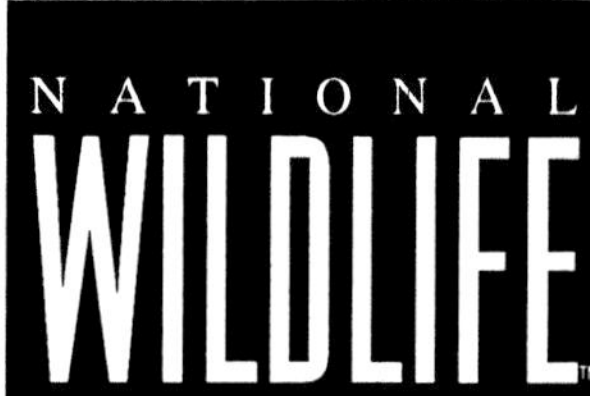

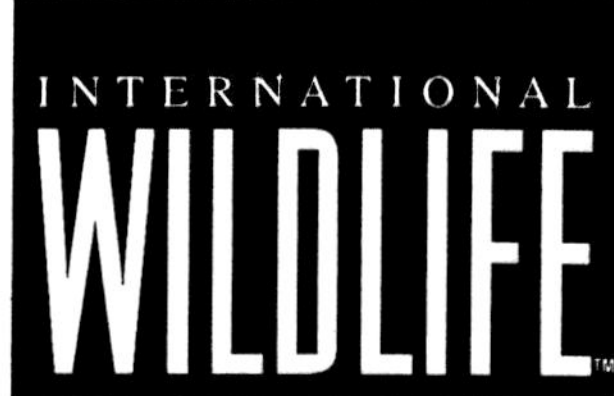

GUIDELINES FOR FREELANCE PHOTOGRAPHERS

National Wildlife and *International Wildlife* are award-winning bimonthly conservation magazines known worldwide for high quality photography and reproduction, depending heavily on contributions from both professional and outstanding amateur photographers.

Both magazines are published by the National Wildlife Federation, the largest private, non-profit conservation education group in the United States. *National Wildlife* is concerned primarily with the wildlife and ecology of the U.S., while *International Wildlife* encompasses the globe. The magazines present all aspects of our environment, ranging from the minute self-contained ecosystem of a tide pool to the wide-ranging effects of global pollution and overpopulation.

Who may send: We are interested in both well-known and lesser-known photographers whose work meets professional standards and is of exceptional quality. *Please, no unsolicited submissions* from those photographers whose work has not previously been published or considered for use in our magazines. However, you may query via mail, including non-returnable samples (tear sheets or photo copies), addressed to: Photo Queries, Wildlife Editorial, 8925 Leesburg Pike, Vienna, VA 22184, USA. Please include a self-addressed, stamped envelope to facilitate our reply.

Where to obtain a recent issue: Please do not send photographic material or samples without prior review of the kind and quality of photos we use in *National Wildlife* and *International Wildlife*. The magazines are available at selected newsstands and your public library, or send $3.00 per issue to: Membership Services, National Wildlife Federation, 8925 Leesburg Pike, Vienna, Virginia 22184, USA.

What to send: The editors are interested in seeing photography dealing with wildlife, including mammals, birds, reptiles, amphibians, insects, underwater life and wild plants. The entire realm of photography is used (photomicrography, macrophotography, close-ups, action, scenics). It is the unusual, dramatic, stimulating, or high-impact photographs which best fill our needs.

We prefer photographers to group their photos into stories about a specific species, ecosystem, aspect of animal behavior, ecological balance, man's role in the preservation of his environment, etc. We also need single photos for front, back, and inside covers, spreads and other individual uses. Photo/text packages are welcome; queries preferred.

Although our primary interest is in color photos, we also have a need for unusual and striking black-and-white photography, stories which use the medium well and would not be as effective in color.

For quality reproduction, we require original color transparencies, 35mm or larger (no duplicates), or 8x10 glossy black-and-white prints. Quality dupes are acceptable for initial review.

Caption information is essential and should be noted on mounts, back of prints, or keyed to accompanying sheets. Specify species, location, behavior, whether wild or captive (wildlife reserve, game park, zoo, studio or otherwise controlled situation).

National Wildlife Federation cannot be held responsible for unsolicited photographs. We carefully handle and give due consideration to all submissions. All photographs are returned. Please allow four weeks of evaluation following receipt of your solicited submission. Payment for the use of photographs is on acceptance and based on one-time rights with limited promotional use. Rates are competitive with other national magazines.

How to package: Package photographs carefully. Place slides in plastic sheets, sandwich photos between cardboard and secure with a large rubberband (do not use tape, slide boxes, or glass mounts).

Be certain your cover letter or delivery memo contains your *street address* and *telephone number* for courier return of any images held. Remember to include a *self-addressed* envelope of the proper size, with sufficient return *postage affixed*, or completed FedEx shipping form for return of your material. We welcome reusable mailers, though self-adhesive address and postage labels must be provided. *We cannot process checks in payment for postage* (use U.S. stamps, U.S. postal money orders, or international reply coupons).

Where to send: Photo Submissions
Wildlife Editorial
8925 Leesburg Pike
Vienna, VA 22184
USA

We appreciate your interest and welcome your submissions. It is through the efforts of freelance photographers that our magazines enjoy increasing popularity and appeal.

THE EDITORS

jm 95

responsibility for solicited material? Are story ideas generated in-house, or do freelancers suggest all the concepts? What rights does the firm want to purchase, in terms of both text and photographs? Are the client's rates competitive with those of other markets, and does it pay on acceptance or publication? For that matter, does the company pay anything at all? Read the guidelines closely.

Marketing Your Work

Now you are ready to start marketing. I think that the best potential markets for beginning nature photographers are small magazines, and that the best thing to sell is an article package or a picture essay of related images. The competition to publish in such magazines as *Sierra*, *Outdoor Photographer*, and *National Wildlife* is absolutely fierce. Only a limited number of pictures can be published in each issue. You have a much better chance of being published in *Wild Bird*, *Farm and Ranch*, and *Ontario Naturalist*, good magazines that don't receive the overwhelming number of submissions as their larger counterparts. When you're just starting out, you don't want to submit pictures to a market that reviews 100,000 transparencies annually. It is better to find a market that reviews only 100 photographs, half of which are your pictures.

Brainstorming

First, come up with some specific ideas that you either already have photographs for, or can go out right now and shoot any necessary extras for. Don't be so esoteric that no one can identify with your material. A picture spread on the edible roots of the Malaysian archipelago might interest you, but I know few magazines that would bite, so to speak. You would be better off with something along the lines of "Why Leaves Turn Red in Autumn," "What's That Sound in the Swamp?—A Journey to a Springtime Frog Pond," or "After the Ice Storm."

Magazine Submissions

Now write a query letter addressed by name to either the editor or picture editor (you received this information in the guidelines package). Send your letter to the publication you think would be specifically interested in your idea. A little market research would help, so check out back issues to make sure that the magazine hasn't done a similar story or photo spread in the past two or three years.

PINPOINTING YOUR MARKETS

Make a list of every item you find anywhere that has pictures printed similar to those you shoot. Think of what this list might include:

Books
coffee-table books
picture books
field guides
textbooks
how-to books
trail guides

Magazines
general-interest magazines
conservation-organization magazines
environmental-action magazines
regional magazines
company magazines
religious magazines

Cards
greeting cards
notecards
postcards

Calendars
wall calendars
desk calendars
pocket calendars
company calendars
corporate-product calendars
promotional calendars

Advertisements
in magazines, books
stand-alone point-of-purchase (P.O.P.) displays

Posters
graphic-arts posters
merchandise posters
corporate posters
event posters

Catalogs
recreational-equipment catalogs
sporting-goods catalogs
natural-food catalogs
garden-supply catalogs

Brochures and bulletins
for religious organizations
fraternal organizations
corporate notices

Newspapers
travel sections
regional papers
advertising supplements

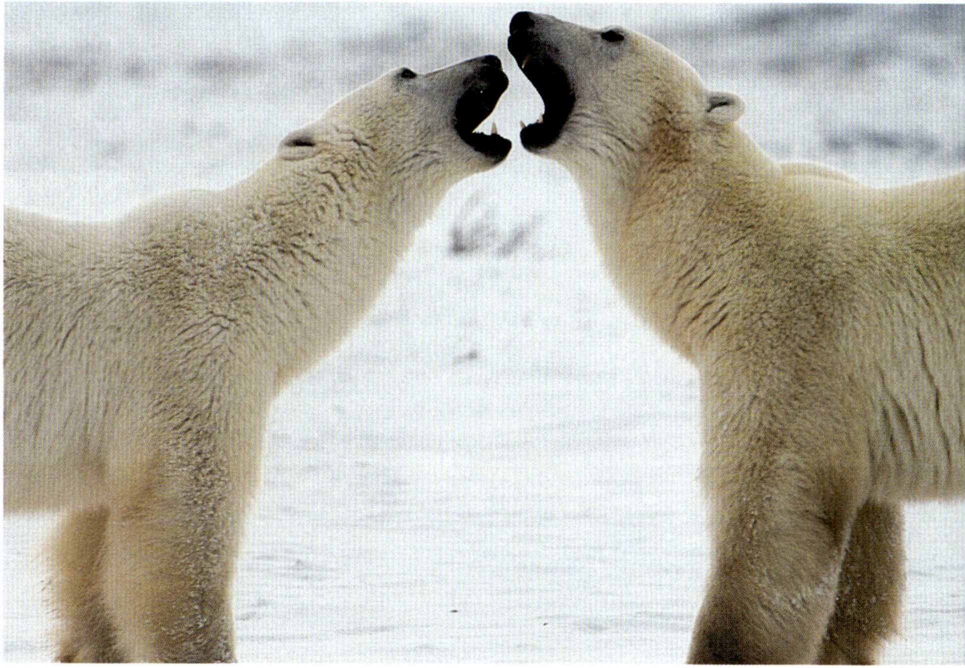

Polar bears, Churchill, Manitoba. Nikon F4, Nikon 500mm lens, Fujichrome 100.

This picture is salable because of the pose of the bears. Their bodies don't overlap while their interaction is obvious.

RESOURCES

Here is a short list of a few resource works; you should be able to come up with more.

American Book Trade Directory

Associated Church Press

Directory of Art Publishers, Book Publishers & Record Companies

Editor & Publisher International Yearbook

Magazine Industry Market Place

Travel Writer's Markets Directory

Writer's Market

A query letter is a brief, simple letter to the editor proposing your idea and explaining how it would benefit the publication. Be sure that your concept is tailored specifically to the market. Even if you send the best query letter ever written on "Dogs Are the World's Best Pets" to *Horse and Rider* magazine, it will be rejected. And any future projects you submit won't be received well.

Never send out an unsolicited package if you value your work. Publications aren't responsible for any material staff members didn't ask to see; consequently if they toss your slides in the trash, you have no legal recourse. Your query letter is the way around the problem. You're asking the publication's staff if they would like you to submit your idea. If it is usable, they'll certainly agree.

Magazines need freelancers because that is where they get their material. Besides, why bother wasting the time and expense of preparing and sending a submission if a publisher doesn't want it in the first place? Send the query letter first. You should hear back in six weeks or so. If you get no response, a simple letter or brief telephone call is okay. If you still don't get a response, don't berate the magazine staff. Just try elsewhere.

Book Submissions

If you want to sell photographs to a book publisher, first arrange to receive the company's submission guidelines. Then write a letter outlining your files. Present yourself in this letter as a professional photographer, explain the subject matter you shoot in broad terms, and give some examples of publishing credits. Include a stock list if you have one (see page 65).

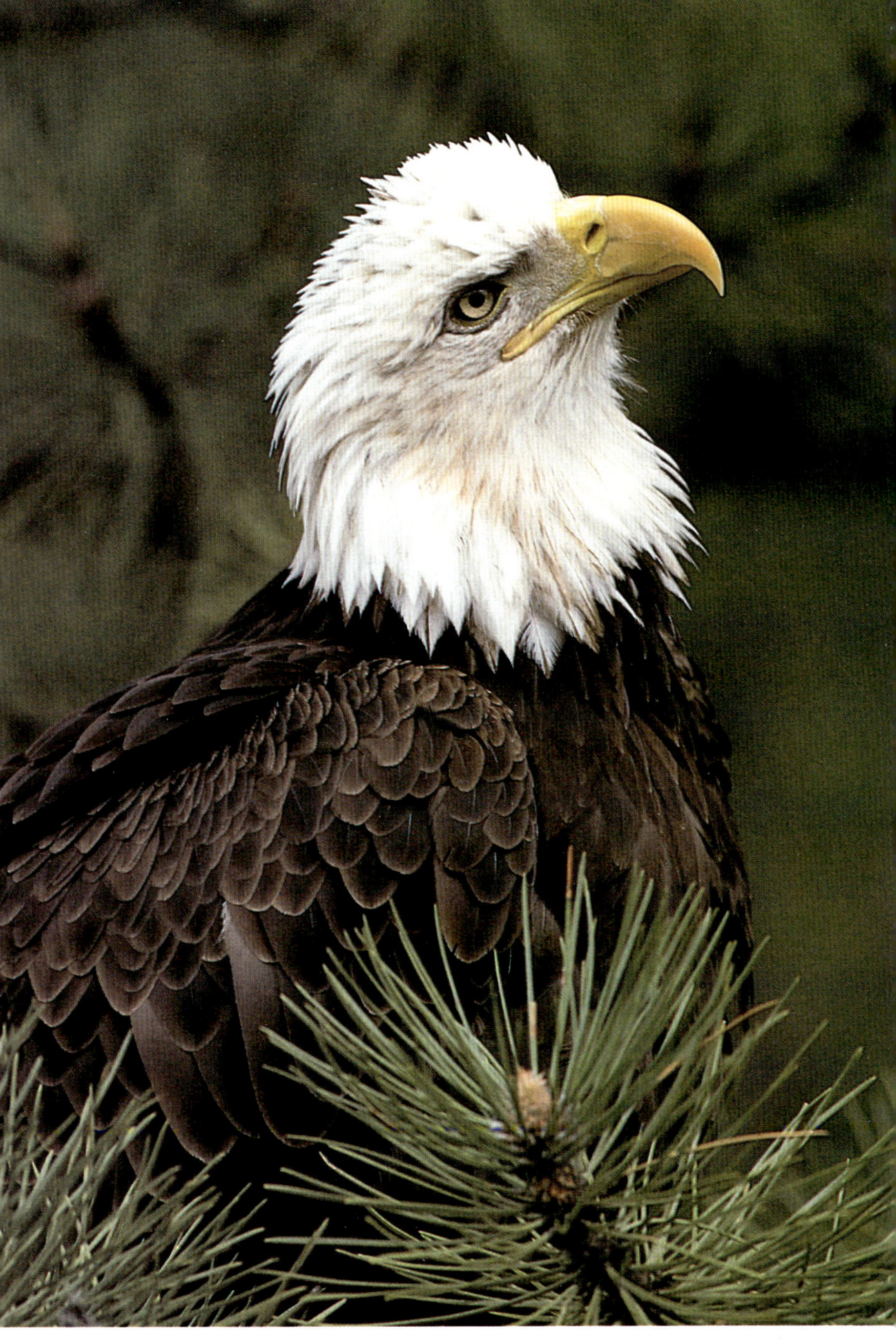

Bald eagle, Colorado. Nikon F4, Nikon 500mm lens, Fujichrome 100.

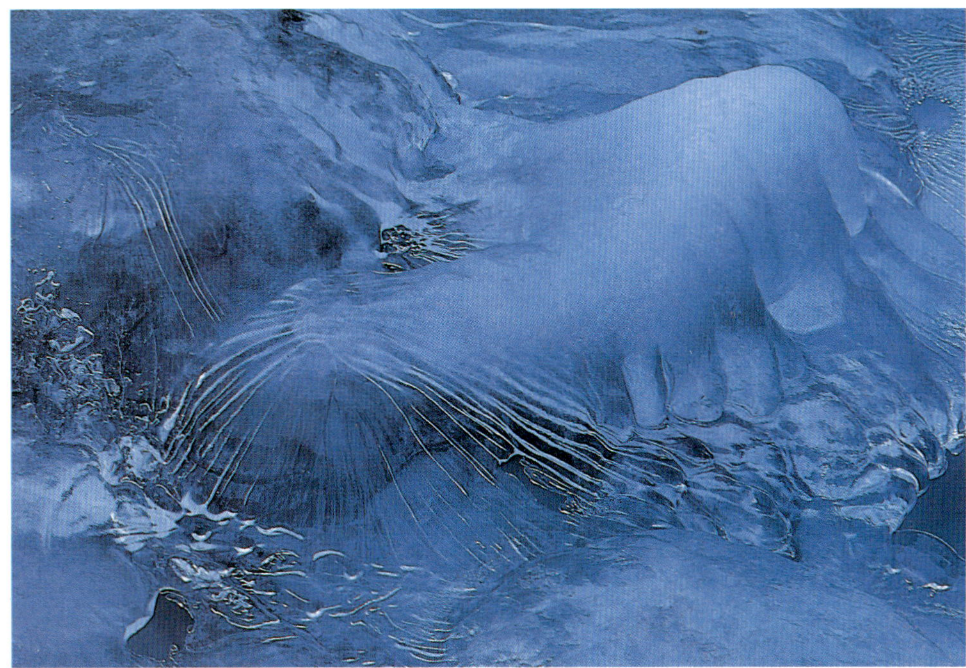

You must have a depth of subjects in your photographic file. Birds, mammals, seasons, closeups—all are necessary if you want to sell more than one or two pictures. This is especially true if you want to submit your work to book publishers.

Ice pattern over stream, Colorado. Nikon F4, Nikon 80-200mm zoom lens, Fuji Velvia.

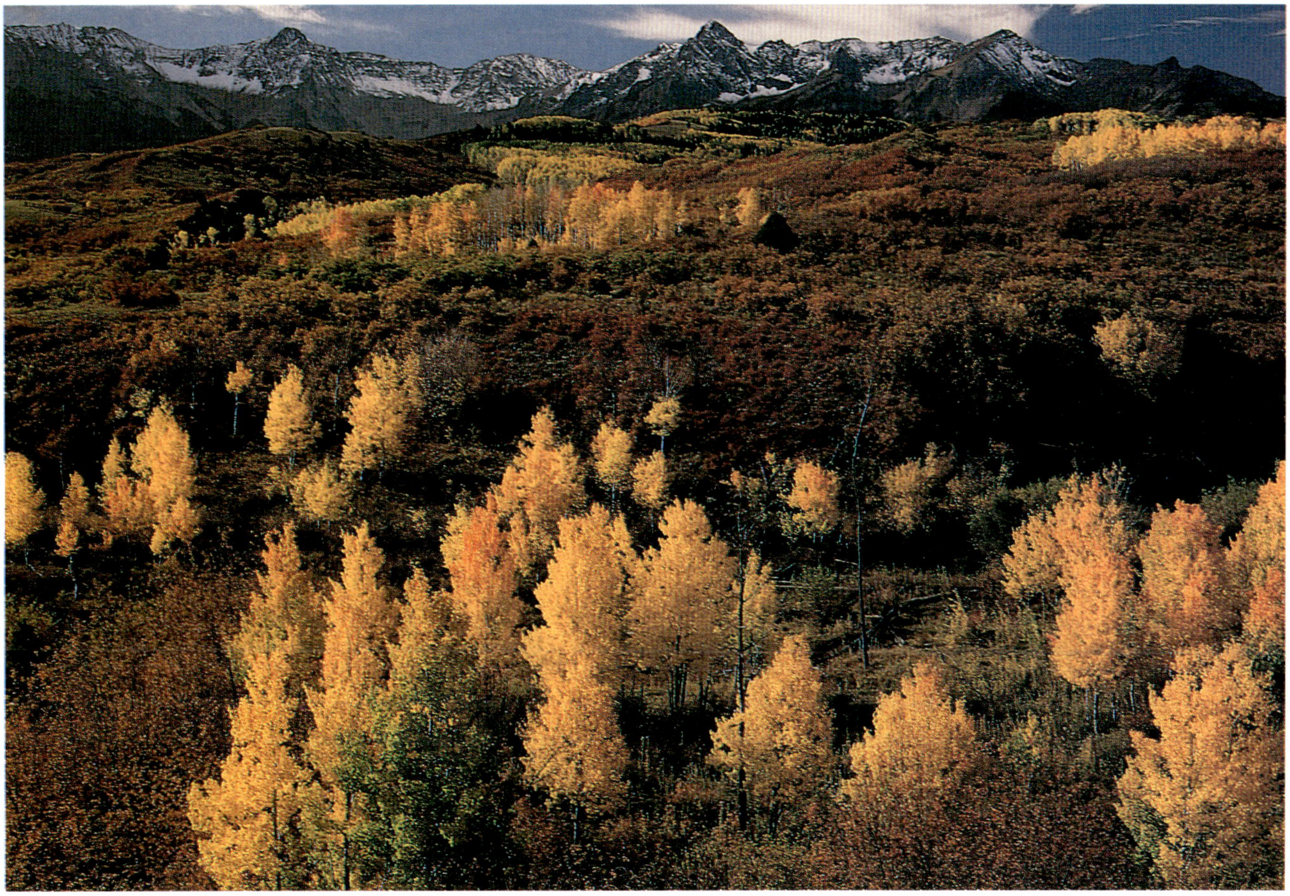

Autumn quaking aspens and scrub oaks, below Sneffels Range, Colorado. Nikon F4, Nikon 35-70mm zoom lens, Fuji Velvia.

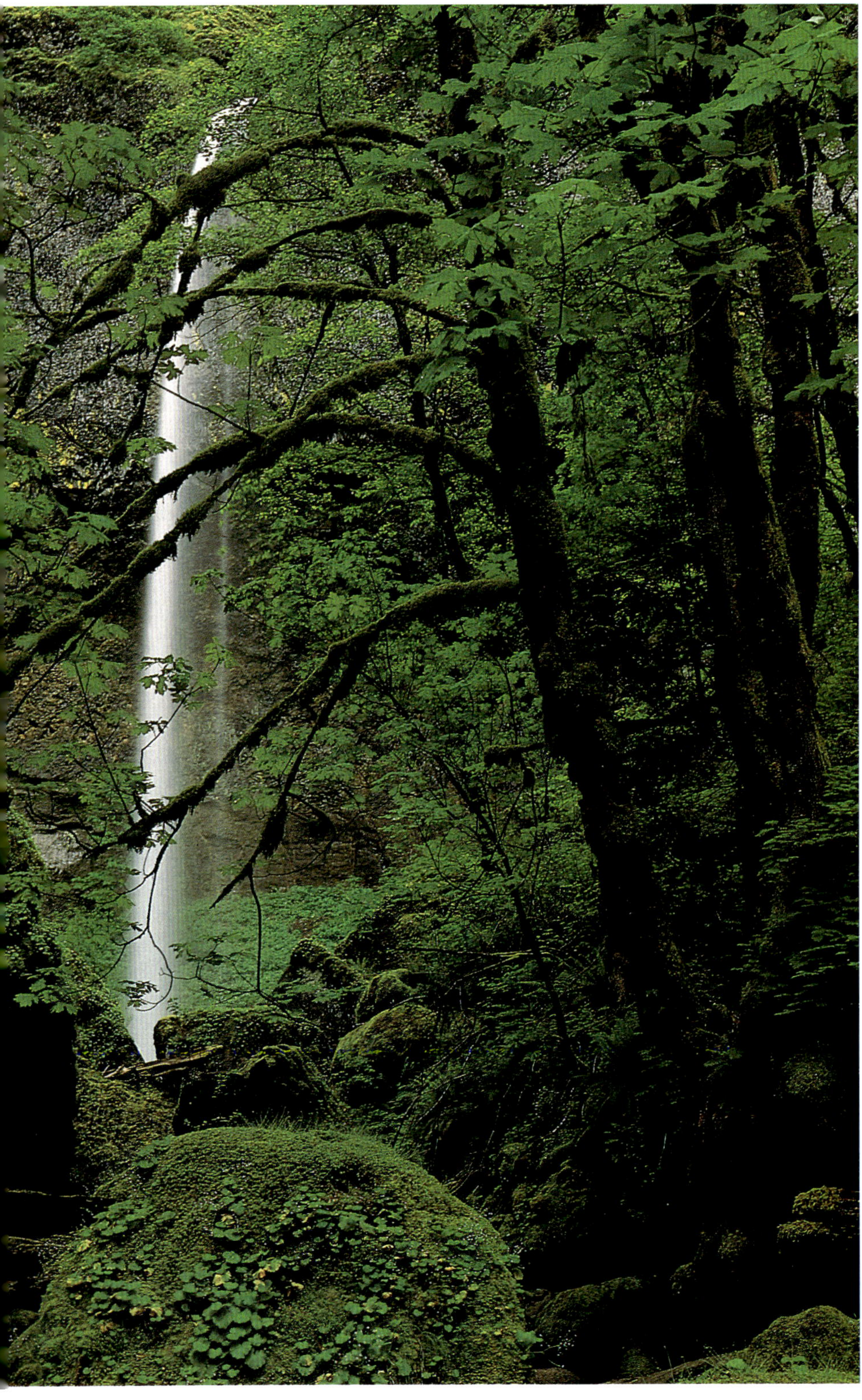

Elowah Falls seen through curtain of leaves, Columbia Gorge Scenic Area, Oregon. Nikon F4, Nikon 50-135mm zoom lens, Fuji Velvia.

This photograph would satisfy a want list calling for a shot of a West Coast waterfall.

Be aware that book companies don't want to deal with unknown photographers who can supply only a limited number of pictures. If your total good-picture file consists of 100 wildflower images, 100 landscape shots, and 100 bird pictures, don't bother contacting book publishers. Go out and take additional salable pictures or concentrate on the small-magazine market.

Think of it this way. If you needed to purchase 197 different grocery items, would you go to a store that stocked only bread, then go to a different store for each of the other items? Wouldn't that be a incredible waste of your time and effort? What would happen if you needed all those items quickly?

The same is true of picture research. Book photo editors don't have the time to contact 197 different photographers to get the 197 different shots they need to publish. That would be a completely inefficient, long, drawn-out process, let alone being a paperwork nightmare, tracking all those transparencies from different sources. Textbook submissions, for example, commonly run into the hundreds of images per photographer. You need extensive files to seriously work the book market. Once you've developed a picture file and started being published, then you can contact book companies. Ask to have your name added to those photographers who receive any "want lists" the company may send out.

Want Lists

A want list, which is also known as a "shot list," is exactly what its name suggests: a list of photographs a picture editor wants to see, and the date they're needed by. In essence, a want list is sort of a cattle call of photographs. Generally it is sent out to selected photographers whose files the picture editor is familiar with, or who specialize in the needed subject matter. It isn't an assignment contract nor will you have time to go shoot pictures; the editor is asking you to pull photographs already in your file.

Book companies, with their long project-development time, can send out want lists to gather photographs. Most magazines don't do so simply because of the much shorter lead times for each issue. Staff members will call around if they need four or five specific photographs. I can think of only a very few nature magazines that ever send out specific want lists at all: *Birder's World*, *Natural History*, and *Ranger Rick*.

If you do get a want list, read it carefully. Even if you don't have what the editors are

CORNELL LABORATORY *of* ORNITHOLOGY

159 SAPSUCKER WOODS ROAD • ITHACA, NEW YORK 14850-1999

EDUCATION & INFORMATION SERVICES • 607/254-2440 • FAX 254-2415

14 November 1994

SHOTLIST FOR *LIVING BIRD* -- SPRING 1995

COVERS -- submissions for front covers should either have a seasonal tie-in or depict species covered in articles within the magazine. Back cover shots usually tell a story; the photos are often humorous, sometimes inspirational, and always visually stunning. Front cover shot must be in a vertical format with room at the top for the *Living Bird* logo.

SPOTLIGHT -- need shots of the following Mexican bird species: White-throated Jay, White-tailed Hummingbird, and Short-crested Coquette.

WHITE IBIS -- need various shots of adult White Ibises flying, foraging, and feeding their nestlings (preferably crayfish and fiddler crabs).

AOU CHECKLIST -- need photos of birds that have had their official names changed in the past (or may have their names changed in the near future) by the American Ornithologists' Union. Species such as Marsh Hawk/Northern Harrier, White-tailed Kite/Black-shouldered Kite, Bullock's and Baltimore Orioles/Northern Oriole, Yellow-shafted and Red-shafted Flicker/Northern Flicker, Whistling Swan/Tundra Swan, Green Heron/Green-backed Heron, etc.

SNAIL KITES -- need various shots of Snail Kites--foraging, flying, nesting, etc.--and their habitat in Florida's Everglades.

ANCIENT DNA -- need scenic shots of habitat in the Hawaiian Islands, also photos of the following species: White-tailed Eagle, White-bellied Eagle, Kiwi, Glossy Ibis, and Laysan Duck.

BIRD NEWS -- need pictures of Brown Jays (nesting activities), Black-capped Chickadees at a bird feeder, female Brown-headed Cowbirds vocalizing. Also need shots of a white oak (close up of leaves and acorns) and white-tailed deer in an eastern deciduous forest.

DEADLINE FOR SUBMISSIONS -- 9 December 1994. Please send slides and prints to: Tim Gallagher, Editor-in-Chief, *Living Bird*, Cornell Laboratory of Ornithology, 159 Sapsucker Woods Road, Ithaca, New York 14850. **(Be sure to include your Social Security number with your submission to expedite your payment in the event that we publish any of your photographs.)**

• A MEMBERSHIP ORGANIZATION FOR THE STUDY AND CONSERVATION OF BIRDS •

This is an actual want list that I received for the Spring 1995 issue of Living Bird *magazine.*

looking for right now, you should shoot the subjects for your file for future submissions. If someone needed a specific image once, chances are some other editor will need the same shot sometime again in the future.

Want lists can describe photographs of the commonplace or the rare. Here are some specific needs from recent want lists that I've received:

- Prairie dog groups
- Whitetail deer herded up in winter
- Foggy scene of Shenandoah National Park
- Any shots of leeches
- Geothermal energy development in New Zealand
- House finches at a wintertime bird feeder
- A shrike sitting next to a skewered insect
- Beautiful landscapes that inspire awe
- Sargassum fish, *Histrio histrio*
- Digger wasp sealing entrance to burrow with pebble

Sometimes want lists are quite specific in their description of photographs. Here is an example: "EASTERN FOREST of oak, maple, and/or beech. If the photograph has a few small pines nestled among the larger deciduous trees, that would be ideal. Verticals only." Now this is a good description. You either have the exact shot or you don't. Very simple.

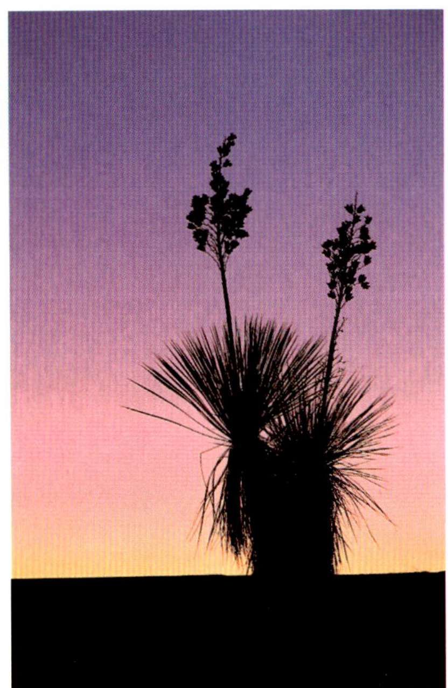

Soaptree yucca against twilight sky, White Sands National Monument, New Mexico. Nikon F4, Nikon 80–200mm zoom lens, Fuji Velvia.

A typical want list might include a specific description, such as "yucca plant at nightfall in Southwestern state."

The following description is less specific. As you read it, think about what is really being requested. "Horizontal view of a pond containing algae and/or water lilies. Pond MUST be surrounded by reeds or cattails, which is then ringed by grasses or shrubs, which is then surrounded by trees. Aerial views, or overviews of the scene, preferred."

This is actually a request for a picture of primary pond succession, showing the changes that occur as you go from water to dry land. Incidentally, an easy way to photograph this exact sequence is along the interstate highways in the northeastern United States. Quite a bit of the median was disturbed during construction of the interstates, so you can see primary pond succession happening where soil and gravel were dug out. Find such a location next to an overpass and shoot low aerials. Think I'm kidding? I took a shot on I-75 in northern Michigan and sold it through a stock agency.

Sometimes want list requests are so esoteric that almost no photographer on earth will have the shot. I've seen a listing for a single fly species found only in certain areas of Borneo. Perhaps a doctoral candidate doing research on that fly might have a picture, but no one else will. I've also seen requests that are really for paintings, not photographs.

Consider the following: "Beautiful Rocky Mountain scene, blue sky, mountain rising in the background (will need the name of the mountain). IMPERATIVE that a *lake* is in the foreground, surrounded on both sides by trees, vegetation, and colorful flowers. IMPERATIVE that there is a deer (no other species) in the foreground. Image is to suggest a total ecosystem. Must crop to square format." Sure, all photographers have that shot in their file.

Marketing Newsletters

Another way to find clients is to subscribe to a marketing newsletter or service that reports picture requests. Rohn Engh at PhotoSource International offers all levels of newsletters from a once-a-month letter to a twice-a-day request sheet sent to you either via a fax machine or E-mail. The charge for these services is between $9 and $55 a month.

Engh also publishes *PhotoStockNotes*, a monthly newsletter on developments and issues of importance to stock photographers and stock-photo buyers. By his own admission, however, Engh's services are geared not to nature photographers but to general shooters. He estimates that only 1 out of 16 of the picture requests that come through his service have anything to do with nature photography. *PhotoStockNotes*, which costs $5 a month, is more general and certainly useful for the established stock photographer who wants to follow stock trends and developments. (For more thorough information, see page 142).

The best marketing newsletter for nature photography and the only newsletter published specifically about this field is *The Guilfoyle Report*. This newsletter is published by Ann Guilfoyle, who previously was photo editor at *Audubon* magazine and senior editor at Chanticleer Press before she founded AG Editions. Let me quote Guilfoyle on the *Report*:

> Since 1982 we have served as a direct link between the world of nature publishing and the photographers who contribute to it. Magazines such as *Natural History* and *Pacific Discovery* regularly run their entire want lists in our reports. Needs from prestigious buyers like *National Wildlife* and the National Park Service appear frequently. Each issue of *The Guilfoyle Report* features 20 to 30 current photo wants from key photo buyers as well as leads on new markets and future trends.

The Guilfoyle Report is published 10 times a year, and each issue contains information to update your list of contacts, news briefs about the nature-publishing world, picture buyers' want lists with deadline dates and contact names, feature articles to identify new markets, interviews with industry professionals, film and equipment reviews, and notices of magazine and book startups. AG Editions also puts out market guides on specific subjects, such as the calendar and greeting-card markets, bird-photography markets, and the art-show market.

Currently the cost of a year's subscription to *The Guilfoyle Report* is $125. In addition, new subscribers get a "Welcome Aboard Pack" of marketing information. Market guides cost between $8 and $20. (For more information, contact AG Editions—see page 140).

SELF-PROMOTION

The business of getting nature photography published isn't the same as the business of a commercial photography studio. You can't take out an ad in the *Yellow Pages* or put a flyer in the Welcome Wagon package and expect picture buyers to come to you. Nature-photography markets are select and, unfortunately, all too few compared to the hundreds of potential customers for a wedding or portrait studio. You need to promote yourself in order to get noticed by photo buyers, but at the same time you must have a good return for the time, expense, and effort that you devote to self-promotion.

Putting Together a Portfolio

Most general texts on selling photographs talk about preparing a portfolio of work and personally taking it around to photo buyers. A portfolio should contain only your very best work, the images that have real impact on viewers. It should also reflect exactly what you actually do as a photographer: what subjects you work, your style, and the quality you can produce. Obviously these should be salable pictures of nature subjects only.

Creating a portfolio of drag-racing shots in order to sell landscapes to *Sierra* magazine is ridiculous, yet there are people who persist in doing just that. *Cat Fancy* doesn't want to see pictures of birds, and *National Wildlife* doesn't care about vacation shots of your family. Study the markets and include only photographs that a working professional would submit to those markets.

You can create a portfolio of 20 to 80 images in many ways. The old standard is a binder with illustrations protected behind plastic pages. Don't use a cheap 3-ring notebook from a discount house; buy a presentation folder at an art-supply store instead. If you don't have copies of published photographs—and obviously you won't when you're first starting out—you should have the best quality prints made. You can even have

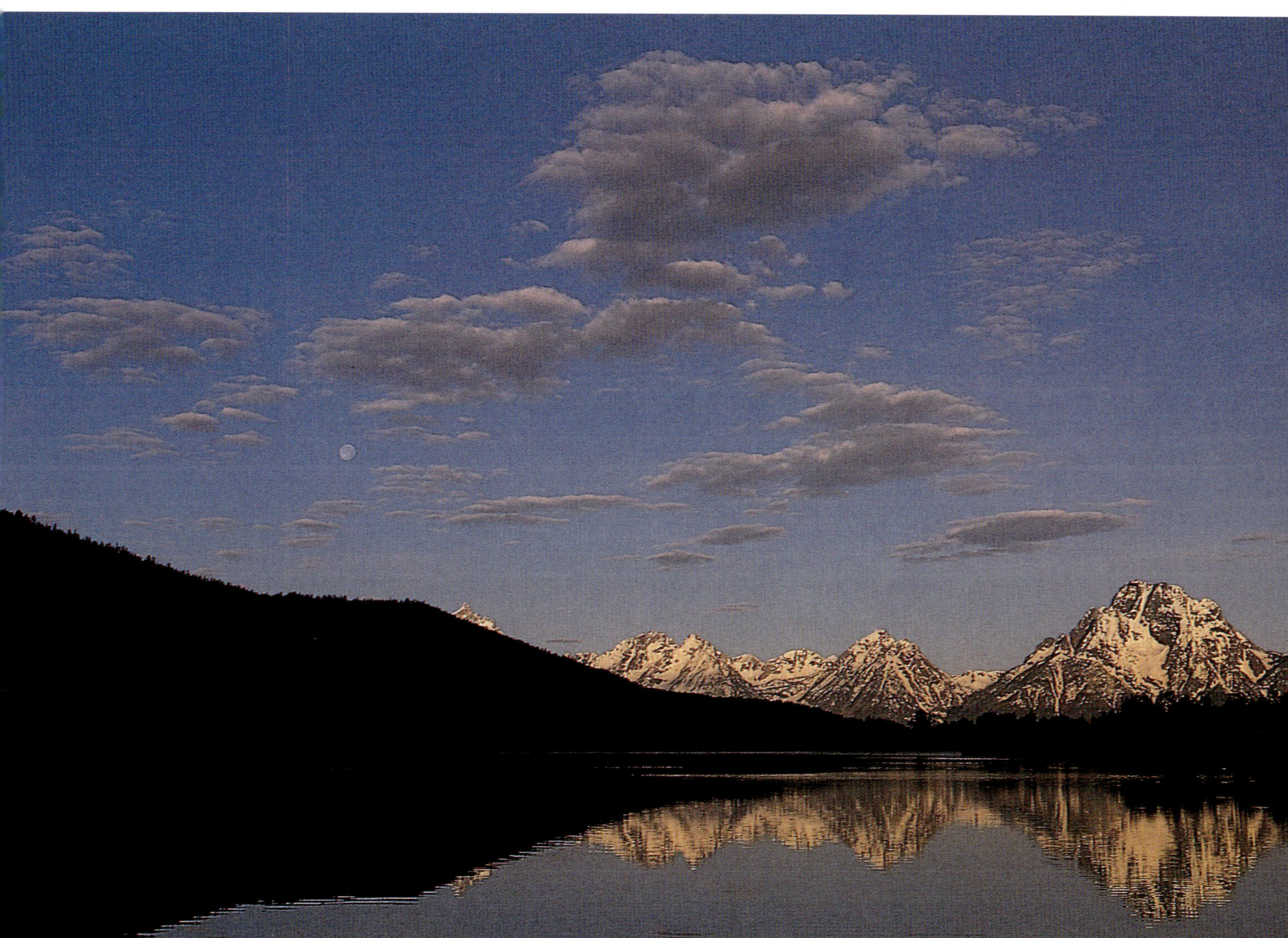

Mt. Moran and Grand Teton Range at sunrise, from Oxbow Bend; Grand Teton National Park, Wyoming. Nikon F4, Nikon 24mm lens, Fuji Velvia.

Having these photographs published anywhere with a credit line accompanying the picture would also be good promotion.

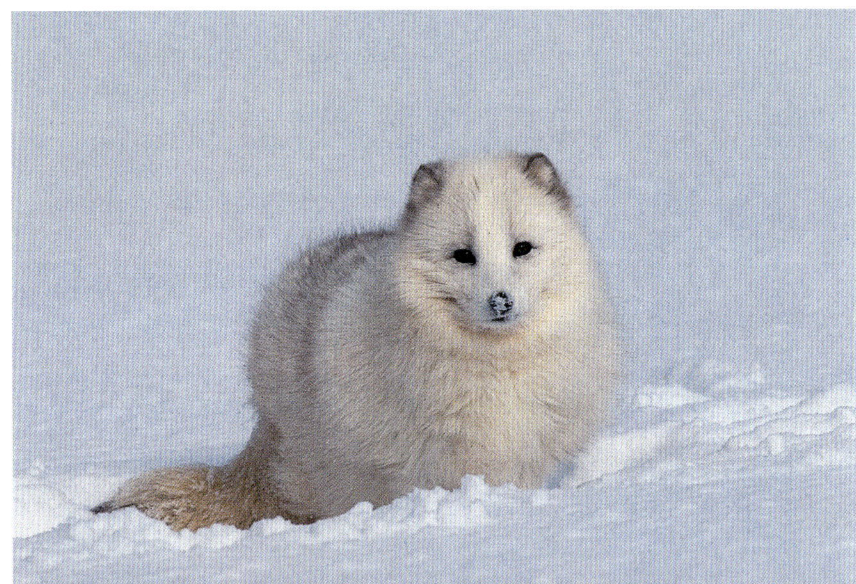

Arctic fox in winter, Alaska. Nikon F4, Nikon 500mm lens, Fujichrome 100.

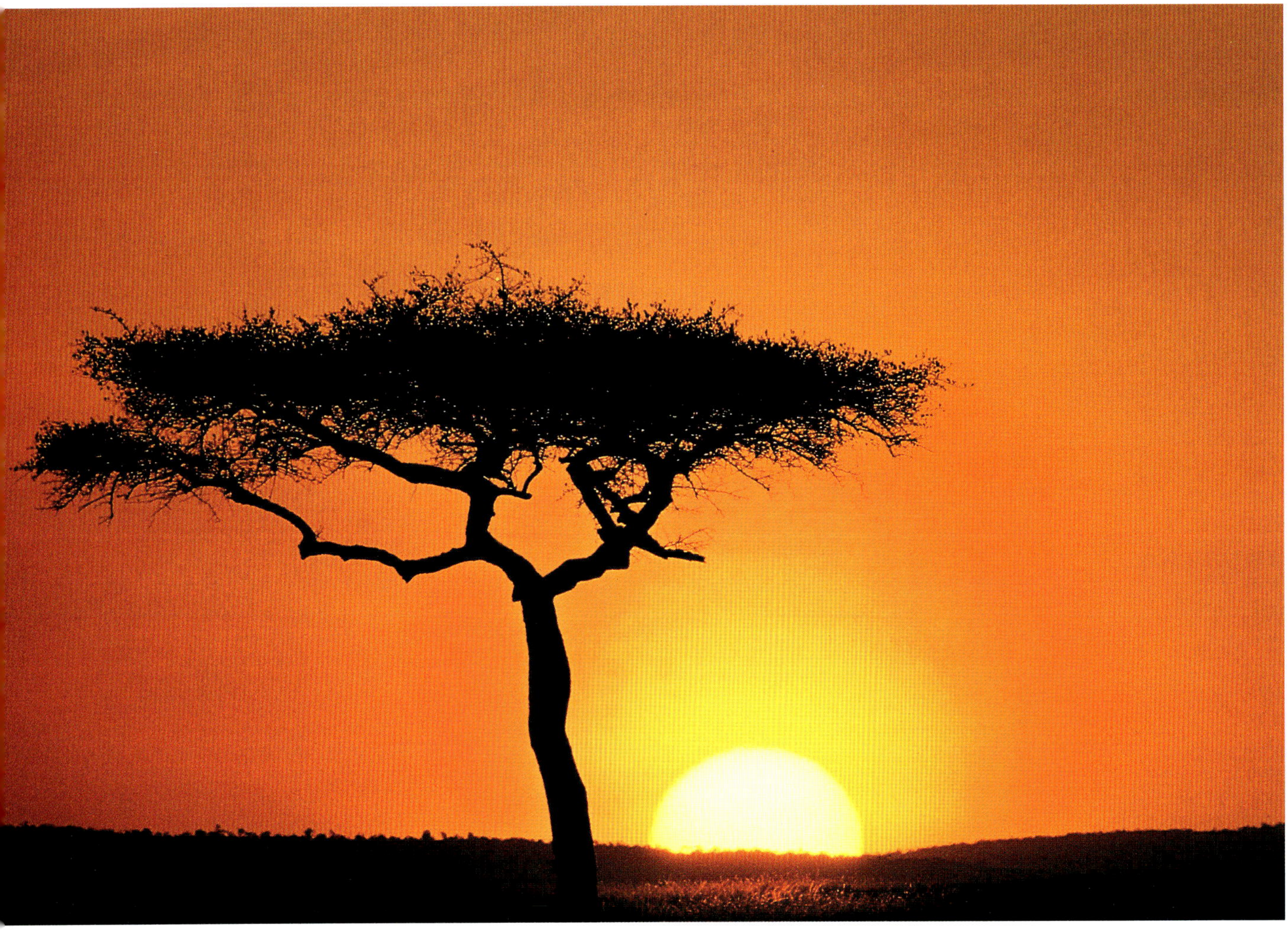

Acacia tree at sunrise, Masai Mara National Park, Kenya. Nikon F4, Nikon 500mm lens, Fujichrome 100.

some of these images mounted and matted as stand-alone photographs.

You can also present a portfolio of images as loose items in a box. Again, not any old box will do. Remember, you want to present a professional image as well as show off your images. Many photographers laminate their tearsheets and prints in order to protect them from becoming dog-eared by repeated handling. Lamination is available in either a high-gloss or matte finish; consider laminating prints with a backing or even a border to set off the images.

Another possibility for a portfolio are slides in a slide tray. Kodak Carousel projectors are the industry standard, so don't even consider using anything else. This approach enables you to present quite a few pictures in a small package, as well as to develop sequences of photographs. Never use original transparencies in a portfolio tray, but rather the best dupes you can possibly obtain. After all, projecting originals damages color film. And furthermore, many disasters might befall unprotected slides.

With my having said all this about portfolios, you're probably assuming that I think you need one. Wrong. To be honest I believe that a portfolio presentation for nature photographers who are just starting out is a waste of time. The day might come when you want to present a portfolio to an advertising agency in order to branch out from doing solely nature work, but just remember what the majority of markets really are for natural-history material. For the most part, books and magazines don't want to review portfolios. They have neither the time nor personnel to do so.

I don't know any working professional nature photographer who even has a presentation portfolio. Nor do I know of any professional nature photographer who consistently makes the rounds of editors in New York City. You would be much better off using the time and money involved to keep taking pictures.

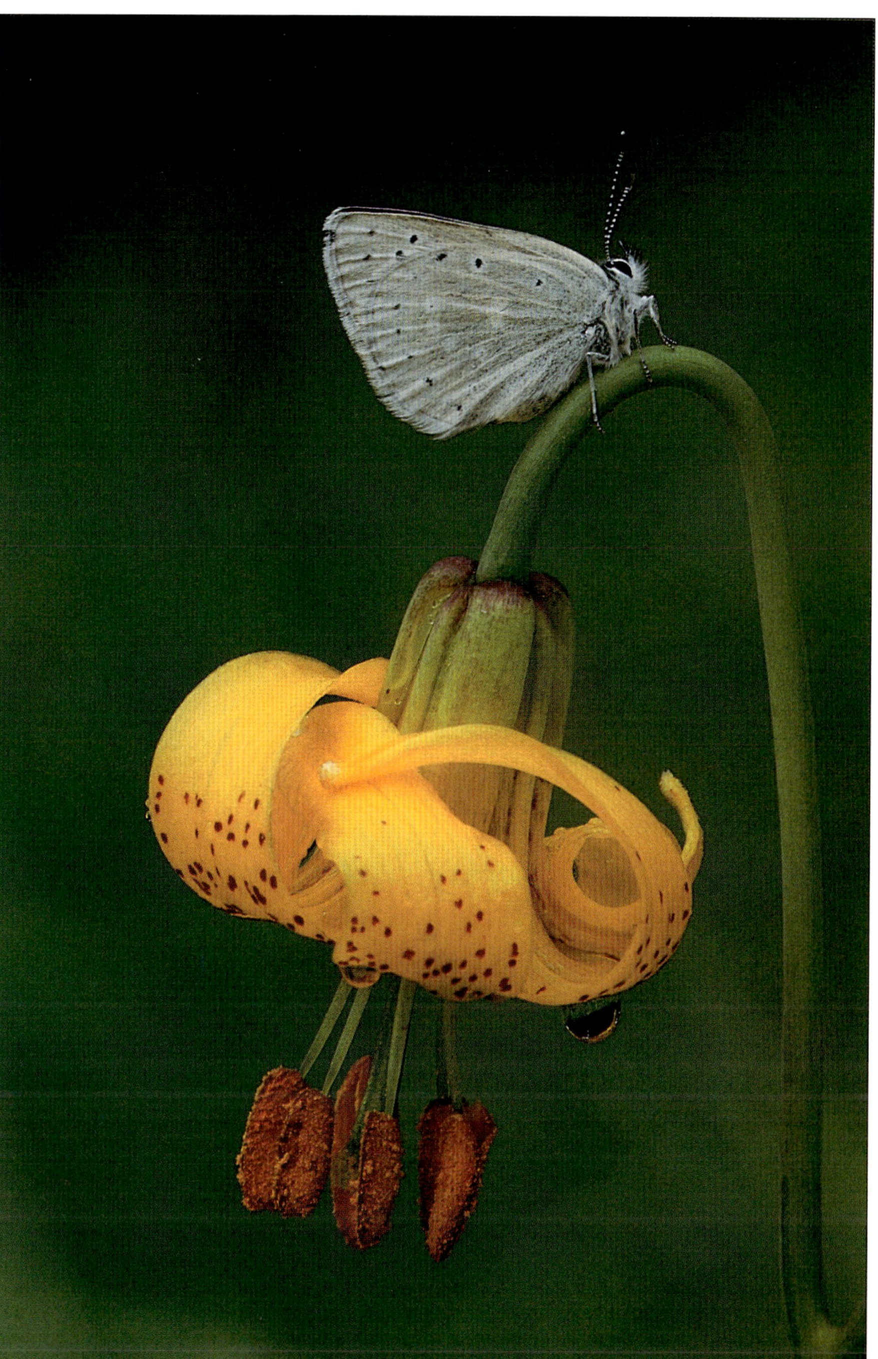

Common blue butterfly on Columbia lily, Olympic National Park, Washington. Nikon F4, Nikon 200mm macro lens, Kodak Lumière 100.

Although this photograph could be included in a portfolio presentation, in terms of business results I would much rather have it printed in a national publication.

Getting Noticed

So how do you make yourself and your work known? Without a doubt, the very best advertising you can have is a credit line printed next to a published photograph. Picture-research people read credit lines and note who shot what subjects. A truism of this business is that the more you publish, the more you'll be published since editors will start coming to you to reuse those shots they saw in print. Time spent submitting pictures and articles will produce far more results in terms of a nature-photography business than time spent putting together a portfolio (for more information, see Chapter 5 on page 94). In fact, a tightly edited submission to a magazine will act like a portfolio of your best work.

I'm certainly not suggesting that you never visit a picture editor in person. Just remember that nature markets are scattered all over the world, so trying to actually visit these markets will consume a lot of your time and money. A quick look through my own Rolodex reveals publishing addresses in New York, Chicago, and Los Angeles (just as you would expect), as well as clients in Michigan, Tennessee, Washington, Georgia, Wisconsin, Texas, and Wyoming. Foreign addresses include listings for Canada, England, Australia, Japan, Scotland, Germany, France, and New Zealand. Almost all of your contacts in this business will take place through the mail, with follow-up communication by telephone, fax machine, and overnight-delivery services.

I recommend a personal visit to an editor only if you have a specific reason for one that goes beyond announcing, "Here I am with some pictures." If you've worked with an editor, and if you can make your visit worthwhile to the editor by suggesting story-lines and photo spreads, go ahead and ask if you can drop by. It certainly is nice to put a face with a telephone voice, but you must remember that editors are always under deadline pressure and can't spend lots of time chatting about your latest adventures.

SUBMISSION REQUEST

Date: __/__/__

Name: ____________________

Address: ____________________

____

____

Phone: ____________________

FAX: ____________________

FedEx #: __________ Airborne #: __________

Project: ____________________

Use/Rights: ____________________

Budget: ____________________

Our Quote: ____________________

Hor [ ] Ver [ ] Both [ ] Date Needed: __/__/__

Description (how to be used, concept, specifics, how many, size):

____

____

____

____

____

____

____

____

____

____

When a picture editor calls you requesting a photographic submission, you'll want to record a lot of information as you talk. All too often some of the pertinent facts will get lost during the conversation. To prevent this, use a telephone submission-request form. A master file of this form is on my computer; I print out a batch of hard copies as needed. Feel free to reproduce and use this form or to modify it to fit your needs.

You can add some promotional materials to any package you send out, even if it is just a query letter. One of the simplest and least expensive items is a Rolodex card with your name, address, and telephone and fax numbers. You might also want to include a few words about your specialties, such as "dramatic light and landscapes," "African wildlife," or "patterns in nature." Any print shop can run some of these, or you can do them yourself if you have access to a laser printer and computer. If you move your office or if the area or ZIP codes change, sending out Rolodex cards is a great reminder for clients to update their files.

(I've moved several times during my professional career, and I don't want clients to lose track of me or not know where to return slides. About six weeks before each moving date, I sent out a pre-move announcement with all the information. I followed this with another announcement and a Rolodex card at the time of the actual move. Six weeks later, I sent out a post-move announcement. Unfortunately, there is always at least one company that still returns submissions to an address I left years ago.)

You can also send out a stock list, which, as its name implies, is a list of the pictures you have in stock to fulfill editorial needs. Stock agencies often send out catalogs of images from their files; the cost for you to do the same would be prohibitive, so a stock list is the next best thing.

Once again a computer with a good word-processing program comes into play; you can generate a list and update it as you add images to your file. You can also tailor your stock list to specific markets. For example, run a list of your coverage of birds and bird-related subjects—for example, nests and nest building, feather patterns, eggs, and bird sanctuaries—to send to birding magazines.

I suggest starting with a broad, all-inclusive list. Make an inventory of your files by subject. Don't list each and every frame as a separate subject, but don't be too broad. Instead of writing only "National Parks," list specifically by name the parks that you have good coverage of. Include concepts and categories also. Compile this list into alphabetical

JOHN SHAW

STOCK LIST

Street
City, State, Zip
Telephone and FAX

Natural History Stock
Geographic Stock
General Stock

abstracts
acid rain
Africa
Alaska
alcids (auks)
amphibians
anatomy, physiology
(of animals and plants)
anhingas
animal behavior
animal sign, spoor, tracks
animal young
Antarctica
Appalachian mountains
Arches National Park
autumn foliage
Banff National Park, Canada
barns
bears, North American
beetles
Big Cypress National Preserve
Blue Ridge Parkway
biology coverage for textbooks
birds
bobcats
bogs
Bryce Canyon National Park
butterflies and moths
cactus
camouflage and cryptic coloration
Canada geese
cardinals
carnivorous plants
caterpillars
chickadees
chipmunks
club mosses
Colorado
Colorado National Monument
Columbia River Scenic Area
Costa Rica
country roads
coyotes
dawn
Denali National Park
deer
deserts
dew
Ding Darling Refuge
dragonflies, damselflies
ducks
eagles: bald, golden
ecosystems
egrets: cattle, great, reddish, snowy
elephants, African
Everglades National Park
falcons: peregrine; gyrfalcon
familiar "backyard" nature
farmscapes
ferns
flies
Florida

Here is the first page of my "complete long-form" version of a stock list.

A STANDARD *GREEN BOOK* LISTING

A typical entry in *Green Book* includes the following information about you and your work:

Your name, along with an identification number that is used throughout the indexes

Your address (mail and/or courier), and telephone and fax numbers

The size and format of your file—for example,
25,000 35mm, 5,000 6 x 7, and 8,000 4 x 5

What natural history material subjects are in your file

General stock coverage

Environmental coverage

Specialties

Geographic areas you've photographed

Most recent coverage

Selected credits

Comments (a brief message from you to the photo buyer)

Noneditorial services, such as workshop instruction, audiovisual production, and cinematography

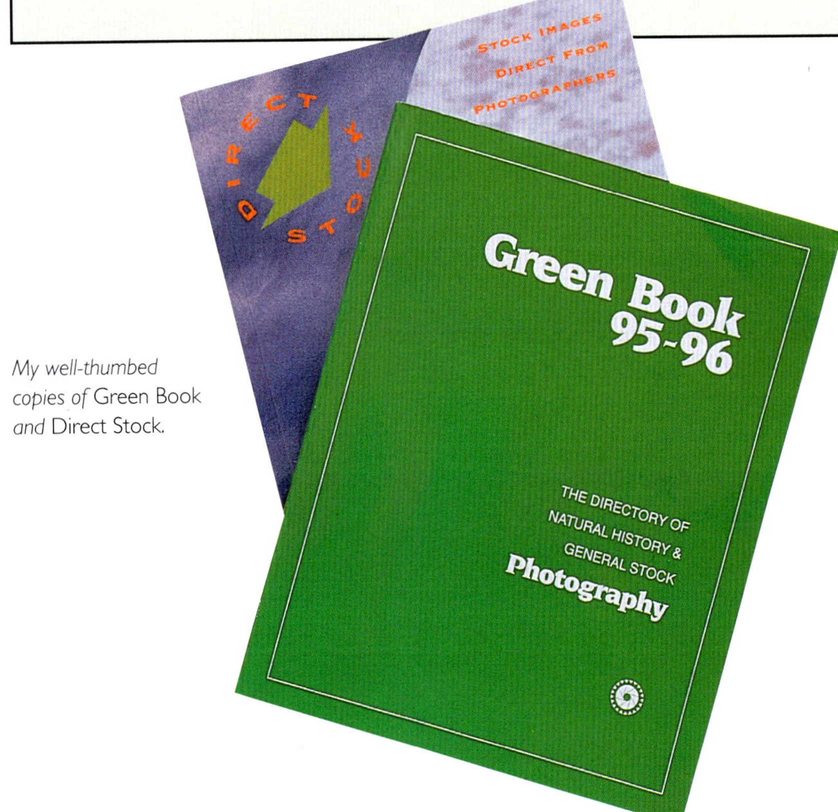

My well-thumbed copies of Green Book *and* Direct Stock.

order, and run it on your business stationery or letterhead created for the list. Incidentally, if your files contain more than just natural history, you might indicate such on your master list, or run separate stock lists for nature work, travel pictures, and general stock.

Once you've sent out your primary list, you might want to update it every six months or so with a short stock list entitled "New Stock" or "New Pictures." This keeps your name in front of editors and picture buyers. It also emphasizes how hard you're working to generate all the pictures they might need.

Another option for promoting yourself and your work is to purchase advertising space in a trade journal or trade publication pitched directly to photo buyers. For the most part, this kind of advertising is quite expensive. As such, it definitely isn't for beginning photographers, generally isn't for stock photographers, and is almost never for natural-history photographers. However, if you want to see what commercial photographic advertising looks like, go to a major library and look through the most current issues of *American Showcase* or *Communication Arts* magazines. While you are at the library, you should also glance at *The Creative Black Book* and *The Stock Workbook*. These are big-buck productions for high-profile photographers and agencies.

My advice to nature photographers starting out in business is simple. Rather than spend your money on advertising, invest in building your picture file, outfitting your office, and buying postage for editorial submissions. Consider advertising only after you have a serious picture file with in-depth coverage and a number of publishing credits to your name.

At that point, you can advertise in two books. One I think is well worth considering, while you should carefully evaluate the other in terms of where you stand as a business. *Green Book*, published every other year, is the only directory specifically designed to list a nature photographer's stock files. You buy a listing in the book and provide a detailed stock description that is worked up using a form supplied to you. Actual images from your file aren't printed, just a textual summation of your business and 220 entries (you can purchase more) in extensive cross-referenced indexes. These indexes are in an easy-to-use, telephone-book format to help researchers locate the photographs they need and the photographer they need to contact.

Copies of *Green Book* are available free of charge to all qualified American and

Canadian picture buyers. Currently it is sent to more than 4,500 picture buyers, including selected advertising agencies and European and Asian publishers. Let me quote from the introduction of the current directory:

> *Green Book* is a directory of stock photography created to meet the needs of editors and researchers. It describes the stock files of photographers, photo agencies, and other stock photo libraries. Most *Green Book* participants are natural history specialists, with subjects covering everything from landscapes to wildlife. Their approaches range from scientific (geology, geography, botany, etc.) to popular. Photo credits are included in the stock descriptions to help photo buyers determine the participant's level of experience and the uses for which their work is best suited.

If you think a listing might be helpful to your business, I would first get a copy of *Green Book,* which is available for about $30 direct from the publisher. Then read through it to help in your evaluation of both the book itself and where you stand in comparison to the other advertisers. As of this writing the cost of advertising in *Green Book* is $700, which includes a one-time setup charge. For past participants, the rate is $600.

You, and photo researchers, can also access *Green Book* online on the World Wide Web. Basic online listing and index service is included as part of *Green Book* participation; custom services, such as updates of information, travel notices, and E-mail links, are available at additional reasonable prices. (For detailed information, guidelines, or a copy of the book, contact AG Editions—see page 140).

Your other option is to purchase space in *Direct Stock,* a color-picture catalog that enables you to display a few of your images—alongside those of many other photographers. This book isn't restricted to nature work, although a number of working professional nature photographers do advertise in it. It definitely isn't appropriate for shooters who are new to the photography business.

You select exactly which pictures and how many pictures you want to include, the size you want the photographs printed, and the general heading(s) you want them printed under. You can also purchase an entire page or multiple pages in order to have your pictures presented side by side with your company logo.

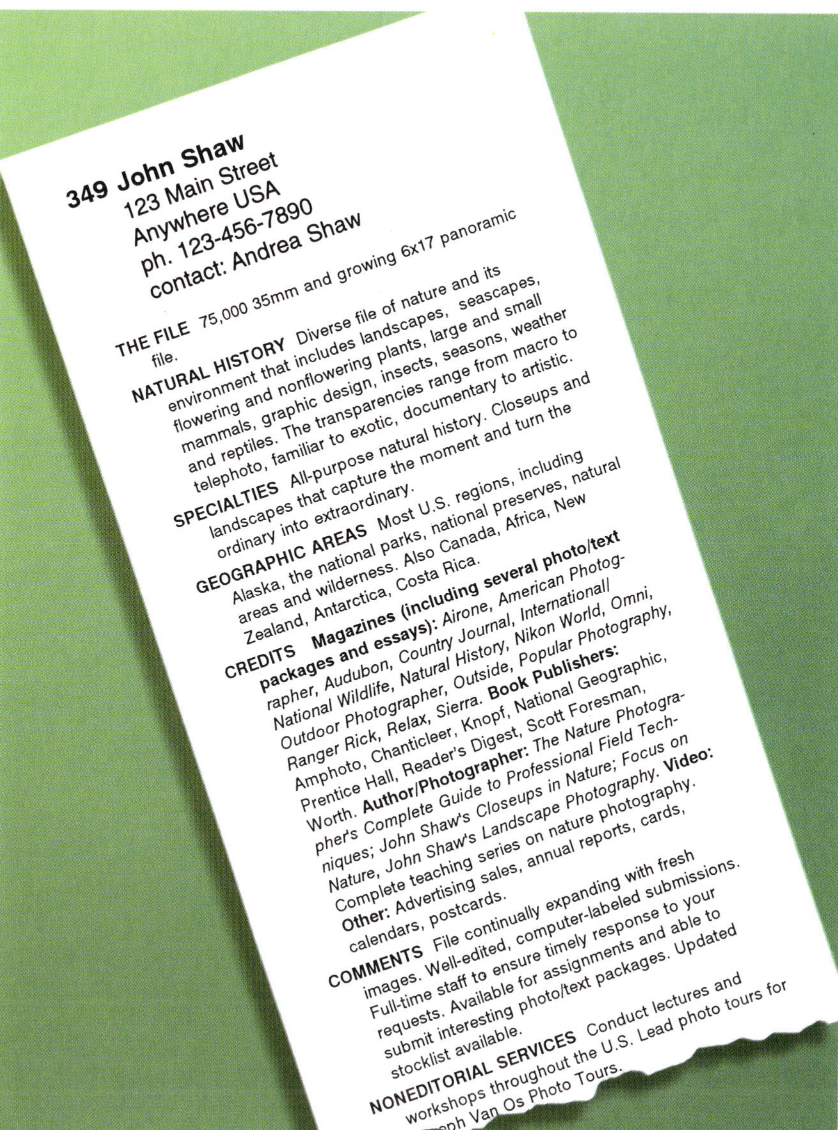

349 John Shaw
123 Main Street
Anywhere USA
ph. 123-456-7890
contact: Andrea Shaw

THE FILE 75,000 35mm and growing 6x17 panoramic file.
NATURAL HISTORY Diverse file of nature and its environment that includes landscapes, seascapes, flowering and nonflowering plants, large and small mammals, graphic design, insects, seasons, weather and reptiles. The transparencies range from macro to telephoto, familiar to exotic, documentary to artistic.
SPECIALTIES All-purpose natural history. Closeups and landscapes that capture the moment and turn the ordinary into extraordinary.
GEOGRAPHIC AREAS Most U.S. regions, including Alaska, the national parks, national preserves, natural areas and wilderness. Also Canada, Africa, New Zealand, Antarctica, Costa Rica.
CREDITS **Magazines (including several photo/text packages and essays):** *Airone, American Photographer, Audubon, Country Journal, International Wildlife, Natural History, Nikon World, Omni, Outdoor Photographer, Outside, Popular Photography, Ranger Rick, Relax, Sierra.* **Book Publishers:** Amphoto, Chanticleer, Knopf, National Geographic, Prentice Hall, Reader's Digest, Scott Foresman, Worth. **Author/Photographer:** *The Nature Photographer's Complete Guide to Professional Field Techniques; John Shaw's Closeups in Nature; Focus on Nature, John Shaw's Landscape Photography.* **Video:** Complete teaching series on nature photography. **Other:** Advertising sales, annual reports, cards, calendars, postcards.
COMMENTS File continually expanding with fresh images. Well-edited, computer-labeled submissions. Full-time staff to ensure timely response to your requests. Available for assignments and able to submit interesting photo/text packages. Updated stocklist available.
NONEDITORIAL SERVICES Conduct lectures and workshops throughout the U.S. Lead photo tours for ...ph Van Os Photo Tours.

Here is my own entry from the 1995–96 edition of Green Book.

Direct Stock is offered to picture buyers who can see the type of work you do. Each photograph has your name and telephone number printed directly underneath it, while an index in the back contains your complete address information. In short, a picture editor deals directly with you; there is no go-between taking a percentage of your sale. Keep in mind, however, that this advertising isn't inexpensive, especially since *Direct Stock* is high-quality color printing on good paper. Rates for the most recent volume (Volume 5) were:

One or two pages	$2,195/page
Three or more pages	$2,095/page

Plus $75 per separation and camera-ready artwork

A one-page minimum is required. You can take this as four quarter-pages in different subject categories, two half-pages, or one full-page.

Think long and hard about the value of purchasing space in this book. A friend who advertises in *Direct Stock* states that he must recoup at least twice the dollar amount it costs him to buy the space in order to make up for the sheer effort of developing the ad. His major concern, as well it should be, is choosing exactly which photographs to include since advertising buyers use the book more than editorial markets do. I suggest purchasing a copy of the book and carefully studying the pictures included before making any decisions. (For more information, contact *Direct Stock* Inc.—see page 140).

SIGNING WITH A STOCK AGENCY

A stock agency is a business that keeps many pictures in-house (in stock, that is), which are available at all times for lease to clients. If you have a file of photographs built up from several years of shooting and you're actively marketing your work, you are in effect a stock agency, albeit a very small operation compared to some of the large companies in the business. If you're marketing your work, you are definitely familiar with most of the hassles of selling pictures. Finding clients, pulling submissions together, meeting deadlines, tracking slides, checking invoices, mounting, labeling, filing—the list goes on and on. Consequently the idea that someone else will sell your work while you sit back and cash the checks can be quite attractive.

Well, yes and no. There are some compelling reasons to find a stock agency willing to push your photographs, and, I believe, some compelling reasons not to do so. First, however, you must always remember that nature subjects are a specialized segment of the overall stock-photography market. Very, very few agencies handle only natural-history material. This is because the biggest dollar accounts are in advertising, while the bulk of nature photographs are used editorially. Most of the advice I've read about stock agencies is written from the perspective of the photographic generalist. Nature stock photography is a niche business.

The Benefits

As far as I'm concerned, there are three major reasons to place images with a stock agency. First of all stock agencies are full-time businesses, always open and ready to send out pictures to prospective clients. Few nature photographers, even working professionals, have a full-time staff to handle requests. In fact, most nature photographers run a one-person business, so when they are in the field shooting pictures needed for their files, just who is helping their clients? Sure, all working professionals have answering machines to take picture-request messages, but you need a real, live person to pull slides and ship them out. A stock agency provides this.

Agencies also find clients that an individual photographer might not be able to reach; in fact, all agencies actively pursue clients on a continuous basis. They have the resources, in terms of both personnel and of money, to do so through advertising, direct client contact, and general promotion. Clients come to know major agencies

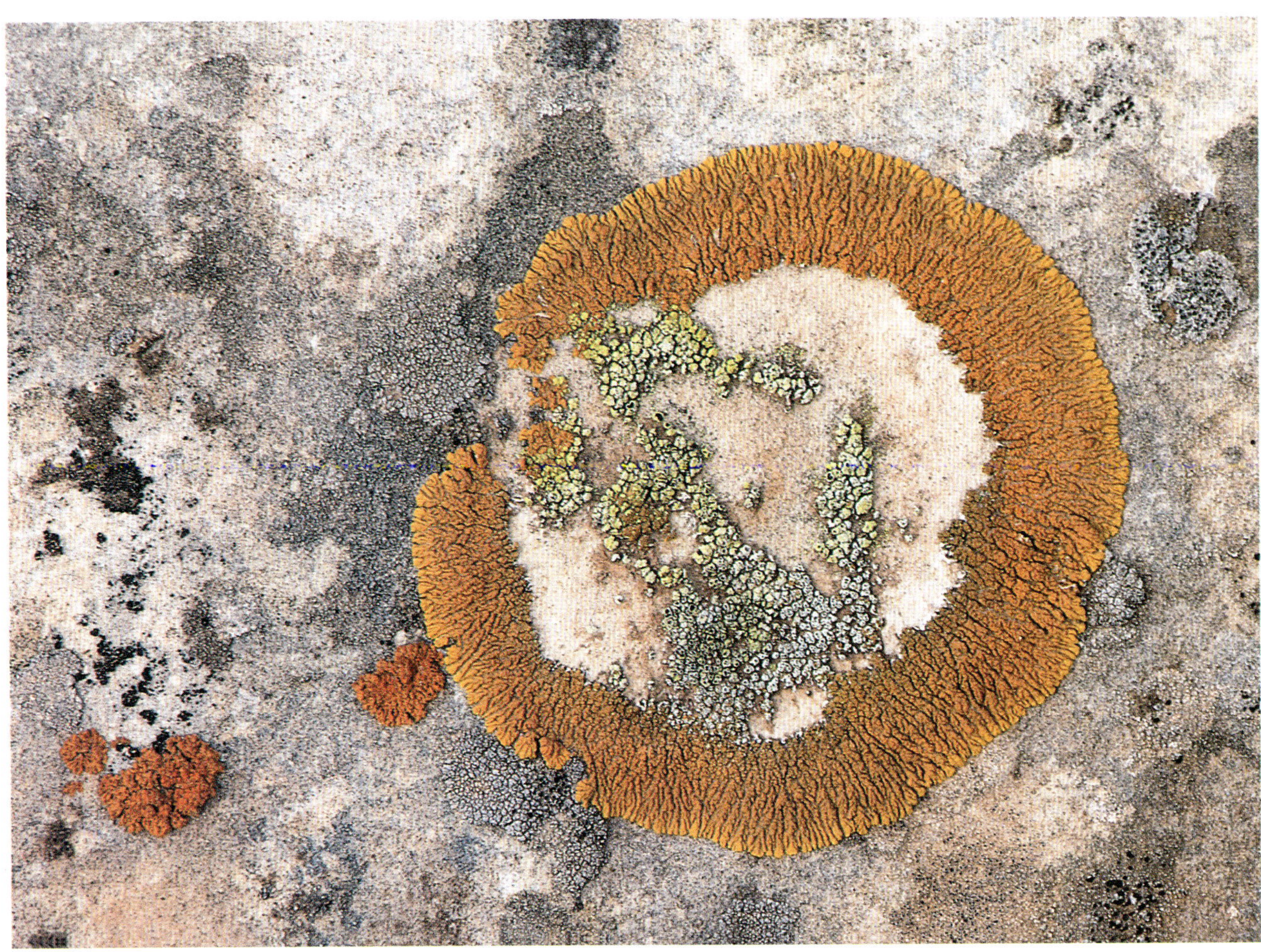

Crustose lichen on rock. Nikon F4, Nikon 200mm macro lens, Fuji Velvia.

This shot of a crustose lichen is sharp, colorful, and clearly defined—all in all a salable editorial photograph.

and what pictures they have on file. It isn't unusual for a client, such as a textbook company, to send a researcher to a stock agency to pull an entire book's photo illustrations. This is particularly true of stock agencies located in the same city as publishers. Agencies keep abreast of what is happening in the publishing world and can respond instantly to developing projects. They can market your work while you are out in the field shooting.

Good stock agencies offer one more benefit: they take care of a lot of the paperwork. Once they've accepted a photograph from you for their file, you don't have to do any more clerical drudgery. They number and file all those pictures, they check the total number of slides in and out of the office, they handle the delivery memos, they remount scanned film, and they keep track of total sales. You simply have to shoot the pictures, label the slides, and cash the checks.

The Disadvantages

For beginning photographers, stock agencies have some drawbacks. First of all, stock photography is a volume operation. That means you have to take many, many pictures each and every month. Over the course of a year, can you produce an average of several hundred different images each month? Most agencies want to see an initial selection of 300 to 500 slides just to determine what sort of photographer you are. If that depletes your good file, don't even consider contacting an agency.

For most nature photographers just starting to think about marketing, my advice regarding a stock agency is quite straightforward: forget it. You probably don't have enough pictures on file, and you probably can't produce enough, to make it worthwhile for an agency to take you on or for you to spend the time looking for one. An agency doesn't want a photographer who will generate a yearly profit to them of $500; they want many pictures of all sorts of subjects in order to generate good money. Consider using an agency once you've built a major file. No one in the nature-photography field makes a living from stock-agency sales alone.

I think you are much better served by starting to market your own work. If you have 5,000 good pictures of a variety of nature subjects, you can reasonably expect $5,000 a year return from them through a stock agency. That is, $5,000 should be yours after the year or so it takes to get the shots into the

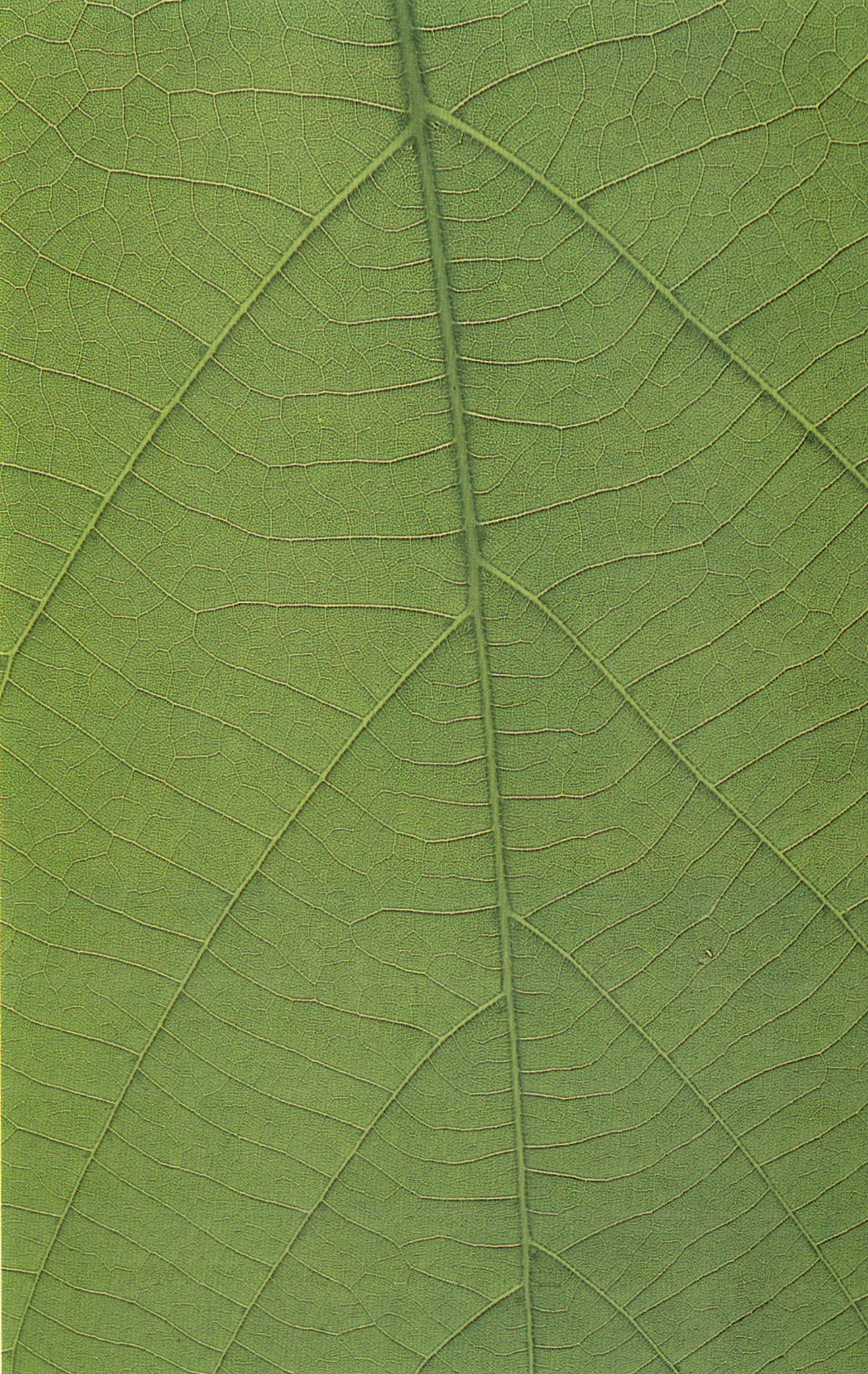

Section of yellow-poplar leaf, Tennessee. Nikon F4, Nikon 105mm macro lens, Fuji Velvia.

This photograph is an example of a stock biological shot. It could be used in a textbook to show the leaf vein pattern of a typical dicot plant, as part of a spread on photosynthesis, or as an illustration of plant structure. It could also be used commercially to represent the concept of networking.

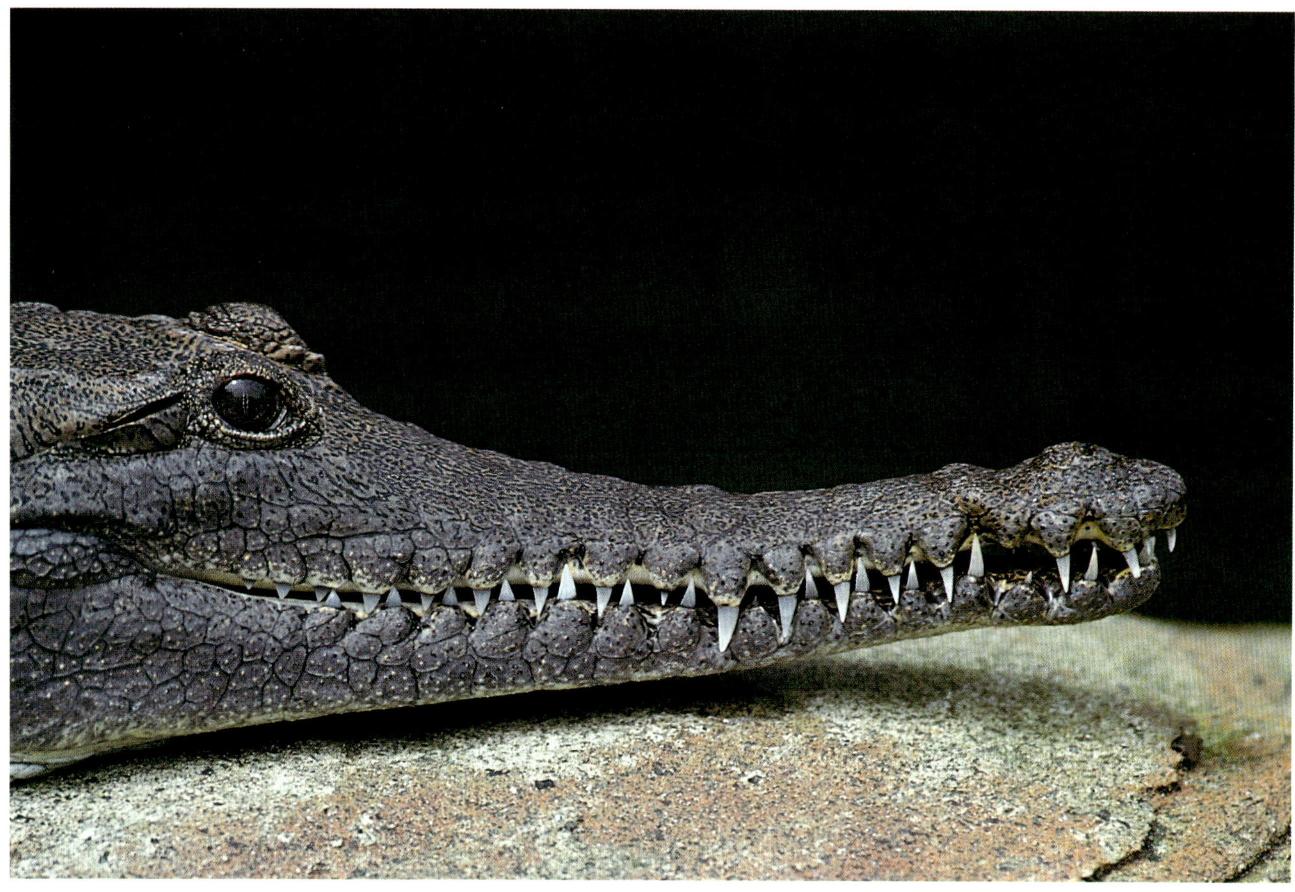

Freshwater crocodile head, Australia. Nikon F4, Nikon 400mm, Fujichrome 100.

This is a good stock photograph because it clearly shows a distinguishing feature of crocodiles: the way the teeth fit into sockets along the outside of the jaw.

Sunrise over lake, Michigan. Nikon F3, Nikon 200mm lens, Kodachrome 25.

This is another picture that has sold well through stock agencies. It is simple and colorful, with plenty of room for type to be dropped in on the image.

agency's file, and then out to clients, and then for the agency to collect for sales and in turn to pay you. Seriously market those same 5,000 photographs to magazine and book clients, and you should have a much better return, even in the first year. Get established, and then look for an agency.

The fact that stock is such a numbers game—big numbers of slides on file with an agency should mean big numbers on the check it sends you—is reflected in an old rule of thumb for editorial stock. You're doing about right if you average $1 per year per transparency on file with the agency.

Suppose you want to make $50,000 a year from your stock agency. You'll need around 50,000 good pictures on file with the agency in order to generate this sort of money. Do you have that many pictures? Remember, stock agencies don't hold every photograph you send them; they edit out what they need. Those 50,000 slides on file probably represent a total submission of 100,000 pictures. Most photographers can't send this number of slides all at once to an agency.

Building up the quantity of pictures you need to make decent money is a long-term proposition. You should also realize that if an agency already has good pictures on file, sending more of the same subject might mean getting your pictures sent right back to you. For example, if an agency already has elk shots and doesn't have enough demand to justify filing more elk pictures, your great images will be returned.

Stock agencies usually take a 50-percent commission on all sales. However, if they have a business relationship with another agency in another country, which is called a *subagency*, you might receive only 30 percent or a bit less from any sale. Often a stock agent charges other fees back to the photographer. Usually the photographs placed with a subagent are reproduction-quality dupes. While it is reasonable to expect a photographer to share in the expense of making these dupes, some agencies assess more than the actual cost of doing so. Be careful. I know of one agency that charges photographers $2 per accepted image as a clerical fee. Place 1,000 photographs with that agency and you're starting out $2,000 in the hole. Average $1 per year per transparency and two years must pass before you break even, assuming you don't place any more pictures with the agency and get even deeper in debt.

Most stock agencies are heavily into producing picture catalogs right now. Who pays for this? Generally the overall cost is

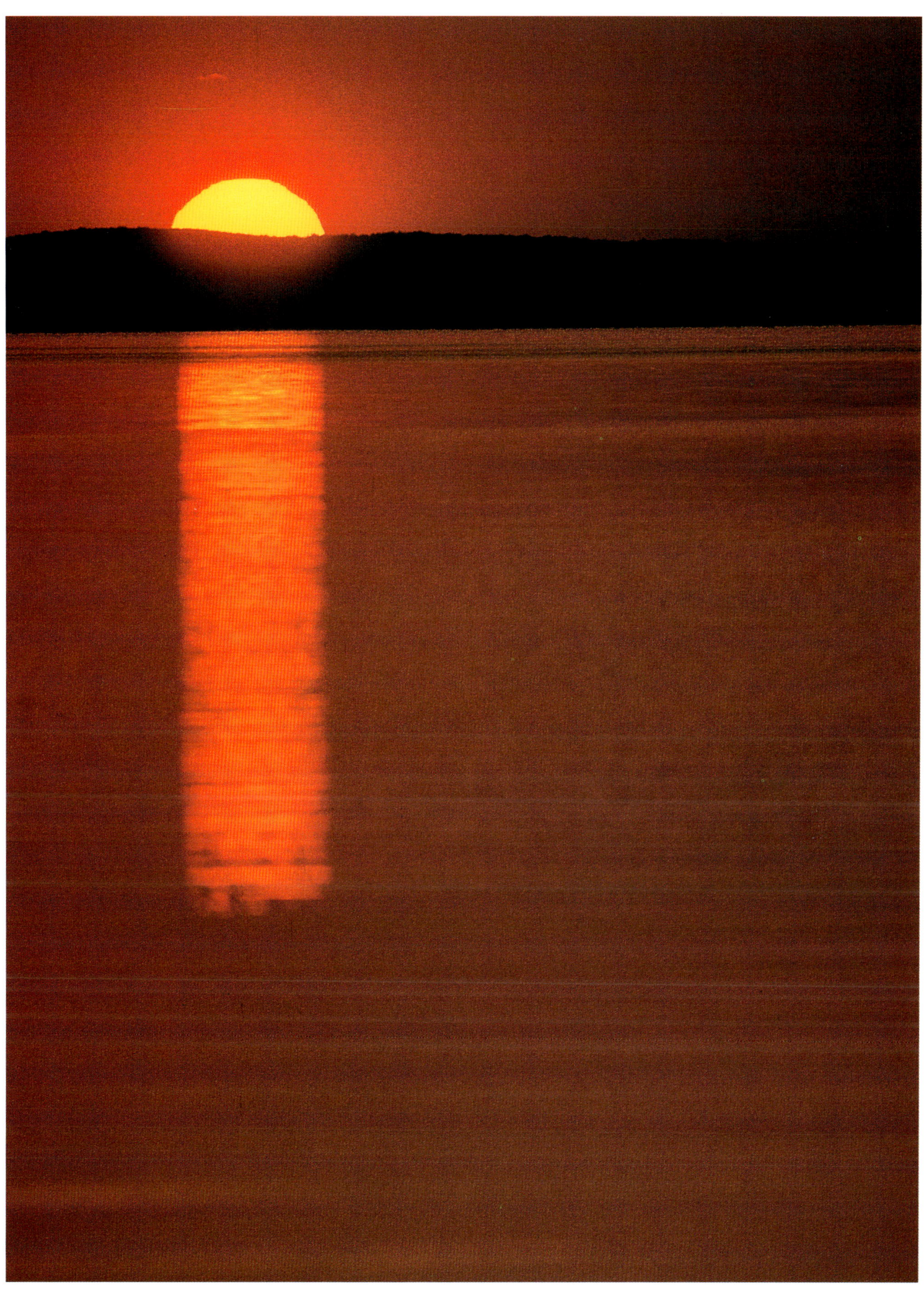

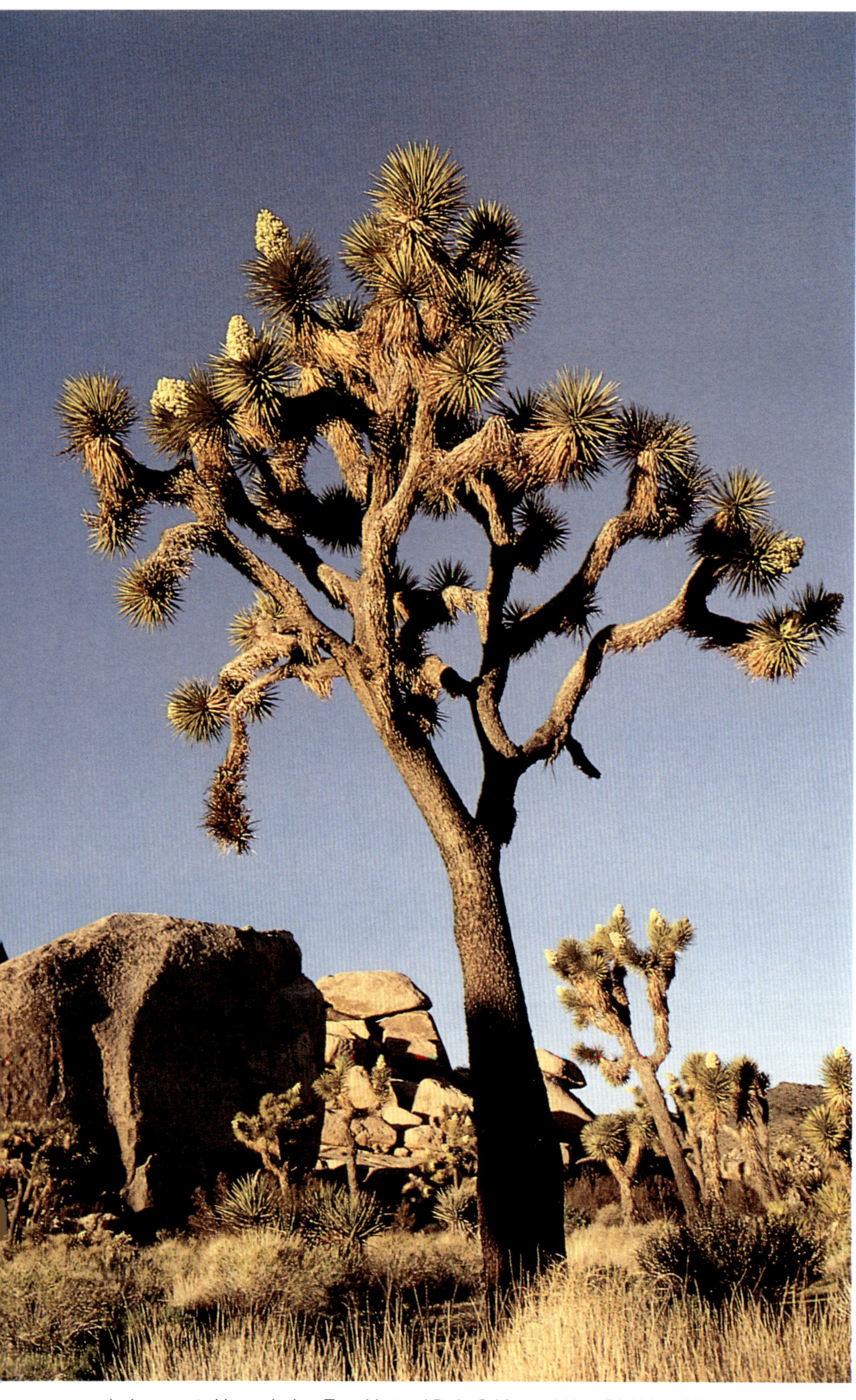

Joshua tree in bloom, Joshua Tree National Park, California. Nikon F4, Nikon 24mm lens, Kodak Lumière.

This photograph could be used various ways. The Joshua tree, which is a form of giant yucca, is a characteristic plant of the Mojave Desert. And Joshua Tree National Park is located in southern California.

split between the agency and the photographer. While you aren't required to place work in a catalog, it is true that catalog shots outsell other images. But only you can decide if the expense is worth the return. While you must spend money in order to make money, be sure you are the one keeping the money in the end and that the agency isn't turning a profit at your expense.

I know one photographer whose gross-sales statement from his stock agency is over $100,000 every year. Not bad, until you figure out his actual net after expenses. Since he is in the field shooting most of the year, he doesn't have the time to edit, label, and submit his work; an office employee does those jobs. Over the course of a year, my friend shoots about 2,000 rolls of 35mm film, and his work takes him all over the world. Airfare and travel expenses for a year add up to about $25,000 (you should realize that an agency won't foot the bill for your production expenses). His agency likes to splash his shots in its catalog; the charge back to him is $150 per catalog photograph with 100 pictures used. So what did my friend have left at end of the year?

Gross sales	$100,000
Office assistant and office expense	-$25,000
Film and processing (2,000 rolls @ $12/roll)	- $24,000
Travel expenses	- $25,000
Catalog photography expenses	- $15,000
Net at the end of the year	$11,000

I think that my friend should look for another job, one that will enable him to buy some extras, like a house, a car, and food. I don't mean to sound like I'm bad-mouthing stock agencies. I definitely believe in them, and I use several agencies around the world to help market my work. They can reach markets that you can't. Most agencies are scrupulously honest in their dealings with both clients and photographers. But as with all business arrangements, you should evaluate the situation before you jump into anything.

Stock agencies work on a contract basis. Read the contract carefully, put it away for a few days, read it again, and then have someone else go over it with you. All contracts are negotiable, but once you sign anything, you're bound by the terms. Here are some points to consider.

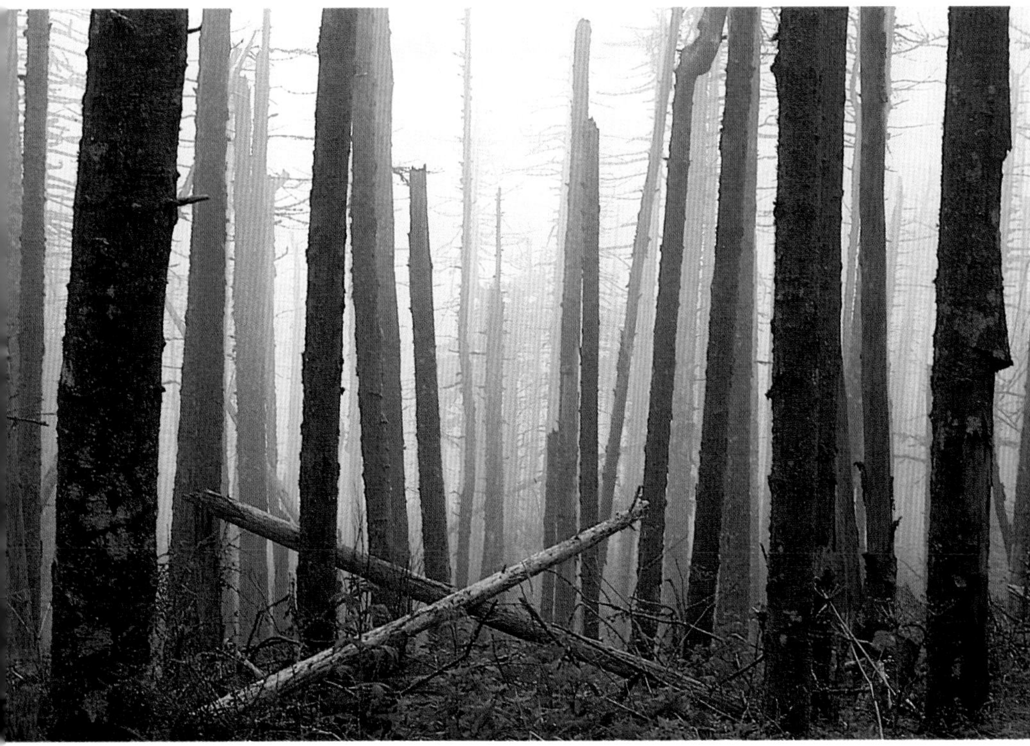

Acid-rain destruction of Fraser fir, Mount Mitchell, North Carolina. Nikon F3, Nikon 105mm lens, Kodachrome 25.

I once had an assignment to shoot the acid-rain damage in the southern Appalachian Mountains. After my client returned the photographs to me, I placed a broad selection of shots with my stock agencies. That was more than 10 years ago, and at the minimum I've made one or two sales of acid-rain-damage shots per quarter ever since. Good stock pictures keep selling.

Representation

Who can sell your work, and where can they sell it? Some agencies ask for "exclusive representation" of your photography. Read the fine print. Can you sell your own work, or is the agency the only outlet you can have anywhere in the world? (The answer is no. You can't sell your own work if the contract says the agency has "sole and exclusive world rights.")

If you're allowed to sell your own work, can you have the same picture in your file as well as with the agency? Can you have another agency if you submit different pictures? Can you have a foreign agency? My contracts state that each agent is the exclusive stock agency in a designated geographic area for pictures placed with it. I can sell my own work, but no other agency in the prescribed area has the same photograph.

Length of Contract

Most stock contracts run for somewhere between three and five years, generally with an automatic renewal clause if there are no written objections. Depending on the exclusivity phrasing, this usually means that you can't have back anything you send to an agency for the stipulated time period. An obvious solution is not to submit work if you think you might need it, although if the agency has complete exclusivity you can't market the images anyway. What happens if you don't want to continue the agency association? How long will it take to get your pictures returned?

Accounting and Payment

How often does the agency pay? Quarterly? Yearly? Only when you submit new work? What is the split between agency and photographer? Is there any proof of sales? Do you receive tearsheets? Do you have the right to audit or inspect your own account? Who pays for repro dupes, catalog pictures, slide pages, and other incidentals? And who actually owns those repro dupes in case the contract is terminated?

Content and Quantity

Most stock-agency contracts don't spell out what you can and can't shoot, but you should consider the point carefully if there is any mention of subject matter. Will you be the only photographer supplying a certain subject, or are you restricted in any way as to what you can submit? Right now you might want to photograph only landscapes, but what happens when you take fantastic bear shots? If your contract says "landscapes only" since the agency already has a "bear photographer," you are out of luck. Do you have to produce a certain number of photographs to be kept on file per year? What are the penalties if you don't reach this number?

If you're interested in agency representation, I strongly suggest that you first read both *ASMP Stock Photography Handbook* and Lou Jacobs's *Selling Stock Photography* (see page 141). These two books give an excellent overview of the general stock-photography business.

By the way, almost all stock agencies put out want lists for their photographers. Reading such a want list is a real education on shooting for the stock-photography business. When you're thinking about signing with an agency, you should definitely ask to see some lists.

Labeling Slides

Most stock houses have a distinct way they want slides to be labeled, so check their requirements carefully. Almost all agencies need at least one wide side and one narrow side of the front of a slide mount for their information (agency name, image number, photographer code, etc.). As a result, you might have to go back and relabel all your work depending on which photographs you want to submit.

For example, Bruce Coleman Inc., one of the agencies I use, asks that photographers begin their slide captions with a set-off, two-letter code indicating general subject matter: MM for mammals, BI for birds, PL for plants, and so on. General landscapes are identified using a similar two-letter code for locality, for example, AF for Africa, AU for Australia, and SA for South America.

CHAPTER FOUR

SENDING OUT SUBMISSIONS

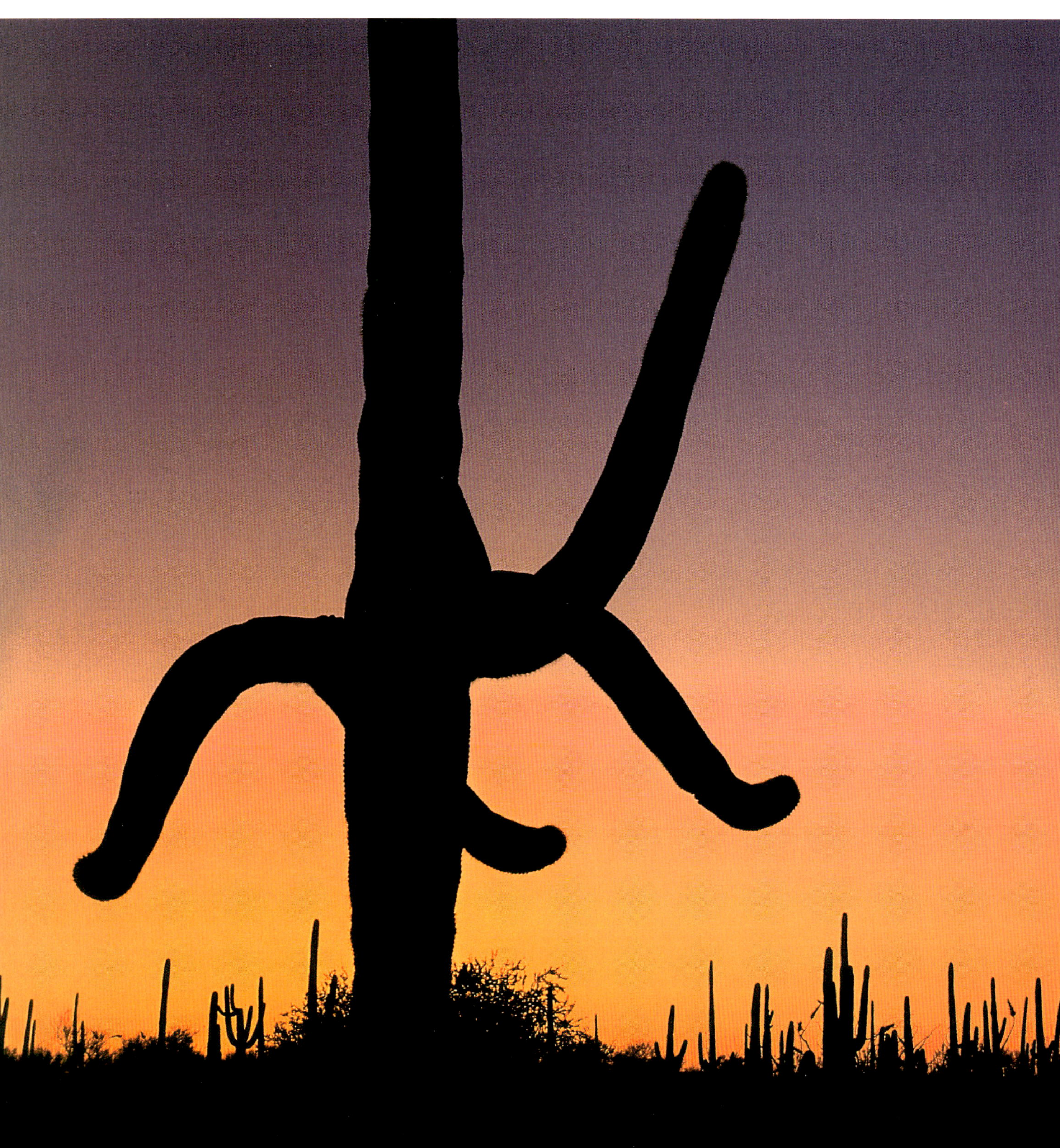

Saguaro cactus at sunset, Saguaro National Monument, Arizona.

CHOOSING SLIDES TO SUBMIT

When you're pulling a submission for a client, don't ever consider sending any image that isn't technically your best work. You shouldn't keep poorly made images in your file. However, there are two more factors that you might not have considered: composition and contrast.

Subject Framing

One of the major differences between amateur photographers—especially camera-club photographers—and working professionals who sell to the print media is the way in which they compose a picture. I'm not talking about the usual graphic elements of line, shape, color, and form, but specifically about how tight the subject appears within the image frame. Beginning photographers hear the same advice over and over: Fill the frame with the subject. This is all well and good because often beginners aren't visually selective. This is particularly true of amateurs using point-and-shoot cameras with their built-in, short-focal-length lenses. Everybody has seen a picture of a deer appearing as just a dark spot somewhere within a shot encompassing the entire North Woods.

However, as photographers continue their education, the "fill-the-frame" rule seems to take strong effect. Subjects are crammed into the frame so that they're almost touching the very edges of the picture format. Actually this seems to be one of the cardinal rules of nature photography in camera clubs. But if you want to sell your work, framing a subject in this manner is absolutely the wrong thing to do. Why? Because editors need some room, some space in the image, with which to work.

Sometimes they need to be able to crop a picture to fit an exact space on the page. Very tight framing precludes this. I've often had requests from editors looking for a specific layout, vertical, horizontal, or even square. If I don't have exactly what they need, they'll usually ask if I have an image that has enough space so that it can be cropped to fit. I've sold photographs taken in a vertical format cropped and published as horizontals, horizontals cropped for verticals, and both versions cropped square. Granted, I would rather shoot both a vertical and horizontal version in the field, but leaving a little room to crop in both versions helps make sales.

The fact that an image just might be cropped means you must start out with technically the very best image possible. Part of the frame is being lost, while enlarging the remaining part of the picture emphasizes any unsharpness or film grain. So I cart around my heavy Gitzo tripod, use the slowest films possible, and purchase the best lenses I can afford. I've had front-cover shots published on national magazines that are vertical layouts pulled from horizontal photographs. I've also had major calendar sales in a horizontal format cropped from a vertical photograph. By the way, picture editors make these decisions, not you the photographer. So don't submit photographs in special slide crop mounts or mask off parts of the frame.

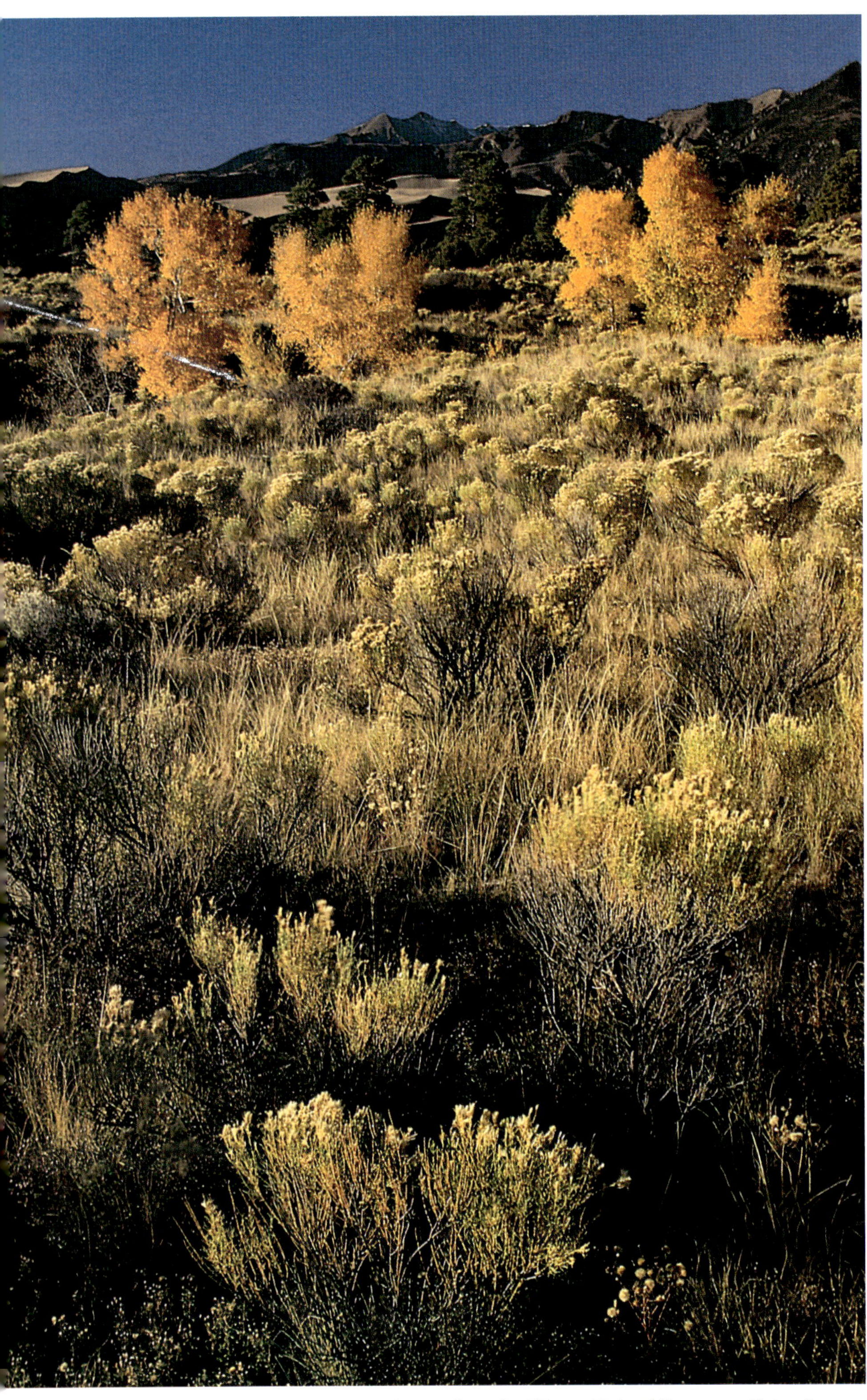

Rabbitbrush and autumn cottonwood trees, Great Sand Dunes National Monument, Colorado. Nikon F4, Nikon 105mm macro lens, Fuji Velvia.

This is a carefully composed image, exactly what a picture editor wants to see.

Completely filling the frame with your subject also means that there is no room left for text, such as a magazine logo. I've heard many editors say that the number-one reason for not using any given image as a cover shot is simply lack of space for the magazine name. Most publications, books and magazines alike, drop type directly onto a picture rather than framing off the photograph separately, like the way a matboard surrounds a print. Study a few covers, and you'll discover that most of the type falls on a rather bare part of the picture. Type running through the main subject or a busy section of an image makes the resulting cover appear disconcerting and chaotic.

You should also realize that the 35mm format with its 1 x 1½-inch proportions doesn't enlarge directly to the standard proportions of books and magazines. When a 35mm image is used as a cover shot, about 1/8 inch is lost from either end of the long dimension of the image on the film. Additionally, most cover shots are printed full bleed. This means that the picture runs off the page on all four sides, so a little more of the image is lost all the way around. If you frame your subject right to the edge of the film, you'll never sell a cover.

I can't really tell you exactly how tight or how loose to frame the subject. No hard-and-fast rule exists. This is best learned by experience, although pretending to drop in type when you're critiquing your work might help. If you're framing tight to the very edge, loosen up a little.

Contrast Ranges

The other factor to always consider when choosing slides for submission is the contrast range within a slide. To put it very straightforwardly, high-contrast shots are hard to reproduce on the printed page while maintaining detail in both highlights and shadows. You must sacrifice one end or the other of the tonal scale.

The difference between the lightest whites and the darkest blacks in an actual real-life scene may be as much as 1000:1. Your eyes can perceive and accommodate this difference; you can simultaneously see detail in the highlight areas and the shadow areas. Photographic film can't handle this range at all. Most films are limited to about a 100:1 range, or 5 to 5½ stops maximum. But even this exceeds what is possible on the printing press. The light-to-dark ratio on a four-color process image on premium paper is approximately 20:1.

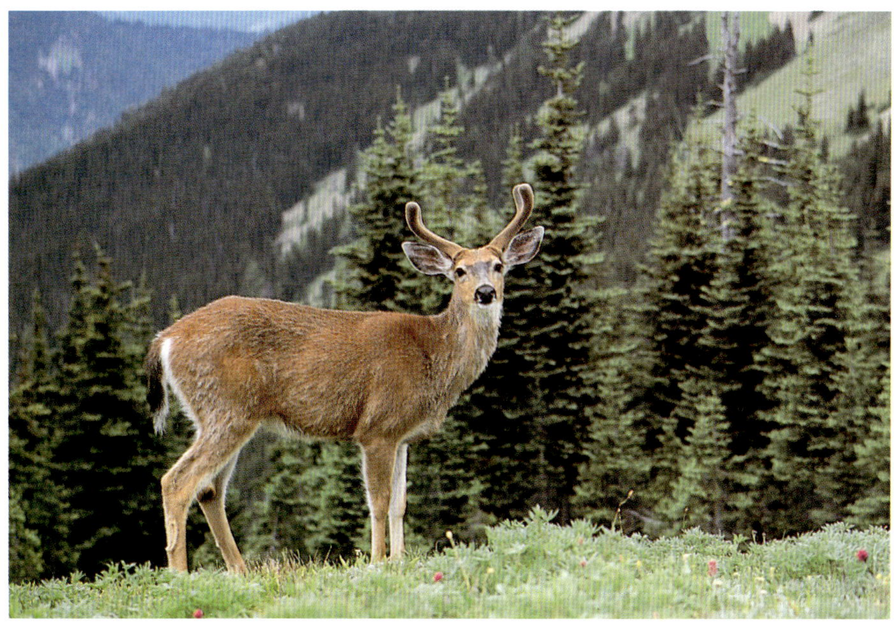

Both of these photographs enable a picture editor to do a bit of cropping if necessary. The two shots also have enough space so that type can be dropped into the images.

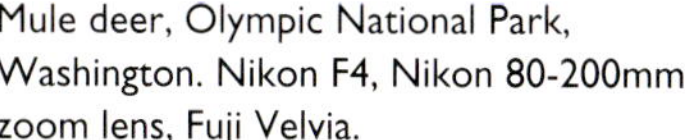

Mule deer, Olympic National Park, Washington. Nikon F4, Nikon 80-200mm zoom lens, Fuji Velvia.

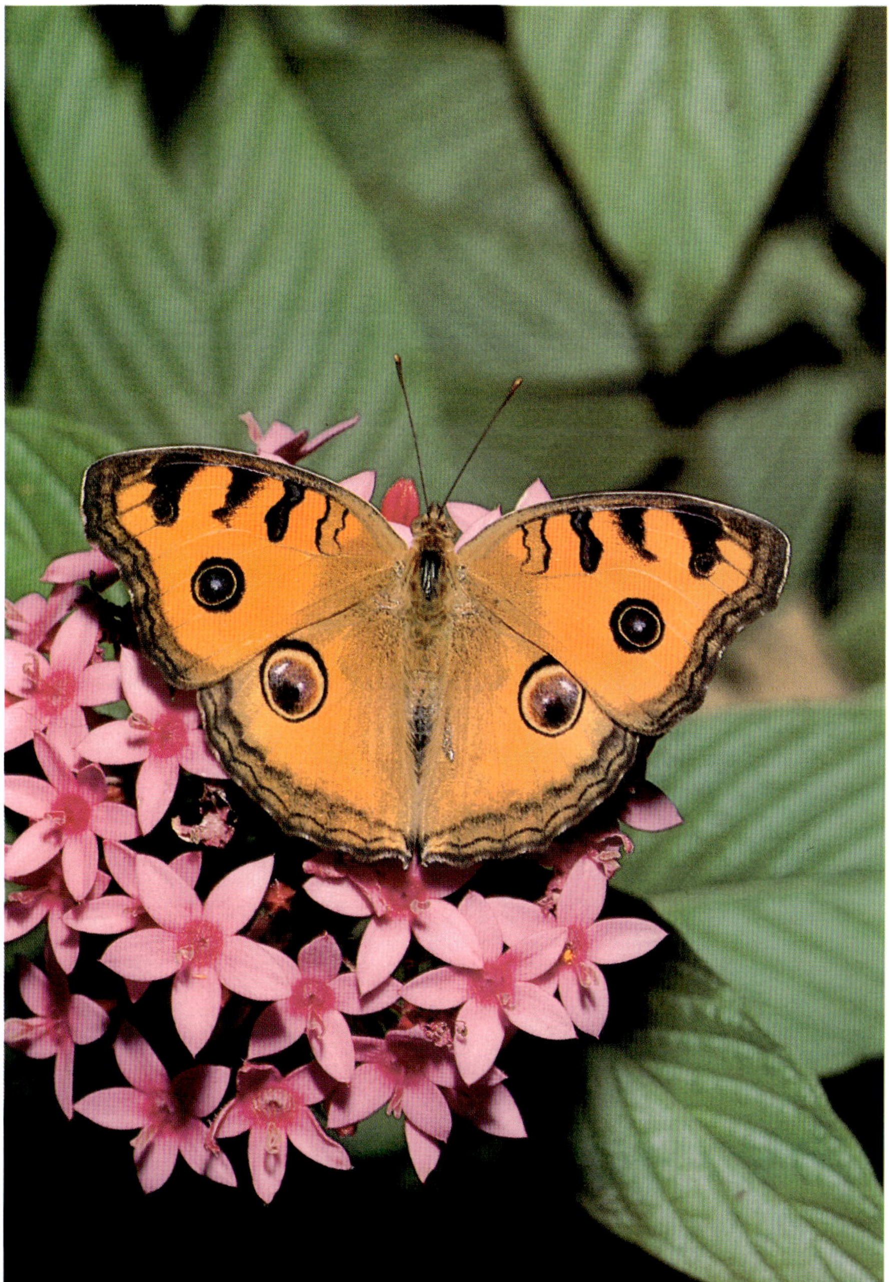

Tropical buckeye butterfly, Florida. Nikon F4, Nikon 105mm macro lens, Fuji Velvia.

Autumn deciduous woods, Green Mountain National Forest, Vermont.

A printer's delight: a low-contrast subject in low-contrast light.

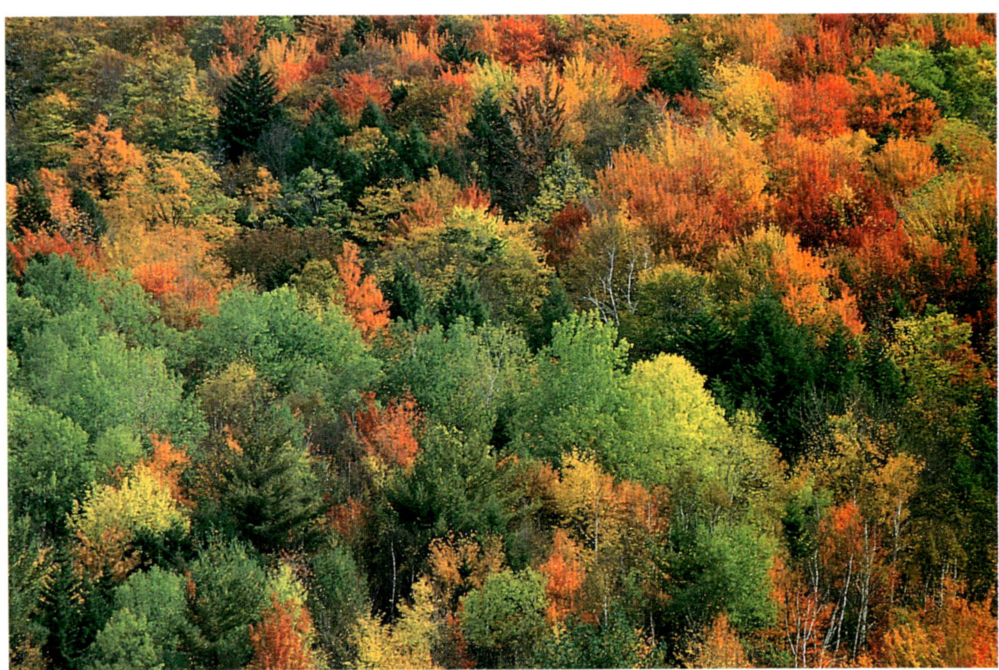

What this means is that tonal compression occurs when the photograph is printed. A picture has less contrast on printing paper than it does as a photograph. And both images have less contrast than what you see in the real world. If holding the whole range of tones is important when the photograph is printed, you need to start with an image that initially has moderate tonal contrast. A slide with all the critical details falling within a maximum four-stop range is great for color printing on quality coated paper. Since the slide doesn't have extreme contrast, it goes through less tonal compression. Consequently when it is printed, it provides greater fidelity of tone and color saturation compared to the original photograph.

Assessing Transparencies

You can assess how a transparency will appear after separating and printing in two ways. One approach is to have a photographic print made. The print will look much more like the printed image will appear than the slide. The slide will be brighter, more vivid, and more detailed.

Of course, you can't make prints of all your slides to evaluate them. So you can try another method, which is far easier. Evaluate your slides for highlight and shadow detail on your lightbox with several inches of illuminated surface surrounding the transparencies. Don't put the film in a wide black mat or examine it using a magnifier with a black skirt that shuts out all extraneous light. Look at the film lying on the lightbox. Even better would be placing the film unmounted on the lightbox, but I certainly don't advocate taking 35mm images out of their mounts just for viewing.

If you have several frames of the same scene that you don't mind playing with, try this exercise. View one frame through your loupe; if the bottom of the loupe is clear, mask it off with black tape. This will give you an accurate view of the image content and its sharpness. Next, view the second frame in its slide mount lying on your lightbox, but don't use your loupe. Now take the third frame, remove it from its mount, place the film on the lightbox, and view it without a magnifier. You'll discover that your perception of the images, as well as of their contrast and detail, changes depending on how you view them. The third method, the unmounted-film way, is the best indicator of how the image will actually appear on the printed page.

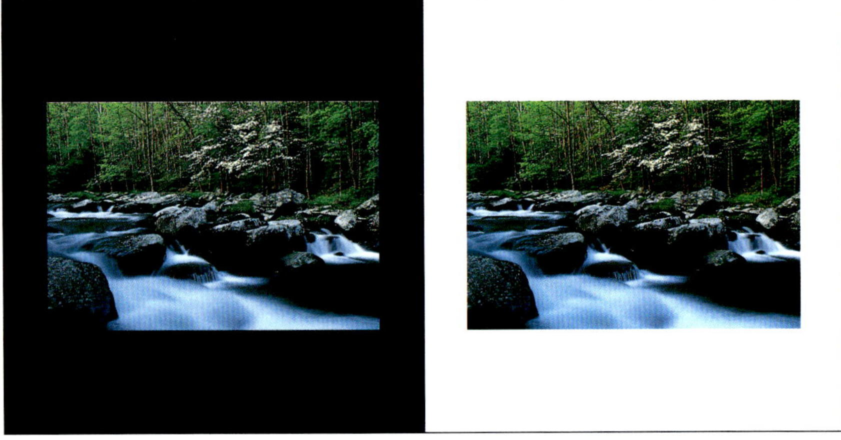

Flowering dogwood along Little River, Great Smoky Mountains National Park, Tennessee. Nikon F4, Nikon 35mm lens, Fujichrome 50.

Even though I shot this scene in overcast light, this slide records a wide contrast range, from the cream of the dogwood blossoms to the dark lower areas of the rocks. Detail is held in both these areas in the original film. Do you notice a slight difference in your perception of the image depending on the surrounding area?

PACKAGING AND SHIPPING SUBMISSIONS

Whether a client has asked for specific shots or you're sending photographs on speculation, submissions of 35mm transparencies are physically handled the same way. A professional presentation of your images can influence a picture buyer in your favor. This is especially true when you're sending pictures to a client by mail. If you can't be there to speak for them, their presentation must do the selling job.

Putting Together the Presentation

Send transparencies in standard, archival slide pages that hold 20 slides. These are the same pages you use to store your slides in a file cabinet or binder. I see no reason at all to use the black-bordered special "presentation" mount boards that hold a limited number of slides. Book and magazine editors are used to slide pages. You especially shouldn't go overboard with your presentation. I heard a picture editor curse a photographer who mounted each and every 35mm piece of film individually in black 4 x 5-inch mounts. This 200-slide submission meant handling 200 separate items, instead of merely 10 slide pages.

Organize your photographic presentations. Make sure the "correct" side of all the slides are facing the picture editors when they place the sheet on the light table. This is where consistency in labeling helps convey a professional image. Remember, you're selling your own image, as well as your images. All of the slide labels should be computer-printed, and all the labels should be placed in the same location on the slides.

When I place slides in a page for submission, I take two additional steps. Horizontal pictures tend to lead the eye into a slide page, while vertical photographs stop it. Picture editors usually start looking at a page of slides at the top-left corner and then proceed to scan across the page, much like the way most people read. Therefore, I ordinarily place horizontal images along the left side of a page in order to lead the editors' vision into the slides. Vertical images placed along the right side of the slide page keep the eye from exiting at the right, thereby forcing attention back to the next line of slides. Combine this with a common tendency for viewers to skip over the lower portion of the page, and you can easily deduce that I always try to place my strongest images in the right center of the top two or three rows.

I also arrange and rearrange slide combinations on my light table until I have a pleasant grouping. I pay close attention to color combinations and contrasts. If I'm sending out a general selection, I mix subjects. I don't lump together all my flower portraits, then all my wildlife shots, and then all my landscapes. Visual variety keeps the presentation fresh, whether on a page of transparencies or in a slide show for an audience.

Does this attention to rather petty details really help in selling pictures? Well, it doesn't hurt. I certainly don't have any research data to support my contentions. But I firmly believe that since picture editors are concerned foremost with visual images, then the best visual presentation of your best photographs is imperative. As I've said before, I'll do anything I can to get a step ahead of my competition.

I complete one more task before I send out my slides, and this is positively mandatory. Before I insert my slides into the pockets on a slide page, I cover each and every image with a 2 x 2-inch transparent, protective sleeve. Slides are protected while they are in the slide pages, but editors pull out any images they want to consider. An unprotected slide is then subjected to fingerprints or scratches or worse. With these protective sleeves over the transparencies, the film remains safe. Absolutely no film leaves my office without first being inserted into a sleeve. I use sleeves made by Filmguard and Proline (see the listings on page 138).

By the way, a sleeved transparency fits easily into a slide-page pocket if you insert the slide into the sleeve the correct way. Sleeves are open on two edges and folded on two. Insert the transparency so that a folded edge goes into the slide-page pocket first. If you do it the other way around, you'll run into trouble. Top-loading slide pages present no problem holding sleeved transparencies, but side-loading pages are difficult to use because the sleeves overlap.

Don't—I repeat, DON'T—ever send out any glass-mounted slides. Shipping these is an invitation to disaster, such as the lethal combination of broken glass and scratched film. Furthermore, most publishers won't accept glass mounts anyway due to liability problems. Don't antagonize editors. Editors also definitely don't want to see slides remounted in odd-sized mounts (the crop mounts available through some camera clubs), sent loose in film boxes, or individually wrapped in tissues. Use standard mounts, such as those from Kodalux and Fuji labs, and slide pages.

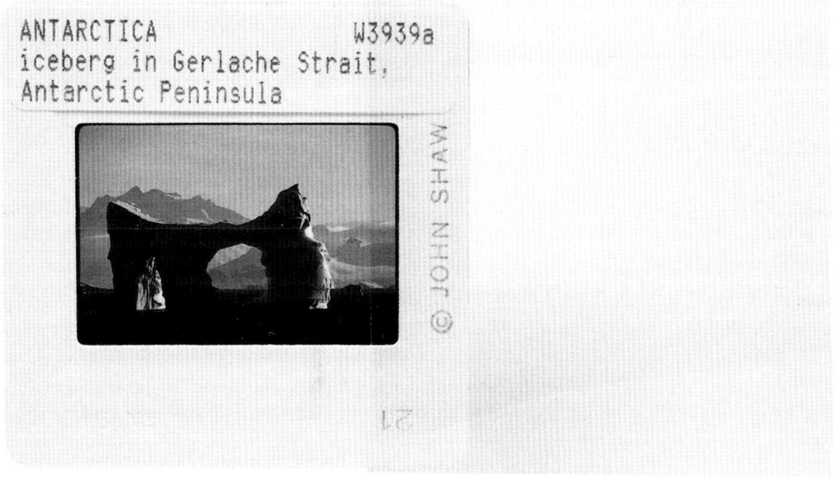

Before I send out a submission I always place each slide in a protective, transparent sleeve. You might notice that this is one of my older computer-generated labels, done on a 24-pin dot-matrix printer.

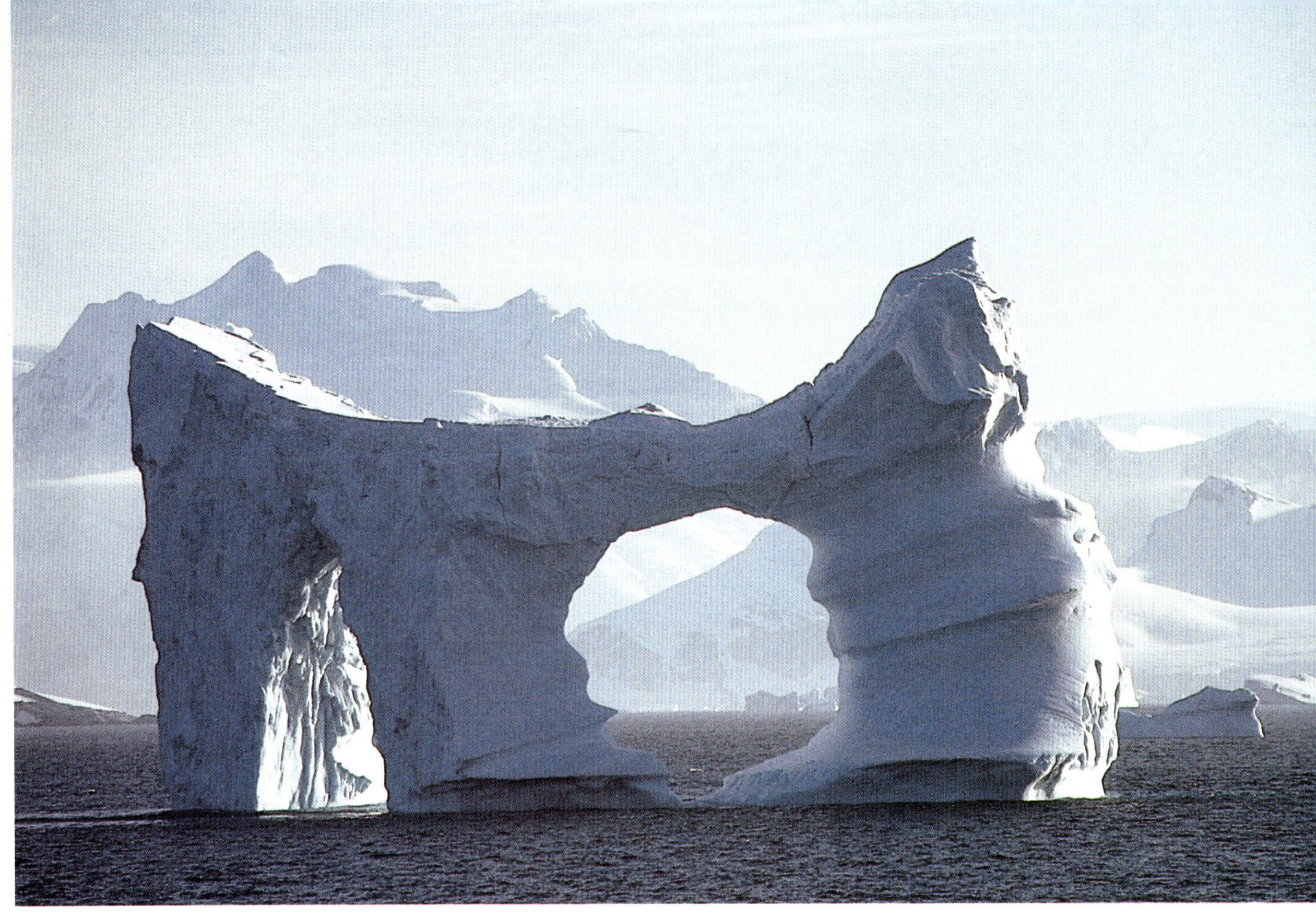

Iceberg in Gerlache Strait, Antarctica. Nikon F4, Nikon 300mm lens, Fujichrome 100.

I shot this picture at a unique moment in time, and it represents quite a bit of effort on my part. I can't go back to the location, reshoot the picture, and duplicate the result. Consequently the film doesn't leave my office without a 2 x 2-inch protective sleeve and careful packaging.

Assembling the Package

Your submission is now sleeved and neatly arranged in slide pages. The next step is to package everything. The easiest way I know is to place the slide pages between two sheets of corrugated cardboard cut to the same size as the pages. Then crisscross two rubber bands catty-cornered to hold the package together. Presto, you have a firmly protected but easy-to-open sandwich of cardboard and slides. No knives or scissors have to be used to get into the package. (Unfortunately, all too often you'll receive the same sandwich back with about 30 yards of sealing tape wrapped around it. Major surgery is the only solution to extracting the film.)

Next, place the cardboard slide package in a sturdy mailing envelope. For additional protection, most photographers use cardboard mailing flats; I buy mine from the Calumet Carton Company in two sizes (see page 138). I then attach a mailing label with my business return address to the outside, and then ship the submission.

For me 9 times out of 10 this means sending the package via the United States Postal Service, certified with a return receipt requested. Using certified mail means I can prove that I mailed the parcel; requesting a return receipt means the recipient has to sign for the submission. I would strongly urge you to ask for return receipts and to save them until the client returns all of your chromes. This way you have a paper trail to prove that the client received the submission.

You might be asking "Why not send submissions via registered mail, which is traceable?" and "What about insurance?" After 25 years in business sending submissions certified, I've never had a package lost in the mail. Not one. I use certified mail since it seems to work, and it costs less than registered mail. On the other hand, registered mail travels under lock and key in its own separate mailbag, and it is signed for at every point along the way.

Only registered mail can be insured. I see little point in insuring packages since, unless you can prove the market value of each slide in the package, you can insure only for the replacement value of the film itself. That means you'll collect about 50 cents per slide, roughly what the insurance costs you in the first place.

At times you'll want to use other carriers besides the United States mail. UPS, Airborne Express, Federal Express, and other services are all alternatives. I urge you to set up a courier account with whichever company best services your area. I use Federal Express; establishing an account didn't cost me anything, and all expenses are charged against my business credit card.

(By the way, if a client calls you requesting a photograph, always ask "May I bill this submission to your Federal Express account?" You might as well have the client pick up the business overhead. If the customer tells you the account number, write it down on the company's Rolodex card for the future. Use it only when you have permission to do so, and don't give out the number to anyone else.)

The Cover Letter

You should always include two more items in the package with your slides: a cover letter and a delivery memo. At times these may be one and the same. A cover letter is just that, a letter on your stationery telling the recipients why they're getting the submission. This can be as simple as one sentence:

> Dear Bill:
> Here are the photographs we talked about last Tuesday.
> Sincerely,
>
> John Shaw

Alternately, the cover letter can be as thorough and complete as you want it to be. Don't assume that busy editors will remember notes they sent you a month ago giving you permission to submit. Remind them.

The Delivery Memo

You should always also include a delivery memo, which is sometimes called a *consignment* or *transmittal memo*, with any submission, no matter how large or how small the submission. It doesn't matter if I send out 200 slides or just 1, I put a delivery memo inside. This is a packing list of what you're sending to the picture editor. Whether the delivery memo is on your letterhead or is a separate business form, it should at the very least give a count of the number of photographs in the package, indicate the format (35mm, 6 x 7cm, etc.), and state if the images are transparencies or black-and-white prints.

The total count is important. What if you send out 20 slides, and the client returns only 19, saying that was the total received. If my photographs are indeed valuable, then I want a paper trail of accountability.

Ideally, you should describe the photographs on the delivery memo. To be useful, the description should have some identifying information. For example, suppose you're sending out some of your mammal shots. If your delivery memo simply states "100 raccoon photographs and 100 bear photographs" then how can either you or the picture editor tell specifically which photos are in the package?

This is where my Nutshell database program, the same one I use for my slide collection, comes back into play. In a file called "Submissions," I've set up a format for my delivery memo. I just fill in the blanks on this form, and then print it onto my letterhead. The front of the page looks similar to the illustration below.

When you look at this form, you notice that right at the top it states that "original transparencies" are enclosed. Ordinarily I send out all originals; the rare times I send duplicates they're noted as such. I strongly

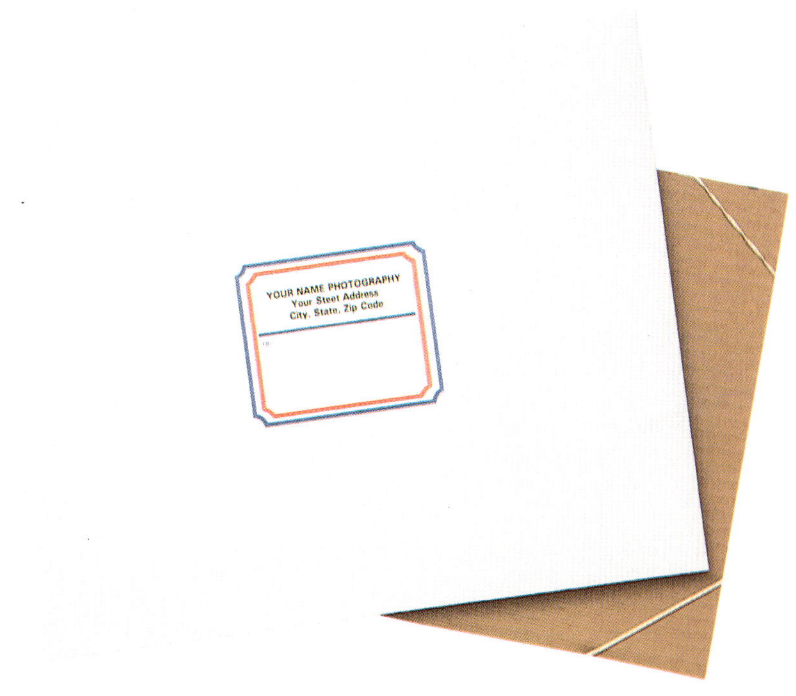

Here is a picture submission and documentation sandwiched between cardboard sheets, ready to be inserted into a cardboard mailing flat.

urge you to use the phrase "original transparencies" on your delivery memo. I once had a client lose some transparencies; its agent said to me, "Why should we pay you anything for this loss? These were only dupes, and you can easily have more made." The agent quickly changed his mind when I pointed out that my delivery memo plainly said "original transparencies" in bold print.

"Transparencies" is a count of the images enclosed. For example, I might send 17 35mm color, 9 6 x 7cm color, and 5 6 x 17cm panoramics. "Shipped via" is obvious: United States mail, Federal Express, etc. "Subject" is a reference as to why the editor is receiving the package; for example, I might write "Wolf photos as per telephone conversation of 11/19" or "Photographs for mushroom article." After I fill in the date and the name of the person or company I'm sending the package to, I simply type in the file numbers of the slides. I list these in the order in which the slides are arranged on the pages. In other words, I create a packing list of exactly what is being sent, and each and every individual piece of film is identified by its file number.

(Another method of keeping track of submissions is to use a personal copier. Simply place a sheet of transparencies face down on the copier, with a 200-watt bulb in a reflector a few inches above the slide page. As you run the copier, the light bulb shines through the slide page. Your final copy sheet shows both the all-important slide-label information and a recognizable image.)

Next, I print two hard copies of this list. I also keep the record in my computer's "Submissions" file. I put one printout in the package for the editor and file the other in a notebook in my office. Usually editors pull some shots and return the rest of the film. As slides come back into the office, I delete their numbers from the delivery memo in the computer. Any slide listed in the "Submissions" computer file is at an editor's office, not mine.

Taking Inventory

I also inventory the returned slides on the hard copy of the delivery memo that I kept; using a felt marker, I yellow out the slide numbers. I can easily read the numbers through the marker color, but I can tell at a glance exactly which images the client is still holding. Pretty high-tech procedure, right? When I receive a shot that was bought and published, I use a blue marker over the slide number to indicate a sale. So numbers on my printed copy are either unmarked (still being held), yellow (not used, but returned to me), or blue (used

J O H N   S H A W

PHOTOGRAPHY

DELIVERY OF ORIGINAL TRANSPARENCIES
SEE TERMS ON REVERSE

Transparencies: ____________________

____

Shipped via: ____________________

Subject: ____________________

Date: __________

To: ____________________

____

____

____

File numbers:

____

____

____

____

____

____

On this version of my delivery memo, I make it clear at the very beginning that I'm sending original transparencies, not dupes.

and returned). I save all of my delivery memos so I can tell who bought what; in fact, I have old delivery memos going back about 15 years.

I do all of this work for two reasons. First is service to the customer. If an editor calls me looking for a specific photograph, I search my database for the file number of that shot. If the editor saw the photograph published previously, I simply look at the old delivery memos kept under that client's name to find what was bought. The rest is simple. The slide is either in-house or out-of-house. If I have the slide, it was filed by sequential number and, thus, easy to find. I pick the telephone back up, and I've made a sale.

If the slide isn't in my office, I use Nutshell to search the "Submissions" file; it tells me who has the image. Both the editor calling and the client with my film are probably located in New York, since so many publishers are there. So I telephone and say, "Send a messenger across town to pick up my film. I'll call and release it to your messenger, and then fax you a delivery memo." The editor stays on the telephone throughout this. Again I've made a sale based on immediate service to the client.

Another reason I carefully track slide numbers and submissions is a worst-case scenario. If all of my slides aren't returned or accounted for, I can specifically describe what is missing thanks to the information in my database, which is keyed to the slide file number. I can say, "There is one slide missing from this return. It is a horizontal shot of the Teton Range from the Snake River Overlook." I've rarely needed to resort to doing this, but on those few occasions my record-keeping has proved its worth.

When published slides are returned, you must have a procedure to get them back into your file as soon as possible. They'll once again be available to editors. This involves three steps. First, physically keep all returned slides separate from your good file until you process them. When slides come back into my office, I immediately check off the film numbers on both the hard copy of the delivery memo and on the computer file. I then place the slides in a "returns" section of a file cabinet. If any question arises about a returned shot or if I need a specific picture again immediately, I know it has been physically refiled or is still in this one drawer.

Also, make sure all the film is yours. Always check all returns by actually looking at the image on film, and not just by any information on the mount. Granted this doesn't happen often, but a few times I've had other photographers' film come back in my mounts. I've also had my film returned to me in someone else's mounts. And I've actually had slides returned that weren't mine and had nothing to do with my office. Carefully check all material as it is returned. Mixups can usually be easily straightened out, so long as the process is started soon after a publishing job is completed. Editors will remember which photographers' images they were viewing soon afterward, but they probably won't nine months later.

The second step involves inspecting all film for scratches, fingerprints, and damage. I learned an easy way to do this a long time ago. Place a black card about 3 x 5 inches big on your lightbox. Hold your film about 12 inches above this card, positioned so that the image lines up with the card. With the lightbox turned on you'll be able to see scratches not readily apparent otherwise.

The last part of the process calls for you to clean, remount, and relabel all the slides. Inevitably some fingerprints and other marks will get on film. Now that Kodak Film Cleaner is no longer available (if anyone has a supply, call me!), use 98 percent or better denatured alcohol on a soft cotton cloth to swab the film. Then remount your slides in the correct orientation, label and name-stamp them again, and refile them in the correct location in your active file.

DELIVERY-MEMO TERMS

When you send photographs to a client you're almost always loaning them the actual pieces of film. Very rarely with natural history subjects will you sell the individual piece of film and its image outright. The client is leasing some sort of specific usage of your picture, but you still own the image on the film and the film itself. If you own it and it's valuable and you're loaning it out, I would certainly have some terms as to the recipient's responsibilities.

If you look at my delivery-memo form, you'll see that right under "Delivery of Original Transparencies" comes the phrase "See Terms on Reverse." Your actual terms can be as casual or as legally complicated as you want them to be. I think that even the most basic delivery-memo terms need to cover at least two points. These are what the client can and can't do with a photograph, and what happens in the event of damage or loss of the photograph. After that, it is up to you to decide how hard-nosed you want to be.

Based on my more than 25 years of selling stock photography, I've found that most nature-photography markets are staffed by decent, careful, hardworking people. Editors and picture researchers aren't sitting out there just waiting to rip off your work or to trash it. They need you and value you, and likewise you need them and should value them. I wouldn't be too tough or mean when dealing with them.

DELIVERY MEMO

Date: ____________

To: ____________

Number of Transparencies: ____________

Subject: ____________

Description of photos:

TERMS OF DELIVERY OF ORIGINAL TRANSPARENCIES

1. All photos are submitted on a 30 day approval basis. A Holding Fee of $1 per day per slide will be charged for all unused transparencies held longer than 30 days unless additional time is asked for and granted.

2. Recipient is liable for damage or loss of transparencies. Payment for loss or damage will be at least three times the client's maximum One Time Use rate.

3. Recipient agrees that the person accepting photos herein is authorized to do so, and in so doing agrees to the terms set forth above.

Here you see my basic delivery memo with terms at the bottom.

Having said that, I still can't imagine sending out any transparencies without some sort of delivery memo included. A picture buyer knows that when packages arrive without any paperwork, they are either from rank beginners or from photographers who don't value their own work. Don't rely on friendly relations with a client and skip the paperwork. After all, most marriages start out as friendly unions, but the malice of divorce court is proof of what can happen.

Oral agreements between photographers and clients often create confusion, misunderstanding, and disagreement, which can lead to you losing a client forever. Put all your terms in writing on your stationery or letterhead with your name, address, and telephone and fax numbers all prominently displayed. Now there are no questionable areas.

I must repeat a warning: *Never, never, never send unsolicited, original photographs to a prospective client.* As far as the recipient is concerned, unsolicited submissions—including your most precious, one-of-a-kind shots—are the equivalent of junk mail and can be tossed in the trash with no liability.

So what exactly should be specified in these terms? That is the subject of a lot of discussion in the photographic community. I believe that nature photographers comprise a special segment of all working photographers and deal with a select group of photo buyers. I don't think standardized terms fit the needs of all photographers perfectly, nor do I think terms based on the commercial/advertising markets fit the nature market. Work up your own terms of delivery based on what you think is best suited for your position. Consider the following suggestions, but—here comes my legal disclaimer—I'm rendering no legal opinion whatsoever about their application.

Here is a copy of my own very first delivery memo, including the terms (left). I no longer use this memo, having gone to more complex and limiting terms. However, I experienced no problems while using them. Feel free to use this form if you want, keeping in mind my legal disclaimer.

Paragraph 1 essentially says that the client has 30 days to decide if it wants to use the photographs. If the client holds any slides longer than 30 days, doesn't actually use the pictures, and hasn't asked permission to keep holding them, then $1 per day per slide will be billed.

I've sold these three shots several times over. All submissions from my office are tracked through a delivery memo and printed terms.

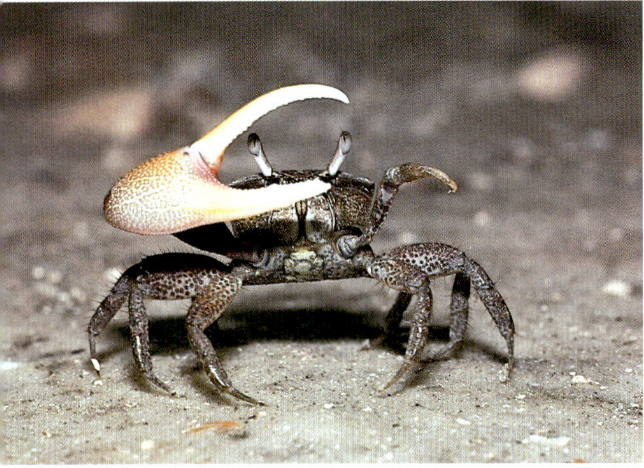

Fiddler crab, Florida. Nikon F2, Nikon 105mm macro lens, Kodachrome 25.

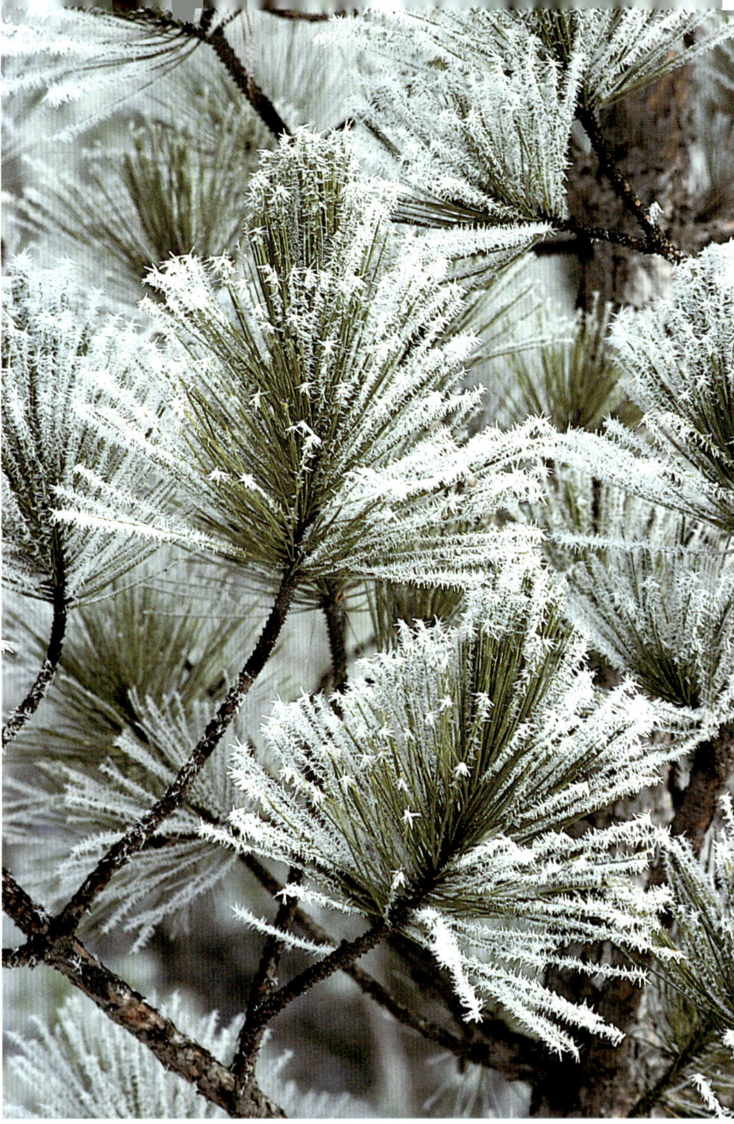

Frost on red pine, Michigan. Nikon F2, Nikon 105mm macro lens, Kodachrome 25.

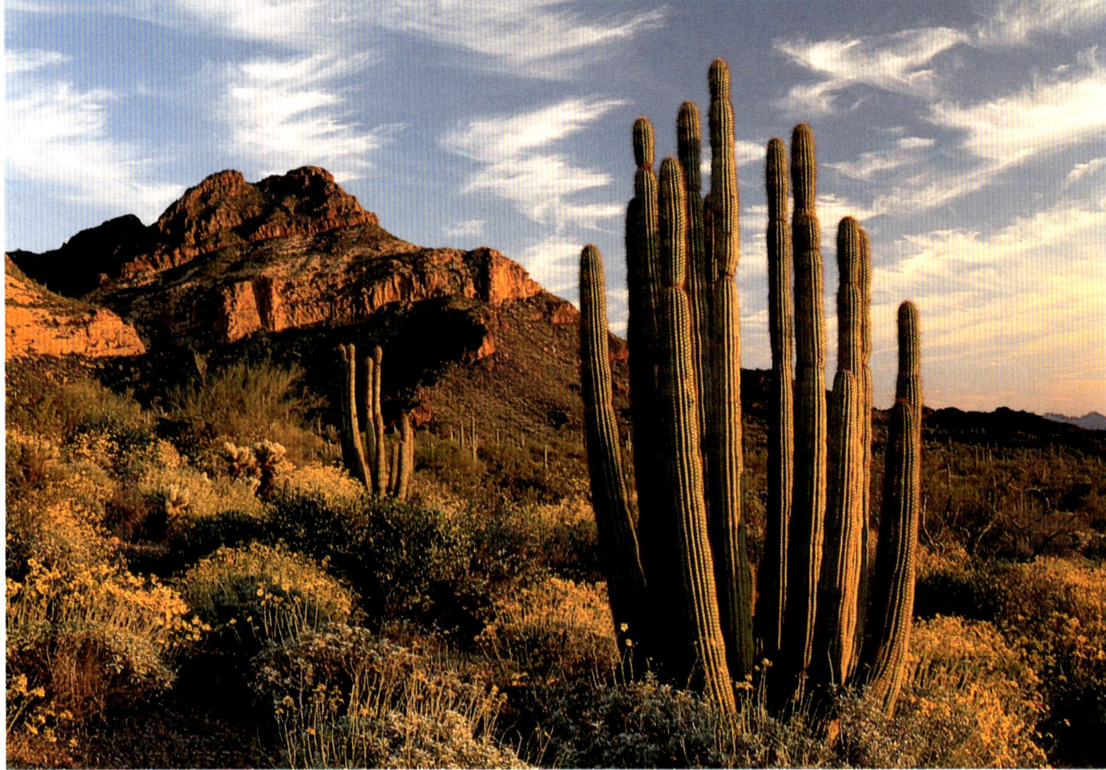

Brittlebush and cacti, Ajo Mountains, Organ Pipe Cactus National Monument, Arizona. Nikon F4, Nikon 35-70mm zoom lens, Fuji Velvia.

Is this enforceable with most nature-photography markets? No. In fact, if you really try to collect this amount, if you actually start billing after 30 days, you'll most likely never do business with that client again.

Part of the reasoning here lies with the most common end users of nature photography, the editorial markets of magazines and books. Almost all magazines are working at least 6 months ahead, if not more. Books minimally take about 12 months of preparation, and most likely 18 to 24 months if the images are solicited from many photographers. It is completely unrealistic to ask these clients to make up their minds within 30 days as to which, if any, of your photographs they'll be using. Editors need to hold your material until the time when final layouts can be completed.

Just for the record, the longest I've ever had photographs held was seven years. Yes, you read those words correctly: seven *years*. The client was a prestigious publication that was published every other month. My photo essay had a strong seasonal theme, and each year it kept getting pushed back and pushed back. I reasoned that as long as no one else immediately needed the pictures simply leaving them with the picture editor was easiest. Besides, it gave me a reason to call and chat with the editor every so often.

Actually, those talks led to better opportunities. Every time I called I mentioned what I'd been shooting and proposed new ideas. I had quite a few photographs published with that client in those seven intervening years. To be truthful when my long-held shots were finally run, I was almost embarrassed to see them in print. By that time I had far better photographs in my file.

So why include the "holding fee" section? If your client objects to the clause, you should graciously waive the fee. Now you've done the client a favor and consequently are perceived as a good guy. On the other hand if the client offers to pay it, you should smile and take the money. Additionally if you need to do so you can always use the holding fee as a bargaining chip.

Once a prospective customer just kept on holding a large submission of my photographs. I hadn't waived the holding fee, and the project was delayed endlessly. When it became obvious to me that the undertaking was at a dead end, I asked for my film to be returned. Nothing happened. A series of telephone calls and letters produced the repetitive response that my entire submission was sitting on a desk and would be shipped back to me the next day. Day

STOCK PHOTO DELIVERY MEMO

TO:

DATE:

The enclosed material, listed below, is submitted for examination ONLY. Photography may not be reproduced, copied, projected, or publicly displayed without express written permission of photographer's invoice, stating the rights granted and the terms thereof. The use of this material as artist's or photographer's reference is specifically prohibited.

TERMS OF DELIVERY

1. Please check count and acknowledge by signing and returning one copy.
2. Submission is conditioned on return of all delivered items safely and undamaged.
3. Reimbursement for loss or damage shall be valued at $________________.
4. Objection to above terms must be made in writing within ten days of receipt of memo. Holding material constitutes acceptance of above terms which incorporate hereby Article 2 of the Uniform Commercial Code and the Copyright Act of 1976.

Received by: ____

Date: ____/____/____

This is a very formal delivery memo with terms.

TERMS OF PHOTO DELIVERY

1. The enclosed photos are for your examination and consideration for future use. We expect this will take a reasonable length of time, up to 30 days. Let us know if you need longer for consideration, otherwise we charge a holding fee.

2. These images represent our best photos for your proposed use. Please treat the photos as though handling valuable papers, cash or similar items. They are worth a great deal over a lifetime of sales. Do Not Project original slides, as they will fade, scratch and damage. Please use signed return receipts and insurance when shipping.

3. Our rates are based on each use, media placement, print quantity, market and similar items. Let us know your planned uses and we'll outline the costs. We understand budgets and value long-term business.

4. We own the copyrights to these images, which remain with us unless negotiated and stated otherwise on our invoice. Your use rights are granted upon payment of our invoice. Nonpayment is an infringement of our copyright. You are expected to provide copyright protection for us, at no charge, for each use. You accept full liability for all uses and indemnify us against all claims for any improper, illegal or outrageous uses. We maintain the right to use these photos in our own promotions and to resell generic and similar images.

5. Model and property released images say so on the mounts.

6. We're in business to sell pictures, not to collect for damage or loss. However, if images are lost or damaged, you are liable to us for their full value.

7. We want to do business with you. If there are questions, please call or fax immediately. No matter how serious a problem, we'd like to discuss and settle it directly with you. Of course, if this doesn't work out, we retain the option of arbitration or other legal action.

Your consideration of my work is appreciated!

(Photo delivery receipt reverse side)

The terms of delivery that photographer/writer Cliff Hollenbeck uses are a great starting point.

after day the slides never appeared. By this time I just wanted my film back. Finally I sent a personal delivery memo in the form of a note to the picture editor, an invoice in her name for $96,000 as the holding-fee charges that had accrued, and a photocopy of her signature on the return receipt. My slides were delivered via Federal Express the very next day.

Paragraph 2 is fairly straightforward: You break it, you've bought it. But reread that second sentence. Here the memo states that for loss or damage the client will be charged "at least (*if not more* is, of course, the implied parenthetical phrase to be inserted here) three times the client's maximum One Time Use rate." What is the maximum one-time-use rate? Payment for the cover.

Suppose the cover rate is $500. Paragraph 2 says that the charge will be at least three times $500, which translates into at least $1,500. If you actually set a figure—and $1,500 has certainly held up in the courts as a stipulated value per image—you might scare off some potential customers in the smaller markets.

Paragraph 3 comes right to the point. Holding of the submission constitutes acceptance of the terms. I don't think this section requires any more explanation.

I've seen some delivery memos in use that are variations of this one. Rod Planck,

This is a copy of a delivery-memo form that photographer Rohn Engh of PhotoSource International uses.

Place your name and address here.....

STOCK PICTURE DELIVERY/INVOICE

TO:

Date:
Subject:
Purchase Order No.:
Client:
A.D./Editor
Shooting Date(s)
Our Job No.:

___Assignment Confirmation ___Job Estimate ___Invoice

RIGHTS GRANTED	MEDIA USAGE			
One-time non exclusive reproduction rights to the photographs listed below, solely for the uses and specifications indicated; and limited to the individual edition, volume, series, show, event, or the like contemplated for this specific transaction (unless otherwise indicated in writing). SPECIFICATIONS (if applicable).	ADVERTISING		EDITL/JOURNALISM	
	Animatic	☐	Book Jacket	☐
	Billboard	☐	Consumer Mag	☐
	Brochure	☐	Encyclopedia	☐
	Catalog	☐	Film Strip	☐
	Consumer Mag	☐	Newspaper	☐
	Newspaper	☐	Sun Supplement	☐
	Packaging	☐	Television	☐
	Pt of Purchase	☐	Text Book	☐
	Television	☐	Trade Book	☐
	Trade Magazine	☐	Trade Magazine	☐
	Other	☐	Other	☐
	CORP/INDUSTRIAL		PROMOTION & MISC.	
	Album Cover	☐	Booklet	☐
	Annual Report	☐	Brochure	☐
PLACEMENT (Cover, inside, etc.) ______	Brochure	☐	Calendar	☐
SIZE (½ pg., 1 pg., etc.) ______	Film Strip	☐	Card	☐
TIME LIMIT ON USE ______	House Organ	☐	Poster	☐
USE OUTSIDE U.S. (specify, if any) ______	Trade Slide Show	☐	Press Kit	☐
COPYRIGHT CREDIT: © 19___ ______	Other	☐	Other	☐

DESCRIPTION OF PHOTOGRAPHS Format:	35mm	2¼	4x5	5x7	8x10	Other	USE FEES
							($)
Total B/W Total Color							

If this is a delivery kindly check count & acknowledge by signing & returning one copy. Count shall be considered accurate & quality deemed satisfactory for reproduction if said copy is not immediately received by return mail with all exceptions duly noted.

SUBJECT TO TERMS ON REVERSE SIDE PURSUANT TO ARTICLE 2, UNIFORM COMMERCIAL CODE AND THE 1976 COPYRIGHT ACT
Acknowledged and Accepted

Signature: ______________________

TOTAL USE FEES: $______
MISCELLANEOUS: ______
Service Fee: ______
Research Fee: ______
Other: ______
TOTAL $______
DEPOSIT: ______
BALANCE DUE: $______

my friend and fellow professional photographer, adds the following terms on his delivery memo (which is reprinted here with his permission):

> Recipient is liable for damage or loss of original transparencies. Payment for loss or damage will be determined by negotiation in good faith based on the uniqueness of the individual photograph. Settlement shall be no lower than $250.00 and no greater than $1,500.00 per image.

Planck also occasionally sends out reproduction-grade duplicates made on 70mm film. To cover these, his memo states:

> Recipient is liable for damage or loss of 70mm repro-dupes. Payment for loss or damage will be limited to $10.00 per image.

Only you can decide exactly what terms and conditions you want to include on your memo. As stated earlier, from my own experience I can state that the markets for nature photography, especially the editorial ones, are fundamentally different from most commercial markets. In many ways this is a niche business; it is small, specialized, and intimate. There are, unfortunately, far fewer markets for nature photography than for the broad field of general

STOCK PICTURE DELIVERY/INVOICE

Terms and Conditions

(1) Except where outright purchase is specified, all photographs and rights not expressly granted remain the exclusive property of Photographer without limitation. Client acquires only the rights specified and agrees to return all photographs by the sooner of thirty (30) days after publication or four (4) months after invoice date, or pay thereafter Five Dollars ($5.00) per week per transparency and One Dollar ($1.00) per week per print.

(2) Submission and use rights granted are specifically based on the condition that client assumes insurers liability to (a) indemnify photographer for loss, damage, or misuse of any photograph(s) and (b) return all photographs prepaid and fully insured, safe and undamaged, by bonded messenger, air freight, or registered mail. Client assumes full liability for its employees, agents, assigns, messenger, and freelance researchers for any loss, damage, or misuse of the photographs.

(3) Reimbursement by Client for loss or damage of each original transparency shall be in the amount of One Thousand Five Hundred Dollars ($1,500), or such other amount set forth next to said item on the front hereof. Reimbursement by Client for loss or damage of each other item shall be in the amount set forth next to said item on the front hereof. Photographer and Client agree that said amount represents the fair and reasonable value of each item, and that Photographer would not sell all rights to such item for less than said amount.

(4) Adjacent credit line for Photographer, and the copyright credit line "© [YEAR OF FIRST PUBLICATION] [PHOTOGRAPHER'S NAME]" must accompany each use, or invoice will be tripled.

(5) Client will indemnify Photographer against all claims, liability, damages, costs, and expenses, including reasonable legal fees and expenses, arising out of the use of any photograph(s) unless a model or other release was specified to exist, in writing, by Photographer. Unless so specified no release exists. Photographer's liability for all claims shall not exceed, in any event, the amount paid under this invoice.

(6) Time is of the essence for receipt of payment and return of photographs. **No rights are granted until payment is made.** Payment required within thirty (30) days of invoice; 2 percent per month service charge on unpaid balance is applied thereafter. Adjustment of amount of terms must be requested within t en days of invoice receipt.

(7) Client shall provide two free copies of uses appearing in print and a semi-annual statement of sales and subsidiary uses for photographs appearing in books.

(8) Client may not assign or transfer this agreement or any rights granted hereunder. Holding or use of the photographs constitutes acceptance of the above terms, which incorporate by reference Article 2 of the Uniform Commercial Code and the Copyright Act of 1976, as amended. No amendment or waiver is binding unless set forth in writing and signed by the parties.

(9) Any dispute regarding this invoice, including its validity, interpretation, performance, or breach shall be arbitrated in [PHOTOGRAPHER'S CITY AND STATE] under rules of the American Arbitration Association and the laws of [STATE OF ARBITRATION]. Judgment on the Arbitration Award may be entered in the highest Federal or State Court having jurisdiction. Any dispute involving One Thousand Five Hundred Dollars ($1,500) or less may be submitted, without arbitration, to any court having jurisdiction thereof. User shall pay all arbitration and court costs, reasonable legal fees and expenses, plus legal interest on any award or judgment.

Note: This delivery memo is based on ASMP Guidelines.

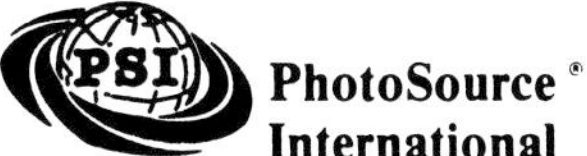

commercial photography. There are also far fewer nature photographers making a living marketing their photographs than there are general photographers. For the most part, nature photography is a close-knit business in that editors and photographers actually know each other. In truth, many working professional nature photographers know each other since they often run into each other on location or at the workshops and programs so many of them conduct. At all such meetings I find that the discussion inevitably turns to shop talk, including any difficulties with picture delivery or handling.

Successful professional photographer Norbert Wu recently made a statement with which I agree:

> I've seen two types of business practices: one which very carefully draws out every detail and pursues every legal detail. The other type cultivates relationships over contracts. I'm sure that either approach has its problems as well as its good points, but I think the more easygoing approach will result in far greater business in the long run.

This doesn't mean that you shouldn't use formal delivery memos and include terms of delivery. Far from it. Not one piece of film goes out of my office without paperwork. But you should definitely tailor your contracts to your clients.

Straight Shooter Studio, Inc.

123 Anystreet, Hometown, ZX 12345 • Telephone: 123-555-1212 • Fax: 123-555-2121

STOCK PHOTOGRAPHY DELIVERY MEMO

Date shipped: ______________ Reference # ______________ Return Images by____________________

Client:

Description of Images:

Qty.	Orig.(O) Dupl.(D)	Format	Photograph Subject/ID No.	Value (if other than $1,500/item) In event of loss/damage

Total Count: ________________

Title in the copyright to all images created or supplied pursuant to this agreement will remain the sole and exclusive property of the photographer. There is no assignment of copyright title, agreement to do work for hire, or intention of joint copyright expressed or implied hereunder. The client is licensed only by subsequent written license on an invoice. Proper copyright notice, which reads: © 19___ Straight Shooter, must be displayed with the following placement: __________________. Notice is not required if placement is not specified. Omission of required notice results in loss to the licenser and will be billed at triple the invoiced fee.

Check count and acknowledge receipt by signing and returning one copy. Count shall be considered accurate and quality deemed satisfactory for reproduction if said copy is not immediately received by return mail with all exceptions duly noted. Photographs must be returned by registered mail, air courier or other bonded messenger which provides proof of return.

SUBJECT TO ALL TERMS AND CONDITIONS ABOVE AND ON REVERSE SIDE

________________________________ ____________________

ACKNOWLEDGED AND ACCEPTED DATE

(Please sign here)

Your acceptance of this delivery constitutes your acceptance of all terms and conditions on both sides of this memo, whether signed by you or not.

TERMS AND CONDITIONS
FOR STOCK PHOTOGRAPHY DELIVERY MEMO

[1] "Image(s)" means all viewable renditions furnished by Photographer hereunder, whether captured or stored in photographic, magnetic, optical or any other medium whatsoever.

[2] Submission is for examination only. Images may not be reproduced, copied, projected, or used in any way without (a) express written permission on Photographer's invoice stating the rights granted and the terms thereof and (b) payment of said invoice. The reasonable and stipulated fee for any other use shall be three times Photographer's normal fee for such usage.

[3] All Images and rights therein, including copyright, remain the sole and exclusive property of Photographer. Unless otherwise provided herein, any grant of rights is limited to one (1) year from the date hereof and to the territory of the United States.

[4] Client assumes insurer's liability (a) to indemnify Photographer for loss, damage, or misuse of any Images, and (b) to return all Images prepaid and fully insured, safe and undamaged, by bonded messenger, air freight, or registered mail, within thirty (30) days after the first use thereof as provided herein, but in all events (whether published or unpublished) within thirty (30) days after the date of final licensed use. Client assumes full liability for its principals, employees, agents, affiliates, successors and assigns (including without limitation independent contractors, messengers and freelance researchers) for any loss, damage, delay in returning, or misuse of the Images.

[5] After 14 days, the following holding fees are charged until return: Five Dollars ($5.00) per week per color transparency and One Dollar ($1.00) per week per print.

[6] Reimbursement by Client for loss or damage of each original photographic transparency or film negative shall be in the amount of One Thousand Five Hundred Dollars ($1,500), or such other amount set forth next to said item on the attached schedule and/or on the face hereof. Reimbursement by Client for loss or damage of each other item shall be in the amount set forth next to said item on the attached schedule and/or on the face hereof. Photographer and Client agree that said amount represents the fair and reasonable value of each item, and that Photographer would not sell all rights to such item for less than said amount. Client understands that each original photographic transparency and film negative is unique and does not have an exact duplicate, and may be impossible to replace or re-create.

[7] Photographer shall receive credit for Images as specified on the face hereof unless no placement is specified.

OPTION: [8A] Client will not make or permit any alterations, including but not limited to additions, or subtractions or adaptations in respect of the Images, alone or with any other material. **OR**

[8B] Client may not make or permit any alterations, including but not limited to additions, subtractions or adaptations in respect of the Images, alone or with any other material, except that cropping, and alterations of contrast, brightness and color balance, consistent with reproduction needs may be made. **OR**

[8C] Client may make or permit any alterations, including but not limited to additions, subtractions or adaptations in respect of the Images alone or with any other material, subject to the provisions as stated in [9] below.

[9] Client will indemnify and defend Photographer against all claims, liability, damages, costs, and expenses, including reasonable legal fees and expenses, arising out of any use of any Images for which no release was furnished by Photographer, or any Images which are altered by Client. Unless furnished, no release exists. Photographer's liability for all claims shall not exceed in any event the total amount paid under this invoice.

[10] Client may not assign or transfer this agreement or any rights granted hereunder. This agreement binds and inures to the benefit of Photographer, Client, Client's principals, employees, agents and affiliates, and their respective heirs, legal representatives, successors and assigns. Client and its principals, employees, agents and affiliates are jointly and severally liable for the performance of all payments and other obligations hereunder. No amendment or waiver of any terms is binding unless set forth in writing and signed by the parties. However, the invoice may reflect, and Client is bound by, oral authorizations for fees or expenses which could not be confirmed in writing because of insufficient time of shooting. This agreement incorporates by reference Article 2 of the Uniform Commercial Code, and the Copyright Act of 1976, as amended.

OPTION: [11A] Except as provided in (12) below any dispute regarding this agreement shall be arbitrated in [PHOTOGRAPHER'S CITY AND STATE] under rules of the American Arbitration Association and the laws of [STATE OF ARBITRATION]. Judgment on the arbitration award may be entered in any court having jurisdiction. Any dispute involving $____[LIMIT OF LOCAL SMALL CLAIMS COURT] or less may be submitted without arbitration to any court having jurisdiction thereof. Client shall pay all arbitration and court costs, Photographer's reasonable legal fees, and expenses, and legal interest on any award or judgment in the event of any award or judgment in favor of Photographer. **OR**

[11B] Except as provided in [12] below, any dispute regarding this agreement shall be adjudicated in [PHOTOGRAPHER'S CITY AND STATE] under the laws of [STATE]. Client shall pay all court costs, Photographer's reasonable legal fees, and expenses, and legal interest on any award or judgment in the event of any award or judgment in favor of Photographer. **OR**

[11C] Except as provided in (12) below any dispute regarding this agreement shall be, at Photographer's sole discretion, either (1) arbitrated in (USE 11A LANGUAGE), or (2) adjudicated in (USE 11B LANGUAGE).

[12] Client hereby expressly consents to the jurisdiction of the Federal courts with respect to claims by Photographer under the Copyright Act of 1976, as amended.

Without a doubt, you can find the most complete treatment of delivery memos and terms in Formalizing Agreements, *a 1995 ASMP publication. Here are two examples of ASMP forms.*

CHAPTER FIVE

WRITING AND PUBLISHING

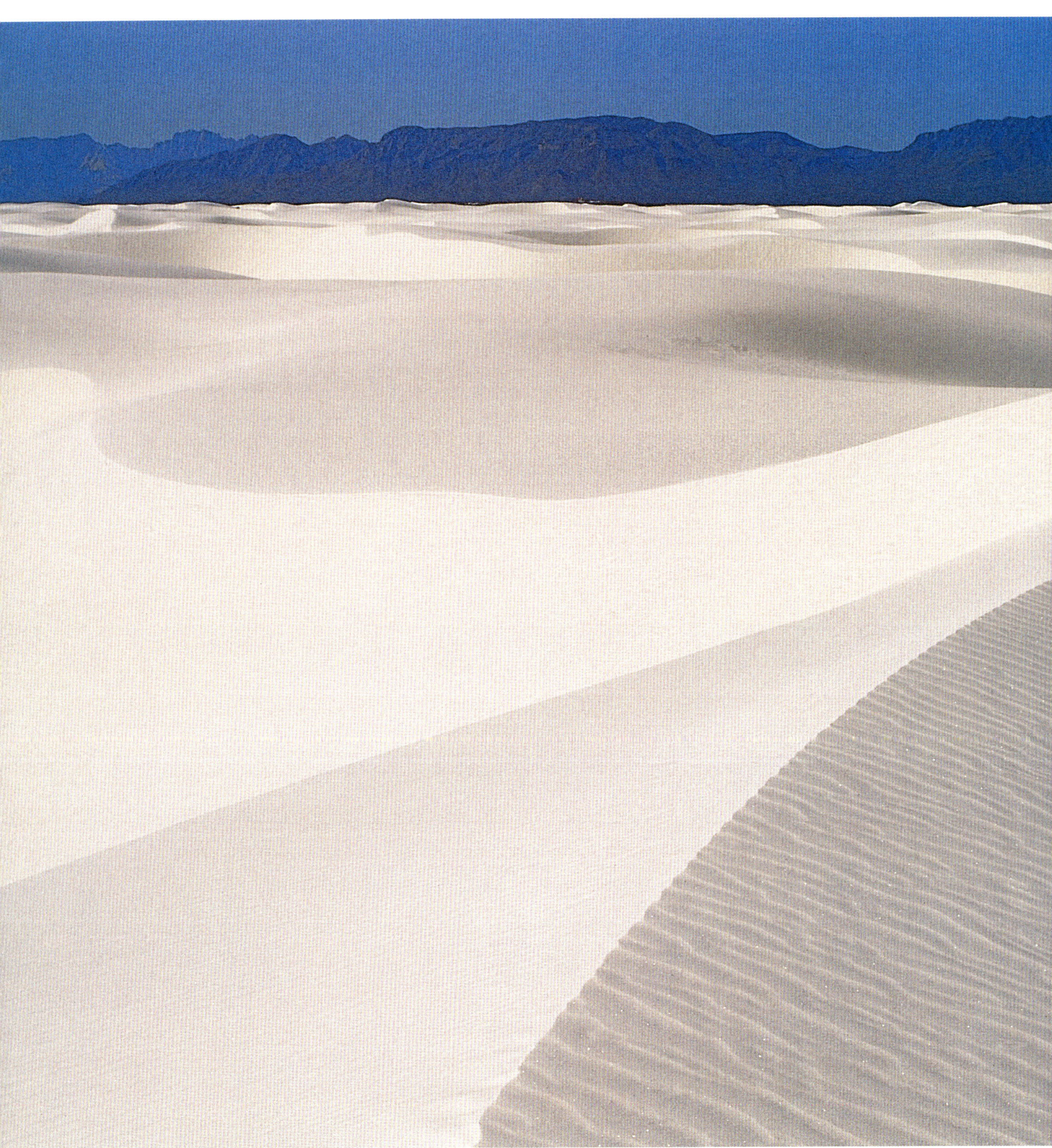

White gypsum sand dunes, White Sands National Monument, New Mexico.

BREAKING INTO THE BUSINESS

When you're first starting to try to market your photography, it is very difficult to sell individual pictures. You probably don't have the thousands of photographs in your file—the broad coverage of a lot of subjects—that book publishers need. The obvious markets for individual shots, the calendar and card companies that use stand-alone photographs, are far too often a once-a-year possible sale. You might think that the magazine market is left, but magazines rarely print a single photograph all by itself.

Suppose you have the greatest fall-foliage shot you've ever seen and decide to send it to a magazine. What will the editors do with the picture? If by pure chance they have a fall-color piece scheduled, and if by chance they need a photograph for the article and your shot fits their criteria, then the magazine might use your shot. But if there is no specific reason to use a single shot, no concrete rational for publishing the photograph, then no matter how great the shot might be it probably won't be published. A few magazines do have a one-picture feature. For example, *Natural History* publishes a photograph called the "Natural Moment." But even with a monthly potential market, your sales are limited to only 12 chances per year. Selling single pictures isn't a good way to get started.

I'm firmly convinced that *the very best way* to break into professional nature photography is to write an article to accompany your photographs. In other words, create a vehicle to carry the pictures. Magazines need articles. Almost all the content of magazines that incorporate natural-history material is obtained from freelancers, not from staff members. You might as well be one of these freelancers. By offering a package you'll be helping the editors fill out their issues, and at the same time you'll be publishing several photographs. You'll also actually be getting paid for the text in addition to the photographs used.

You don't have to be a professional author to write a magazine story. Most publications will work with you to shape the words into what they want, so long as the basic concept and construction are acceptable to them. Stylistically, don't write in the passive voice, don't refer to yourself as "the author," and don't use large words when simple, straightforward ones will work. Write so the text sounds like a letter to your mother, and definitely not like a tax form. The following is an example of bad writing: "It was then determined by your author that the peregrinations of the gargantuan, bovine mammal circumnavigated the mead." What was that again? Be clear and direct: write "The big cow walked around the meadow."

I believe that it is better, or at least easier, to think of yourself not as a writer, but rather as a photographer who writes. If each individual word in your story is precious to you, you'll have problems with editing since all text must fit into allotted column space. Also, your text style must conform with the magazine's preference. Just as serious photographers don't like to see their images cropped, real writers don't like having words changed or deleted.

How you physically present your story is pretty basic. All manuscripts should be typed or printed, double-spaced, with at least 1-inch margins all around the page. Once again I'll urge you to get a computer along with a full-featured word-processing program. Writing and editing text are far easier to do on a computer than on a typewriter. I know this from experience. My first book was actually written on a manual typewriter. Since then I've worked with WordPerfect on my computer, and the contrast in ease of writing is like the difference between night and day.

If you can't write a sentence in standard grammatical form, take an adult-education course in basic writing. I know this doesn't sound like fun. In fact my advice to write in order to sell photographs is starting to sound like work. Well, the business of nature photography is just that, a business you must work hard at. While you're taking that adult-ed class, you should also learn to touch-type if you missed picking up that skill at some point during your education.

Print your manuscript on good-quality, white, standard-letter-sized office-supply bond paper. If you're typing or using a dot-matrix printer, make sure you use a new ribbon (black ink, of course). If at all possible, you should avoid using a 9-pin dot-matrix printer because the output can be difficult to read. At the bare minimum, you should work with a 24-pin printer in its "letter-quality" mode, never in "draft" mode. A far better choice would be to buy an inkjet or laser printer for your office. Remember that to some degree you yourself will be judged by the presentation of your work.

A real godsend in most serious word-processing programs is the "spelling-checker" feature. Editors don't like to see dozens of misspelled words in a manuscript. If you don't have access to such a program, pick up a "speller" book and keep it on your desk. This is simply an alphabetical list of words correctly spelled and syllabicated; it is like a dictionary without definitions.

Some grammatical problems are sure to arise in your writing, such as the old "two/to/too" and "there/their/they're" confusion. Text editors will tolerate a few grammar faults (or at least I trust they will since I continually have problems with "that" and "which." Is it "the photographs *which* book publishers need" or "the photographs *that* book publishers need"?). You must also have standard subject-verb agreement, consistency in verb tenses, and complete punctuated sentences in order to be taken seriously as a writer.

STARTING TO WRITE

When you're first starting to try to market your photography, it's extremely difficult to sell individual pictures. You probably don't have the thousands of photographs in your file, the broad coverage of a lot of subjects, which book publishers need. The obvious markets for individual shots, the calendar and card companies that use stand-alone photos, are far too often a once-a-year possible sale. What's left? The magazine market, except magazines rarely print a single photograph all by itself.

Consider this: suppose you have the greatest fall foliage shot you've ever seen. Send it to a magazine and what will they do with the picture? If by pure chance they have a fall color piece scheduled, and if by chance they need a photo for the article and your shot fits their criteria, then the magazine might use your shot. But if there is no specific reason to use a single shot, no concrete rational for publishing the photo, then no matter how great the shot might be it probably won't be published. A few magazines do have a one-picture feature. *Natural History*, for example, has a photo called the "Natural Moment." But consider that even published monthly, your potential sales are limited to only 12 chances per year. Selling single pictures is not how to get started.

I am firmly convinced that the very best way to break into professional nature photography is to write an article to accompany your photographs. In other words, create a vehicle to carry the pictures. Magazines need articles. Almost all the content of magazines which use natural history material is obtained from free-

This is a basic manuscript presentation, with good, white bond paper, legible type, double-spaced text, and clean printing.

I want to repeat something I said earlier. I believe that the best way to break into print, and indeed the way to continue selling photographs and consequently get your name known by picture buyers for future sales, is to write articles for magazines. The first picture sale I ever made wasn't a single photograph, but rather a "story" to *National Wildlife* magazine back in the 1960s.

I had very few decent slides in my file, but after reviewing all of my pictures dozens of times, I realized that I did have 20 or so good shots of green things in the spring. I grouped these photographs, and thought and thought until I finally realized I could write about the color green itself. People tend to think of green as a cool, calm, quiet color, but this isn't true in springtime. Then green is alive, vibrant, intense, vivid, and bursting with life! My text was about two manuscript pages, and the pictures showed new beech leaves unfolding, fern fiddleheads, cattails freshly emerged in a swamp, and green darner dragonflies perched on new shoots. The magazine used my text and seven photographs and paid me $500, which at the time seemed like a fortune.

I will also state that years later, when I became quite serious about writing as a means of selling pictures, my gross income doubled within a year. Writing is hard work; there is no doubt about that. I definitely agree with the old adage that I hate writing, but I enjoy having written. After all, my writing helps sell my photographs and enables me do exactly what I want to do: to spend time in the field photographing nature.

QUERY LETTERS

Before you write one word of an article, you should first make sure that a market for your idea actually exists. Notice that I said "idea" here, not "subject." Magazine articles derive from specific ideas, not general topics. "Trees" is a general topic, while "Why Tree Leaves Turn Color in the Autumn" is a precise concept. If indeed there is a market for your idea, you also have to find out specifics about how your client wants the piece. After all, why bother writing a 20,000-word treatise if a magazine wants only 1,000 words and extended captions?

So your very first order of business is to write a query letter. This is exactly what its name suggests: a letter presenting your idea to potential purchasers and inquiring if they would be interested. Address this letter to the magazine editor by name. (You might want to review the section on "Finding Clients," where I talked about obtaining guidelines for writers and photographers. Each publication's guideline should list the editorial address; if it doesn't, check the masthead in a current issue of the magazine.)

A query letter should be to the point. For a magazine article I think it should be a maximum of two pages; one page of two or three paragraphs is much better. You

Here is a copy of the actual query letter that I sent to Outdoor Photographer *magazine concerning an article on the Pribilof Islands.*

J O H N S H A W

P H O T O G R A P H Y

January 11, 1991

Mr. Steve Werner, Editor
OUTDOOR PHOTOGRAPHER
12121 Wilshire Blvd., Suite 1220
Los Angeles, CA 90025

Dear Mr. Werner:

I would like to propose an article for use in *OUTDOOR PHOTOGRAPHER*.

THE PRIBILOFS

St. George and St. Paul Islands are two of the premiere wildlife photography locations in the world. These are the major islands in the Priblof Archipelago, a chain of islands in the Bering Sea north of Alaska's Aleutians. Because of the great abundance of seabirds, arctic fox, and northern fur seals, the Pribilofs are often compared by naturalists as northern counterparts to an island chain in the southern hemisphere, the Galapagos.

On the sheer cliffs of the Pribilofs millions of birds nest every year. It is estimated that on St. George alone roughly a million thick-billed murres can be found; this is the largest seabird colony in the northern hemisphere. Other bird species nesting on the islands include horned and tufted puffins; parakeet, crested, and least auklets; and red-legged kittiwakes.

I propose a photo/text destination piece centering on St. George Island, which is the more remote of the two islands. In fact, this is about as remote a spot as you can find. But what makes it such an outstanding photographic location is the incredible access one has to such a variety of subjects. Seals, foxes, and birds are all within a five minute walk from the one-and-only hotel on the island. Based on my knowledge gained by four trips to the Pribilofs, I'll discuss when to go, how to get there, what photo equipment to take (long lenses!), and what to expect.

I've enclosed a SASE for your convenience.

Best regards,

John Shaw

need to immediately hook the editor with a strong concept and a strong lead sentence. I once actually sold a picture/text spread about a New Zealand backpacking trip simply because I'd written a compelling opening sentence: "I was standing on the top of the bottom of the world." Always explain exactly what your story idea is and why the subject would be of interest to the readership. If you have some special expertise that relates to the story, you should definitely mention it.

When you've finished writing, proofread your query letter, and then proofread it again. This letter is the first impression a potential client has of your ability to write, so you don't want it to contain any errors. Check your spelling carefully, including the spelling of names of both the magazine and the editor. Make sure that your sentences are indeed sentences and not just phrases. As with a manuscript, the letter should be typed or printed and presented as neatly as possible. After all, you're proposing a business deal.

Don't send original photographs with your query letter. Remember, publishers aren't responsible for unsolicited material, whether manuscripts or photographs. In essence, if they didn't ask for the material, it is for all practical purposes junk mail and thus can be thrown out. You can send duplicate transparencies with your query letter, or even color copies, but be sure these are marked as such. Don't suggest picture layouts to the editor or create a pasted-up article.

Group these photographs together, and you should have some ideas for a query-letter topic. The possibilities range from the scientific "How do icicles form?" to the more poetic "After the ice storm."

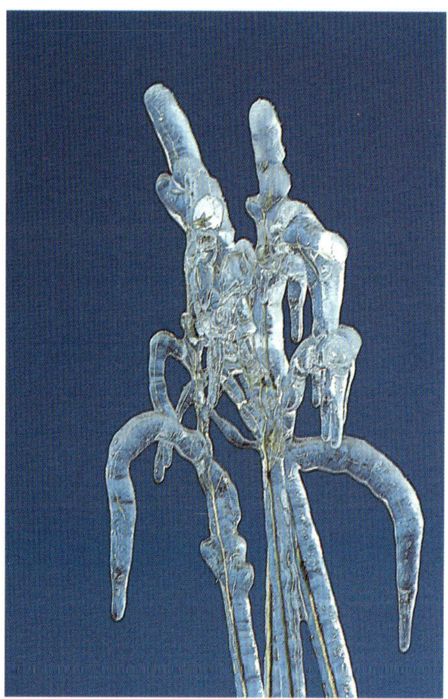

Ice-covered meadow grass, Michigan. Nikon F3, Nikon 80-200mm zoom lens, Kodachrome 25.

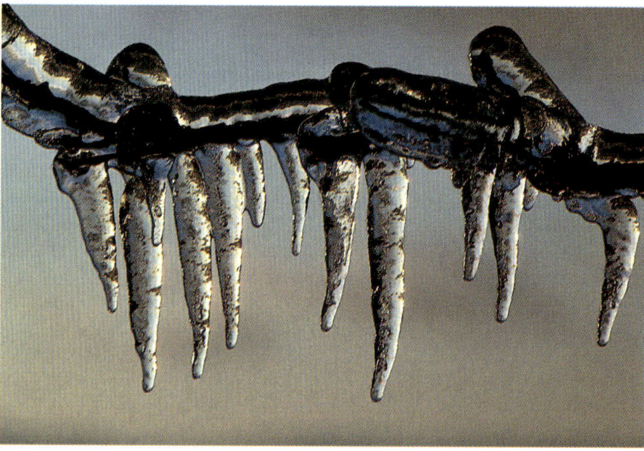

Icicles on branch after ice storm, Michigan. Nikon F3, Nikon 80-200mm zoom lens, Kodachrome 25.

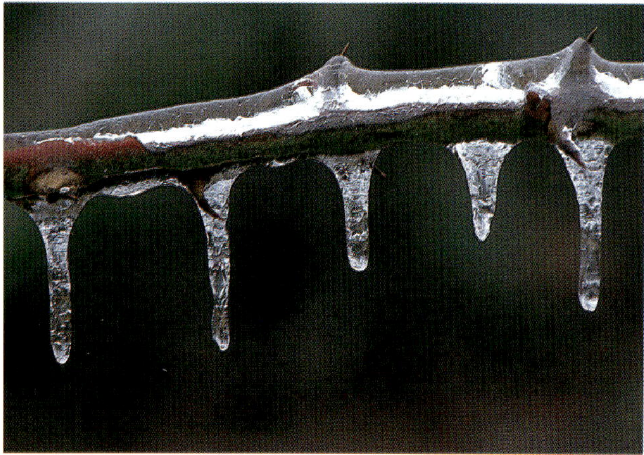

Icicles on wild rose cane, North Carolina. Nikon F4, Nikon 105mm macro lens, Fuji Velvia.

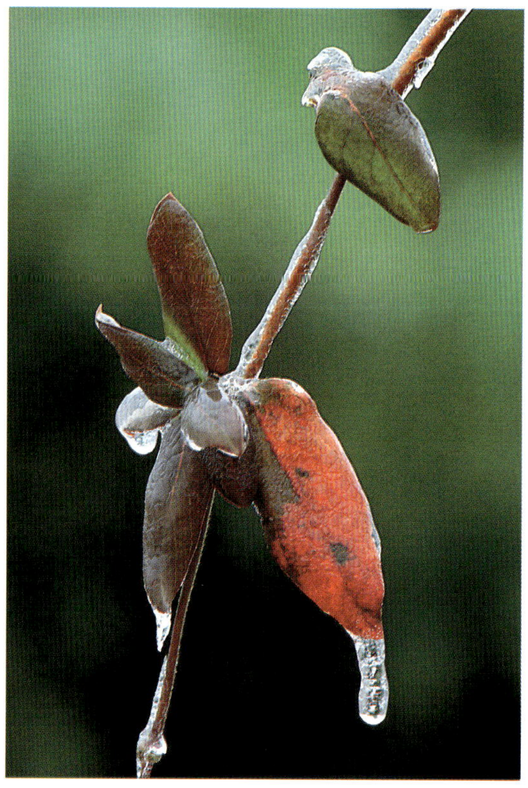

Icicles on honeysuckle, North Carolina. Nikon F4, Nikon 200mm macro lens, Fuji Velvia.

But what exactly is this idea that you want to present? Make it unique and different from what would be the standard idea pitched to the magazine. Do some market research to make sure that your idea hasn't just been published. Check out back issues of the magazine to see what articles have been published. If you don't subscribe directly, you'll be able to find old copies at most libraries.

For example, a piece on "Gathering Edible Mushrooms of the Great Smoky Mountains" won't be salable if your intended market just ran a similar piece within the last couple of years. Pay attention when going through back issues, and you'll probably gather a few additional pointers. For example, you might notice a number of how-to pieces being used, which would lead you to change your fungi concept to "10 Sure-fire Recipes for Cooking Wild Mushrooms." And one magazine's articles could suggest possible pieces for you to do for another magazine.

I actually do an additional form of this "market research" every few months. Whenever I have the chance, I go to a large bookstore and quickly scan magazines and books, just to keep myself current on what is being published. I note what sort of images are being used, if any subjects seem to be in favor at the moment, and the names and addresses of any new publications.

A series of examples should illustrate what a salable idea is. Consider the following package proposal for *Outdoor Life* magazine, a publication devoted to hunting and fishing. This magazine receives many proposals along the lines of "How I Caught the Big Fish," so you should try to hook them (no pun intended) with a different approach. Outdoorsmen often state that what they really like is just being out in nature, so I would suggest an article entitled "I Did NOT Catch My Limit."

Imagine a piece on fishing that doesn't talk about catching fish. What is it like to be out on a great trout stream at first light on the opening day of the season? What did you see as the light came up? What were your feelings as you waded the stream? The accompanying pictures could include an opening shot of a beautiful stream with mist rising off the water in the early morning, a deer peeking around a thick shrub, a dew-covered dragonfly on a wild iris, baby ducks swimming behind their mother—everything you saw *except* fish and fishermen.

I have a friend named John Ray who wanted to gross enough money publishing his pictures to pay for his photography hobby, including all of his travel overhead and his purchase of new lenses. He realized that the competition was fierce to publish individual photographs in such venues as the Sierra Club calendar line, or even to sell articles to major national magazines.

So when Ray started out he specifically concentrated on targeting articles to the small-magazine market. His first sale was a package about the wild orchids of the Great Lakes area. People tend to think of orchids as exotic, tropical plants, yet Michigan alone has more than 60 species, including the showy lady's slipper, the largest blossom of all North American orchids. A regional car magazine bought the package even though the article had nothing to do directly with cars. It did, however, suggest an activity you could do with your car: take a drive to wild areas and search out spectacular orchids. Ray's total sale was four inside pages (seven photographs) plus the cover shot of a dew-drenched lady's slipper flower; he was paid $2,000 for the package.

Ray's next sale was to a backpacking magazine that usually gets proposals for "I hiked the Trails of Yosemite." The name of his article was "Hiking with a Train." A railroad runs directly though the Agawa Canyon wilderness area, and simply by your asking the conductor, the train will stop anywhere you want along the line. Ray got off, hiked and camped for a week in the wilderness, and then returned to the railroad and flagged down the train. Now that is a salable article idea.

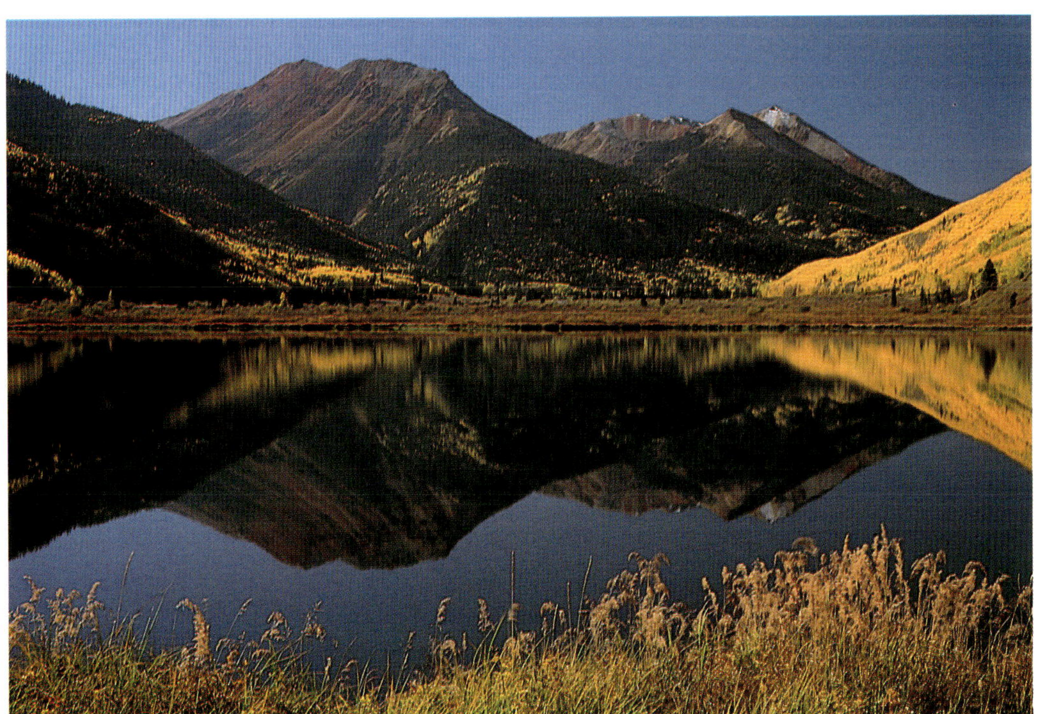

Reflection of Red Mountain and autumn quaking aspens in Crystal Lake, near Ouray, Colorado.

This shot of the San Juan Mountains reflecting in a lake readily lends itself to a magazine submission. I could use it as a springboard for an article on such topics as the spectacular colors of nature, dramatic light, and reflections.

Magazine articles don't have to be complex and esoteric. These three photographs are the beginning of a piece on patterns in nature. But it is definitely a salable idea to a magazine that hasn't run such an article recently.

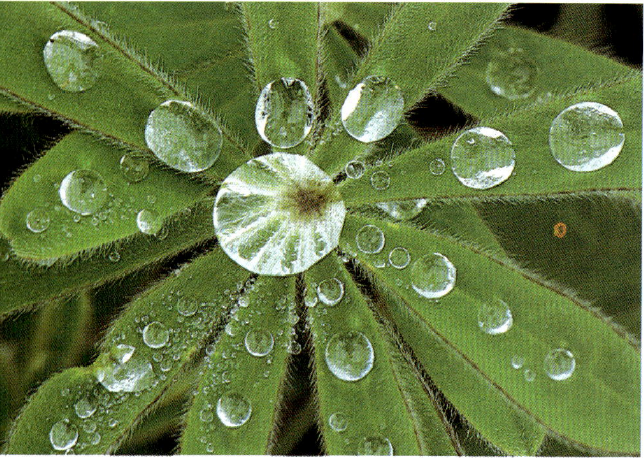

Raindrops on lupine leaves, Olympic National Park, Washington. Nikon F4, Nikon 200mm macro lens, Fuji Velvia.

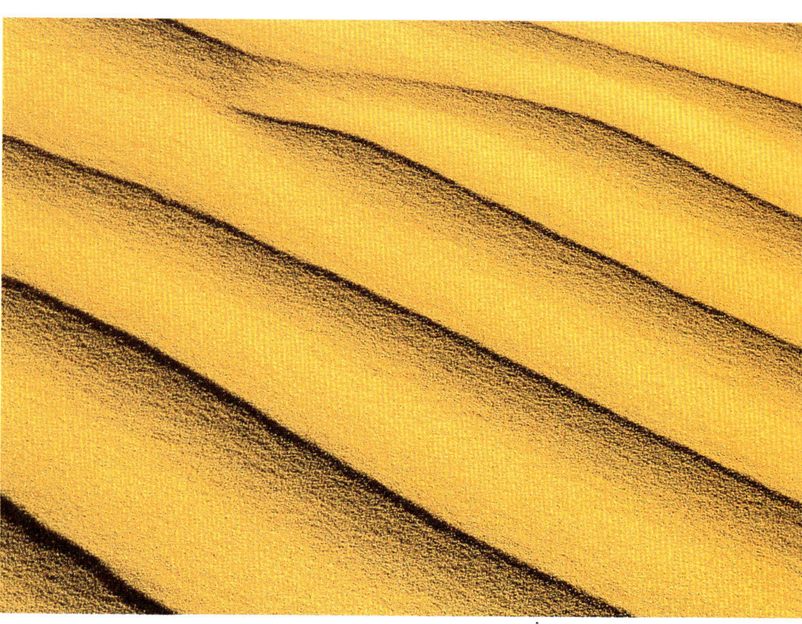

Ripples in sand, Colorado. Nikon F4, Nikon 105mm macro lens, Kodak Lumière 100X.

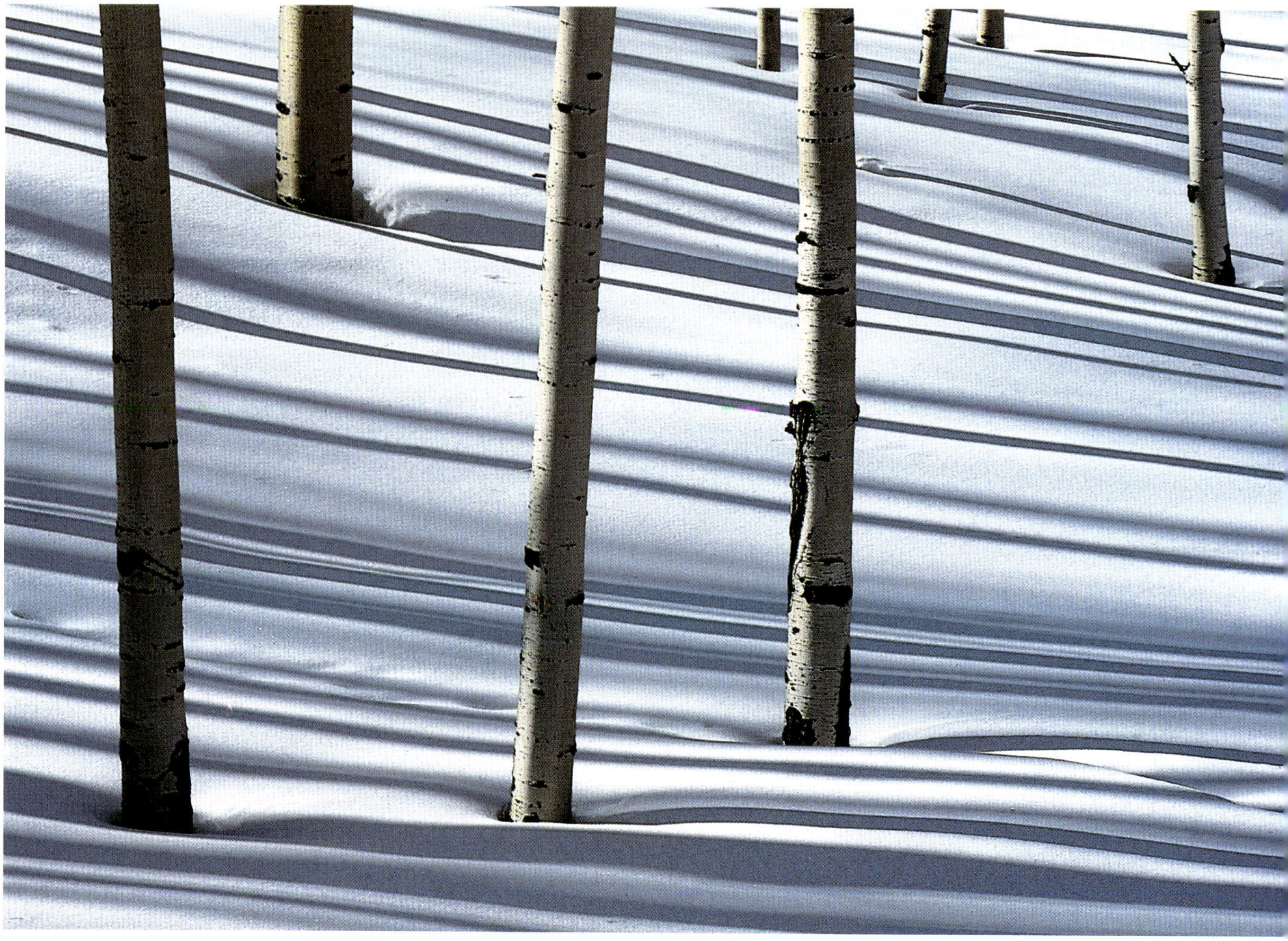

Winter aspen trunks and shadows on snow, Colorado. Nikon F4, Nikon 50-135mm zoom lens, Fuji Velvia.

Ray's third sale was to an airline in-flight magazine. This was a piece about a man with an esoteric occupation: me. Being a professional nature/wildlife photographer isn't your standard, run-of-the-mill way to make a living. He interviewed me and wrote an article about what I do, and photographed me in the field with my camera equipment. Actually this sale really irritated me because the airline broke down Ray's payment into separate amounts for the text and the photographs. The company used only one of his pictures, a shot of me, but paid him $500 for it as a full-page feature. The airline used three of my pictures, but paid me only $250 per shot!

How-to articles are always in demand. Take the phrase "photographing while ______," and fill in the blank with as many activities as you can think of. Each of these phrases should describe a specific topic that is salable to a special-interest magazine.

Here are 10 possible answers:

. . . backpacking

. . . hunting

. . . fishing

. . . skiing

. . . traveling

. . . snowmobiling

. . . bicycling

. . . traveling in an RV

. . . gardening

. . . raising a dog

Every special-interest magazine will buy an article specifically about how to shoot that special interest. For example, for a travel-magazine article you could write about and, of course, illustrate these ideas: What are the lightest weight, most compact, and most versatile lenses to carry when traveling? Should you take a tripod? What is the easiest way to carry equipment? What light is best for landscapes? How do you take a picture of a cityscape after dark? Which films are best? What are some of the best destinations for traveling photographers?

Remember, although these answers might be obvious to you, the responses might not be to your readers—unless they are photographers as well. To the uninitiated, the difference between Kodacolor and Kodachrome is a mystery that needs to be explained. Of course, any one of these ideas can lead to many more ideas.

POSSIBLE SPECIAL-INTEREST MAGAZINE IDEAS

Take the "Photographing with an RV" concept. One obvious piece would be to write about the basic camera equipment you should take on an RV adventure. Here are some other ideas off the top of my head, which you could pitch to an RV magazine. These aren't farfetched topics. Just recently while waiting in my dentist's office, I stumbled across a published piece about setting up a complete darkroom in an RV.

The 10 most scenic national parks

The 10 least-visited national parks

Following the seasons across the United States in your RV

Wildlife photography from your RV (using it as a blind)

A guide to the flora and fauna of the interstate-highway median strip (what was that big white bird, anyway?)

A photographer's guide to buying an RV

The 10 best wildlife-viewing destinations in the United States accessible via an RV

The best RV campgrounds in Colorado for autumn aspens

How to photograph your RV so the picture looks great!

Photographing winter from your RV

You can sell the same idea several times to different magazines so long as the publications aren't direct competitors and/or the article won't appear in the same general time period. However, you can't sell the exact same text because magazines generally buy specific rights to the text. No problem; just rewrite your original copy for the second magazine with its own distinct journalistic slant.

Most photographs are, of course, bought on a one-time basis, and each magazine will determine what pictures it wants to use. I once sold a photo/text package to *Outdoor Photographer* magazine about photographing the wildlife of the Pribilof Islands in Alaska. A year later I sold the same idea to *Relax*, a magazine concerned with physicians' free time travel. And a year after that, a German photography magazine picked up the same story idea.

When you send your query letter you should have already completed all of the required research and have a good selection of photographs on hand to illustrate your feature. What if the magazine responds that it wants the material in two weeks, but you have never been to 10 national parks, let alone determined which ones are the least visited? Be prepared to immediately start writing. Just don't actually do so until you have a client.

There are a number of articles I would like to do, from the very simple to the extremely complicated. Flying into New York City I once noticed how many rooftop gardens were below me. I've always thoughy it would be fun to do a piece on a scenic fall color tour . . . of the skyscrapers of New York. I've never queried any publication on this idea since I don't live in New York City, nor do I have any images for the article. However, if you are a photographer in the New York area who wants to work with this idea, feel free to do so.

I've also always wanted to do a piece on blimps. I have an ulterior motive: I think a blimp would be an ideal shooting platform for aerial photography. In truth, I just want to spend a week flying on a blimp while it crosses the United States. Armed with a selection of fast lenses, hundreds of rolls of film, and lots of batteries, I would crank out as many stock aerial shots as I could. A blimp piece could be my ticket. Right here I must admit that I've pitched this idea every way I can think of and so far no one has taken me up, so to speak:

Most people like blimps. The response on seeing a blimp is usually a joyful "Oh wow, there's a blimp!" I can't imagine anyone saying disgustedly, "Rats, a blimp is coming." Since blimps are fun, I've proposed a fun piece on blimps about the human-nature side of blimps. Where do blimps go at night? Are all airports also blimpports? How do you go about becoming a blimp pilot? How many certified blimp pilots are out there anyway? Talk about an esoteric job; the only job more esoteric is that of the person who tests blimp pilots for their licenses.

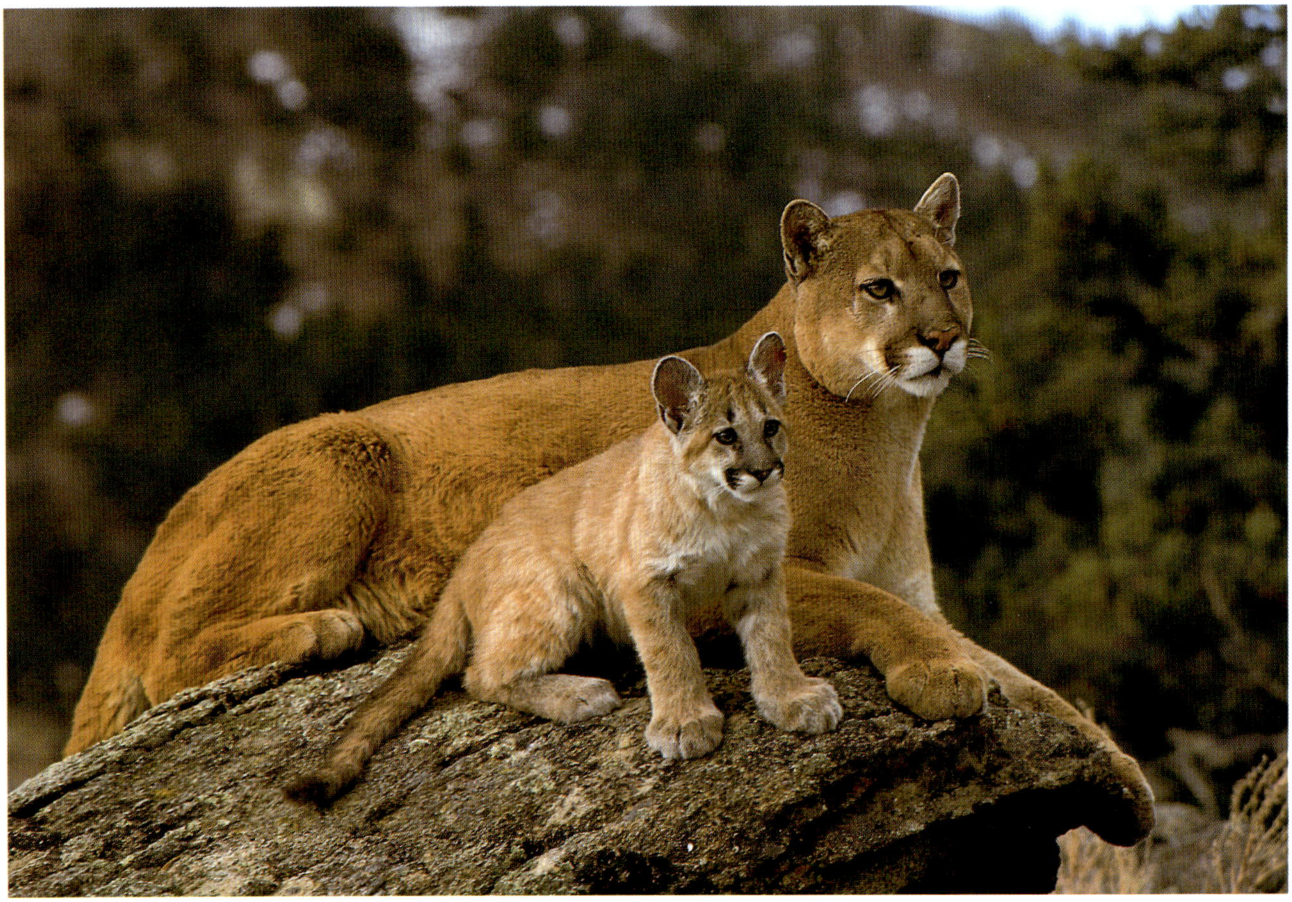

Mountain lion adult with cub, Montana. Nikon F4, Nikon 400mm lens, Fuji Provia.

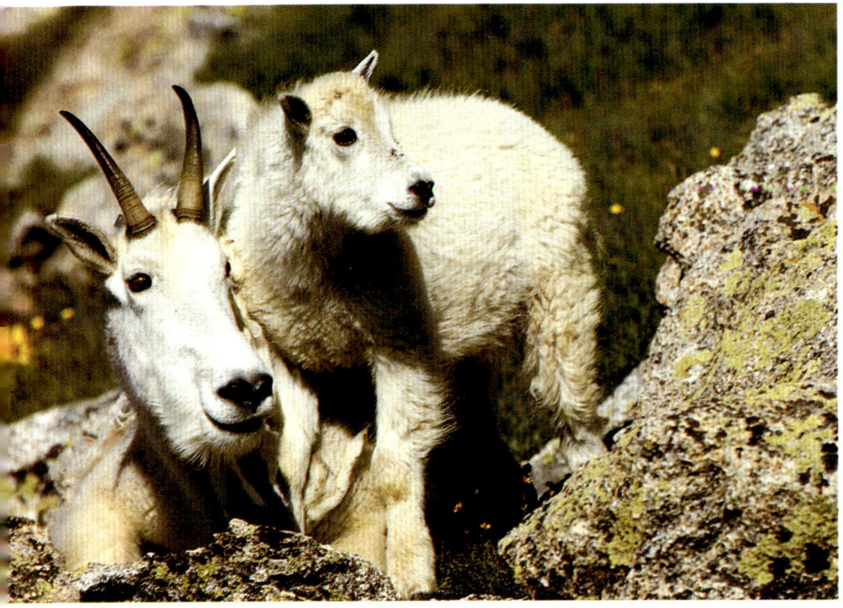

Mountain goat (female) with young kid, Colorado. Nikon F4, Nikon 500mm lens, Kodak Lumière 100.

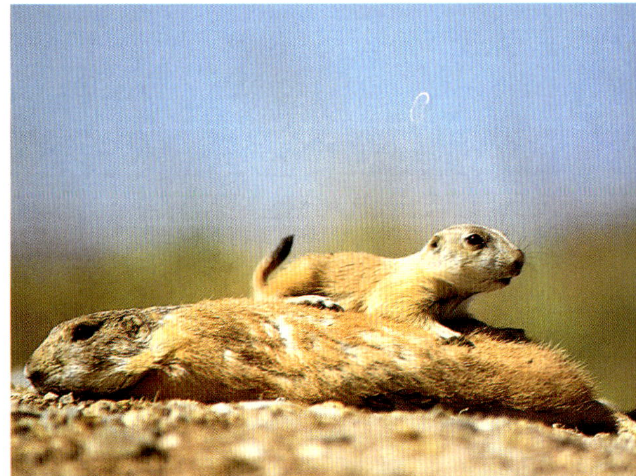

Black-tailed prairie dog adult with young, Arizona. Nikon F4, Nikon 400mm lens, Fujichrome 100.

See an obvious article idea here? If you were to include about seven or eight more photographs along with some text, you would have a magazine submission.

SHAPING A MAGAZINE ARTICLE

Understanding the step-by-step process of doing an entire magazine submission from start to finish is important. For example, I have an "Autumn Color" section in my slide-filing system. Autumn is my favorite season to photograph because of its cool days and spectacular colors. I've lived in both the eastern and western sections of the United States, and I've photographed the fall-color display extensively in these two regions. Almost every general-interest magazine uses some sort of autumn piece every year, so every year in midwinter I comb my files over and over to come up with several autumn ideas to propose.

Developing Ideas

After searching through my photographs and viewing them carefully, I noticed some differences in my pictures depending on the geographic region in which I'd shot them. I concluded that how photographers actually work—the equipment they use, the time of day they photograph, their subject matter—was location-dependent to some degree. Aha! An article idea.

At the same time I realized exactly how much I enjoy shooting autumn aspens in Colorado. When I first moved here, learning the state in photographic terms was a big undertaking. It took me a couple of autumn seasons to discover a few great back roads with extensive aspen stands—wow, another article possibility.

Writing the Proposal

Since these two ideas were photography related, they seemed to be perfect for a photography magazine, such as *Outdoor Photographer*. So I wrote a query letter, mailed it off, and waited for a reply. The actual proposal is shown at right.

You'll notice several things about this letter. First of all, since I've developed a working relationship with *Outdoor Photographer*, I was a little more casual in the letter ("Dear Steve") than I would be with a new client. My proposal was also slightly shorter than it might have been if it were going to other magazines. The *Outdoor Photographer* staff was familiar with my photography and my writing style; indeed, I've published quite a number of articles in the magazine, so the editors more or less know what to expect.

Note the date of the letter. Most magazines work at least six months ahead of the publication date. For example, the autumn issue of *Outdoor Photographer* is planned during late winter/early spring, so I always time my proposals with this in mind.

I didn't receive a letter back from the magazine. Instead, after about six weeks I got my own letter faxed back to me with handwritten instructions that I should proceed with my first idea of "Autumn East/Autumn West." A deadline of June 1 and a text length of around 2,000 words, plus caption cut-lines, were set. My second idea, for a Colorado autumn-aspen guide, was turned down. Well, one sale out of two proposals isn't bad. Besides, I'll recycle that idea to another publication soon, perhaps one of the travel magazines.

J O H N   S H A W

PHOTOGRAPHY

January 17, 1995

Steve Werner, Editor
OUTDOOR PHOTOGRAPHER
12121 Wilshire Blvd., Suite 1220
Los Angeles, CA 90025

Dear Steve:

Here are two article proposals for your consideration. Please call me if you would like to discuss these in more detail.

1. AUTUMN EAST/AUTUMN WEST

Autumn is one of the most spectacular seasons for color photography, but geography plays a major role is this activity. I propose comparing and contrasting the opportunities to photograph fall foliage in different parts of the US. I would make suggestions as to some of the best photo locations, the peak color times, photographic equipment needed, films, etc. And I would show the differences that geography plays in the availability of photographic opportunities, and in the styles of photographs usually taken in each location.

2. COLORADO AUTUMN ASPENS

Colorado, with its combination of mountains and aspens, is well known as a fantastic destination for western autumn color. But for the non-resident, the sheer size of the state is overwhelming. I propose a where-and-when article: a guidebook to some of the best locations in Colorado for aspen color, and a timetable (both time of month and time of day) for being at those locations. Photo tips would also be included.

I've enclosed a SASE for your convenience.

Best regards,

John Shaw

This is the original query letter that I submitted for my "Autumn East/Autumn West" article.

Writing the Text

I would like to say that I immediately sat down and knocked out the text for *Outdoor Photographer*, but the truth is that my very next step was to procrastinate for a couple of months. As far as I'm concerned there is no doubt that writing is quite a chore. Instead I went photographing, shooting winter around Telluride and taking a trip up to Yellowstone, telling myself that I was just "mulling over the concept." Sure.

Finally I got to work. I went through my slide files and pulled a grouping of pictures for the two aspects of autumn color. I find it much easier to write this kind of article if I have actual, specific photographs on the light table. I can glance at them from time to time to help gather my thoughts. All the transparencies were inserted into protective sleeves, then placed in archival storage sheets. A separate hanging folder in one filing cabinet is for "submissions in progress," which is where the pages ended up. I could take them out and scan them whenever I wanted to.

The next step was the actual writing of the text. After much gnashing of teeth and pulling out what little hair I have left, I produced the text. I proofread it several times and ran a spell-check with the program built into WordPerfect. Finally I printed out a hard copy.

Here is the follow-up letter that I sent along with my "Autumn East/Autumn West" submission. Below is the opening spread of the article, which appeared in Outdoor Photographer magazine.

from the office of
John Shaw Photography

May 4, 1995

Steve Werner, Editor
OUTDOOR PHOTOGRAPHER

Dear Steve:

Enclosed are the text and photos for the AUTUMN EAST/AUTUMN WEST piece which you have scheduled for the October issue.

I would be glad to write extended captions once you pick which shots you're using. Just call or fax me my photo file numbers from the slide mounts.

Best regards,

John Shaw

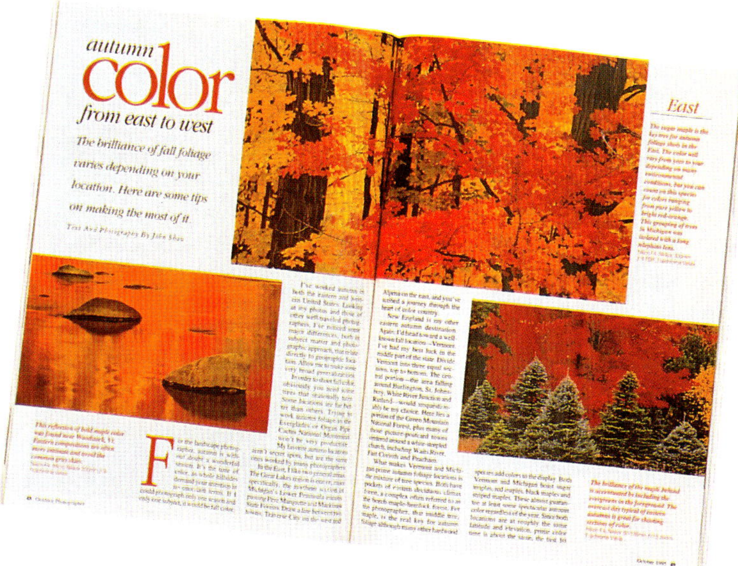

autumn
color
from east to west

The brilliance of fall foliage varies depending on your location. Here are some tips on making the most of it.

East

Preparing the Submission Package

At this point, I was ready to pull together the whole submission as a package. I typed my slide-file numbers into my "Submissions" file in my database, and then printed out two copies of my delivery-memo form on my letterhead. My terms of delivery are in a file on my computer, so I simply turned the paper over and ran it through the printer a second time. For a cover letter to remind the magazine editors why they were receiving this package, I jotted a few sentences on a note format (which is also on my computer). To the left is a copy of the note.

Then it was time to actually pack the material. Between two sheets of corrugated cardboard I placed the slide pages, the manuscript, the delivery-memo form, and my note. I used a couple of rubber bands to hold the assembly together and then inserted it into a cardboard mailer. The mailer was addressed to *Outdoor Photographer* using a self-adhesive label with my business address preprinted on it. After sealing the mailer with heavy-duty mailing tape, I affixed a Federal Express form to the opposite side, and then dropped it off in the nearest Federal Express box.

The piece was published in the October issue of the magazine, just as agreed upon. My entire submission of photographs, the shots used and those not printed, was returned in late October. I checked the transparencies that were used for major scratches or cuts, remounted the film in cardboard mounts, and relabeled the mounts with new slide labels. I marked off the returned pictures on the hard copy of my delivery memo, noting the ones that had been bought, and deleted the computer copy from my "Submissions" file. Two weeks later a check arrived.

And, thanks to computer technology, should I ever need to access the text again I can do so in a matter of seconds. In my word-processing program on my computer I have a directory labeled "OP." This directory has a file of every letter, every proposal, and every article I've sent to *Outdoor Photographer*. I can keep track of which essays I've suggested, review old manuscripts for possible conversion for other markets, and follow my business relationship with the magazine.

A BOOK OF YOUR OWN

Sooner or later all photographers want to have a book of their photographs published. There are three possible ways this might actually happen. First, a publisher could come to you, pleading to let the company show the world your great work. Trust me, this isn't going to occur unless you have verifiable photographs of the return of Elvis—even better would be if the Loch Ness monster were in the background!

A second way to have a book of your work published is to publish it yourself. A word of caution: can you name 10 successful, money-making, nature-photography books that have been self-published? Can't do it? How about five self-published books on any topic that have been profitable? If you can't—and that is very likely—then you should think twice about self-publishing (see page 109).

The third possible way to have a book published is for you to convince a publisher that it should invest quite a bit of time and money in producing, advertising, marketing, and distributing your work. In many ways the procedure involved is similar, although on a much grander scale, to the procedure for placing magazine articles.

Creating a Proposal

To start you must have a book idea. This has to be far more concrete and specific than "here is a portfolio of my pretty pictures." Indeed, picture books—books of pictures all by themselves—are almost impossible to sell. Go into any bookstore, and look at the remainder table. This is where you find the sale books that the store is trying to unload. You'll inevitably discover picture books in the pile. Few publishing houses today will even consider a picture-only book. You must have a point, a purpose, or an intent for readers to buy the book.

Next, write a proposal. In it you need to cover several particulars. Describe these in detail for the book company.

Explain your idea

Be as specific, and as thorough, as you can be. Write a sample chapter or at the very minimum 5 to 10 sample paragraphs to illustrate your point. This will also prove that you actually are able to put together a

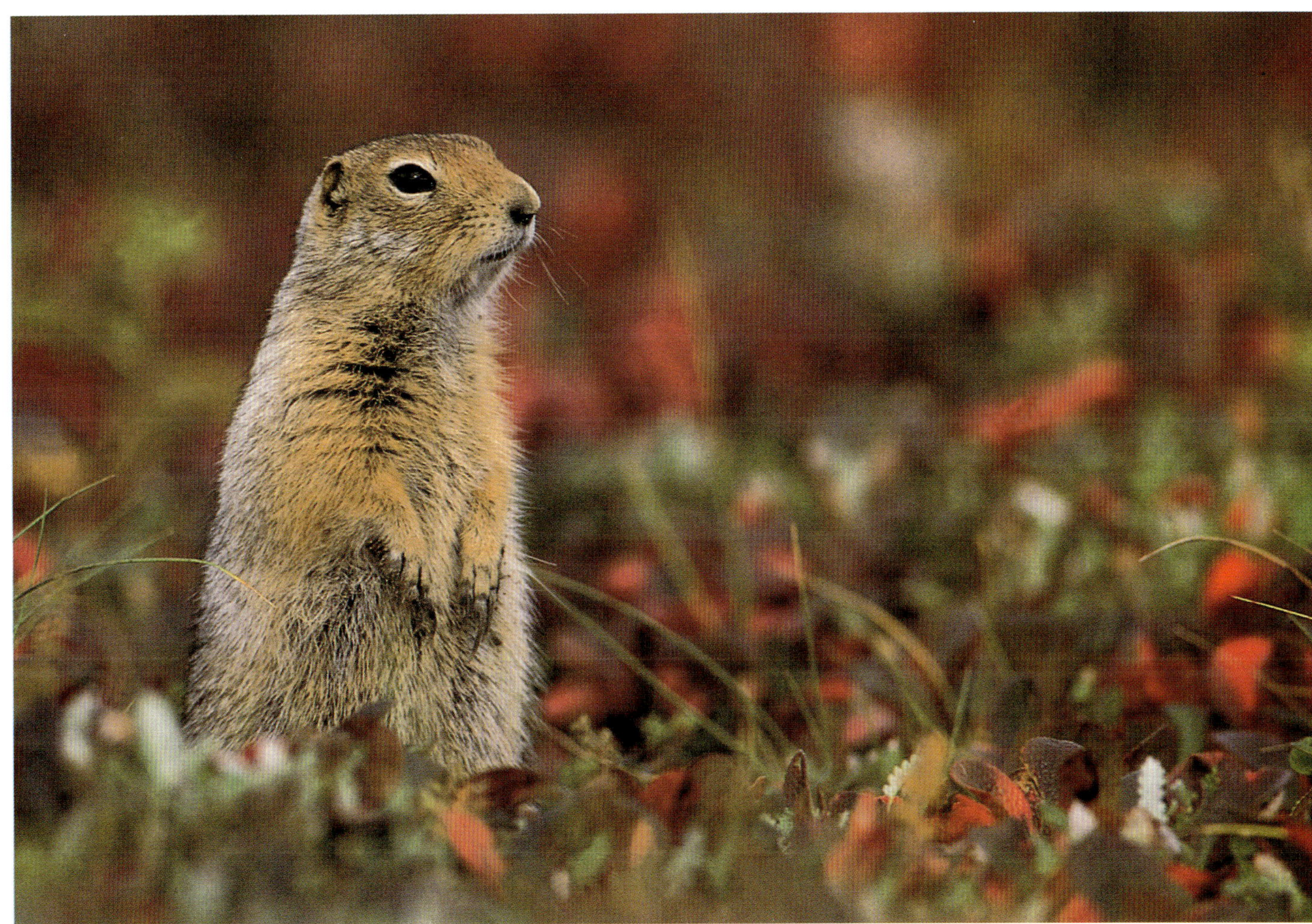

Arctic ground squirrel on autumn tundra, Denali National Park, Alaska. Nikon F4, Nikon 500mm lens, Fujichrome 50.

Here is a photograph from one of my earlier books, John Shaw's Focus on Nature *(Amphoto, 1991). Amphoto offered me a contract for this title when I submitted a written concept for the project.*

standard English sentence. However, if your idea is unique enough—and marketable—an editor will help you through some writing difficulties.

Outline the book

Show what you're going to include and explain why. The outline should exhibit some logical progressive development. The second section of your book should reasonably follow the first, the third should reasonably follow the second, etc.

Describe your qualifications

Explaining to the publisher exactly why you're qualified to write the book you're proposing should be easy to do. After all if you have no special qualifications, why are you even suggesting a book idea? List some of your publication credits here.

Discuss the book's salability

The book publisher is interested in selling books, not just in publishing your "art"—however good your pictures might be. If there is no market for the book, no publisher will want to handle it. It is a good idea to

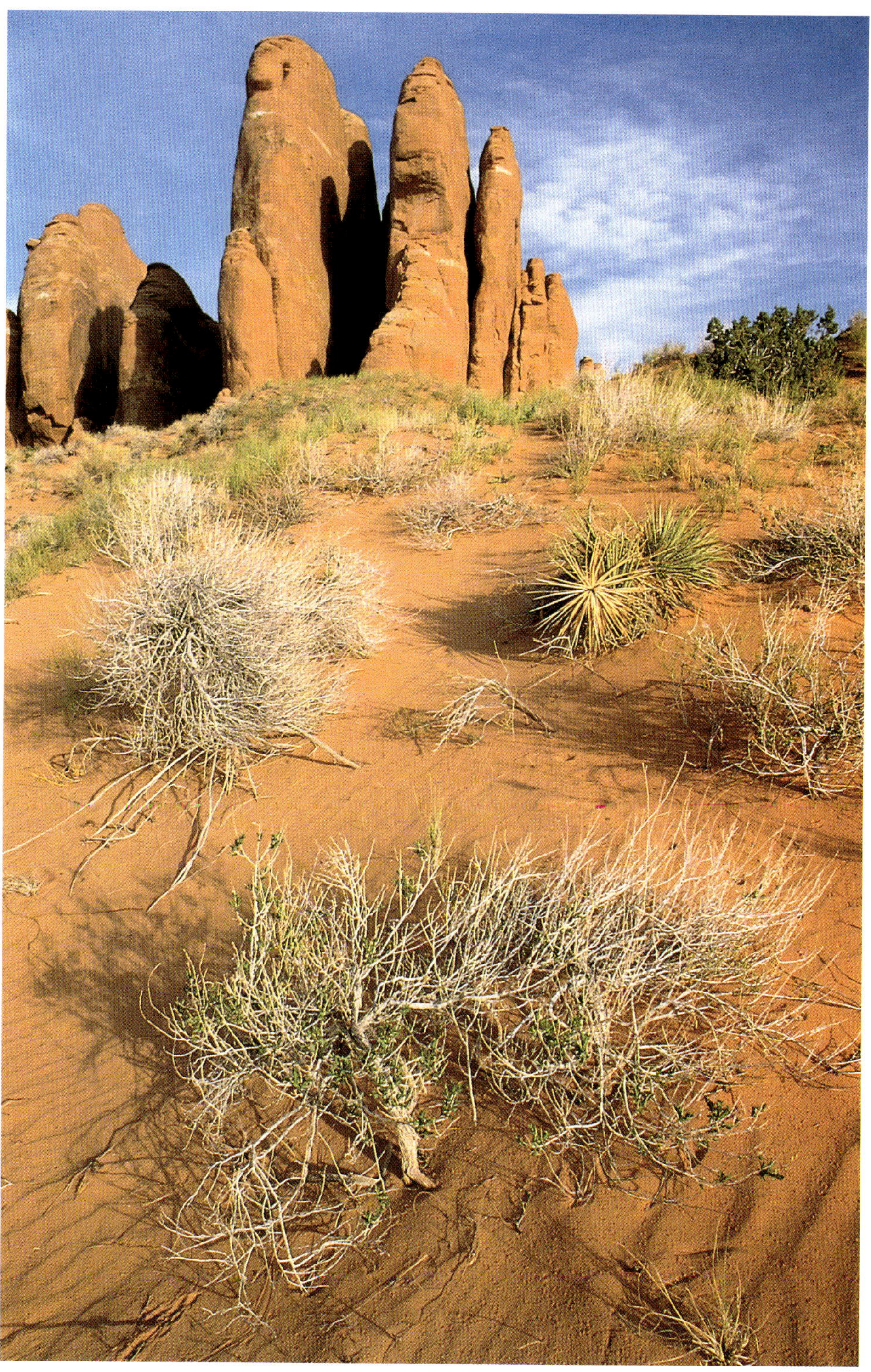

Sandstone fins in Fiery Furnace, Arches National Park, Utah. Nikon F4, Nikon 24mm lens, Fuji Velvia.

This photograph was used as the title-page opener in my last book, John Shaw's Landscape Photography *(Amphoto, 1994). "How-to" is a much-used book concept, testified by the hundreds of instructional books on the market today.*

review the competition here. What other similar books are currently on the market? What are the shortcomings of those books? How will your work be different? Why would anyone want to spend money on your book? Be realistic. If the potential market is too small, your idea might not be publishable as a book or you might have to look for a small, specialty book publisher.

For example, *A Field Guide to the Low Elevation Flowers of Costa Rica* might be an interesting idea, and you might have terrific photographs of the subject. But in truth very few people in the United States would buy this book. Remember, no potential sales translates into no interest on the part of publishers.

State a time frame for completion

If you have all the photographs in-house and you've done all the necessary research, say so. But be realistic about what you can and can't do. Few photographers/writers can suddenly drop everything and devote all their time to producing a book-manuscript package on a tight deadline. Most nature photographers, especially those trying to make a living through photography, must keep shooting to update and expand their files in order to keep selling pictures.

This is particularly true about seasonal events. If you're locked into a tight publishing deadline, you won't be able to work in autumn color, spring bird migration, alpine summer flowers, or other seasonal events that occur—not if you want to make your deadline and keep your editor happy.

Be especially realistic about the time required to produce any images you need for the book. *Winter in the Rockies* might be a great book idea, but if you don't already have good photographs, how many winters will it take to produce them? What if the coming winter is mild? Conversely what if the season is so harsh that you can't get to locations to shoot? I suggest having most of the images in your files before you make a book proposal.

Locating a Publisher

Now you need to find a publisher. Evaluate what is on the market and the type of material each book company handles. Send your proposal to a publisher with a line of books that your title would fit. For example, a company that specializes in how-to books about photography probably won't want to see a proposal on the intricate biological life of the old-growth forests of the Northwest.

A simple way to check publishers is to peruse the largest bookstore in your area. Check out a bookstore that has several feet of shelf space devoted to the general realm of your idea. You should also go through the "Book Publishers" section of the most recent edition of *The Photographer's Market* (see page 141).

Negotiating a Contract

If the day comes when a book company accepts your proposal, you'll be offered a contract. This is a legal agreement, so read it carefully. Remember that as in all businesses, all points of a book contract are negotiable, but the degree to which they are negotiable is the major sticking point in contract talks.

A fairly standard book contract states that by such-and-such a date, you'll furnish all final artwork and text, usually both a hard copy and a copy on computer disc. You give the company the exclusive right to publish, distribute, promote, and sell the work in book form. The format, style, design, editorial treatment, and number of books printed is ordinarily up to the publisher. You can certainly offer suggestions, but you must remember it is the publisher's money, not yours, being spent to produce the book.

In exchange the company will offer you a percentage of the profits made by the work in the form of a royalty, and will give you an advance against these royalties. The advance money is yours to keep as long as you actually produce a book acceptable to the publisher. Publishers often pay advances in three parts: 1/3 of the money when you sign the contract; 1/3 when you deliver the work; and 1/3 upon publication.

The amount of the advance and the percentage you'll receive are two major negotiating points. Most authors would like the really big money up front because they have a nagging, dualistic thought: "My book concept is great, and I should be paid a huge amount for it! But if the book just doesn't sell, I still want to rake in as much money as possible for my time and effort."

If the publisher offers an advance of $3,000 and you counter with a demand for $300,000, you might not receive a second offer. No nature-photography book is going to merit an advance as large as those given for potential best-sellers. How many copies will a nature-photography book sell? I don't think any have been on the *New York Times* best-seller list or made into a television miniseries.

Your royalty, which is the part of the book's profits you receive, and the dollar value it is based on are also open to discussion. Many publishers offer a sliding scale of a certain percentage paid on the first so-many copies sold, a slightly higher percentage on the next so-many copies, and perhaps a third percentage on copies sold thereafter. The gamble for both parties is, of course, on how many books will actually be sold. The percentage figures offered vary depending on exactly what number you're talking about taking a percentage of. Is it the list price of the book or the money received?

Consider the following example. Suppose your book has a list price of $30 and a royalty payment of 10 percent. At 10 percent of $30, you'll receive $3 for each copy sold. Great! Sell 10,000 copies, and gross $30,000. Sounds simple. But 10 percent of money received is a different situation. Most publishers sell books to bookstores at about 40 to 45 percent off the list price; after all the bookstore has to make a profit, too. That $30 book discounted to 45 percent off list price translates into a sale figure of $16.50, and 10 percent of that figure means that you'll get $1.65 per copy sold. So if those same 10,000 copies are sold, you'll get $16,500. But remember, you'll receive additional money only after you've earned back your advance payments.

A little more math here helps keep things in perspective. If you're getting a royalty of $1.65 per book sold, the book needs to sell more than 60,000 copies in order for you to gross $100,000 from it.

Carefully read any section of the contract that concerns your royalty on books sold at a discount beyond the standard bookstore discount. Such sales might be based on a temporary promotional price or on a deal with a book club. If you're getting a percentage of monies received, you certainly want to make sure the figure is as high as possible. Of course, you receive no royalty at all for complimentary copies, such as those the publisher sends out to reviewers. This applies to the 10, 20, or however many copies your contract stipulates are yours as author's copies.

So to make serious money from a book—to be able to write just one book and then sit back, relax, and rake in the profits—you must either get a huge advance or produce a work that will sell many, many copies. Keep in mind that having a book published nationally, available through any bookstore, gives you instant credentials for other projects. *This* just might be worthwhile in and of itself.

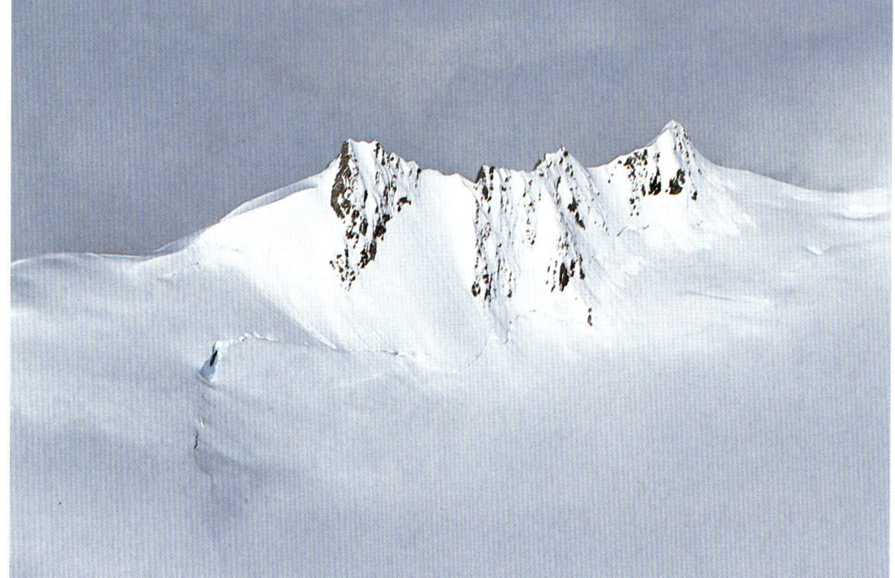

Mountain ridge and clouds, Southern Alps, New Zealand (aerial photograph). Nikon F4, Nikon 35-70mm zoom lens, Fujichrome 100.

Moeraki Boulders, South Island, New Zealand. Nikon F4, Nikon 20mm lens, Fuji Velvia.

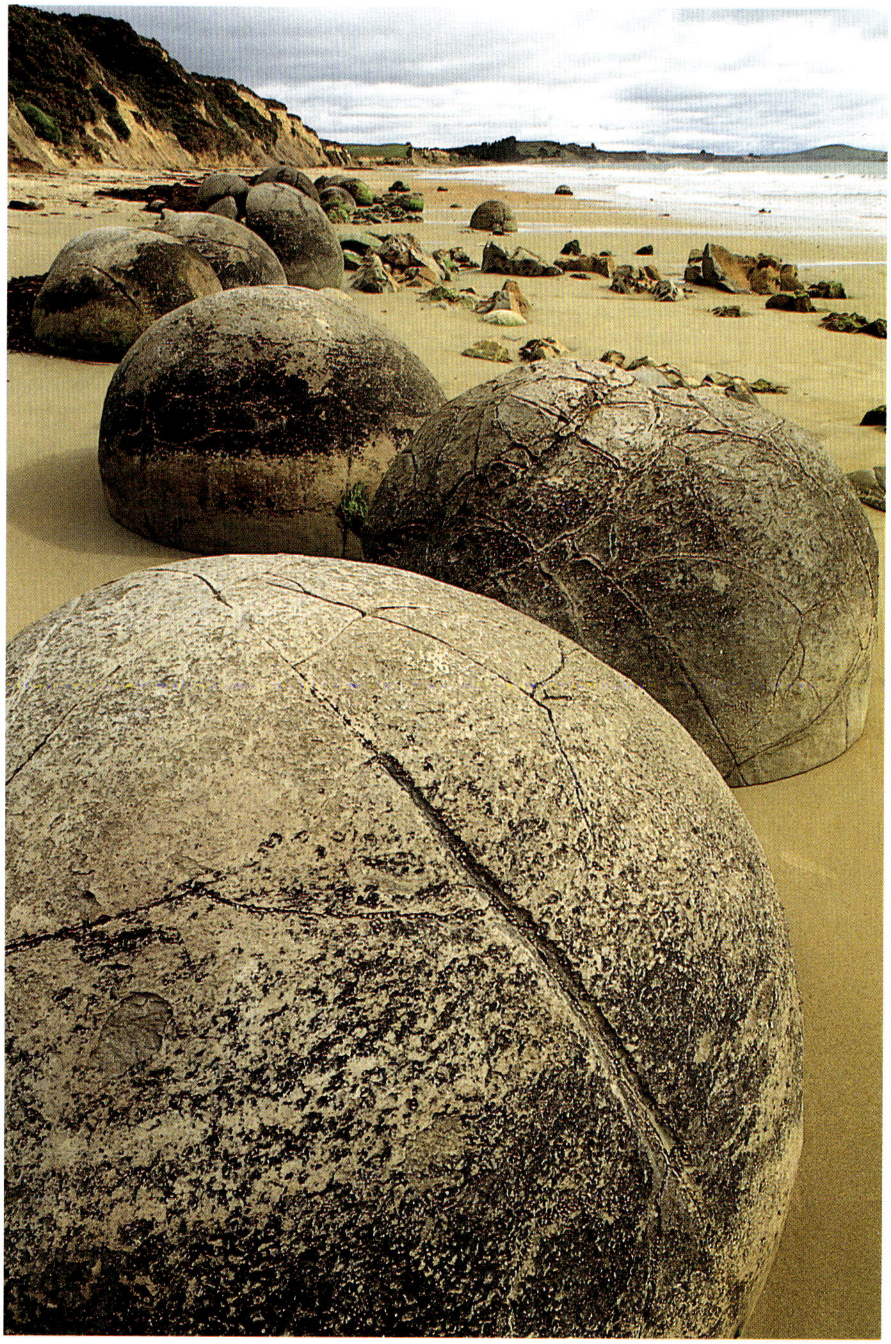

I made both these shots in South Island, New Zealand. What possible book concepts do they suggest? Assuming that I have many more pictures of this area, I might write a traveler's guide or a naturalist's guide to New Zealand. I also might propose pieces on: South Island, New Zealand; how-to photograph New Zealand and where to go; and/or patterns in nature.

SELF-PUBLISHING

Depending on your budget, you can self-publish anything, from cards to calendars to a complete pictorial history of your development as a photographer. But right up front you need to make a firm decision: Are you self-publishing principally because you want to have something in print, or are you self-publishing as a business venture? These reasons aren't necessarily one and the same.

Choosing a Product

There is certainly nothing wrong with printing a card, a calendar, a poster, or even a book simply because you want to do so. Spending your own money to create a product is nothing new; for many years authors have supported the so-called vanity-press industry. On the most basic level, almost every greeting-card shop offers a picture-frame card into which you can slip a small print. One step up are calendar forms on the top of which you affix a larger print. Another option is to spend quite a bit more money and create a press run of posters, cards, or whatever. If money isn't an issue, you can play to your heart's desire.

But publishing for profit is different. Certainly having complete editorial control of the images used and showcasing your work for promotional purposes are valid reasons to self-publish, but as a business the bottom line is profitability. Only you can decide how much return is worth the effort. Exactly how much money do you want to net: $1,000, $5,000, $10,000, $50,000? Is self-publishing going to be an adjunct to your selling photographs to other markets or your only source of photographic income?

Begin by answering these three important questions. First, which product do you want to sell? Second, how will you distribute the product? Finally, how much time and money are you willing to put into the project?

Most self-published products are either cards, posters, calendars, or books; all are retail items that someone has to sell. Of the four choices, I would dismiss calendars immediately out of hand because there is one major drawback to creating a calendar for your first publishing project. Calendars have a distinct time frame in which you can sell them. A mass of new calendars appears about mid-September annually, and the numbers seem to increase exponentially year after year. Calendars on every subject imaginable, of every size and shape, flood the market through Christmas. But what happens to calendar lines that don't sell out? Nothing is more worthless than a left-over calendar. If you wait until the end of January to buy a calendar, you'll find a stack of remainders marked down to about 75 percent off list price at every bookstore. This isn't a good way to make money.

I think it is far wiser to start with cards or posters simply because they are still salable even if you don't sell out within one year. They are timeless in that you can carry over an inventory from one year to the next. But be warned: every profitable self-publishing photographer I've talked with has stressed the same two basic points over and over. Don't jump into self-publishing in a big way; start small. And be prepared to spend far more time and effort than you'd originally budgeted for on production, distribution (packing, shipping, invoicing, etc.), and marketing.

Market Research

First you need to determine which images and products are actually salable, so do some market research. Visit every card and poster shop you can, and evaluate what is being sold, how it is designed, and how it is presented to potential buyers. Pay attention to the quality of paper used and the physical size of the product. I heard a horror story about a beginning self-publisher who produced a color notecard only to discover that it wouldn't fit into any standard-sized envelope. One fact you'll recognize instantly: you're going to publish in color whether you decide to do a card, poster, or book. Very few black-and-white nature products are on the market; one notable exception is the Ansel Adams line.

You'll also discover that printing four-color is quite expensive. All continuous-tone color photographs you see printed have been made from four separations of the subtractive, secondary colors: cyan, magenta, yellow, and black. Photographs are printed using very fine dots of these colors; the finer the dot pattern, which is called *lines to the inch*, the better the picture looks. Exact registration of each color is mandatory, as is good paper stock to prevent the fine dots of color from bleeding together. All this must be run through a quality printing press operated by a skilled operator.

In short, this is an expensive procedure. You can expect to pay a minimum of $300 per photograph for color separations, plus everything else. Consequently the only way to keep the per-unit cost of production low is to have a print run of about several thousand for cards, of about 5,000 for posters, and of about 10,000 copies for books.

Distribution

Now you face the real problem with self-publishing: distribution. This is where the daydream of having photographs in print runs headlong into hard reality. You have 3,000 copies of a single notecard sitting in

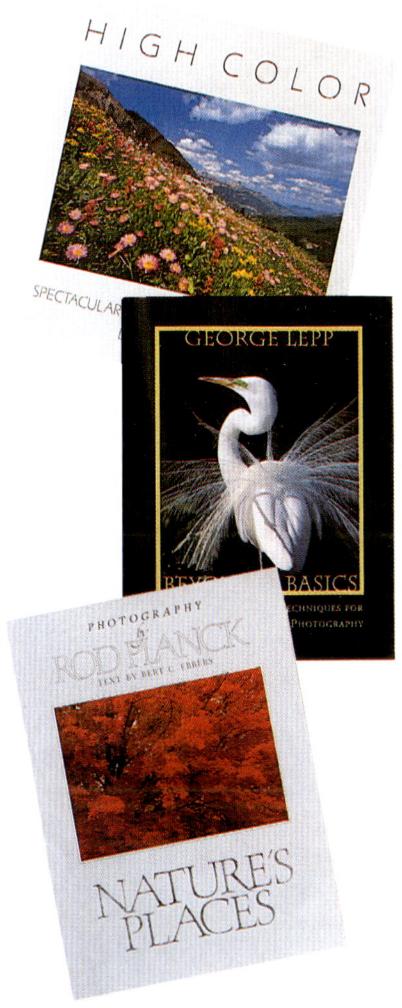

These successful, self-published books are part of my library. They are the work of three photographers: High Color *by Linde Waidhofer (top),* Beyond the Basics *by George Lepp (center), and* Nature's Places *by Rod Planck (bottom).*

boxes in your bedroom. What do you do with them? Unless you already have an outlet where you can directly market the cards yourself, you'll have to sell them at a wholesale rate to someone else to retail. Almost no retailer will purchase a single card design from a supplier; you might have to go back into production for additional cards. You could hire a sales representative to handle your card series; you can find reps through greeting-card trade publications. But reps charge about 20 percent of the wholesale price for their service.

Suppose that you plan to sell your notecard for $1.50. This translates into a wholesale price of about half, or 75 cents. This figure has to cover your production costs, marketing, office overhead, and shipping, among other expenses. It is perfectly clear that you have to sell quite a lot of cards in order to earn a day's pay.

Imagine that you have 10,000 copies of your book filling your garage. You have three choices. You can sell directly if you have an outlet, such as workshops and lectures. You can also take out ads in relevant periodicals and hope for orders—read "overhead expense eating into profits" here.

Another possibility is to sell retail. This means going to individual book outlets, convincing them to carry your title, and then selling it to them at a discount of at least 40 percent off the list price. No one bookstore is going to take all 10,000 copies off your hands, so you'll have to pound the pavement going from bookstore to bookstore. Look at some numbers. Even if every bookstore were to buy 20 copies from you, you would still have to reach at least 500 separate stores in order to place those 10,000 copies. This is going to take some time and effort on your part.

A third possibility is to sell the book at wholesale, but first you have to find a wholesaler who wants to carry it. You may have to sell at 50 to 55 percent off the list price. In addition, you might have to pay the wholesaler an upfront fee or a periodic maintenance/restocking fee to manage your book.

Of course, book publishing involves a major cash outlay right in the beginning, before you ever even run into the possibility of distribution problems. Most publishing houses calculate that they must price a book at between four and six times its actual production costs. A self-publisher with no fancy office and limited overhead

Look at these distinct photographs from a self-publishing viewpoint. Which, if any, would make a good poster? What about a marketable card? What if you needed to drop type into the frame? What sort of caption, if any, would be usable for each shot? Are there other products for which these photographs would be more appropriate?

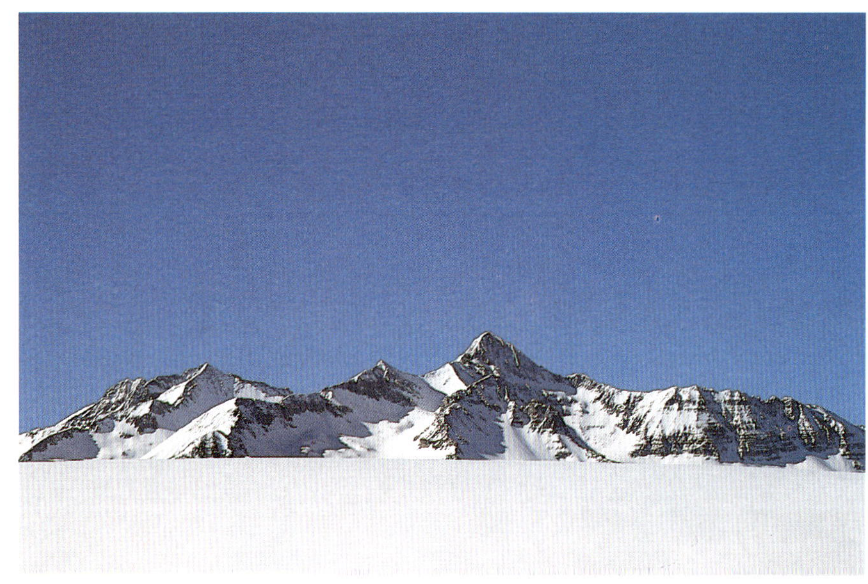

Mt. Wilson one winter morning, Colorado. Nikon F4, Nikon 80-200mm zoom lens, Fuji Velvia.

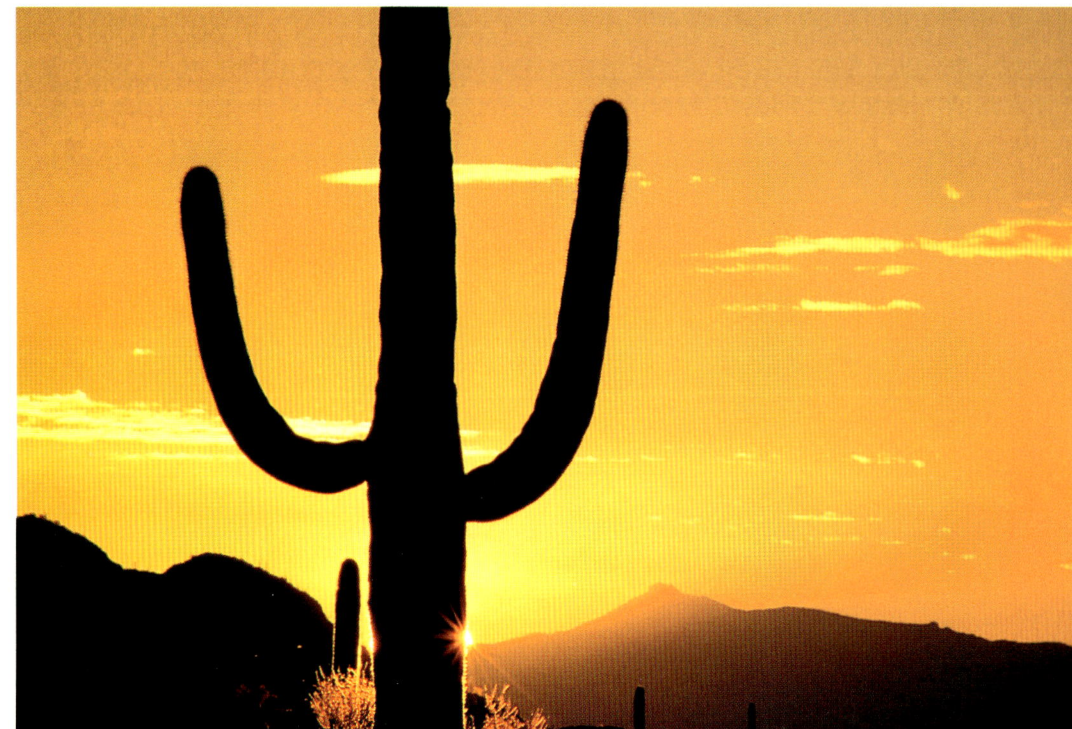

Saguaro cactus at sunrise, Saguaro National Monument, Arizona. Nikon F3, Nikon 50-135mm zoom lens, Fujichrome 50.

can work on a lower margin. But this mark-up still means a book with a $20 cover price actually costs about $5 per copy. And 10,000 copies equals $50,000 upfront.

Self-publishing sounds great when you first say the words. I don't mean to sound discouraging: quite a number of nature photographers have done well financially with their own line of products. But do your homework carefully and thoroughly. Looking into a few resources, including printers and reference books, is a good way to begin (see page 141).

Hiring a Print Broker

One way to minimize production overhead involved with self-publishing is to print your product overseas. But if you live in Kansas and want to use a printer in Hong Kong, you're facing a big problem. The solution is to hire a broker, a go-between who can watch over your project. You might want to discuss your plans with a management company, such as Bolton Associates. This full-service, print-brokering and production-management firm utilizes printers in South Korea and Hong Kong for the production of flyers, brochures, promotional pieces, posters, calendars, and full-color, softcover and hardcover books. In addition Joanne Bolton is a photographer herself and can speak the language of photography. Consequently she understands your concerns about printed reproductions of your work. All such companies can guide you through all the stages of book manufacturing, from camera-ready art to proofing and final production (see page 139).

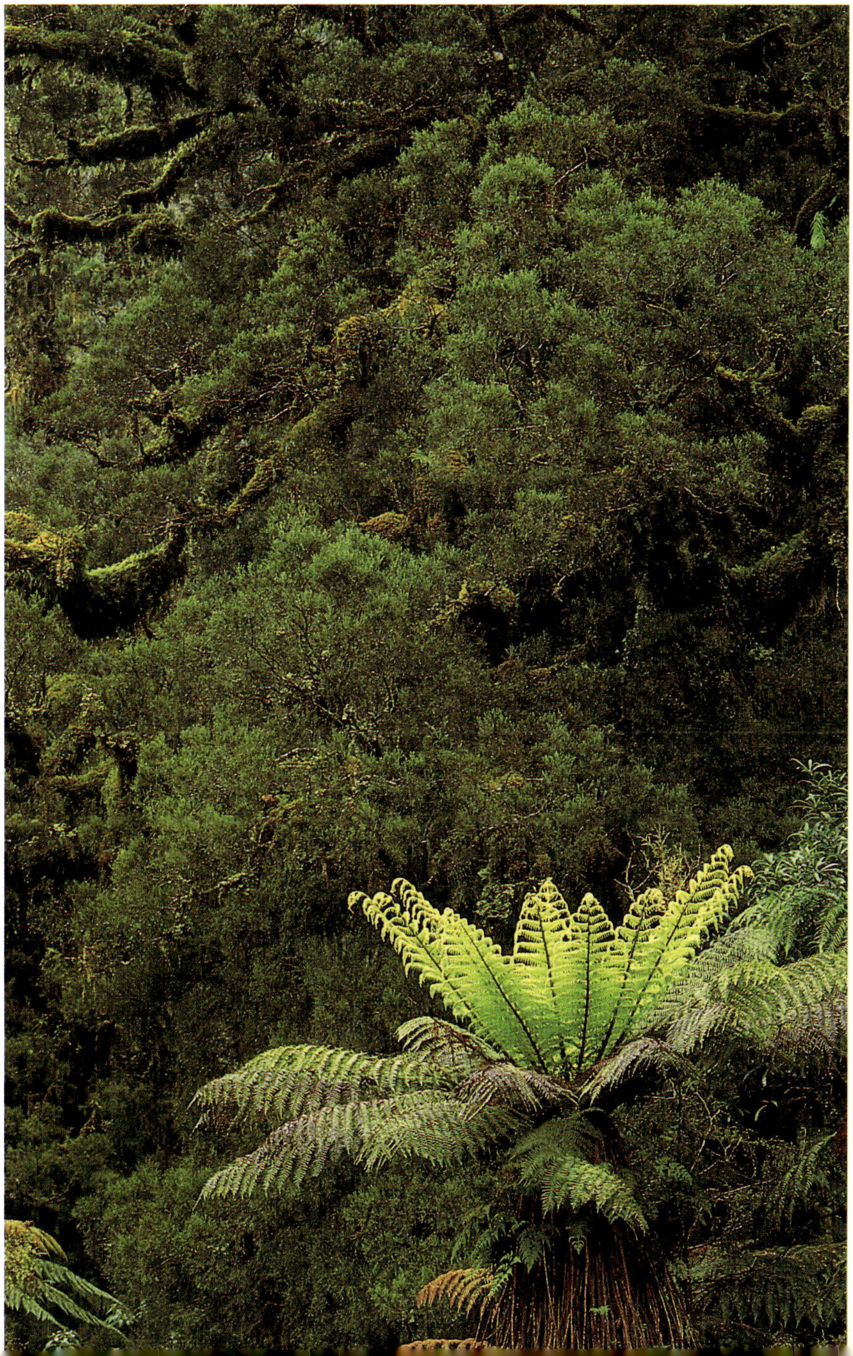

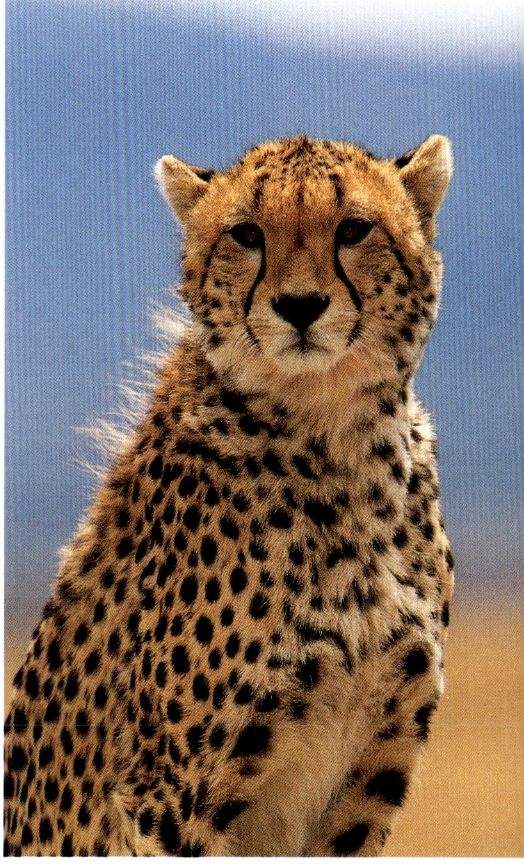

Cheetah, Kenya. Nikon F4, Nikon 500mm lens, Fuji Velvia.

Tree-fern and moss-draped beech in rain forest, New Zealand. Nikon F4, Nikon 80-200mm zoom lens, Fuji Velvia.

CHAPTER SIX

MONEY MATTERS

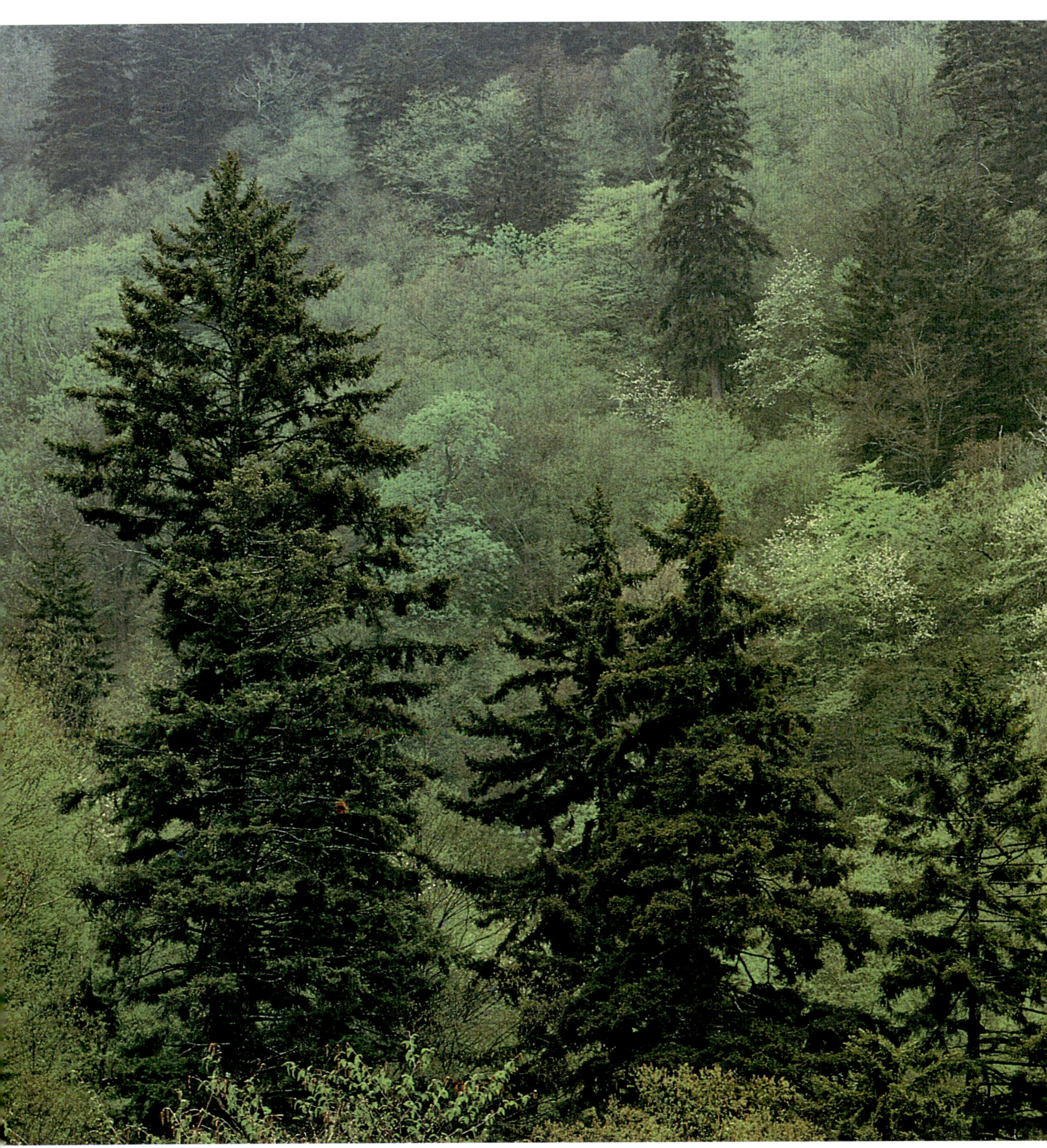

Spring leaves, Great Smoky Mountains National Park, Tennessee.

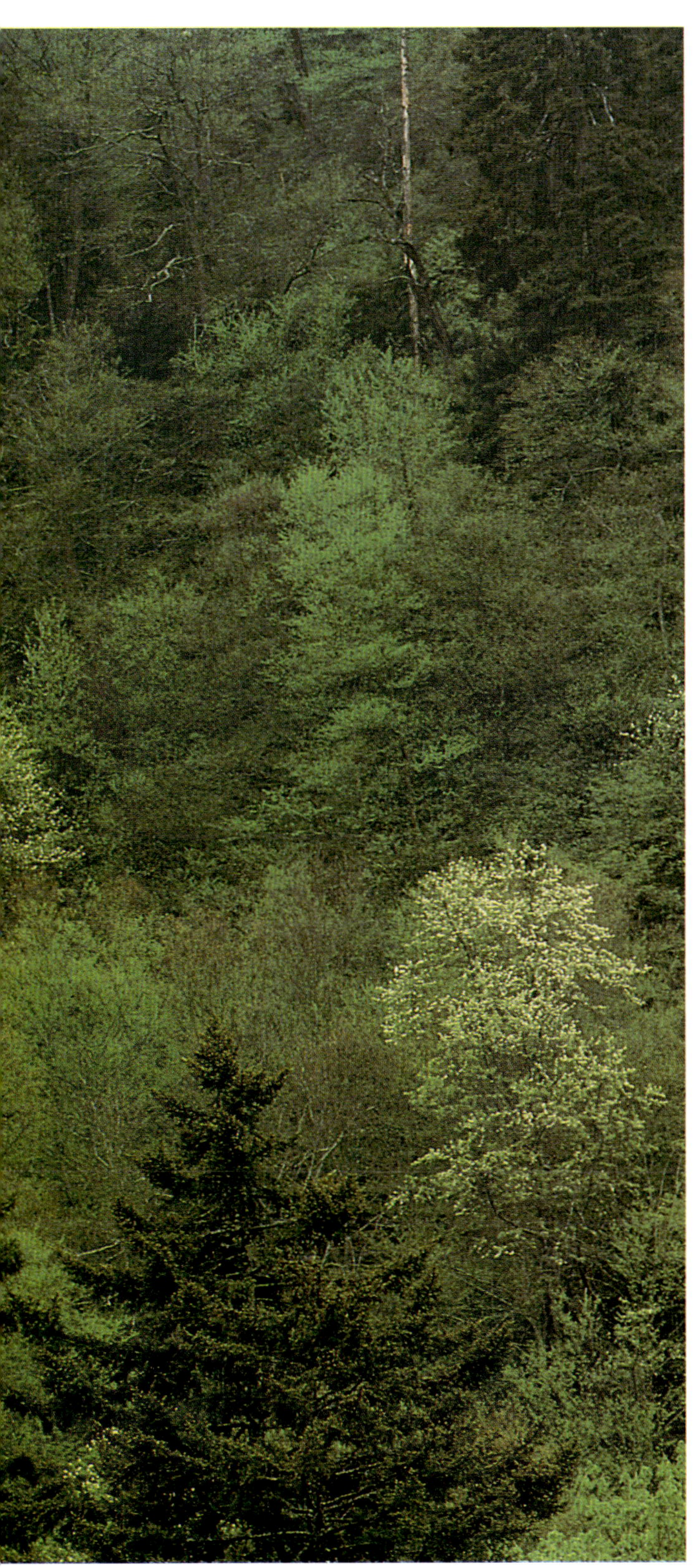

PRICING AND PAYMENT

As I've already pointed out, the best places to start publishing nature photographs are the editorial markets: magazines, books, calendars, and cards. Generally editors in this field aren't going to think about your photographs, or any photographs for that matter, along the lines of "fine art." Instead, even though editors are certainly searching for the best visuals available, they're faced with publishing deadlines. So they'll consider photography more in terms of a physical space on a page that must be filled.

Payment Structures

This editorial mind-set influences the payments you'll receive for your images. The fees paid for the editorial use of a photograph depend on several factors.

How large a photograph is printed

The usual breakdown runs along these divisions: 1/4 page or less, 1/2 page, 3/4 page, full page, double page, back cover, and front cover. The smaller a shot is printed, the lower the payment is; the larger a shot appears, the higher the payment is. A front-cover use pays the most money since, for most magazines and books, this is the first impression the consumer has of the product. Some publishers also have special rates for chapter openers or inside cover shots.

The circulation of the product

The bigger the circulation or press run, the better the payment should be. Small publications that have a modest subscriber base or that charge low rates for advertising, don't pay as well as magazines with huge circulations. But few natural-history pictures are used on the cover of *TV Guide* or *Time*. A magazine with a circulation of fewer than 20,000 is considered very small, as is a book with an initial press run of fewer than 10,000 copies.

The rights purchased

The basic sale of a photograph ordinarily includes "one-time rights." Actually you'll rarely sell a photograph outright; most of the time you're leasing your pictures for a specified usage. One-time rights means that the purchaser is buying the right to use the photograph once in any way it wants. A one-time-rights sale pays the least money, although this doesn't mean you'll get only 1/4-page payment. After all, a cover shot quite often involves a one-time use.

Selling Rights

You can sell rights to your images numerous ways. My most basic rights for purchase are "one-time, nonexclusive, North American, English-language rights." Exactly what does this mean? The buyer gets to use my photograph once, it might not be the exclusive user, it can publish the photograph in the North American market only, and it will appear in an English-language publication. If the purchaser wants to do anything else with my shot, it must purchase additional rights. Consequently the price goes up.

Some other rights that can be purchased include the right to publish in other languages or in other locations. Today many

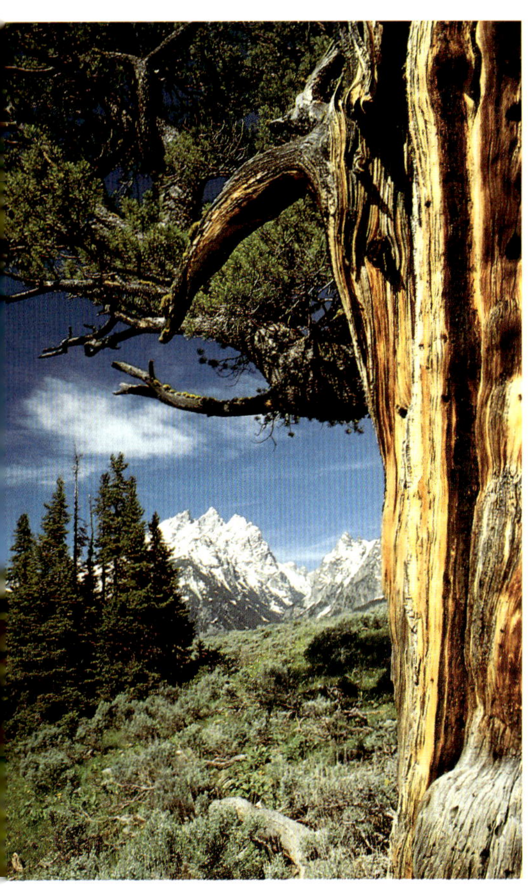

Old limber pine, Grand Teton National Park, Wyoming. Nikon F4, Nikon 24mm lens, Kodak Lumière 100.

This old limber pine is about a mile off the main road in Grand Teton National Park. I walked out to it and photographed it using several different lenses, shooting various compositions in both horizontal and vertical formats. I wasn't particularly thinking about how salable a photograph of the tree might be; I just liked the tree.

United States publishers ask for either English- and Spanish-language rights or European rights. Most calendar companies purchase very specific "calendar rights." For example, if a company wants "exclusive calendar rights for 1997," that photograph couldn't be used in any other calendar in that year. You could still sell the image for use on a card or to a magazine or for some other publication use, but not to a calendar.

Card companies sometimes buy rights for a specific length of time, such as "greeting-card rights for three years." Poster publishers often buy "exclusive poster rights." "First rights" means that the picture hasn't been published before; in other words, the buyer gets to use it before anyone else does. "World rights" lets the client use the photograph in the international marketplace.

You need to keep track of what rights you sell if they are anything other than one-time rights. After all, the client is paying extra money for a special usage of your photograph. However, there is nothing wrong with selling the exact same shot to several different picture buyers at exactly the same time if—and this is a huge if—you aren't selling conflicting rights *and* the purchasers are noncompeting markets. Examples of noncompetitive markets are *Popular Science* and *Field and Stream* magazines, and *Outdoor Photographer* and *Power Boat* magazines. Similarly, you could let an image be used as a greeting card and as a book's chapter opener.

The strangest rights I ever sold were to a consumer-products company, which wanted "exclusive, world, key-chain-fob rights." This meant that the company had the exclusive right to use my photograph worldwide on a key-chain fob. I almost laughed when it initially asked if such rights were available.

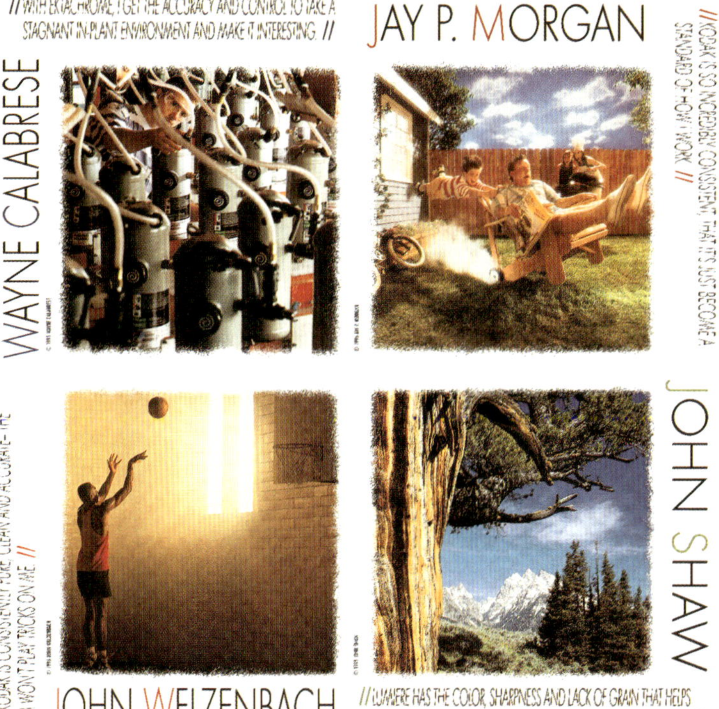

Sometimes you get lucky. Less than a month after I shot the photograph at left in Grand Teton National Park, it appeared in a Kodak brochure, a detail of which appears here. (Notice that Kodak flopped the image when preparing the layout.) In fact, the total time from pressing the shutter until I cashed a check was less than two months. That is a very short amount of time in the nature-photography business.

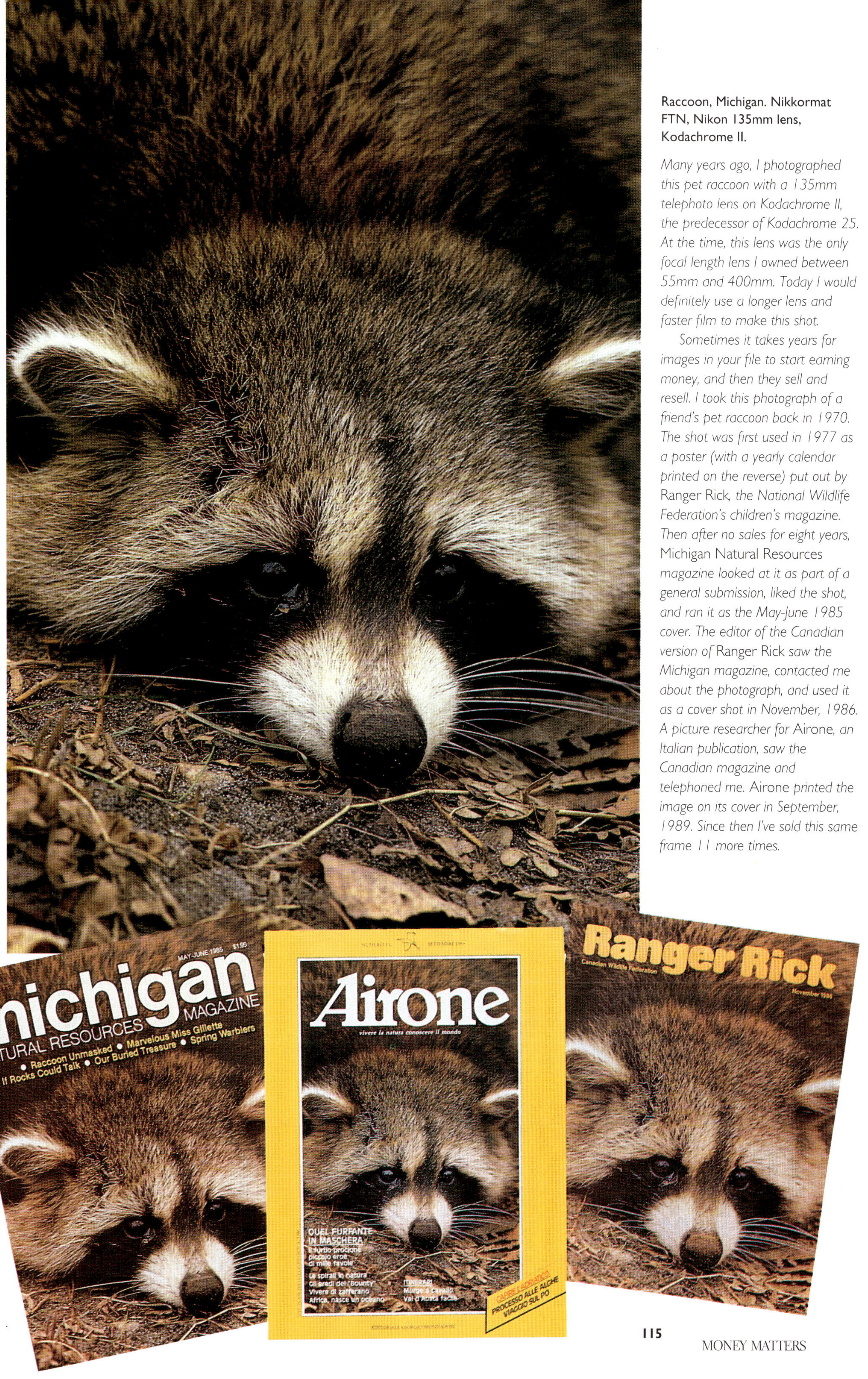

Raccoon, Michigan. Nikkormat FTN, Nikon 135mm lens, Kodachrome II.

Many years ago, I photographed this pet raccoon with a 135mm telephoto lens on Kodachrome II, the predecessor of Kodachrome 25. At the time, this lens was the only focal length lens I owned between 55mm and 400mm. Today I would definitely use a longer lens and faster film to make this shot.

Sometimes it takes years for images in your file to start earning money, and then they sell and resell. I took this photograph of a friend's pet raccoon back in 1970. The shot was first used in 1977 as a poster (with a yearly calendar printed on the reverse) put out by Ranger Rick, *the National Wildlife Federation's children's magazine. Then after no sales for eight years,* Michigan Natural Resources *magazine looked at it as part of a general submission, liked the shot, and ran it as the May-June 1985 cover. The editor of the Canadian version of* Ranger Rick *saw the Michigan magazine, contacted me about the photograph, and used it as a cover shot in November, 1986. A picture researcher for* Airone, *an Italian publication, saw the Canadian magazine and telephoned me.* Airone *printed the image on its cover in September, 1989. Since then I've sold this same frame 11 more times.*

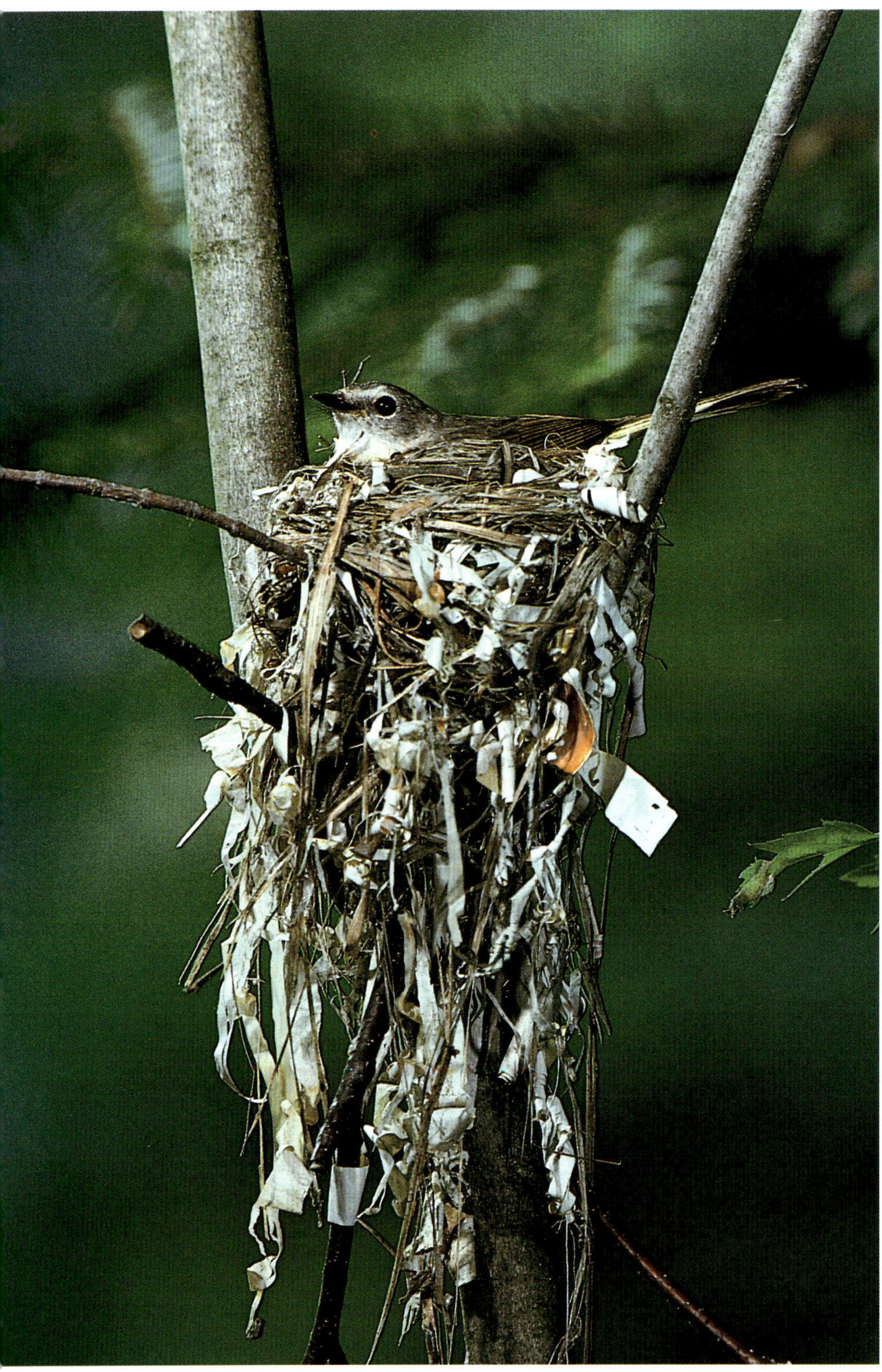

American restart (female) on birchbark nest, Michigan. Nikkormat FTN, Leitz 400mm lens adapted to Nikon, Kodachrome II.

I took this photograph years ago in Michigan's Upper Peninsula at a time when I still photographed songbirds at the nest. For well over 20 years four sharp frames of this bird languished in my slide file. Who would possibly want a rather nondescript photograph? Well, in 1995 I received a telephone request: Did I have any pictures of a bird on a nest made out of birchbark strips? I submitted the picture, and it ran as a full-page illustration. One month after publication, another editor called; he'd seen the shot, and he wanted it. This turned into another full-page sale. You never know which image is going to sell, or when it will sell.

Uniqueness

To some degree how unique a picture is determines its value. Certainly a publisher will pay more for a shot that is available from only one source than for a shot that almost every photographer on earth has on file. A picture of Mt. Saint Helens erupting is unique in comparison to a picture of a fallen autumn leaf.

Payment Rates

For the most part, editorial markets will tell you what they pay. Often this is presented in a take-it-or-leave-it manner, but I can unequivocally state that in business everything is negotiable. However, published payment rates give you an idea of what to expect, or at least point to an area of negotiation. For example, if a client states that payment is $150 for one-time rights, you would be rather foolish to insist that your picture fee is $1,500 for 1/4 page or less. Based on my experience, if you are fair with publications when discussing rates, they'll be fair with you. If you are hard-nosed and argumentative, you'll lose repeat business.

You can easily see that grossing $50,000 when you're receiving only $250 per check isn't an easy way to make money. If you want to earn a living selling nature photographs, you must sell lots of pictures. Obviously this means that you must have lots of pictures to sell. And you need to find a better way of making sales rather than relying on "1/4-page or less" rates.

Devising a Financial Strategy

I've always found it helpful to look at my income as a series of $5,000 increments I need to accrue. To gross $50,000 I just need to find 10 $5,000 clients. To gross $100,000 I need to have 20 $5,000 clients. The obvious question here is how can you find one $5,000 client, let alone 20. The answer isn't complicated: Diversify.

Have as many potential markets, potential sources of income, and potentially salable pictures as possible. Don't try to sell photographs only directly from your office; use stock agencies and write articles. Rather than photograph only one subject, work as many different subjects as possible. You can't earn a living taking only elk pictures, no matter how good your shots are. Making a livable income through stock nature photography is a numbers game. The more good pictures you have, the more subjects you have, the more thorough your coverage, the more potential markets, the more in your paycheck.

A truism of publishing is that if your pictures are good, the more you publish, the more you will publish. Eventually photo-research people will come to you for images since they'll have seen your shots in print. And when a publisher asks you to name a fee for picture use, remember that if you quote high, you can always come down. But if you quote low, you're stuck with the price.

I strongly recommend that when the time to quote prices does arrive, that you purchase one additional computer software program. FotoQuote is a pricing-and-negotiating program for stock photography. Although the software wasn't written specifically for nature photographers, it is a great help in determining prices. FotoQuote leads you through a series of steps to determine the value your images have to a client, as well as the uniqueness of the pictures in the marketplace. This very simple program is available in DOS, Windows, and Mac versions (see page 136).

The program is set up as a series of choices, starting with how a picture is to be used: Advertising, Corporate, Editorial, or Other. Then each of these topics is broken down further. For example, the Editorial usage list contains the following divisions:

- Consumer magazine
- Newspaper
- Sunday supplement
- Network television
- Cable television
- Textbook
- Retail book
- Picture book
- Encyclopedia
- Electronic book
- Filmstrip
- Educational poster
- Retail poster

Within each of these categories you pick the size the image will be used, the press run, the rights to be purchased, and whether the image is common, average, or unique. Then with just a click of your mouse, you have a suggested price for starting negotiations.

You should determine with your clients if you need to send them invoices. Surprisingly, many of the editorial markets don't need you to do this. A check made out to you mysteriously appears in the mail one day. Consequently waiting for each day's mail delivery becomes a big event for most freelance photographers! Nevertheless you should definitely keep a log of which company owes you what amount, the date of any telephone agreement as to payment, the name of the person you spoke with, and any other pertinent details.

For those markets that do call for an invoice, you should send one immediately. I'm always amazed that some photographers actually forget to stay on top of administrative procedures, such as mailing out invoices. Develop a system for tracking invoices, which ones customers have paid and which ones are past due. If a client owes you money and the check doesn't come and doesn't come, you'll usually find that making a telephone call to the picture editor is all it takes. Don't hire an attorney yet. You'll have to establish how valuable a client is in relation to how much hassle you might experience in getting paid.

In all truthfulness I do have a blacklist of clients that I'll never deal with again, either because of payment problems or because of their handling of my photographs. Not many names are on the list since most publishers are quite straightforward and honest. But I'm dismayed that some major nature publications demand payment for advertising immediately, yet they let their payments to photographers slide for months. This is just the reality of the business.

EDITORIAL PHOTOGRAPHY RATES

The following are some average editorial rates in the nature-photography press as of 1995.

Calendars

Major, national calendar lines, such as those the Sierra Club and the National Audubon Society publish, pay:

$400-$450 for a photograph in a wall-calendar format

$225-$300 for a photograph in an engagement calendar

$100 additional if the photograph is used as a cover

Small calendar companies pay:

$150-$250 for a wall calendar

$100-$150 for engagement calendars

Magazines

National magazines with circulations between 750,000 and 1,000,000 pay:

1/4 page or less	$150-$300
1/2 page	$200-$350
3/4 page	$275-$425
Full page	$300-$500
Double page	$350-$700
Front cover	$500-$800

Small-circulation magazine rates can be quite modest, possibly as little as half of the low magazine figures listed immediately above.

INVOICE

YOUR NAME
Street Address
City, State, Zip Code
Phone Number
Social Security #: XXX-XX-XXXX

Number:

Date:

SOLD TO:

REFERENCE:

TERMS: 30 days net plus 1½% per month past due.

PHOTOS USED	DESCRIPTION	AMOUNT

One-time, non-exclusive, North American English language rights only, unless otherwise specified.
No electronic rights granted.

Credit Must Read: © YOUR NAME

Here is a fairly simple invoice form. Feel free to use it, modify it, or add to it as you see fit.

KEEPING YOUR MONEY

One of the best ways I know of showing a profit in nature photography, or in any business for that matter, is to minimize your overhead expenses. Grossing $10,000 with only $1,000 of business costs is far better than grossing $100,000 while spending $101,000. I once casually spoke with an aspiring photographer who insisted that he was a professional. He started talking financial figures and informed me that he'd grossed a total of $6,000 through November of that year. Since we were in Alaska at the time and he was from Texas, I asked about his expenses to date. His reply was "$32,000." I am sure he was quite offended when I suggested that perhaps his business would do better if he could reverse the figures.

SPEND WISELY

My advice is to be extremely careful with business overhead. Don't scrimp, but don't spend unwisely. I heard of another aspiring photographer who decided to turn pro. Even though he'd never made a submission or sold a photograph, he quit his job. Figuring he would be on the road shooting pictures, his first acquisitions were a new Chevrolet 4-wheel-drive Suburban, complete with a cellular phone, and a 28-foot-long Airstream trailer fitted out with a computer, fax, and modem. This beginning photographer started his career by completely depleting his financial resources. Within a year he was searching for a job after selling off the vehicle, the trailer, and all of his camera equipment. He certainly didn't have a very realistic business plan.

To shoot professionally you do need quality photography equipment, which is quite expensive. But you probably don't need to update all your lenses at once, or to replace your 20mm, 28mm, and 35mm lenses with a 20-35mm zoom lens right now. Justify your expenses. I've always said you should write down 10 reasons why you need a new lens before you buy one. (Nonetheless, I've often had a bad case of "lens lust," which as far as I'm concerned counts for 9 out of the 10 reasons required.)

You'll certainly need office space, but this doesn't necessarily mean one in a fancy office plaza. Indeed, most of the professional nature photographers I know have their offices right in their homes. Even then, most of the office furnishings are generally from a discount store rather than the executive line.

REDUCING EXPENSES

You can cut expenses all sorts of ways. When I am on the road I avoid high-priced hotels, staying in inexpensive chains or even camping out in the back of my truck. More

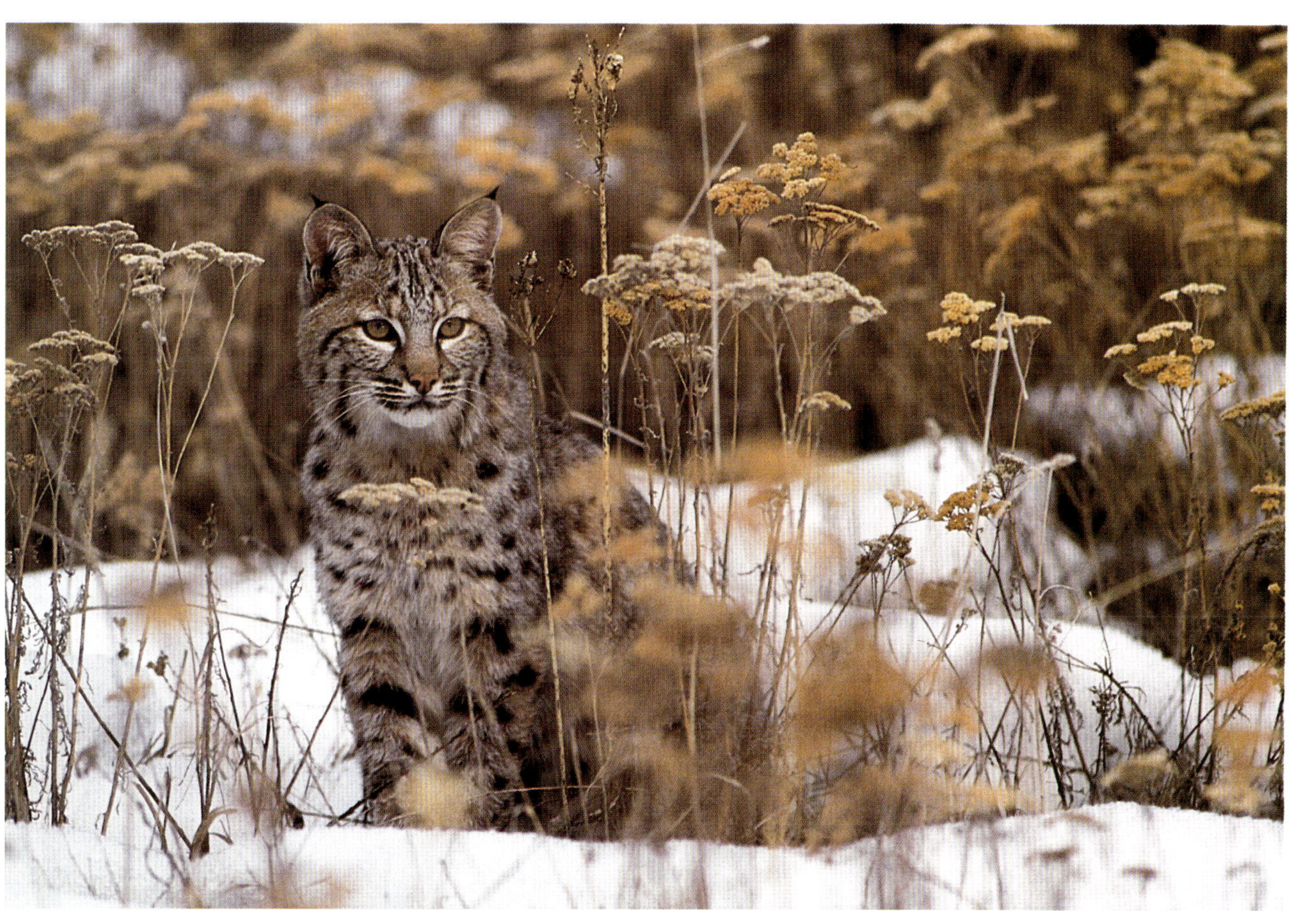

Bobcat in winter, Montana. Nikon F4, Nikon 500mm lens, Fujichrome 100.

Taking pictures like this with a sharp, quick-handling, long lens is great fun. But this lens is quite expensive. Do you take the volume of wildlife photographs, and do you sell enough of them, to justify purchasing such costly equipment?

often than not meals come from my ice chest rather than from a restaurant. I'm not suffering; by choice I would much rather be on location in the best shooting light than waiting for a meal at the Marriott.

Film costs, of course, are unavoidable. But purchasing film in quantity through a reliable discount house can knock off a dollar or two per roll. You can reduce processing expenses by using prepaid mailers. My local professional lab currently charges $7.25 to process one 36-exposure roll of E6 film. When I add the expense of driving to the lab to drop off the film and then driving back to pick it up—the entire round trip is about 25 miles—suddenly the cost is around $10 per roll for processing, not including the expense of my time.

Prepaid processing mailers bought from a photo discount house are currently around $4.50 per mailer plus postage. I can drop off the mailer at my local post office, which is about 2½ miles away, or at my own mailbox, which is about 80 yards from my office. For every 1,000 rolls of film I shoot, the difference in overhead adds up to roughly $4,500. So I patronize the local lab when I need fast turnaround time; otherwise I use prepaid mailers. That extra $4,500 goes right into my retirement fund.

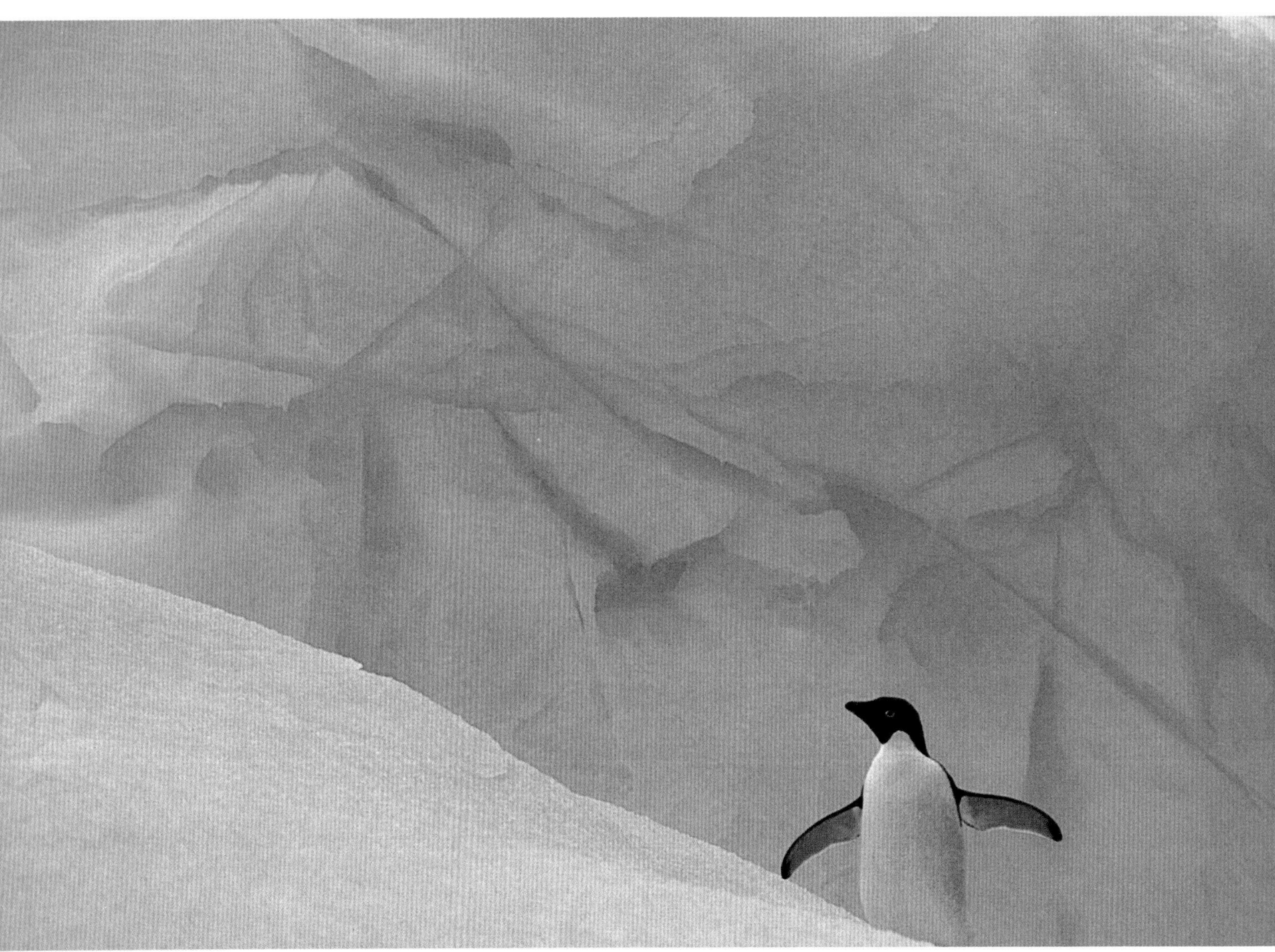

Adelie penguin on iceberg, Antarctica. Nikon F4, Nikon 80-200mm zoom lens, Fujichrome 100.

Antarctica is a great photographic destination, and being there is an incredible experience for a naturalist. But going there for anything beyond the most superficial tour is also quite costly. Will the resulting picture sales justify this expense?

These two appealing shots are of beautiful locations where the nearest lodging of any sort is miles and miles away. In order to be on location in good light I camped in my truck.

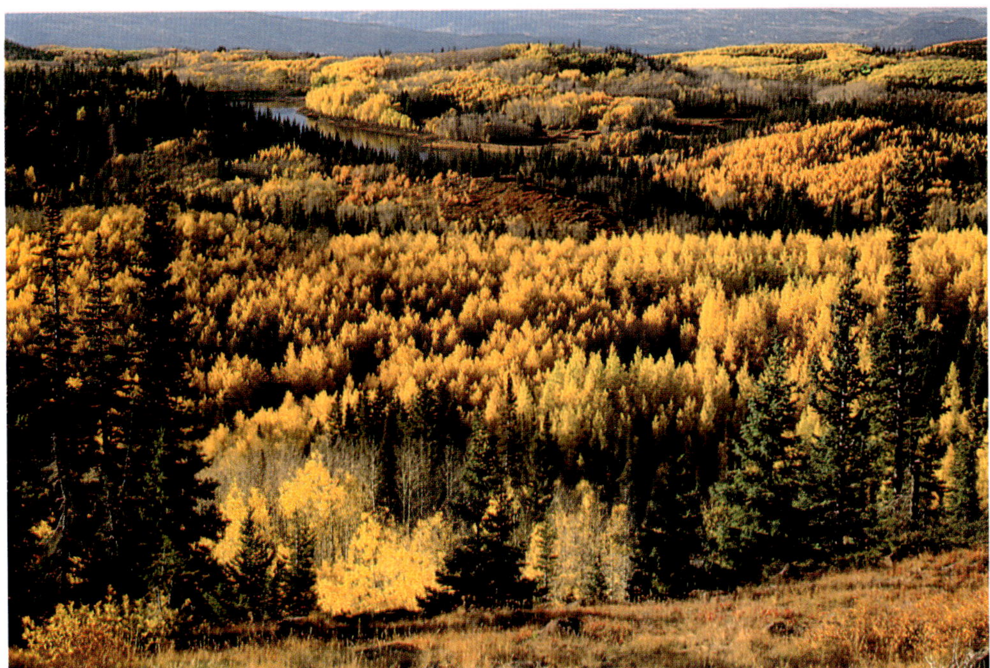

Autumn aspens, Grand Mesa, Colorado. Nikon F4, Nikon 35-70mm zoom lens, Fuji Velvia.

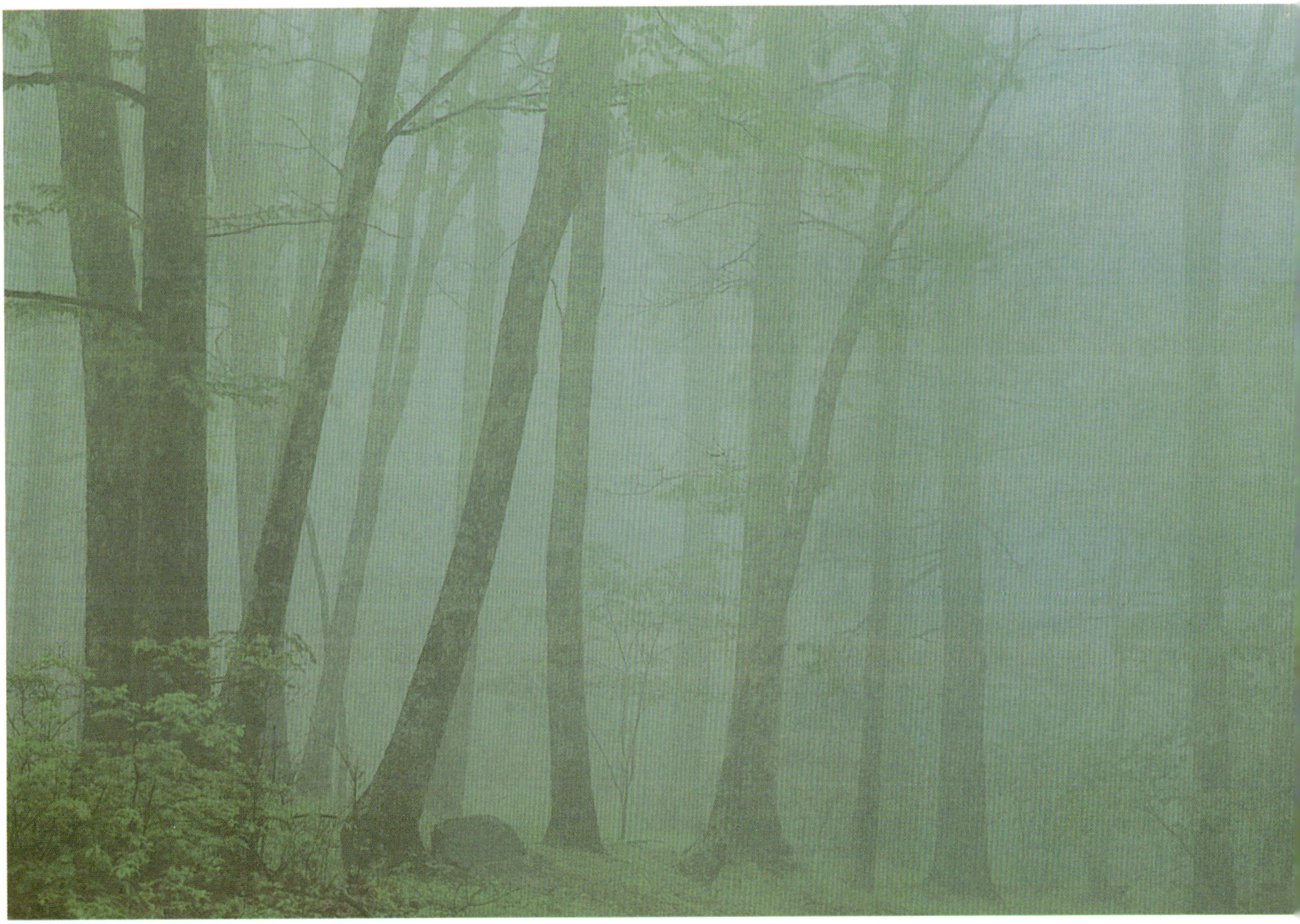

Trees in summer fog, Shenandoah National Park, Virginia. Nikon F4, Nikon 50-135mm zoom lens, Fuji Velvia.

LEGAL CONSIDERATIONS

When you begin thinking seriously about getting more than just one or two photographs published, you should realize that you're actually thinking about starting a small business. The extent to which the business grows is completely up to you, but in terms of business there is far more to photography than simply the ability to take good pictures. Marketing and business procedures don't take care of themselves; only you can do that. In fact, given comparable technical skills, what separates the successful photographer from the failure, the professional photographer from the amateur, is the ability to take care of business.

Successful businesses remain profitable by paying attention to four areas: producing a quality, professional product; pricing that product at a competitive level while still maintaining profitability; providing service to the nth degree to all clients; and researching and complying with all legal matters.

Three of these are obvious. Your photographs must be on the best films and of the best technical and aesthetic quality possible if you want to be paid professional prices for your work. If you're asked to quote fees for the use of your photographs, the amount must be in line with what markets will bear but that will still enable you to show a profit at the end of the year. Accurate bookkeeping and careful evaluation of expenses are necessary for an overview of finances and profitability. Service means following up when you make promises, sending submissions promptly, attending to necessary paperwork, meeting publishers' deadlines, and being as courteous and helpful as possible.

The legal considerations involved with going into business might not be so obvious. I strongly urge you to consult with your local Better Business Bureau, the Small Business Administration, and both state and federal revenue agencies (see page 128 for information on IRS tax matters). Most of these organizations have startup guidelines for small businesses, including licensing and tax information. Keep all this information on file, including the names of the individuals you spoke with and the dates of your conversations.

Generally most nature-photography businesses that don't sell photographic prints locally but rather license the use of photographs to publishers, are unique organizations in terms of local and state regulations. Explain exactly what it is you do, the product you sell (licensing use rights), whether or not you have local clients coming to your place of business, and whether or not you're selling publishing rights in-state or out-of-state. In short, be as specific as you can be. You should thoroughly investigate at least three specific areas.

Licenses and Permits

Find out if you need any state or local business licenses. If so, make sure you get them before you start operations on a large scale. Depending on where you live you might not need any license at all, or you might need quite a few licenses.

In the three states I've resided in as a working professional, I haven't needed any special paperwork to run my business. But I haven't sold work under an assumed business name, sold photographs locally either as prints or to local publishing clients, done local commercial work, or operated a place of business that clients could come to. Furthermore I made all my sales to out-of-state customers. Don't overlook any forms, permits, or regulations that may apply to your business because governmental bodies don't accept ignorance of the law as an excuse for noncompliance.

There definitely are some restrictions as to where and when you can photograph. It is simply good business ethics for you to learn these regulations and to abide by them. At the most basic level, some locations have a "No tripods" and/or a "No flash" rule. Some areas, such as critical nesting or denning habitats or revegetation areas, may be closed to the public. Demanding that you have certain privileges as a photographer or, even worse, simply ignoring these regulations is both elitist and unethical.

If you plan to run nature-photography workshops or tours, or to do any sort of advertising photography, be aware that most locations, including national parks, monuments, and wildlife refuges, require that you obtain a "Commercial Use Permit" before the event. Ordinarily this involves your providing proof of liability insurance and paying a fee for the permit.

Some state and national parks have restrictions on vehicle use. Alaska's Denali National Park, for example, limits the use of private automobiles on most of the park's roads. Professional photographers can obtain a permit to use their own vehicles for a limited time period, but they must follow an established procedure, This involves a lot of prior paperwork. Don't show up and whine about the regulations; plan ahead. As fundamental as it sounds, one option is simply to shoot elsewhere; go to a location without such limits. Is it imperative that you photograph in Denali? Are the subjects you want to photograph found only at Denali? Is access with your vehicle the only choice?

Sales Taxes

Be sure that you inquire specifically about whether or not you must pay state or local sales taxes. Explain carefully and thoroughly what you specifically do as a business. Not doing so could lead to rulings against you for back taxes. Consider the following short note from *The Guilfoyle Report* (December 1995):

> TAX ADVISORY
> According to *Photo District News*, several Vermont photographers have recently been audited and billed for back taxes and penalties because they failed to report sales taxes on their work. Under Vermont law, any transfer of title possession—including rental, lease, license to use or consume—is taxable. This applies to residents as well as photographers with a "business presence" in the state (which can include photographers there on assignment).

Model and Property Releases

If you're photographing people or privately owned property that is recognizable as such—for example, a building, a racehorse, or a sailboat—and you want your photographs to be available for advertising use, you should carry model and property releases and get them signed. A release is basically a document that in effect says the person being photographed or the person who owns the property not only has given you permission to take the photograph, but also to use it in some manner.

Obtaining a signed release lowers the probability of legal action for the typical commercial use of a photograph. This also protects you against invasion-of-privacy lawsuits, which is the unauthorized use of a photograph of a person for trade or advertising, and libel suits, in which the person in the picture claims to be demeaned by the publication of it. If you photograph people or personal-property items, you should read

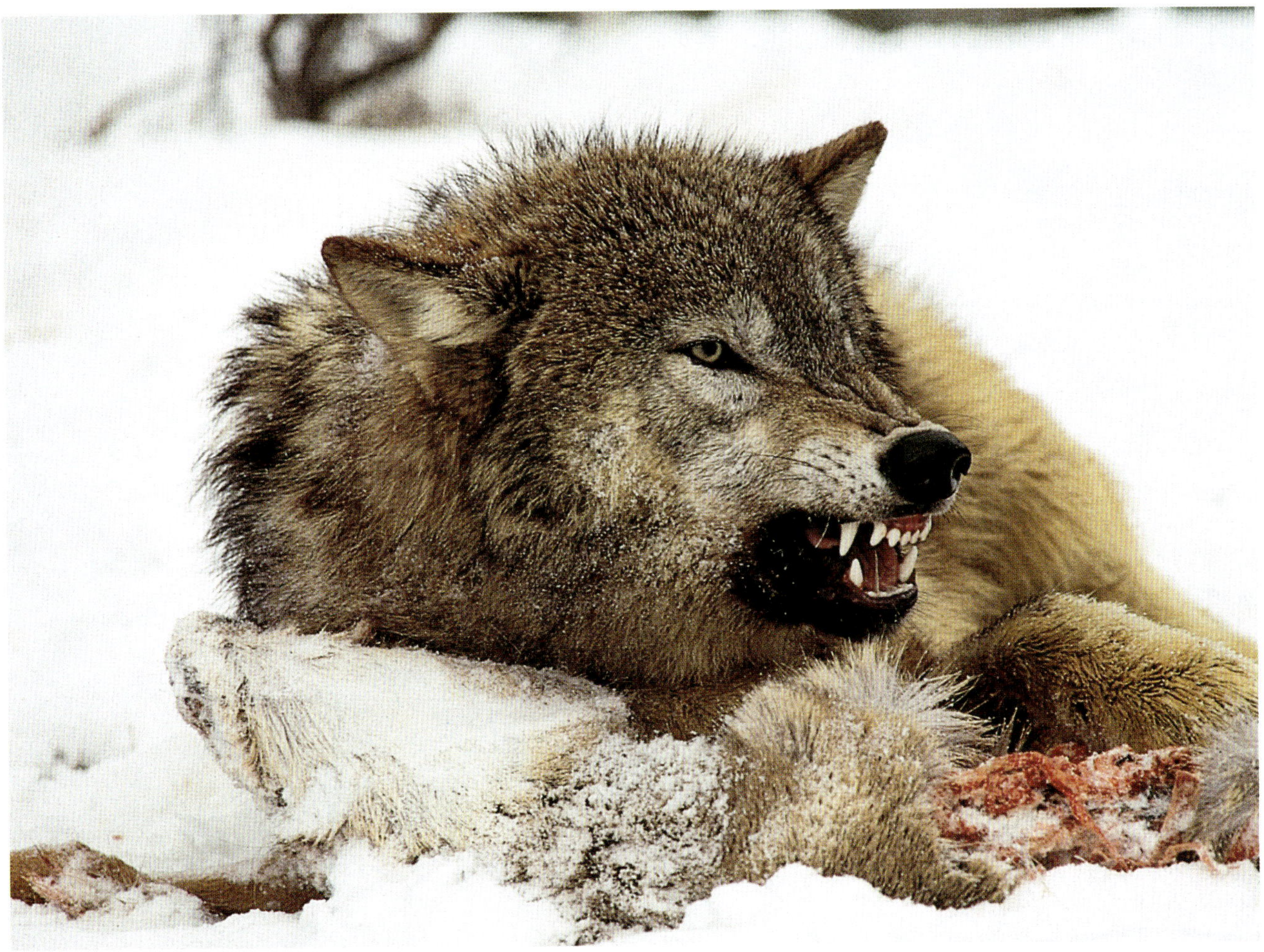

Wolf on deer carcass, snarling at other wolves, Montana. Nikon F4, Nikon 400mm lens, Fujichrome 100.

I made this shot while on an animal-model photo shoot. I have a signed release from the wolf's owner, keyed to my image file number. This release enables me to use the pictures from the shoot for commercial gain.

the ASMP publications concerning releases very carefully and follow their advice.

But what do you do as a nature photographer? Do you need a release to publish a fall scenic or even a complete picture essay in a magazine, such as *Outdoor Photographer*? No, you don't need anything for the editorial use of photographs. What about a shot of another photographer, illustrating the use of certain equipment? Once again, you don't need a release as long as the photograph is for editorial purposes.

Having said this, I strongly suggest getting a signed release whenever possible if you have people in your pictures. This is particularly important if there is even the slightest possibility that your photograph will be used in an advertisement, as promotional material, or in any manner that could be deemed embarrassing or compromising. When in doubt, get a release signed.

You can purchase pamphlets of generic model releases through most camera stores. You can also duplicate one of the following examples if you wish. You need to develop a system to tie any signed release to the actual photograph, either a note in your database, a model-release numbering system, or an explanation written on the release as to which photographs it covers. Be explicit here. A note on a release that reads "Photo of man with tripod" doesn't indicate which one of your 178 different pictures of this subject is the released picture. In addition you should make some notation on the slide mount in order to let editors know it is a released shot. Standard abbreviations are:

- MR Model release
- PR Property release
- NR No release

I have very few released photographs in my file simply because of the type of pictures I take. This isn't to say that I don't ask for releases whenever possible; I do. Actually, most of my releases aren't for people. I've photographed a number of animals at game farms that specialize in animal models, and I have a signed release from each of the farms just in case the photographs are picked up for advertisements.

I do carry releases and ask people to sign whenever I photograph them. For example, on my last trip to the Masai Mara in Kenya I photographed cheetahs momentarily sitting on top of a vehicle. The people inside were identifiable in the frame, so once the shooting opportunity was over I drove up and asked them to sign a release, which they did.

I carry a release form printed on the back of my business cards. A friend who shoots for a large stock agency showed me this trick. If

Red house and autumn maple, Vermont. Nikon F4, Nikon 24mm lens, Fuji Velvia.

Driving around Vermont one autumn I found this bright red house and a maple tree. I thought it would make a good stock shot for my "Buildings" file, as well as a good image to place with an agency. Luckily the owners were home at the time and were more than happy to sign a release. Actually they were absolutely thrilled that a photographer would want to shoot their house.

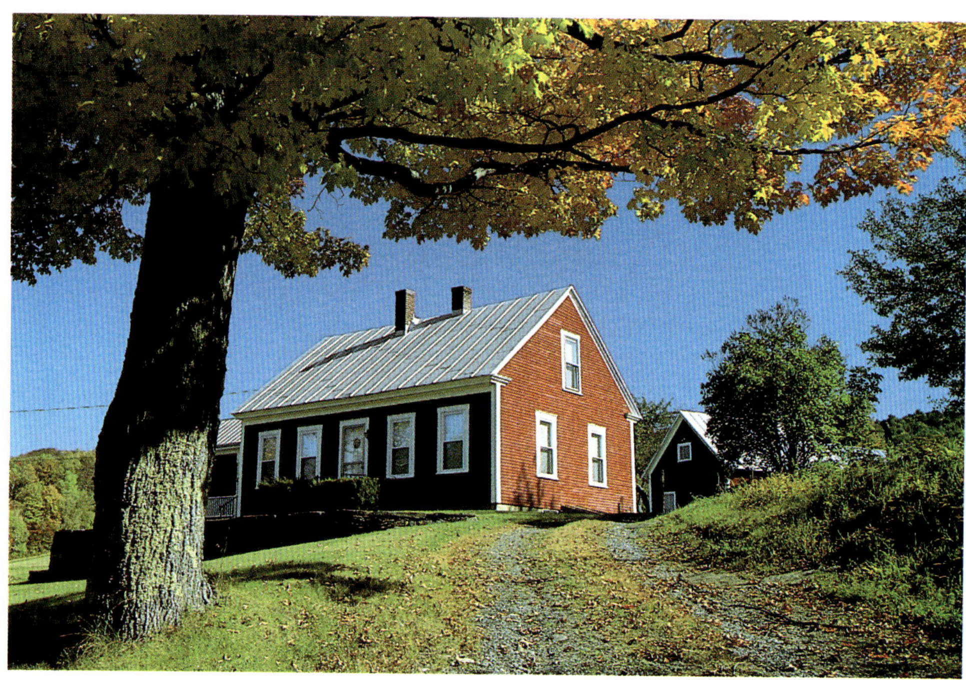

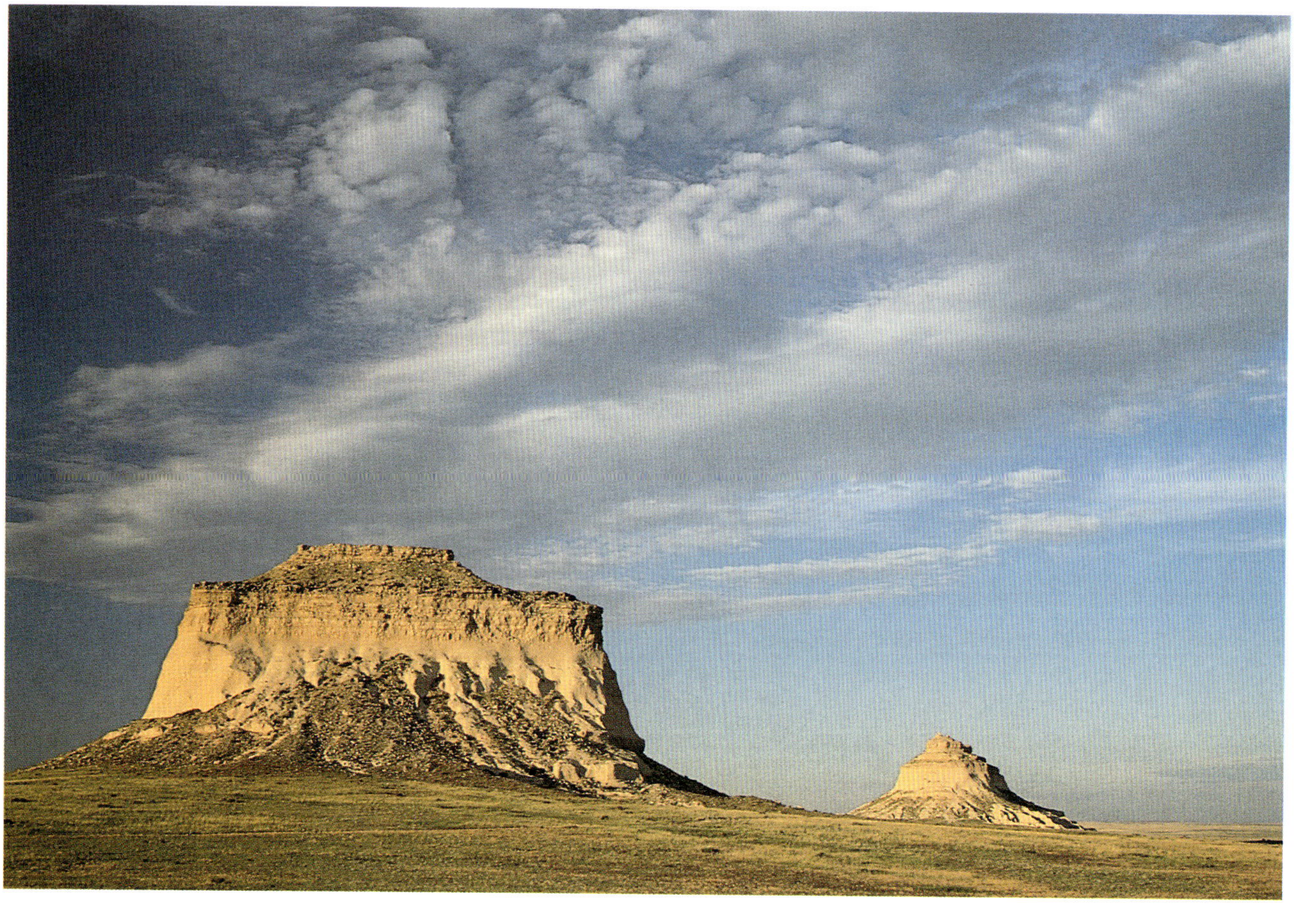

Pawnee Buttes, Pawnee National Grasslands, Colorado. Nikon F4, Nikon 35-70mm zoom lens, Fuji Velvia.

I don't have a release, nor do I need one, to sell this photograph to any buyer for any use.

you have a laser printer you can easily produce these yourself using the laser business-card forms manufactured by Avery (form #5371) and other paper companies. I've never had anyone refuse to sign one of my business-card forms. I believe this is partially so because a card isn't an intimidating piece of paper, whereas a full-page model release can be. However, if I specialized in people pictures or even took more of them than I do currently, I would use another form.

Printed here are several versions of releases, including my business-card form. Read these carefully before you decide which forms you want to use.

National Park Service Permits

After several years of discussions, ASMP won a clarifying statement from the National Park Service about regulations regarding professional photographers. The following statement was released with a letter, dated 4/6/90, from the Secretary of the Interior directing any misunderstandings to the Park Service's professional public-affairs staff.

NATIONAL PARK POLICY STATEMENT

It is the policy of the National Park Service to permit and encourage photography within the National Park System to the fullest extent possible consistent with the protection of resources and the enjoyment of visitors.

As a general rule, permits are not required for either commercial or noncommercial photographers. This is true whether or not the photographer uses tripods, flashbulbs, strobe lights, or interchangeable lenses.

Permits can be required when the photography involves product or service advertisements or the use of models, sets, or props, or when such photography could result in damage to the resources or significant disruption of normal visitor uses. Permits shall be required for photographers granted access to areas normally closed to the visiting public except that oral approval can be given for such access to a photographer engaged in bona fide news-gathering activities.

Photographers should not need a permit to go anywhere that members of the public are generally allowed to go without a permit. Nor should a permit be needed for photographers to do anything that members of the public are generally allowed to do without a permit.

If a photography permit is deemed appropriate in any particular situation, NPS personnel should impose only those conditions necessary to accomplish the needed resource protection, visitor use, or legal limitation. For advertising photography, it is appropriate to impose a permit condition that prohibits implied or stated Service endorsement of the advertised product or service.

Care should be taken that conditions are reasonable. Liability insurance requirements and other limitations should not be made unduly burdensome.

Photo Release

I give (Your Name) permission to photograph myself and/or property, and to use or sell the materials as he wishes.

Signed ____________________

Name (Print) ____________________

Address ____________________

City ____________ State ______

Zip Code ____________ Date ______

Minor Photo Release

I give (Your Name) permission to photograph the below named minor, and to use or sell the materials as he wishes.

Signed ____________________
(Parent/Guardian)

Minor's Name ____________ Age ______

Address ____________________

City ____________ State ______

Zip Code ____________ Date ______

Property Photo Release

I give (Your Name) permission to photograph the below-named property, to which I have ownership and/or legal control, and to use or sell the photos as he wishes.

Description of property:

Signed ____________________

Name (Print) ____________________

Address ____________________

City ____________ State ______

Zip Code ____________ Date ______

Photographer/writer Cliff Hollenbeck uses these model releases.

Photographer Rohn Engh devised this model release.

Model Release

RELEASE

In consideration for value received,* I hereby authorize ________________ (the photographer) and or parties designated by the photographer (including clients, purchasers, agencies and periodicals or other printed matter and their editors) to use my photograph in conjunction with my name (or fictitious name) for sale to or reproduction in any medium the photographer or his designees see fit for purposes of advertising display, audiovisual exhibition, or editorial use.

I affirm that I am more than 18 (21) years of age.

Signature ________________________________

Date ________________________________

- -

Guardian's consent (for model release)

RELEASE

I, ________________ parent/guardian of ________________________, a minor, in consideration for value received,* assign to ______________ it's customers and representatives, the exclusive right to copy and reproduce for the purpose of illustration, advertising, and publication in any manner whatsoever any photograph of said minor in its possession.

Signed ________________________________

Address ________________________________

Witness ________________________________

Date ________________________________

*compensation the model receives might be a dollar, a copy of the publication the picture appears in, etc.

This is the model release that is printed on the back of my business cards.

STOCK-PHOTO MODEL RELEASE

I hereby give John Shaw or his assigns permission to use and publish photos in which I appear without incurring any debts or liabilities of any kind.

Name (print) ________________________________

Address ________________________________

City/State/Zip ________________________________

Signature ________________________________

Parent or guardian's signature ________________________________

Stock pictures are photos made available for client use. The photos in which you appear may be used for editorial or advertising purposes.

ADULT RELEASE

In consideration of my engagement as a model, and for other good and valuable consideration herein acknowledged as received, I hereby grant to ____________ ("Photographer"), his/her heirs, legal representatives and assigns, those for whom Photographer is acting, and those acting with his/her authority, and permission, the irrevocable and unrestricted right and permission to take, copyright in his/her own name or otherwise, and use, re-use, publish, and re-publish photographic portraits or pictures of me or in which I may be included, in whole or in part, or composite or distorted in character or form, without restriction as to changes or alterations, in conjunction with my own or a fictitious name, or reproductions thereof in color or otherwise, made through any medium at his/her studios or elsewhere, and in any and all media now or hereafter known for illustration, promotion, art, editorial, advertising, trade, or any other purpose whatsoever. I also consent to the use of any published matter in conjunction therewith.

I hereby waive any right that I may have to inspect or approve the finished product or products and the advertising copy or other matter that may be used in connection therewith or the use to which it may be applied.

I hereby release, discharge and agree to save harmless Photographer, his/her heirs, legal representatives and assigns, and all persons acting under his/her permission or authority or those for whom he/she is acting, from any liability by virtue of any blurring, distortion, alteration, optical illusion, or use in composite form, whether intentional or otherwise, that may occur or be produced in the taking of said picture or in any subsequent processing thereof, as well as any publication thereof, including without limitation any claims for libel or invasion of privacy.

I hereby warrant that I am of full age and have the right to contract in my own name. I have read the above authorization, release, and agreement, prior to its execution, and I am fully familiar with the contents thereof. This release shall be binding upon me and my heirs, legal representatives, and assigns.

______________________	______________________
DATE	NAME
______________________	______________________
WITNESS	ADDRESS

SIMPLIFIED ADULT RELEASE

For valuable consideration received, I hereby grant to __________________ ("Photographer") the absolute and irrevocable right and unrestricted permission in respect of photographic portraits or pictures that he/she had taken of me or in which I may be included with others, to copyright the same, in his/her own name or otherwise; to use re-use, publish, and re-publish the same in whole or in part, individually or in any and all media now or hereafter known, and for any purpose whatsoever, for illustration, promotion, art, editorial, advertising and trade, or any other purpose whatsoever without restriction as to alteration; and to use my name in connection therewith if he/she so chooses.

I hereby release and discharge Photographer from any and all claims and demands arising out of or in connection with the use of the photographs, including without limitation any and all claims for libel or invasion of privacy.

This authorization and release shall also inure to the benefit of the heirs, legal representatives, licensees, and assigns of Photographer, as well as the person(s) for whom he/she took the photographs.

I am of full age and have the right to contract in my own name. I have read the foregoing and fully understand the contents thereof. This release shall be binding upon me and my heirs, legal representatives, and assigns.

______________________	______________________
DATE	NAME
______________________	______________________
WITNESS	ADDRESS

This photography release appears in Formalizing Agreements, *an ASMP publication.*

TAX MATTERS

Before you start seriously marketing your nature photographs, you should get ready to face more tax forms and preparation. Since selling photography is a business, you must report gross sales and total expenses in order to determine your tax liabilities. Even if photography is just an additional means of income as far as you're concerned, it still is a taxable source of income as far as the Internal Revenue Service (IRS) is concerned. However, having your own full-time or even part-time business enables you to take some substantial deductions to counterbalance taxable income.

Business or Pleasure?

First you need to determine if photography is really a business or just a hobby for you. The answer will affect how you report income. Many people have moneymaking hobbies that they would like to claim as businesses in order to take the largest deductions possible. You can deduct *hobby expenses* only up to the amount of income the hobby yields. You can claim *business expenses and deductions* over the total income that your business produces.

According to the IRS the difference between a business and a hobby is the primary intent of the activity. If your intent is primarily to have pleasure, even if the activity produces income, then the activity is a hobby. But if the intent is primarily to make money, then the activity is a business and you can deduct all the expenses ordinarily incurred to operate such a business.

For example, you are serious about your photography, and you sell some shots to a regional magazine. If your primary intent was having fun taking pictures and enjoying seeing your work published, then your photography is a hobby. If you get paid a total of $500 total for your pictures this year, you can deduct up to $500 for hobby expenses, such as film and processing. But if you're really trying to sell photographs and you are serious about publishing, your goal is to make money. So your photography is a business.

But—and this is a big "but"—the IRS will need proof that supports your claim that you're trying to run a business. One sure way is to report a profit in at least three out of five years. Even if you fail to do this, the IRS might still recognize you as a business. After all, it certainly isn't un-American to be a bad businessperson; many major American corporations are living proof of this fact. However, you'll have to convince the IRS during your audit that you are indeed serious about making a profit, and that you can afford standard living expenses while showing a net business loss for so many years.

Some of the best ways to avoid problems are also the most basic. First, give yourself a business name. This doesn't have to be fancy; mine is "John Shaw Photography." Then open a separate business checking account in this name. Have some business stationery and business cards printed. Set up a specific bookkeeping account for the business to track all income and expenses. Illustrate consistent picture submissions with a file of delivery memos. Keep careful records of business use of personal-type assets, such as your car, which are used for both business and pleasure.

You might also want to consider getting an employer identification number (EIN) from the IRS even if you don't have any employees. This costs nothing and remains your unique number as long as your business is in operation. All these steps are basic proofs that your photography is more than a hobby. Consequently you'll avoid most IRS questions.

If the IRS challenges your "intent" to make a profit and sends you a notice disallowing your business deductions, you have 60 days to file Form 5213, "Election to Postpone Determination." This delays the decision until the end of a five-year period, during which you can show a profit and substantiate your claims. Get a copy of IRS Publication #334, "Tax Guide for Small Businesses" (see page 139).

Organizing Your Financial Recordkeeping

In truth most problems you might have with the IRS are the result of your not paying attention to basic organization and recordkeeping. Careful recordkeeping means that you can avoid paying any unnecessary taxes. Remember that it is legal to *avoid* taxes, but illegal to *evade* them. Paying taxes in full and on time should be just another part of standard business procedures.

Maintaining financial records for your business, even if it is a one-person business, will be greatly simplified if you have a separate business account. Find a local bank you trust, and talk with a representative about accounts and establishing a line of credit *before* you need any money. Since you probably won't be opening a studio, building a separate office, or hiring designers and models, you won't have the overhead or credit needs of a commercial photographer. Still, it is better to know what money is available before you have an immediate need.

A business credit card is one of the easiest ways to simultaneously obtain quick credit and provide the expense records you need at tax time. But credit cards are also one of the easiest ways to get into serious debt, as far too many people know. Be judicious about your purchases, and pay off the balance every month in order to avoid finance charges.

I run my entire business through one credit card, which also simplifies accounting records. I use the card to cover every business expense possible, and I never pay cash if I can avoid doing so. Every month I reconcile the account with my receipts, and then I file away the credit-card statement with the receipts for tax purposes. In December my issuing bank sends out a yearly summary statement totaling all expenditures on the card. I file this document, too.

Regarding the IRS, most nature photographers set up their businesses as *sole proprietors*, an arrangement that can also include a spouse. This is by far the easiest way to run a small business and probably the best way to start out. Before you consider anything more complicated, such as a partnership or a corporation, consult with a good tax lawyer and accountant. The actual business will run on the cash basis of accounting, which means that you report income when a check is received and deduct an expense when the money is spent. If you're selling usage rights to books and magazines, you don't have to account for "starting and ending inventory."

Tracking Your Finances

Cash accounting is the simplest way to track finances. About the only problem you'll encounter occurs at the start of each new year. How do you record a check dated in December that you receive in January? Every client you have will be sending Form 1099, "Miscellaneous Income," to both you and the IRS. On this form the check will be

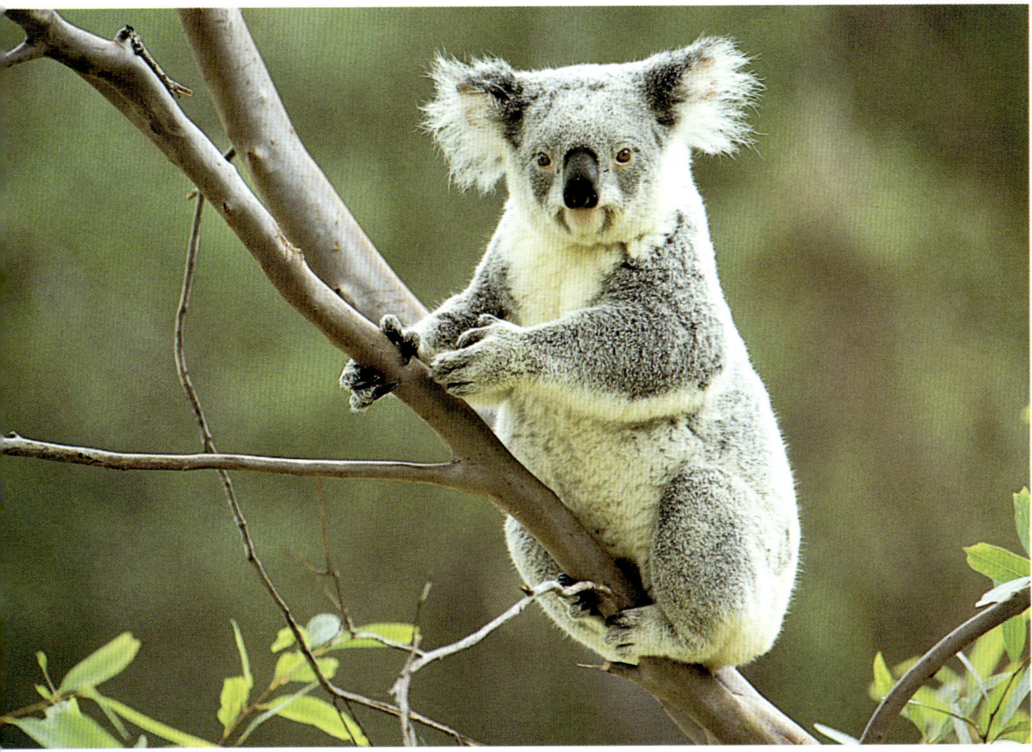

If you're truly interested in photographing nature, most likely you enjoy traveling to far-off places. The IRS considers the cost of travel a legitimate business expense if you can prove that the trip wasn't just a vacation.

Koala, Australia. Nikon F4, Nikon 400mm lens, Kodak Lumière 100.

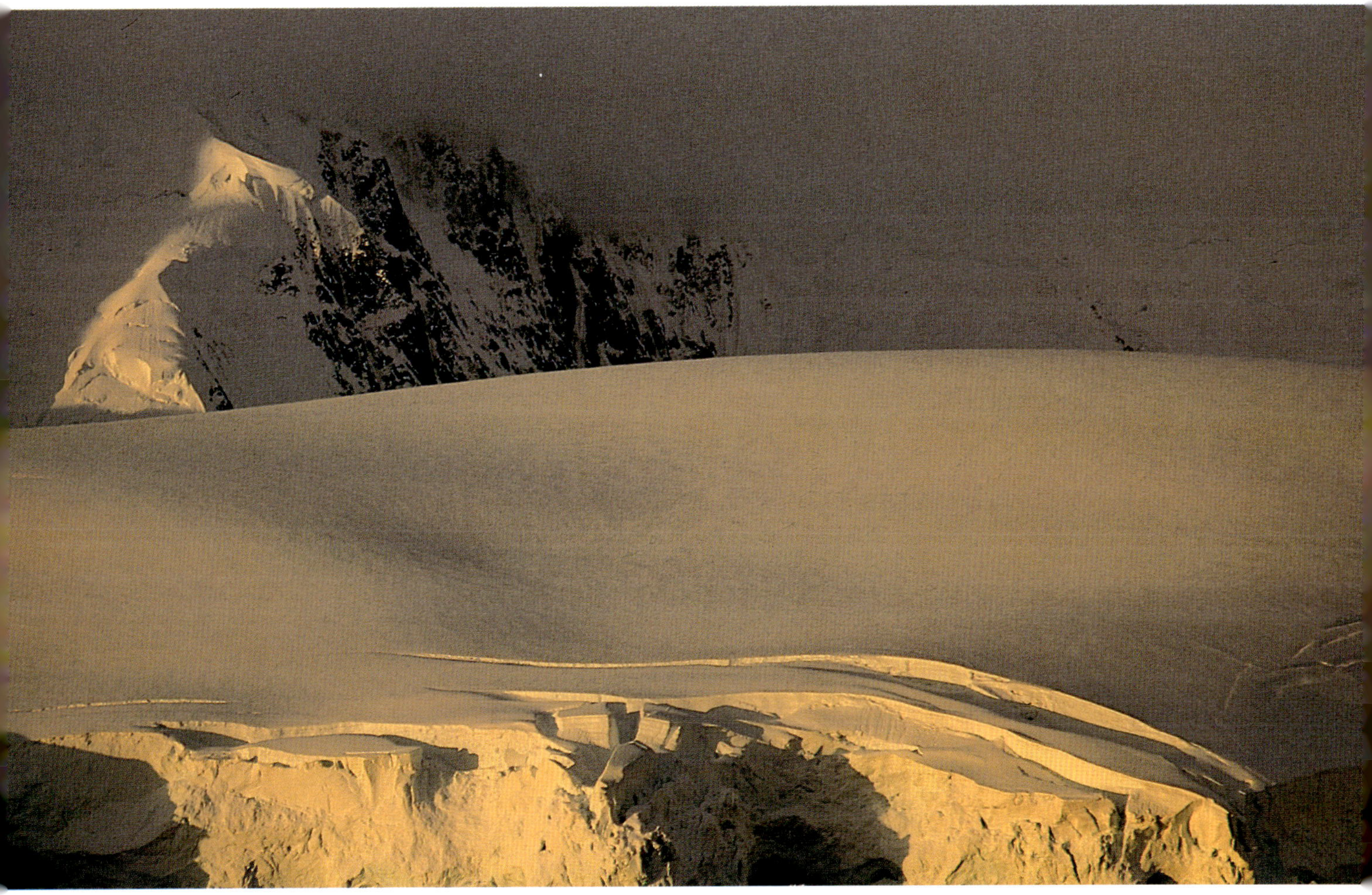

Glacier in Neumayer Channel, Antarctica. Nikon F4, Nikon 80-200mm zoom lens, Fujichrome 100.

Actively marketing your pictures from Alaska and Florida substantiates writing off travel expenses.

included in the issuing year's total payments. This is how I report the money even though it wasn't actually available for my use until the following year. Be consistent in your reporting. (By the way, usually you should report deductible credit-card purchases in the tax year in which the purchases were made, not the year in which you pay the card's charges.)

As a small business owner, you'll probably do your own books. Complete and accurate recordkeeping is the foundation of all good business administration. This is actually pretty easy for most starting nature-photography businesses, but it is time-consuming. Set up an accounting system by deduction category, get a receipt for any expense over $25, and file it.

The simplest way I know to keep track of your business finances is to use a computer money-management program that shows income along with the general deduction categories that the IRS set up. The categories are listed in IRS Schedule C, "Profit or Loss from Business," which you'll have to file with your 1040 return. I use *Quicken* as my bookkeeping software program, and I give it my highest recommendation. A cash account in *Quicken* basically works just the way your checkbook does. You track both income and expenses by categories that you devise, and then by name within each category.

For example, if I receive a check from a stock agency, I enter it as income under my "Agency" category with the agency's name as payee. I enter non-agency payments by client name in my "Direct Photo Sales" category. Expense categories include:

- Film and processing
- Postage
- Photo equipment
- Office expenses
- Travel

Whenever I want, I can run all kinds of reports to show me exactly how much income I've received and where it has gone. I can easily determine how much money I've made from each client, which stock

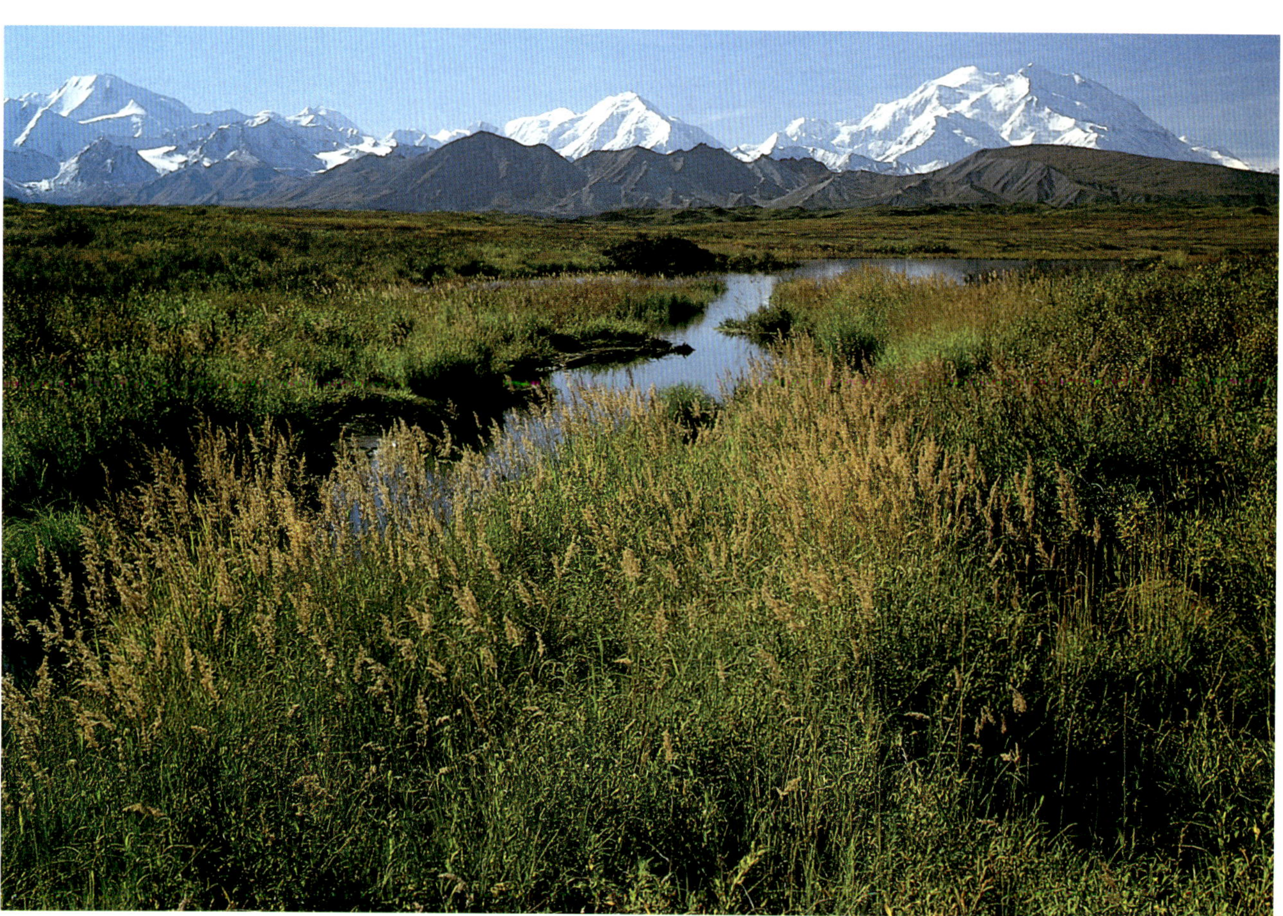

Mt. McKinley and beaver pond, Denali National Park, Alaska. Nikon F3, Nikon 50-135mm zoom lens, Fujichrome 50.

agency produces the best return, and how much I've spent on film this year compared to last year. *Quicken* is a good program, easy to learn and easy to use. Just set up as many income and expense categories as your situation calls for. (The company that offers *Quicken* also has a tax software program called *TurboTax*. With it, you can directly transfer the income and expenses you record with *Quicken* onto your federal tax forms.)

If you look at Federal Schedule C, you'll see exactly what the IRS deems acceptable expense deductions. I've included some of these here, skipping ones that probably won't apply to a small nature-photography business. Remember, the definition of a deduction is "an ordinary and necessary expense" to the process of conducting business.

Advertising

This deduction might or might not apply to you. It is the direct cost of any advertising you purchase, not the expense of putting the ad together. For example, you would need to report a listing in *Green Book* or *Direct Stock* here.

Car and Truck Expenses

These are pro-rated on business use, so you can either deduct actual expenses (gas, oil, basic maintenance) or take a mileage allowance (much easier). A third option is to depreciate the vehicle itself. Be careful: auto expenses are one of the first items examined during an audit. You must be able to prove business use versus personal use. Having a company car that is driven only for business is one solution, but a logbook for recording dates, business mileage, and destinations is acceptable.

Commission and Fees

Your stock agency might be taking a 50-percent "commission" for handling your work, but ordinarily agencies take this amount off the top before they issue you any money. Therefore, you can't claim their half of the sales figures as a commission expense. Stock agencies don't report the gross amount of sales as your income, just the portion actually paid to you. Since you don't receive the gross amount as income, you can't deduct their half as an expense.

Depreciation

This is a huge, complicated area that involves the cost of your photography equipment, office furniture, office equipment, and all other capital expenses. Even though you paid out the full amount of these items this year, the cost must be depreciated over their useful life. And the length of that "life" varies by item. Read the tax literature carefully.

Currently another choice is to expense up to $17,500 of business equipment—tangible personal property, that is—in a single year rather than depreciating it over several years. You might try figuring out Schedule C with the standard depreciation and then again with an amount expensed to see which works better. You can only elect to expense an amount equal to your taxable business income. So if your taxable income is $10,000, you can deduct $10,000 and carry any excess over to the following year.

Keep in mind that home computers must be used at least half of the time for business in order to be considered business equipment. If this applies, you can deduct

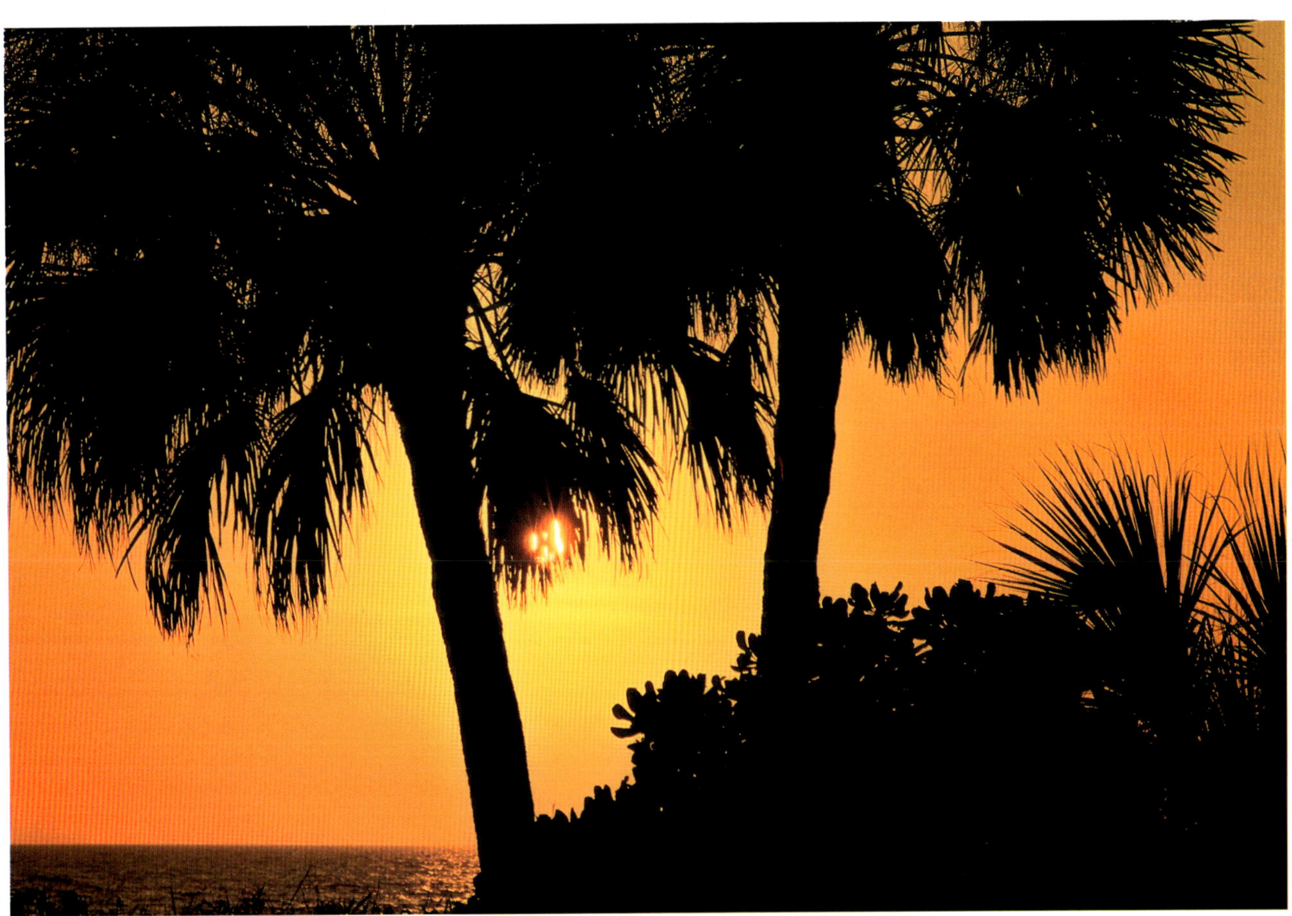

Sunset and coconut palm, Florida. Nikon F4, Nikon 50-135mm zoom lens, Fuji Velvia.

that proportion of the cost or depreciate that amount over the life of the computer. Your business software may also be deductible.

Insurance

You can deduct camera insurance and any business insurance, but not health or life insurance. Check the current tax forms for reporting health-insurance premiums for the self-employed.

Legal and Professional Services

The costs of lawyers, certified public accountants (CPAs), bookkeepers, and models are reported here. These people must be in business and offer similar services to others. For example, the $50 you gave your brother Bill to do your taxes isn't deductible here unless he is legitimately in the tax-preparation business.

Office Expenses

All the usual office expenses are reported here, such as stationery, postage, business cards, and copier and fax paper.

Repairs and Maintenance

You can report repairing any business equipment that is worn or broken, but you can't deduct the expense of just making improvements.

Supplies

These are non-office supplies necessary for business in general but not for a specific project. Batteries for your camera's motordrive seem to fit this description.

Taxes and Licenses

If you paid any business taxes or license fees, you can report them here.

Travel Expenses

These expenses refer to what it cost you to go shoot pictures, other than your business-vehicle expenses. This category includes such expenses as car rentals, airline tickets, and lodging expenses. The IRS closely examines this area, so make sure that you have receipts and can support your deductions. Claiming that you needed a two-week beach-front rental in Hawaii in February to shoot stock pictures might be questioned. In fact, it *will* be questioned unless you can prove how you produced lots of stock sales and articles. Sure.

Meals and Entertainment

You can deduct half the actual cost of meals while on the road shooting, or you can take a standard per-diem deduction. I doubt that you'll have much to report as "entertainment," unless you take an editor to lunch. Perhaps those sunflower seeds you bought for bird-feeder shots would fall under this category.

Utilities

A separate business-telephone line is deductible. If you have only one line for both your home and office, the cost of local service isn't deductible.

Other Expenses

Be sure to report film and processing under this miscellaneous category.

Home Office Expenses

You'll have to fill out Form 8829 in order to figure out this deduction. If photography is a sideline business for you, you'll have to be careful. Home-office space must be an area that you use exclusively for business. Home-office deductions are another audit trigger area for the IRS. Showing a profit is one step in alleviating their concerns. If your only source of income is nature photography and you have no other office for your profitable business, you shouldn't have a problem.

Additional Tax Forms

Schedule C isn't the only tax form you'll need in order to report business income. If any of your equipment depreciated, you'll have to work through Form 4562, "Depreciation and Amortization." (This is also where you explain vehicle use and expenses.) Keep in mind that when an item has been fully depreciated, it may still have some value. If you sell it, you must report the income on Form 4797, "Sale of Business Property." Suppose, for example, you had an old zoom lens that fully depreciated, but then you sold if for $100. You can report this sale on Form 4797 rather than as photography-business income to avoid paying unnecessary self-employment taxes.

Speaking of self-employment tax, this is another way of saying "Social Security tax." And, of course, since you are the sole proprietor of your business, you are both employer and employee. And as such you must pay both halves of this amount. See Schedule SE.

If your business income is more than $500 in a given year (and after all a much larger number called profit is exactly why you are in business), you're required to pay estimated income taxes. Unlike a standard job, where taxes are deducted from your take-home pay—this is called *withholding*—the income you receive as a photographer is just gross income. Consequently four times a year you must ante up what you think you owe the government. Get Form 1040-ES, do the math, and write a check. To avoid penalties for potential underpayment, pay at least the same amount that you owed your last tax year. If you believe your business is going to grow, take the amount of last year's tax due and add $100.

These are some of your federal tax considerations. Almost every state also has special forms and procedures, including payment of state estimated taxes. If you want more complete information, contact the IRS. Direct your requests to one of the regional form-distribution centers, which offer all sorts of free publications (see page 139).

Having provided all this information about taxes, I want to state, loud and clear, that I am not a tax lawyer, I am not an accountant, and I am not a tax expert. I am just a photographer who, like everyone else, has to pay taxes.

AN OVERVIEW OF DIGITAL IMAGING

When the term "digital imaging" is spoken to photographers, usually one of two concepts come to mind. First is the idea of using a completely digital camera to capture images on disc, bypassing film altogether. Several of these cameras are on the market, including versions from Canon and Nikon working in conjunction with Kodak and Fuji. While this technology holds much promise for the future, if you're interested in marketing nature pictures today (1996), I see little immediate need to take digital pictures.

First of all, the cost of the cameras is quite high, upward of $10,000. But this is only your starting expense. Once you capture an image ("push the shutter release" seems out-of-date for a digital camera), what do you do with the digital information? You must either download it into a computer in order to send out the file, or output the information as a hard print through a dye-transfer sublimation thermal printer. Either way you'll need to buy some more expensive hardware. At this point you can't simply submit digital files to clients since not all of them have the means at their end to deal with images received in this manner. Sending actual prints to clients, even a non-darkroom print, isn't acceptable. Right now, stick to shooting film.

The other typical reaction to "digital imaging" is that it should really be called "digital manipulation of images." Instead of dodging, burning, cropping, and spotting prints in a darkroom, you can work on an image using a computer. Basically digital manipulation has two major applications. You can create an entirely new picture out of elements from several other photographs. You can also "repair" a single photograph by removing scratches, taking out offending elements, or adding highlights to animals' eyes. Again you end up with a data file, so again you face a decision as to how to present the image to a client.

While I don't think there is much pressing need in nature photography for a digital camera, I definitely see a use for the digital repair of images—using computer technology for practical purposes as a digital darkroom. The questions are really quite simple: Should you do the work yourself or hire an outside source? And since repairing even a single slide is expensive, how much money do you want to spend?

The Step-by-Step Process

Digital manipulation isn't something you would do to every image in your file. Far from it, unless all you want to do is sit in front of a computer day after day after day. Consider, for a moment, just a few of the necessary steps in the process.

First, you need hardware and software. I'm assuming that you're serious about your work and that you want to be able to output salable film images. Digital manipulation breaks down into: (a) scanning your film to convert it into digital form; (b) inputting that digital information into a computer loaded with the correct software; (c) working on the image through the software; and (d) outputting the manipulated image back onto film. Generally it is easier and far more cost effective to have someone else make the scans for you unless you're going into digital manipulation full-time. Of course, that would mean you wouldn't be in the field photographing.

Scanning Options

Most scans that service bureaus, which are in essence digital photo labs, produce for professional photographers are either made via a drum scanner or in the Kodak Photo CD format. The latter has two levels, Photo CD and Pro Photo CD. Expect to pay about $75 or more per image for a drum scan, roughly $20 per image for a Pro Photo CD scan, and around $3 for a Photo CD scan. A drum scan or a Pro Photo CD scan should yield a file in the neighborhood of 72 megabytes (megs), while a Photo CD is 18 megs. Which scan you need is partially determined by what format you start with (35mm, 6 x 7cm, 4 x 5 inch) and what you want to eventually output (again, 35mm, 6 x 7cm, 4 x 5 inch). By the way, all scans aren't created equally; the quality of the scanner operator determines the quality of the scan. The better the scan, the better your end results will be.

Getting Set Up

Several points are immediately obvious. First, a large amount of money is already involved. To have 100 slides scanned on Pro Photo CD at today's prices, you must spend about $2,000. And this is only the first step in the process. Second, if you want to work on digital images, you better become a computer jockey. You'll need to learn the language to follow the procedures.

Suppose that you've had one of the Photo CD scans made. Next, in order to input the picture into your computer, you need one with a Photo CD-compatible drive. However, the odds are that the computer you already own for word processing isn't powerful enough for digital manipulation, nor does it have enough random access memory (RAM). For that matter, unless you have one of the latest speed machines, your computer probably isn't fast enough either—unless you like to take a lot of coffee breaks while waiting for your computer to finish a job.

The most popular machines for image manipulation are the high-end Macintosh computers (Macs) and personal computers (PCs) with fast chips. You'll need a lot of disc storage space. After all, where are you going to put all those image files you create if they are between 18 and 72 megs each? A hard drive in the gigabyte range is a definite plus. Add as much RAM as you possibly can; 48 megs is about the minimum for working with Photo CD data, while 148 megs will enable you to play with fewer restrictions.

Of course, you'll also need special-image manipulation software; Adobe Photoshop is the most popular program. Be aware, though, that being able to fully utilize Photoshop isn't a skill you learn in a few hours or even a few days. To be proficient you must continually work within the program. The total expense for the hardware (excluding a scanner) and software is somewhere in the neighborhood of $10,000 through mail-order discount houses, and even more if you purchase these items locally. And you have to factor in the amount of time you spend learning to use the software.

Once you've worked on an image, you still have to get it back onto film. Unless you want to purchase a film recorder, you'll need a means of taking the data file back to a service bureau. Your choices are either a SyQuest removable drive, a ZIP drive, or a CD write drive. In other words, you have to buy more hardware. At the service bureau your data file is turned back into film. The cost for this ranges from around $5 for a single 35mm transparency (although there is almost always a minimum charge of about $25) to between $100 and $200 to output it as a high-end 4 x 5-inch image.

An alternative is to do what I do. If I wanted to be a computer operator, I wouldn't be a photographer, but all I want to do is to

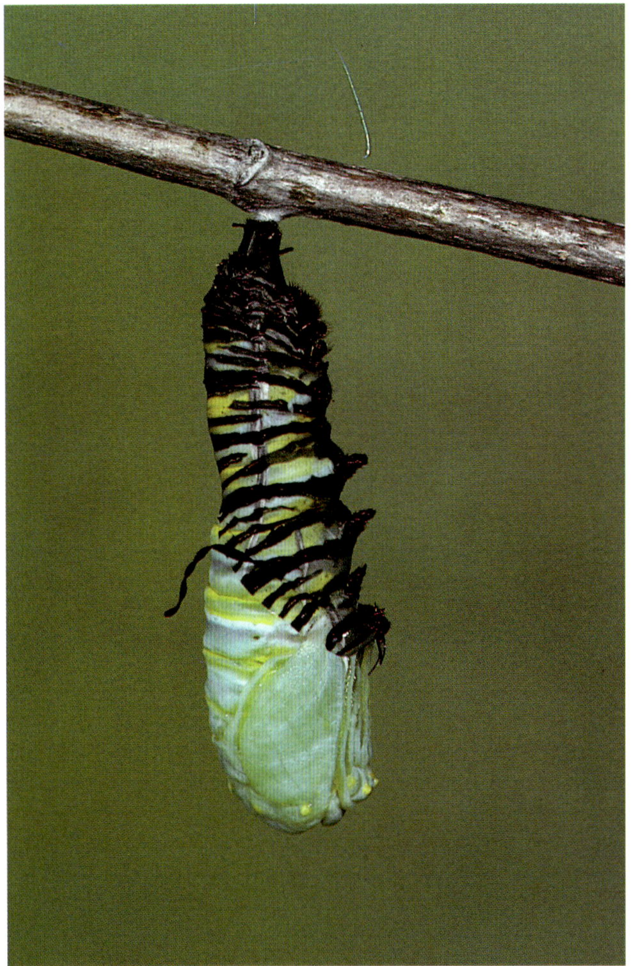

Monarch butterfly larva pupating, scratched version. Nikon F3, Nikon 105mm macro lens, Kodachrome 25.

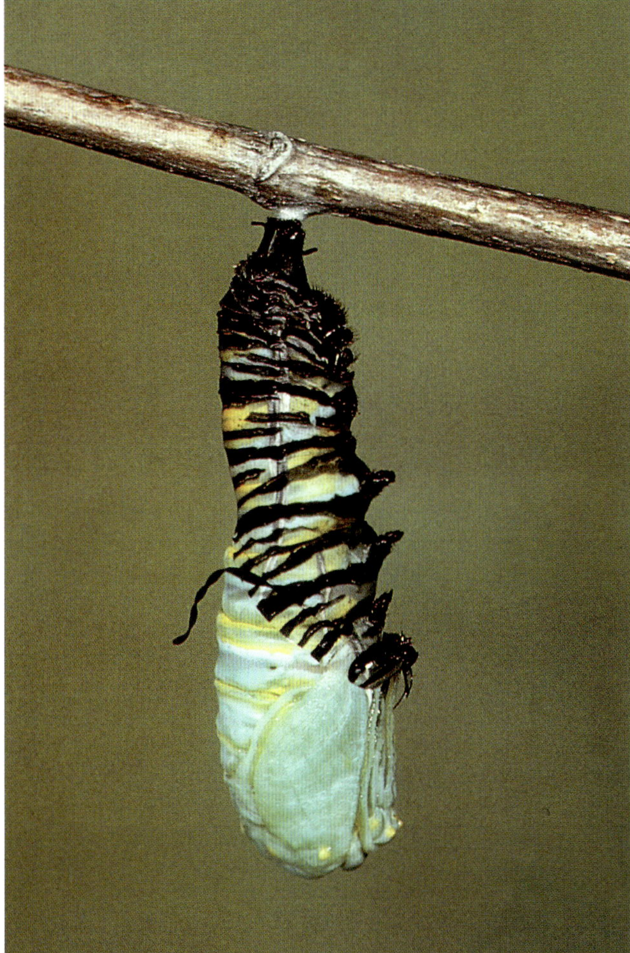

Monarch butterfly larva pupating, scratch repaired.

The original slide was severely damaged, so I had it scanned and repaired digitally. Actually the "repaired" version was presented to Amphoto Books, the publisher of this book, not as an actual piece of film but as digital information on a SyQuest disc running on a Mac platform. The times, they are a changing.

take pictures. So I haven't done the little digital manipulation that I've tried on my images—and this has been only to fix scratches on slides. I think it is far more efficient and cost effective to have a skilled operator fix any problems than for me to spend hours learning another program on additional, expensive computer hardware.

If I need to have a salable image repaired, I take the damaged film to a digital lab and simply say, "Fix this." The service bureau is going to go through all the same steps with the same equipment, although they'll have top-of-the-line scanners and computers. Consequently fixing one small scratch on one slide is still going to be expensive. Expect to pay a minimum of $50 to get one quality 35mm slide back.

Creating an entirely new picture from graphic elements taken from other photographs is another story. Plan on hours of computer time if you want the resulting image to look right. Can you justify the expense? This is a direct business decision. Is the potential return worth the cost of the procedure? Advertising shots are reworked extensively, but they are generally only one final picture and usually have big budgets standing behind the work. In nature photography ordinarily you'll be paying the bill for the image manipulation, and adding a few hundred dollars overhead per image isn't always smart.

(By the way, magazine and book publishers don't digitize pictures and then rework them extensively. The publishers might eliminate a small, distracting element if it is easy to do—as they would have done in a darkroom in the old days—but no typical end user of nature pictures has the time or finances required for full computer manipulation. Consider that the average issue of a magazine might have 75 to 100 photographs in it. Spending a couple of extra hours per photograph in digital work adds up to hiring one more full-time person on staff doing nothing but digital imaging eight hours a day, five days a week.)

So picture manipulation is thrown back onto photographers' shoulders. I think that this creates some additional problems. First of all, I'm starting to see some awful pictures that have obviously been put together, appearing to all the world like a cut-and-paste paper collage. Unless the operator is quite skilled with Photoshop, the results don't always look right. For example, edges between objects aren't quite realistic, or the light on different portions of the scene comes from different angles; the latter is identical to the old problem of a double-exposed full moon over a sidelit foreground.

Remember when desktop publishing first became popular? Everyone suddenly produced a newsletter, some of which were just horrible. People seemed to believe that if they had the option to use 19 different fonts and graphic borders, they were obligated to do so. Some digital pictures look like this: they lump together lots of elements from different scans ("Hey, I've got this neat wolf silhouette, and here's a full moon, and boy this tree looks nifty, and maybe I'll turn the sky magenta, and some geese in flight up there at the top . . ."). Enough.

But I've also seen some high-quality work in print. This is where I believe photographers need to develop some guidelines about presenting images to editors. I think that photographers need to distinguish between a natural-history photograph, a recording of something that is actually in front of you, and a digitally combined or created picture.

Is It Manipulation?

I want to make some distinctions here. I see nothing wrong with using filters to enhance a photograph. Is this manipulation? Is it falsifying a photograph? I wouldn't consider it as such. Suppose you use a graduated neutral-density (ND) filter in a shot. What you're actually doing is compressing the tonal range so that the film is capable of recording more of the subject. But you're still working with only the elements of what is there.

However, I think that digitally adding a different sky or a mountain, or an animal or two, is another matter. You've created something that didn't exist at that moment in time. Is this wrong? No, not as far as I'm concerned—so long as the resulting image is clearly and prominently marked as a manipulated computer graphic, and it isn't presented as a natural-history fact.

What worries me is that the end user of a photograph might not know the difference since editors aren't naturalists. For example, I saw a photograph depicting several humpback whales breaching simultaneously. Do humpbacks actually display such behavior in unison? What about an image depicting different species of animals interacting? Do they? Truth in captioning—stating outright that an image is a digital expression and not a recording of an actual event—would alleviate most of my concerns.

Tony Stone Images, a major stock agency, is starting to do just that. The firm has introduced the practice of identifying all images that have undergone significant digital manipulation. The label "DC," which stands for "Digital Composite," indicates an image with a component that has been moved, removed, or added. An image that has been either digitally enhanced, such as by stretching, distorting, changing textures or density, or selectively enlarged, is labeled "DE," for "Digital Enhancement." The "CE" label, an abbreviation for "Color Enhancement," signifies that the image's colors have been significantly modified or altered via digital means. These notations appear on slide mounts and alongside pictures in the company's stock catalog. If these identifiers were to come into common use and to be published in printed picture captions, I would be much happier.

SOFTWARE OPTIONS

Some software programs are designed specifically for photographers. These include captioning programs, database programs, and full-featured programs that generate delivery memos, invoices, and more. This list is by no means a complete directory of all the available software, nor is it an endorsement of any program. I haven't tried all of these programs; in fact, I've actually seen only one or two of them in operation. The programs I use (Nutshell as a database, WordPerfect for all word processing, and Quicken for accounting) work fine for me, and I'm used to them.

And just as there isn't only one camera brand for all professional photographers, there isn't only one program for office procedures. Contact the suppliers for more information about the specific features of each program and the computer equipment needed to run the software.

Obviously you'll need some general software. If you have a computer you're probably already working with software that can be used in a nature-photography business. Today most computers are sold with a fairly extensive software package already installed.

Aperture 5.0 (PC or Mac)
Horizon Software
P.O. Box 549
Helena, AL 35080
205-525-5333

Cradoc Captionwriter (Mac or PC)
Photo Management System (Mac or PC)
Perfect Niche Software
6962 East First Avenue
Suite 103
Scottsdale, AZ 85251
602-945-2001

File-a-Foto (PC)
Tropich Software
529 Central Avenue
Scarsdale, NY 10583
914-472-0278

Full Spectrum Pro (Mac)
ProFiler (Mac)
Stock Module (Mac)
Parahelion
P.O. Box 107
Cornish Flat, NH 03746
603-675-2966

LABELbase (PC)
LABELmate (Mac or PC)
LABELware (Mac or PC)
LASERware (Mac or PC with laser printers)
QuickStock (Mac)
Image Innovations
7685 Washington Avenue South
Minneapolis, MN 55439
800-345-4118

Label Power (PC)
Caption Power (PC)
Power Software
702 Gist Avenue
Silver Spring, MD 20910
301-589-1690

MacStock Label (Mac)
MacStock X (Mac)
MacStock X+ (Mac)
Stock Express 3.0 (Mac)
Photo Agora
Hidden Meadow Farm
Keezletown, VA 22832
703-269-8283

Norton Slide Captioning System (PC)
Boyd Norton
P.O. Box 2605
Evergreen, CO 80439
303-674-3009

Nutshell
Nutshell Plus II
Ultra-Press
Fairhaven Software
295 Phillips Avenue
New Bedford, MA 02746
508-994-6400

Phototrack (PC)
SuperLabel (Mac)
Phototrack Software
6392 South Yellowstone Way
Aurora, CO 80016
303-690-6664

Proslide II (PC)
Ellenco
P.O. Box 159
Tijeras, NM 87059
505-281-8605

SlideBase Pro (PC)
Multiplex
1555 Larkin Williams Road
Fenton, MO 63026
800-325-3350

HANDLING REJECTION

Not making sales is just part of the business of nature photography. Indeed, the vast majority of what you send out won't be purchased by clients. After all you might send a submission of 100 transparencies to satisfy the needs of an editor who has space for only two shots. In fact, 98 percent of your submission will be returned unused.

Receiving photographs back unused isn't necessarily a comment on the quality of your work but on the realities of publishing. Obviously if you *never* make a sale, I suggest that you reexamine how you're shooting and how you're presenting your pictures to the markets.

Most of the time you'll get submissions returned with little or no explanation as to why the material wasn't used. Editors generally don't have the time to write out a rationale as to why they purchased one picture and not another. Years ago *Audubon* magazine had a "Returns Form" on which picture editors could quickly check off some points, thereby letting photographers know where they stood. Although the magazine's staff members no longer use this form, I've included it here since much can be learned from it.

AUDUBON

Thank you for submitting material to AUDUBON. We are returning your material enclosed herewith, for one of the following reasons:

_____Terms of Delivery Memo too restrictive

_____Unacceptable format (___prints ___dupes ___in Kodak boxes)

_____Material needs editing, too many images

_____Currently overstocked
___try resubmitting same material in _____ months
___try submitting new material in _____ months

_____Too similar to material on hand or recently published

_____Inappropriate subject matter
___study magazine, then query or submit different subject

_____Quality of material does not meet our standards
___technical quality good, concept too ordinary for us
___work shows promise, try again
___based on submission, we cannot be encouraging

When submitting material, please remember:

1. to include sufficient postage to insure the safe return of your photographs
2. we are not responsible for unsolicited material
3. seasonal material should be submitted at least six months ahead

Date:_______________ Reviewed by:_______________________________

Additional comments:____

____

____

The picture editors at Audubon used to fill out this form and return it with a rejected submission, thereby letting photographers know exactly why their work wasn't accepted.

SUPPLIERS

Some of the unique supplies you need to run a nature-photography business aren't easy to find. You can't just run down to your local office-supply store to pick up slide mounts. However, you can easily order all such specialty items by mail or telephone. Here are some companies I use.

Calumet Carton Company
P.O. Box 405
16920 State Street
South Holland, IL 60473
708-333-6521
Calumet Carton offers heavy-duty, cardboard mailing envelopes, called "Stay-Flat Mailers" in both white or kraft finishes. The #3 Stay-Flat envelope is 11 x 13 inches, which is perfect for a submission of up to five or six 35mm slide pages (100 to 120 slides), plus sheets of protective cardboard on either side. The #4 Stay-Flat envelope is slightly larger at 12 x 15 inches; it easily holds 20 filled 35mm slide pages (400 slides) with cardboard. Both mailers are available in cases of 100. For serious marketing, get a case of each size in white.

Calumet Photographic
890 Supreme Drive
Bensenville, IL 60106
800-225-8638
Calumet Photographic leans toward supplying the large format and commercial markets. It is a good source for light tables, loupes, and other general supplies. Request a copy of its full-line Photographer's Catalog.

Filmguard
P.O. Box 788
Escondido, CA 92033
800-777-7744

Proline
Kleer Vu Plastics Corporation
P.O. Box 449
Brownsville, TN 38012
800-677-3686
Both Filmguard and Proline manufacture the 2 x 2-inch protective sleeves that fit over mounted 35mm slides. Filmguard makes archival polypropylene sleeves, while Proline offers a diacetate version. Both companies sell sleeves in minimum 500-count boxes. If you are serious about marketing, you'll need to place a basic order for three or four times this number. Both companies also offer polypropylene sleeves for large-format films, plus polypropylene slide pages, slide mounts, and other items. The two manufacturers also offer volume discounts.

Print File
P.O. Box 607638
Orlando, FL 32860
407-886-3100
Many companies offer polypropylene slide pages, but I particularly like this company's heavyweight, top-loading pages, style number 2x2-20HB. Print File also offers many other styles, including pages for other formats.

SlideScribe Products
Image Innovations
7685 Washington Avenue, South
Minneapolis, MN 55439
800-345-4118 or 612-942-7909
SlideScribe markets what I consider to be the best labels available for 35mm slide mounts. What makes these particular labels so good is not only the archival quality of the label paper cut with radius corners, but also the strong-bonding pharmaceutical adhesive. Put simply, these labels don't fall off your slides, even when the slides are run time after time through the heat of a projector. The labels are 1⅞ x 7/16 inches, which is just a bit smaller than the wide side of a slide mount, so they are easy to position. They are available in rolls for use with typewriters or tractor-feed printers, as well as in sheets for laser printers.

SlideScribe also offers a variety of other products, including slide mounts, different-size labels, and software programs. You should definitely request a catalog.

The Stock Solution
307 West 200 South, #3004
Salt Lake City, UT 84101
800-777-2076
The Stock Solution offers more sizes of quality, self-sealing transparency mounts than any other manufacturer I know. The mounts range from standard 35mm to 6 x 17cm panoramic formats, including all the medium-format sizes: 6 x 4.5cm, 6 x 6cm, 6 x 7cm, and 6 x 9cm). You have your choice of standard white mounts or black mounts.

If you're shooting medium-format film, you might be interested in the "flap-free" polypropylene sleeving that the Stock Solution sells. The standard sleeving that most processing labs use to return 120 or 220 film has a folded flap to keep the film from slipping out of the sleeve. However, this same flap protrudes into the image area when you mount the film. When you use this "flap-free" sleeve and then place the sleeved film in a Stock Solution self-sealing mount, both the film and the sleeve are held securely.

Also available from The Stock Solution is an "Anti-Rip-Off Seal." This is a small transparent seal that you can place around the open sides of protective film sleeves. In the old days, you had to remove film from its mount in order for it to be scanned so that a publishing house could use it.

This isn't true with the digital revolution. How do you know for sure if a client has scanned your slides? Scanners don't work well through film sleeves, and this little seal must be slit open to remove the film from the sleeve. The seal reads: "Copyrighted image. No unauthorized use. $250 minimum fee if any seal is broken." Of course, you can negotiate this fee with clients if for some reason the wording disturbs them.

MISCELLANEOUS RESOURCES

IRS Regional Form-Distribution Centers

Central Area Distribution Center
P.O. Box 8903
Bloomington, IL 61702-8903

Eastern Area Distribution Center
P.O. Box 85074
Richmond, VA 23261-5074

Western Area Distribution Center
Rancho Cordova, CA 95743-0001

IRS Publications

#334: Tax Guide for Small Businesses

#463: Travel, Entertainment and Gift Expenses

#505: Tax Withholding and Estimated Tax

#529: Miscellaneous Deductions

#917: Business Use of a Car

Maps

DeLorme Mapping
P.O. Box 298-5200
Freeport, ME 04032
800-227-1656
These are absolutely the best, most detailed maps available. They show back roads, scenic features, waterfalls, nature trails, etc. Check local-area bookstores or contact the company directly.

Printers

MCG McGrew Color Graphics
Box 19716
Kansas City, MO 64141
A high-quality, high-gloss color printer that will do smaller print runs at reasonable prices.

Printing/Production Broker

Joanne Bolton—Bolton Associates
222 Jewell Street
San Rafael, CA 94901
415-454-8778
415-454-9603 fax
Bolton Associates is a print-brokering and production-management service that helps self-publishers keep costs down by working with printers in Hong Kong and South Korea.

Custom Quick-Release Plates and Accessories

Kirk Enterprises
107 Lange Street
Angola, IN 46703
800-626-5074

Really Right Stuff
P.O. Box 6531
Los Osos, CA 93412
805-528-6321
These two companies have specialized, custom-made quick-release plates and clamps in the professional standard Arca-Swiss design. Both companies offer excellent products at competitive prices.

GLOSSARY

ADVERTORIAL: A combination of advertisement and editorial, the term describes an advertising supplement or section designed in the editorial style of the magazine in which it appears.

APPROVAL: A picture buyer may ask to hold pictures "on approval," a stipulated time period before a use decision is made.

ART REFERENCE: The use of a photograph in respect to artwork. A picture is used as a source of information for the artwork, but the photograph isn't recognizable in the final artwork.

ART RENDERING: The use of a photograph in respect to artwork. A version of a photograph or portion thereof in which the original photograph is recognizable.

BLEED: Printing that extends to the very edge of the paper after it is trimmed. A photograph actually runs off the page a little bit. A "full-page bleed" means the illustration "bleeds" on all four sides.

BUTTING: In graphic-arts production, placing images together with no space in between them.

BUY-OUT: Either (1) a complete transfer of all rights in and to a photograph, from the photographer to the purchaser, including the copyright; or (2) the purchase of certain rights for an exclusive use for a certain time period or geographic area. Carefully study any arrangement in which a "buy-out" is mentioned in order to make sure of meanings.

CHAPTER OPENER: A book-publishing term for a photograph used to mark or begin a new chapter in a book. A textbook often also has unit openers and/or section openers.

CMYK: An abbreviation for Cyan, Magenta, Yellow, and Key (black), which are the four process, or printing, colors.

COMP: A layout showing all the essential elements in place. When a photograph is used this way, a "comp fee" is often charged. If the comp is approved and goes to production, a "reproduction fee," which usually eliminates the "comp fee," is then charged.

COPYRIGHT: The legal ownership in a work protecting it from unauthorized use. The holder of the copyright, usually designated by the symbol © with a name, has the legal right to reproduce or sell a creative work.

CONSIGNMENT MEMO: A delivery memo.

CONTENTS PAGE SPOT: The use of a photograph, or part of a photograph, on the table of contents page.

CONVERSION: A black-and-white image made from a color one. Usually the buyer does this and pays for the cost of doing so, but no additional use rights are granted. By the way, you can easily make your own black-and-white negatives from 35mm color slides if you use a slide copier. Overexpose a fine-grained, black-and-white film by a couple of stops, underdevelop it by about 30 percent, and use a compensating developer.

DELIVERY MEMO: A list of photographs submitted to a client, including all terms and conditions of the transaction. Often this is the only proof of such a delivery and is therefore a record of the location of the photographs.

DISTRIBUTION RIGHTS: The granting of the right to reproduce a photograph in a publication intended to be distributed in a defined geographic area.

DUMMY: A mock-up of either a book or a magazine.

DUPLICATE: An exact copy, made either by photographically coping an original or by shooting a second exact frame in the field.

EDITORIAL USE: All uses of an image other than in advertising or promotion.

FLAT FEE: A single payment to cover certain use rights; no royalties are involved.

FRONTISPIECE: A photograph printed in the front matter of a book, usually facing the title page.

GUTTER: The part of a book or magazine where the pages meet in the binding. If you hold a magazine open, the gutter will be where the left-hand page and the right-hand page come together.

KILL FEE: A cancellation fee.

LAYOUT: The organizational plan of a page or pages.

MASTHEAD: The list of owner, publisher, and editorial personnel at a newspaper or magazine, printed on the "masthead page."

NONEXCLUSIVE RIGHTS: The granting of use rights to a photograph for which the user doesn't have exclusivity; therefore, there are no restrictions on granting the same use rights to another buyer.

PACKAGER: An independent producer of books that are distributed by a third party.

PAGE RATE: Also called "space rate," this is how much per page a magazine or book pays for photographs. Ordinarily this figure is broken down into increments of a page: 1/4 page or less, 1/2 page, 3/4 page, full page.

RELEASE: Written permission to publish a photograph of a person (a "model release") or private property (a "property release").

RESEARCH FEE: A service fee for researching and pulling a picture request.

REUSE: Printing a photograph for a second time from the same separations. This usually entails additional rights and fees.

SASE: Self-addressed, stamped envelope. Incidentally, an easy way to enclose funds for the return of a submission is to open your own Federal Express account, then include a shipping form already made out with your name, address, and account information.

SERIAL RIGHTS: Rights to use a photograph in a magazine.

SIMILARS: Photographs taken at the same time or in the same manner as others.

STOCK: Photographs already taken and available for a client to use.

STOCK AGENCY: A company that maintains a library of existing photographs and markets and licenses their use for a percentage of the money collected.

TRADE BOOKS: Books published for the general market, as opposed to textbooks.

TRANSPARENCY: A color positive; an image viewed by transmitted light, not reflected light.

WORK FOR HIRE: A work agreement in which the employer owns all rights to a work, including the copyright. Basically two kinds of work for hire exist: work done as a regular employee of a company, and commissioned work in which the photographer signs a written agreement relinquishing all rights to the photographs taken.

WRAPAROUND: A book or magazine cover that wraps around the entire outside, so that one image is continuous on both front and back.

BIBLIOGRAPHY

ASMP Stock Photography Handbook
American Society of Media Photographers
14 Washington Road, #502
Princeton, NJ 08550
609-799-8300
609-799-2233 fax
No two ways about it: buy this book. It has some of the best information available on the general business of photography, although it isn't oriented toward professional nature photography in the least. The handbook includes a list of stock agencies, a discussion of pricing stock photography, and a variety of forms and contracts. A well-read copy should definitely be in your office if you're planning on photographing professionally.

ASMP also publishes what I believe should be two other standard reference guides for your office if you're serious about selling photographs:Formalizing Agreements and Professional Business Practices in Photography.

(If you decide on a full-time career in photography, you should consider membership in ASMP. Information is available from the address above.)

Big Bucks Selling Your Photography
Cliff Hollenbeck
Amherst Media
P.O. Box 586
Amherst, NY 14226
716-874-4450
716-874-4508 fax
Despite the title, you should definitely buy this book. Although it is written for the general commercial photographer, not the nature photographer, it contains a wealth of information and presents it in an easily readable manner.

The Complete Guide to Self-Publishing
Tom and Marilyn Ross
Writer's Digest Books
1507 Dana Avenue
Cincinnati, OH 45207
513-531-2222
513-531-4744 fax
I think that this is probably the best book available on the totality of self-publishing, even though it concentrates on text and not photographs.

Directory of Book, Catalog, and Magazine Printers
Ad'Lib Publications
Box 1102
Fairfield, IA 52556
This is a great sourcebook of addresses and information on both domestic an foreign printers. It lists specialties, such as "coffee-table-book" production.

Direct Stock
Direct Stock Inc.
10 East 21st Street, 14th Floor
New York, NY 10010
212-979-6560
212-254-1204 fax
This is a color-picture catalog in which photographers can purchase space to showcase their work. It is similar to the stock-photography catalogs that stock agencies put out, but it promotes many individual photographers rather than one agency.

Getting It Printed
Mark Beach
North Light Books
1507 Dana Avenue
Cincinnati, OH 45207
This is a thorough introduction to printing, from reproduction processes to paper to ink, explained in a clear, easy-to-read manner.

Green Book
AG Editions
41 Union Square West, #523
New York, NY 10003
212-929-0959
212-924-4796 fax
E-mail: 102400.1444 @ compuserve.com
Online: HTTP://www.AG-editions.com
Newsletters, too
This directory of nature photographers, which includes a description of their stock files, is distributed to photo editors throughout the United States and Canada. Picture subjects are extensively cross-indexed for convenience.

Literary Market Place
Reed Reference Publishing (previously RR Bowker Company)
121 Chanlon Road
New Providence, NJ 07974
908-464-6800
908-464-3553 fax
Every good-sized library should have this standard work in its reference section. This title probably contains the most extensive listing of book publishers available, including names, addresses, and publication information.

Negotiating Stock Photo Prices
Jim Pickerell
110 Frederick Avenue, Suite A
Rockville, MD 20850
301-251-0720
301-309-0941 fax
A worthwhile read on a subject spelled out in the title, although it is slanted toward commercial photography.

On Writing Well
William Zinsser
HarperCollins (formerly Harper & Row)
10 East 53rd Street
New York, NY 10103
212-207-7000
Even if you don't plan on writing magazine articles or book manuscripts, you still need to produce business letters and captions. The better written your material is, the better received it will be.

Photo District News
1515 Broadway
New York, NY 10036
212-536-5222
212-536-5224 fax
A "newspaper" that is the trade paper for the photography industry. It is slanted heavily toward commercial photography—and, I find, the big-city photography scene—but it will help you keep abreast of what is happening. It is particularly helpful for professionals because of its coverage of business and legal news.

Photographer's Market
Writer's Digest Books
1507 Dana Avenue
Cincinnati, OH 45207
513-531-2222
513-531-4744 fax
Treat this yearly publication as a reference source for names and addresses of photography buyers. This isn't oriented to nature photography, but it is well worth using as a sourcebook. Included are sections on book publishers, stock agencies, calendar and card markets, and both consumer and trade publications.

Photography Best Sellers
James Ong
Moore & Moore
488 Madison Avenue
New York, NY 10022
This book contains 100 images that have sold and sold and sold. Take a look just to evaluate what top-selling commercial stock images are all about. The book includes some information on number of sales and price, but not on who purchased what rights. Although this book is out of print, you can probably find a copy in most large libraries. It is well worth a look.

PhotoSource International
PhotoSource International
Pine Lake Farm
Osceola, WI 54020
715-248-3800
Newsletters
Although not directed specifically toward the nature-photography markets, PhotoSource International puts out a wealth of information on general photographic direct marketing. It offers various services, including PhotoBulletin, PhotoDaily, PhotoLetter, and PhotoMarket.

Pocket Pal
International Paper
Box 100
Church Street Station
New York, NY 10046
This is a very basic primer on paper selection and printing. It has been around in one edition or another for more than 20 years.

The Professional Photographer's Guide to Shooting & Selling Nature & Wildlife Photos
Jim Zuckerman
Writer's Digest Books
1507 Dana Avenue
Cincinnati, OH 45207
513-531-2222
513-531-4744 fax
This book contains is a broad discussion of many areas of selling natural-history photographs. Some of the information is rather general, but all in all the book is well worth a read.

Publishing Your Art As Cards, Posters & Calendars
Harold Davis
The Consultant Press Ltd
163 Amsterdam Avenue
New York, NY 10023
212-838-8640
212-873-7065 fax
This is a specific discussion of all the steps required for publishing images as cards and posters. It is helpful to anyone considering self-publishing either of these items.

The Self-Publishing Manual
Day Poynter
Para Publishing
Box 2206
Santa Barbara, CA 93118
As its title indicates, this book answers most of the questions of first-time publishers.

Sell & Resell Your Photos
Rohn Engh
Writer's Digest Books
1507 Dana Avenue
Cincinnati, OH 45207
513-531-2222
513-531-4744 fax
If there is such a thing as a standard reference for general stock sales, especially to the smaller editorial markets, this is it. First published in 1981 and updated and revised several times, this book offers a good overview of the process of marketing your own work. While this book doesn't target the nature markets, it provides a lot of useful information. I think it is particularly helpful for those individuals just getting started in stock photography.

Selling Stock Photography
Lou Jacobs, Jr.
Amphoto
1515 Broadway
New York, NY 10036
212-736-7400
Jacobs is a past president of ASMP, a professional photographer, and a writer whose work covers a wide range of photographic subjects. This book contains lengthy interviews with a number of working photographers of various specialties, as well as interviews with a number of major stock-agency personnel. It provides a good overview of what the professional stock photographer actually does.

Stock Agency Directory
Picture Agency Council of America (PACA)
P.O. Box 308
Northfield, MN 55057
800-457-7222
507-645-7066 fax
This is a catalog of all the members of the Picture Agency Council of America (PACA). Most of the stock agencies in the United States are associated with PACA. Each agency has a one-page summation of its activities with names, addresses, and photo specialties (nature, hard news, historical pictures, travel, etc.). In addition agencies are listed by geographic region, which is a help if you're looking for local representation.

Reed Reference Publishing (previously RR Bowker Company)
121 Chanlon Road
New Providence, NJ 07974
908-464-6800
908-464-3553 fax
A number of specialized titles on the printing and publishing industry are available from Reed Reference. Many of these works are directories and reference sources that you probably won't want to purchase, but having correct information will help when doing market research. For example, Reed Reference offers the two-volume set Publishers, Distributors & Wholesalers of the United States 1995–96, *a listing of more than 80,000 publishers, wholesalers, distributors, software firms, and museum and association imprints. Write Reed Reference for a catalog.*

INDEX

Accessories, additional, 18, 19
Accounting, 35, 136
  by agency, 77
  See also Financial entries; Money
Adobe Photoshop, 133, 135
Advertising, 59, 67
  by photographers, 70–71, 131
AG Editions, 64, 71
Airborne Express, 34, 84
Airone, 115
American Showcase, 70
Amphoto Books, 105, 106, 134
Answering machines, 34
Arca, 18
ASMP, 93, 123, 125, 127
ASMP Stock Photography Handbook, 77
Assembling package, 84
Audubon, 137
Avery, 125

Beginnings, 11–13
Better Business Bureau, 122
Biomes, 31
Birder's World, 62
Bogen, 17, 18
Bolton, Joanne, 111, 139
Bolton Associates, 111, 139
Book(s), 59, 60, 61, 62, 67, 80, 89, 109, 110–111, 134
  your own, 105–108
Books in Print, 53
Brainstorming, 59
Breaking into business, 53, 95–96
Brochures and bulletins, 59
Bruce Coleman, Inc., 77
Business expenses. *See* Expenses

Calendars, 59, 99, 109, 114, 117
Calumet Carton Company, 34, 84, 138
Calumet Photographic, 138
Canon, 133
Captioning slides, 39–42
Cards, 59, 109–110, 114
Car expenses, 131
Catalogs, 59
Cat Fancy, 65
Chicago, 68
Circulation, of product, 113
Clients
  contacting of, 53–64
  finding of, 52–77
Commissions, 131
Communication Arts, 70
Composition, 24, 25, 79–80, 81
Computers, 35, 41, 47–51, 68, 96, 104, 117, 133, 136
Consignment memo, 85
Contacting clients, 53–64
Content, agency and, 77
Contracts, 76–77, 92, 107
Contrast ranges, 26, 80, 82
Copyrights, 39
Costs. *See* Expenses

Cover letters, 84–85, 104
The Creative Black Book, 70
Credit lines, 66, 67
Custom quick-release plates, 139

Damage, 90, 91
Databases, 35, 47–51, 136
Deductions, 128–132
Delivery memos, 85, 86
  terms of, 87–93
DeLorme Mapping, 139
Depreciation, 131–132
Depth-of-field preview, 16
Developing ideas, 103
Digital imaging, 133–135
Direct Stock, 70–71, 131
Display capability, of Nutshell, 50
Distribution, 109–111
DOS, 35, 50, 117

Eastman 5247, 23
Editing slides, 36–38
Editors
  requirements of, 24–26
  visits to, 68
Employer identification number (EIN), 128
Engh, Rohn, 64, 90, 126
Equipment
  office, 34–36
  photographic, 14–19
Expenses, 11–12, 76, 128–132
  film, 14
  hobby vs. business, 128
  reduction of, 119–120
  See also Finances
Exposure, 16, 24, 25

Farm and Ranch, 59
Fax machines, 35
Federal Express, 33, 34, 48, 84, 85, 90, 104
Fees, 131
Field and Stream, 114
Filing slides, 43–46, 47–51
Filmguard, 83, 138
Films, 16, 20–23, 115
  amateur vs. professional, 22–23
Film speed, 20, 22
Finances, tracking of, 128, 130–132
  See also Accounting; Money
Financial recordkeeping, organizing of, 128
Financial strategy, 116
Focus, 24–25, 38
Formalizing Agreements, 93, 127
FotoQuote, 117
Framing, subject, 79–80, 81
Freelancing, 25, 60, 95
f-stops, 16, 17
Fuji, 22, 23, 83, 133
Fuji Provia, 16, 20
Fuji Velvia, 20, 21, 22

Generalist approach, 31
Getting noticed, 67–71

Getting started, 10–31
Gitzo, 17, 18, 79
Golden Guides, 40
Green Book, 70–71, 131
Guidelines, 53–59, 60, 97
Guilfoyle, Ann, 64
The Guilfoyle Report, 64, 122

Hasselblad, 14
Heads, tripod, 17–18, 19
Hobby expenses, 128
Horizontal composition, 24, 25, 41, 79, 83
How-to articles/books, 101, 106

Ideas
  developing of, 103–104
  explanation of, 105–106
  salable, 99–102
Income, 11–12, 128, 130–131, 132
Indexing capability, of Nutshell, 50
Insurance, 132
Interlibrary Loan Service, 53
Internal Revenue Service (IRS), 122, 128–132, 139
Inventory, 85–86
Invoices, 117, 118
ISO ratings, 16, 20, 21, 22, 23

Jacobs, Lou, 77

Kirk Enterprises, 18, 139
Kodachrome, 20, 21, 23, 115
Kodak, 22, 23, 46, 114, 133
Kodak Carousel, 67
Kodak Ektachrome, 20
Kodak Film Cleaner, 86
Kodak Lumière, 16, 22
Kodak Photo CD, 133
Kodalux, 83

Labeling, 41–42, 77
Large-format cameras, 14–15, 17
Legal considerations, 122–127, 132
Lenses, 15, 17, 19, 115, 119
Lepp, George, 109
Letters
  cover, 84–85, 104
  for guidelines, 53
  query, 59–60, 68, 97–98, 101, 103, 104
Licenses, 122, 132
Lightboxes, 36
Line, Les, 39
Literary Market Place, 63
Living Bird, 63
Los Angeles, 68
Loss, 90, 91
Loupes, 36–37

Macintosh, 50, 117, 133, 134
Magazines, 62, 67, 68, 80, 89, 114, 117, 134
  articles for, 53, 59–60, 95–96, 97–98, 99–102, 103–104
Maps, 139

Marketing, 59–62, 64, 73–74, 77, 130
See also Salability
Market research, 99, 109
MCG McGrew Color Graphics, 139
Meals and entertainment, 132
Michigan Natural Resources, 115
Microsoft, 35, 36
Model releases, 122–125, 126, 127
Money, 112–132
keeping of, 119–121
See also Accounting; Financial entries
Movement, representation of, 38

National Audubon Society, 117
National Geographic, 25, 40
National/International Wildlife, 13, 54–55, 58, 59, 64, 65, 96
National Park Service, 64, 125
National Wildlife Federation, 115
Natural History, 62, 64, 95
Nature Photographer, 56–57
Newsletters, marketing, 64
Newspapers, 59
New York City, 67, 68, 101
Nikon, 133
Nutshell, 48, 50–51, 136
Nutshell Plus II, 48, 50

Office equipment, 34–36
Offices
home, 33, 132
physical space of, 33–35, 119
work in, 32, 36–51
Office supplies, 33–34, 132
Ontario Naturalist, 59
Organization
of financial recordkeeping, 128
of slides, 43–46, 49
Outdoor Life, 99
Outdoor Photographer, 59, 97, 101, 103, 104, 114, 123
Outline, book, 106

Pacific Discovery, 64
Packaging, 83–86, 104
Payment, 113–118
rates of, 116, 117
Payment structures, 113
PCs, 35, 50, 133
Peak 4x, 37
Permits, 122, 125
Peterson series, 40
Photo District News, 122
The Photographer's Market, 53, 107
Photographic equipment, 14–19
Photographs
number of, 11–12
salable, 12–13, 24–26
size of, 113
stock, 11
PhotoSource International, 64, 90–91
Physical space, office, 33–35, 119
Planck, Rod, 90–91, 109
Popular Science, 114
Portfolios, 65, 67, 68
Postal Service, United States, 34, 84, 85
Posters, 59, 109, 110
Power Boat, 114
Presentation, putting together of, 83
Pricing, 113–118
Printers, 35, 41, 96, 104, 125, 139
Print File, 138
Print/production brokers, 111, 139
Product
choice of, 109
circulation of, 113
Professional services, 132
Projectors, 36, 67
Proline, 83, 138
Property releases, 122–125
Proposals
book, 105–107
magazine article, 103
See also Query letters
Publishers, location of, 107
Publishing, 94–111. *See also* Self-publishing

Qualifications, in proposal, 106
Quality, agency and, 77
Query letters, 59–60, 68, 97–98, 101, 103
Quicken, 35, 130–131, 136

Ranger Rick, 54, 62, 115
Ray, John, 99, 101
Really Right Stuff, 18, 139
Rejection, 137
Releases, 122–125
Repairs and maintenance, 132
Representation, 77
Resources, 60, 139
Rights, 113–115
Rolodex, 34, 68, 84

Salability, 12–13
book, 106–107
See also Marketing
Salable ideas, 99–102
Sales taxes, 122
Scanning, 133, 134
Schneider 4x, 37
Self-employment tax, 132
Self-promotion, 65–71
Self-publishing, 105, 109–111
Selling rights, 113–115
Selling Stock Photography, 77
Services, legal and professional, 132
Shipping, 83–86
Shot lists, 62–64
Shutter speeds, 16
Sierra, 59, 65
Sierra Club, 99, 117
Signing, with stock agency, 72–77
Size, of photograph, 113
Sleeves, 83, 84
Slide mounts, 21
Slides
assessing of, 82
captioning of, 39–42
choosing of, 79–82
editing of, 36–38
organization of, 43–46, 49, 77
SlideScribe Products, 41, 138
Small Business Administration, 122
Social Security tax, 132
Software, 35, 41, 47–50, 117, 130–131
list of, 136
Sole proprietors, 128, 132
Specialist approach, 27, 31
Spending wisely, 119
Stock agencies, 68
signing with, 72–77
Stock lists, 60, 68–70
Stock photographs, 11
The Stock Solution, 23, 238
The Stock Workbook, 70
Storing slides, 46
Straight Shooter Studio, Inc., 92
Subagencies, 74
Subject framing, 79–80, 81
Subjects, 27–31
Submissions, 78–93
packaging and shipping of, 83–86, 104
Suppliers, list of, 138
Supplies
general, 132
office, 33–34, 132
SyQuest, 133, 134

Taxes, 128–132
as deductions, 132
sales, 122
Telephone submission-request form, 68
30 day approval, 87, 89–90
35mm system
advantages of, 14–15
essentials of, 16–19
selection of, 15–16
Time frame, for book completion, 107
Tony Stone Images, 135
TRAC Slidetyper, 41
Transmittal memo, 85
Transparencies. *See* Slides
Travel expenses, 129, 130, 132
Tripods and heads, 17–18, 19
Truck expanses, 131
TurboTax, 35, 131

Ultra-Plus, 48, 50
Uniqueness, 116
Unsolicited material, 60, 87, 98
United Parcel Service (UPS), 84

Vertical composition, 24, 25, 41, 79, 83

Waidhofer, Linde, 109
Want lists, 62–64
Wild Bird, 59
Windows, 35, 117
Withholding, 132
WordPerfect, 41, 50, 96, 136
Word-processing programs, 35, 47–48, 68, 96, 104, 136
World Wide Web, 71
Writing, 94–111
of captions, 39–42
of magazine articles, 53, 59–60, 95–96, 97–98, 99–102, 103–104
of proposals, 103, 104
Wu, Norbert, 92

ZIP drive, 133